W9-CUH-594

TREASURY OF LITERATURE

VOICES AND REFLECTIONS

SENIOR AUTHORS

ROGER C. FARR
DOROTHY S. STRICKLAND

AUTHORS

RICHARD F. ABRAHAMSON
ELLEN BOOTH CHURCH
BARBARA BOWEN COULTER
BERNICE E. CULLINAN
MARGARET A. GALLEGO
W. DORSEY HAMMOND
JUDITH L. IRVIN
KAREN KUTIPER
DONNA M. OGLE
TIMOTHY SHANAHAN
PATRICIA SMITH
JUNKO YOKOTA
HALLIE KAY YOPP

SENIOR CONSULTANTS

ASA G. HILLIARD III
JUDY M. WALLIS

CONSULTANTS

ALONZO A. CRIM
ROLANDO R. HINOJOSA-SMITH
LEE BENNETT HOPKINS
ROBERT J. STERNBERG

HARCOURT BRACE & COMPANY

Orlando Atlanta Austin Boston San Francisco Chicago Dallas New York
Toronto London

Portions of this work were published in previous editions.

Printed in the United States of America

ISBN 0-15-301238-2

1 2 3 4 5 6 7 8 9 10 048 97 96 95 94

Acknowledgments continue on page 623, which constitutes an extension of this copyright page.

Acknowledgments

For permission to reprint copyrighted material, grateful acknowledgment is made to the following sources:

Atheneum Publishers, an imprint of Macmillan Publishing Company: From "The Great Shut-Eye Mystery" in *Bio Amazing: A Casebook of Unsolved Human Mysteries* by Judith Herbst. Text copyright © 1985 by Judith Herbst. ". . .And Then the Prince Knelt Down and Tried to Put the Glass Slipper on Cinderella's Foot" from *If I Were in Charge of the World and Other Worries* by Judith Viorst. Text copyright © 1981 by Judith Viorst.

Ballantine Books, a division of Random House, Inc.: Cover illustration from *Black Star, Bright Dawn* by Scott O'Dell. Copyright © 1988 by Scott O'Dell.

Bantam Books, a division of Bantam Doubleday Dell Publishing Group, Inc.: From *Men from Earth* by Buzz Aldrin and Malcolm McConnell. Text copyright © 1989 by Buzz Aldrin and Malcolm McConnell.

Barron's Educational Series, Inc.: Cover illustration by Daniel Maffia from *Marie Curie and the Discovery of Radium* by Ann E. Steinke. Copyright © 1987 by Eisen, Durwood & Co., Inc.

Gregory Benford: "What Are You Going to Be When You Grow Up?" by Gregory Benford from *Spaceships & Spells: A Collection of New Fantasy and Science-Fiction Stories*, edited by Jane Yolen, Martin H. Greenberg, and Charles G. Waugh. Text copyright © 1987 by Gregory Benford. Published by HarperCollins Publishers.

Bradbury Press, an Affiliate of Macmillan, Inc.: Cover illustration by Neil Waldman from *One-Eyed Cat* by Paula Fox. Copyright © 1984 by Paula Fox. From *Dogsong* by Gary Paulsen. Text copyright © 1975 by Gary Paulsen. From *Woodsong* by Gary Paulsen, cover photograph by Ruth Wright Paulsen. Text copyright © 1990 by Gary Paulsen; cover photograph copyright © 1990 by Ruth Wright Paulsen.

Broadside Press: From *Report from Part One* by Gwendolyn Brooks. Text copyright © 1972 by Gwendolyn Brooks Blakely. "When Handed a Lemon, Make Lemonade" from *Beckonings* by Gwendolyn Brooks. Text copyright © 1975 by Gwendolyn Brooks Blakely.

Gwendolyn Brooks: "The Bean Eaters" from *Blacks* by Gwendolyn Brooks. Text copyright © 1987 by The David Company, Chicago.

Curtis Brown, Ltd.: "Great Grandfather Dragon's Tale" by Jane Yolen from *Dragons & Dreams: A Collection of New Fantasy and Science Fiction Stories*, edited by Jane Yolen, Martin H. Greenberg, and Charles G. Waugh. Text copyright © 1986 by Jane Yolen, Martin H. Greenberg, and Charles G. Waugh. Published by HarperCollins Publishers.

Judith Gwyn Brown: Cover illustration by Judith Gwyn Brown from *The Callender Papers* by Cynthia Voigt. Illustration copyright © 1983 by Judith Gwyn Brown. Original art is in the collection of the Boston Public Library.

Chelsea House Publishers, a division of Main Line Book Co.: Cover illustration by Jane Sterrett from *Phyllis Wheatley: Poet* by Merle Richmond. Copyright © 1988 by Chelsea House Publishers.

Childrens Press: "Tornado Power" from *Disaster! Tornadoes* by Dennis B. Fradin. Text copyright 1982 by Childrens Press,® Inc.

Clarion Books, an imprint of Houghton Mifflin Company: "Ms. Phyllis Shaw," "Tammy Yarbrough," "Kwang Chin Ho," and "Belinda Enriquez" from *Back to Class* by Mel Glenn. Text copyright © 1988 by Mel Glenn. From *The Great Ancestor Hunt* by Lila Perl. Text copyright © 1989 by Lila Perl.

Cobblestone Publishing, Inc., Peterborough, NH 03458: "Charles Richter: 'Earthquake Man'" by Catherine Plude from *Cobblestone* Magazine, April 1986. Text © 1986 by Cobblestone Publishing, Inc.

Don Congdon Associates, Inc.: Cover photograph from *Growing Up* by Russell Baker.

Congdon & Weed, Inc. and Contemporary Books, Inc., Chicago: From *Growing Up* by Russell Baker. Text © 1982 by Russell Baker.

Joan Daves Agency, on behalf of The Heirs to the Estate of Martin Luther King, Jr.: From "I Have a Dream" speech by Martin Luther King, Jr. Copyright 1963 by Martin Luther King, Jr.; copyright renewed 1991 by Coretta Scott King.

Delacorte Press, a division of Bantam Doubleday Dell Publishing Group, Inc.: Cover illustration by Jody Lee from *Song of the Gargoyle* by Zilpha Keatley Snyder. Illustration copyright © 1991 by Jody Lee.

Dell Books, a division of Bantam Doubleday Dell Publishing Group, Inc.: Cover illustration by Michael Tedesco from *Johnny Tremain* by Esther Forbes. Copyright © 1943 by Esther Forbes Hoskins; copyright © renewed 1971 by Linwood M. Erskine, Jr.

Dutton Children's Books, a division of Penguin Books USA Inc.: Cover illustration by Michael Hays from *The Drackenberg Adventure* by Lloyd Alexander. Illustration copyright © 1988 by Michael Hays.

David Allan Evans: "Bus Depot Reunion" by David Allan Evans from *Shenandoah: The Washington and Lee University Review*, Volume XXV, Number 2 (1974).

Farrar, Straus & Giroux, Inc.: "The Parakeet Named Dreidel" from *Stories for Children* by Isaac Bashevis Singer. Text copyright © 1984 by Isaac Bashevis Singer.

continued on page 623

Dear Reader,

Look again at the cover of this book. Can you see the reflections in the pond or imagine voices coming through the trees? Those voices and reflections, along with the many voices and reflections of authors and characters in the selections in this anthology, inspired the title *Voices and Reflections*.

Listen to reflections about growing up, families, adventures, dreams, and friendship. The authors' voices will invite you to distant shores and to nearby communities just like your own.

You will hear many voices that have contributed to the richness of our country's heritage. Early American patriots such as James Forten, a young African American sailor, and Abigail Adams, the wife of John Adams, may give you a new perspective on the complex struggle for American independence. A tradition of respect for nature echoes in the poetry by Native Americans. Hispanic writers speak from a tradition of intense family loyalty. Japanese American voices reflect determination and the spirit of hard work.

Some of the voices in this anthology will connect you with the past. Others, such as that of Dr. Martin Luther King, Jr., will challenge you with a vision of the future. As you read, you may reflect on the importance of your own heritage and your place in it. You may also be led to reflect on your future and on the potential of your own unique voice. Once you have recognized its value, you, too, will be able to speak out and inspire others.

Sincerely,
The Authors

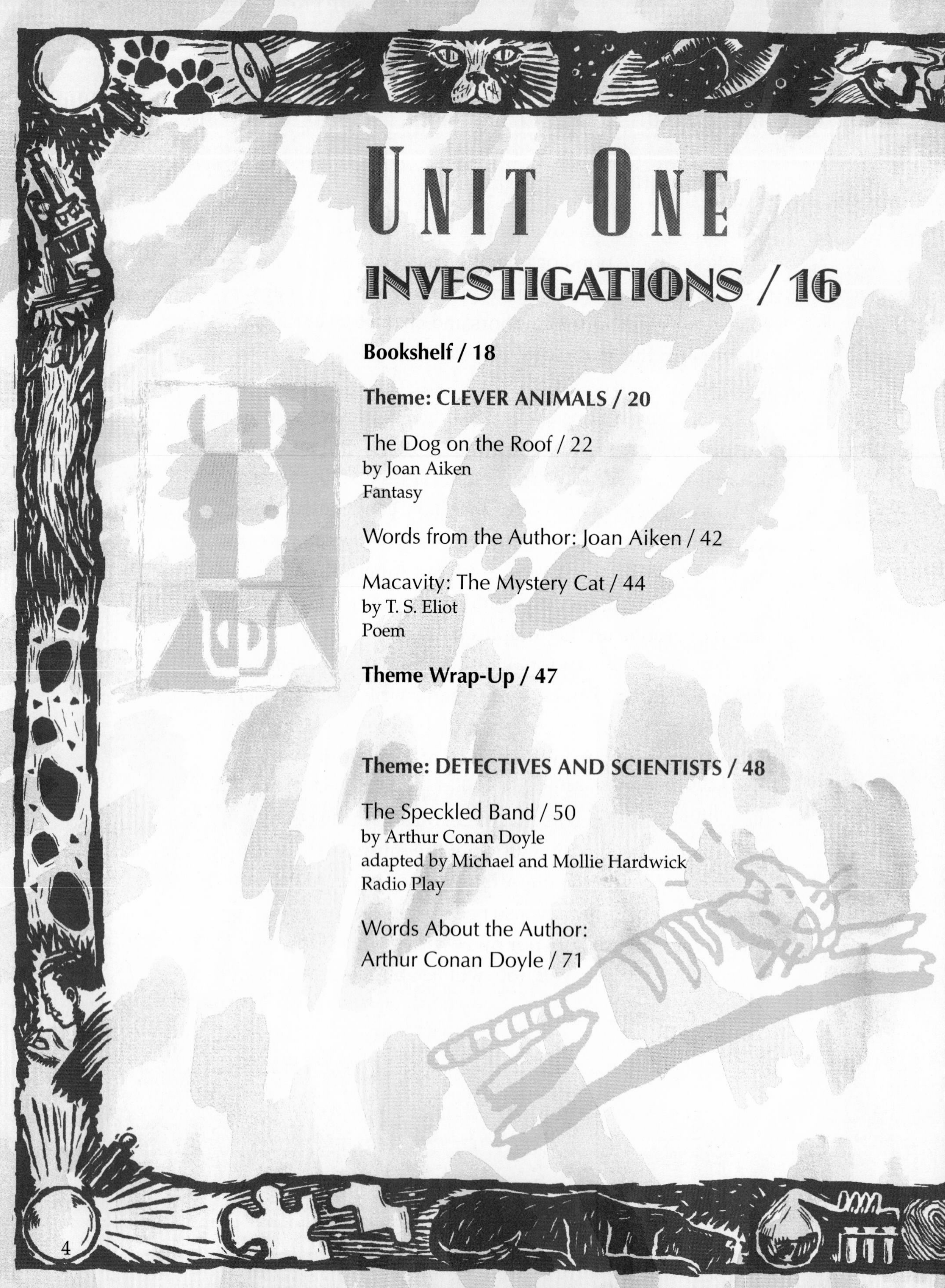

UNIT ONE

INVESTIGATIONS / 16

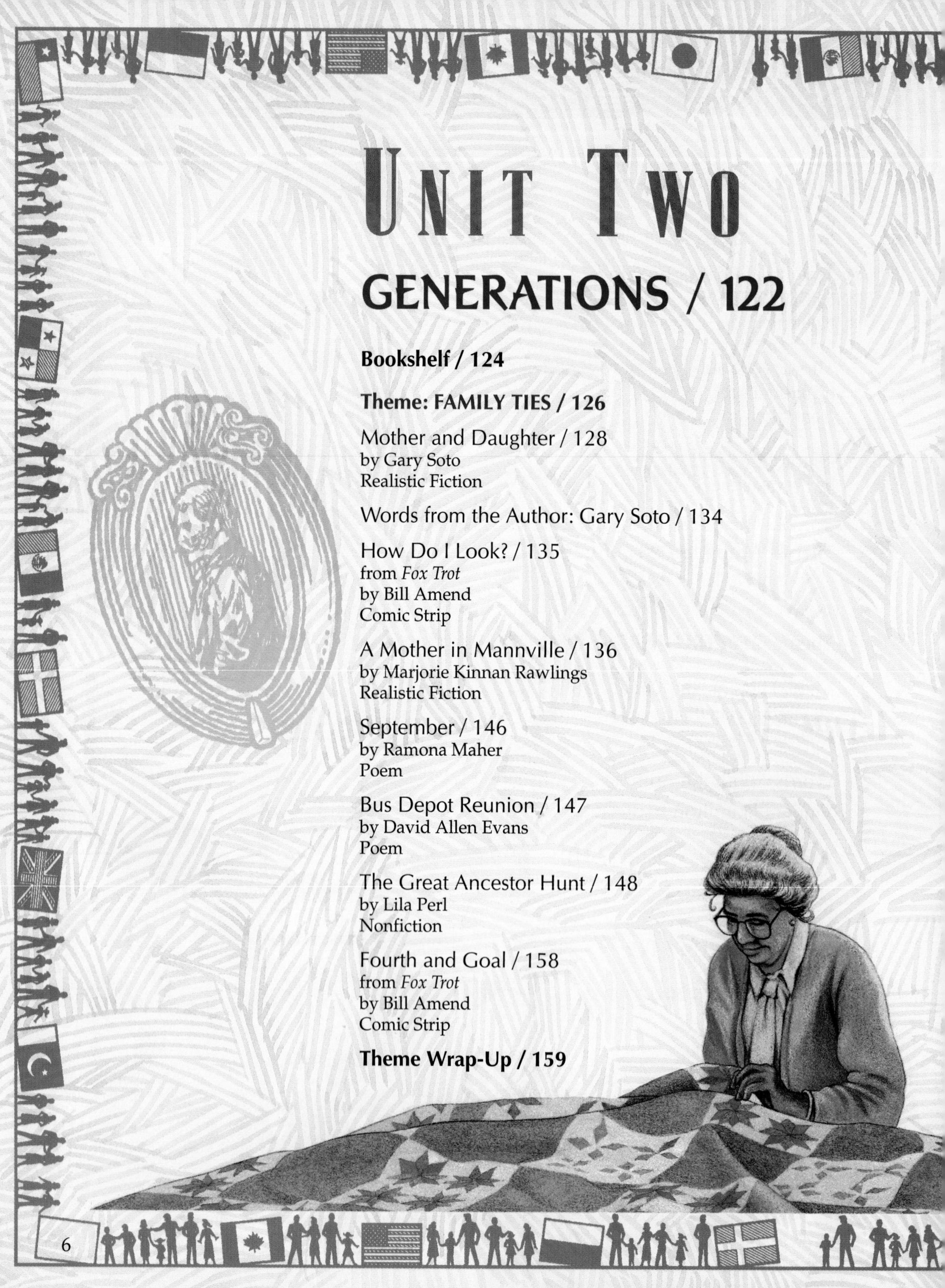

UNIT TWO

GENERATIONS / 122

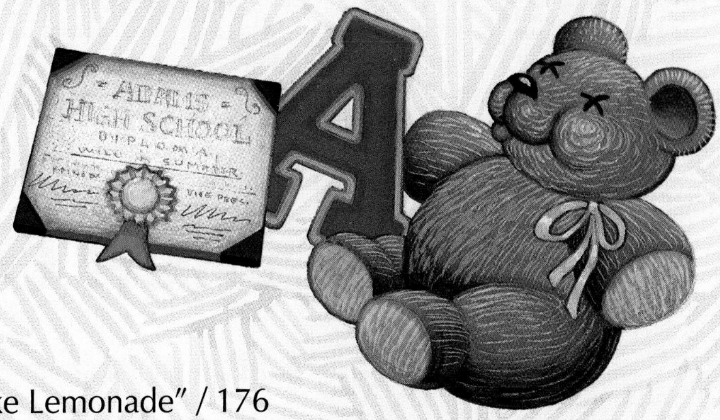

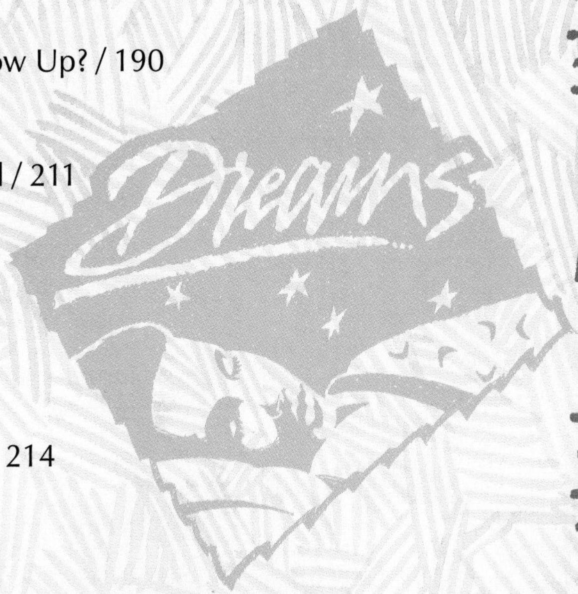

UNIT THREE

A NEW COUNTRY 218

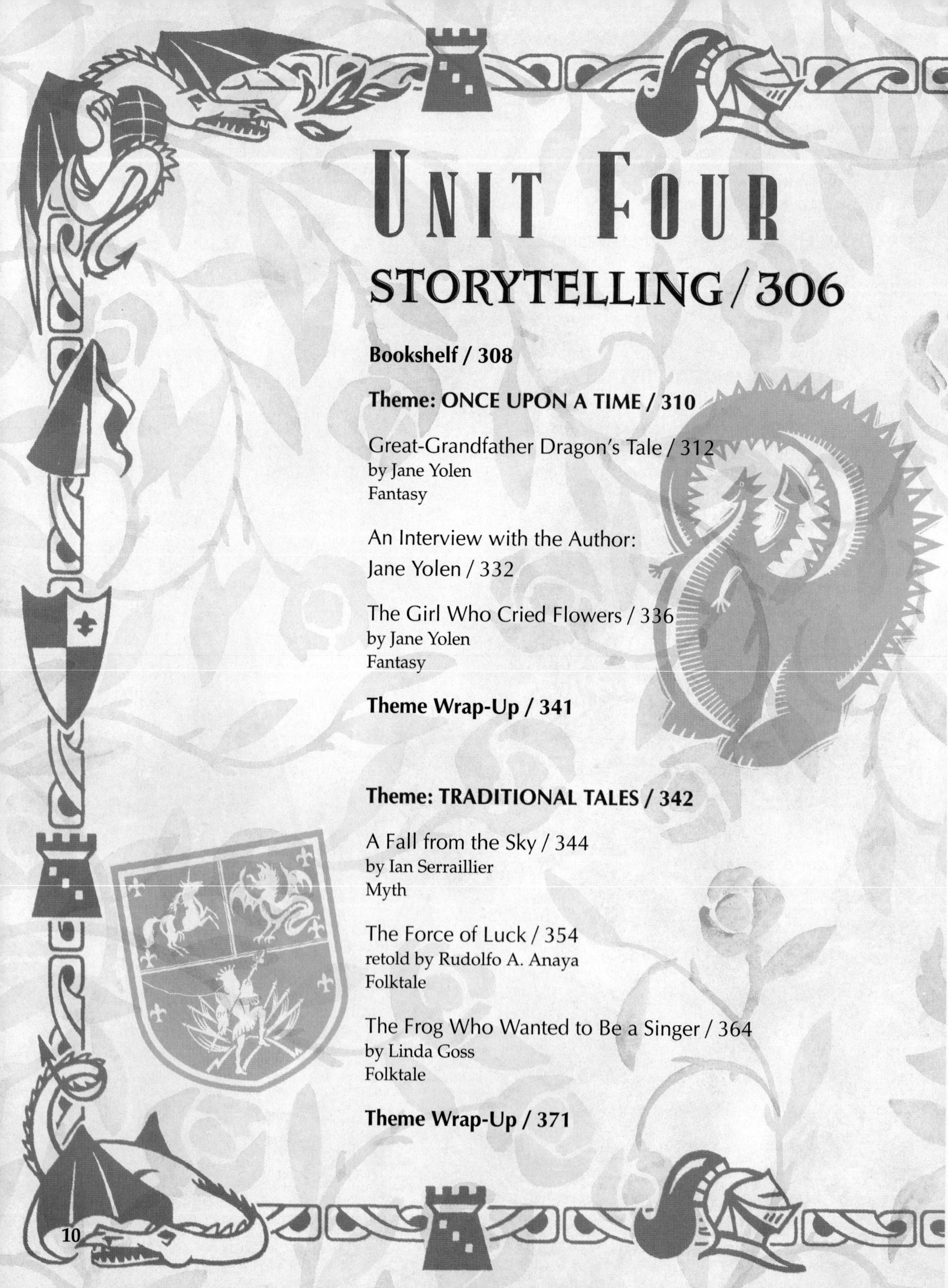

UNIT FOUR

STORYTELLING / 306

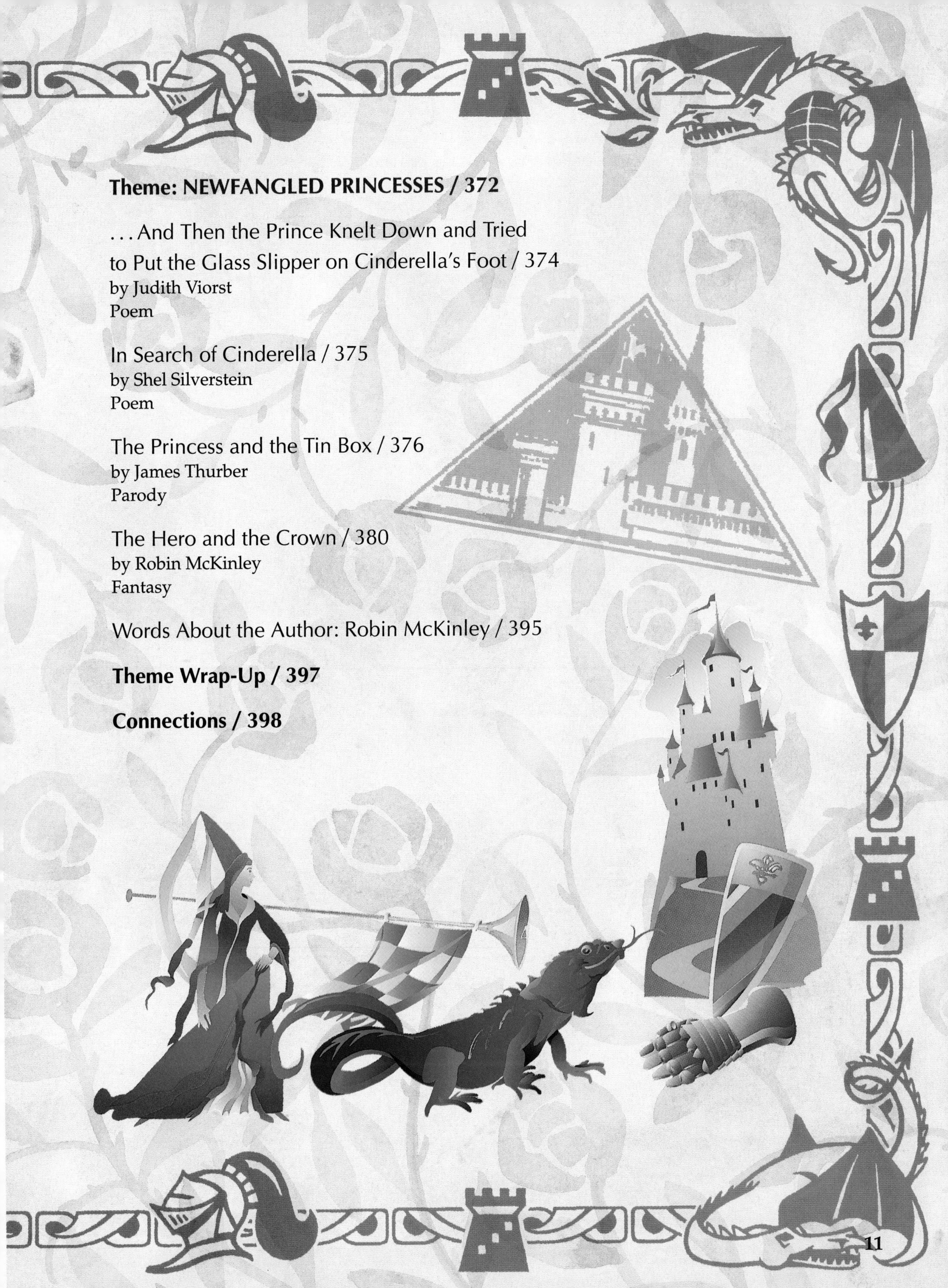

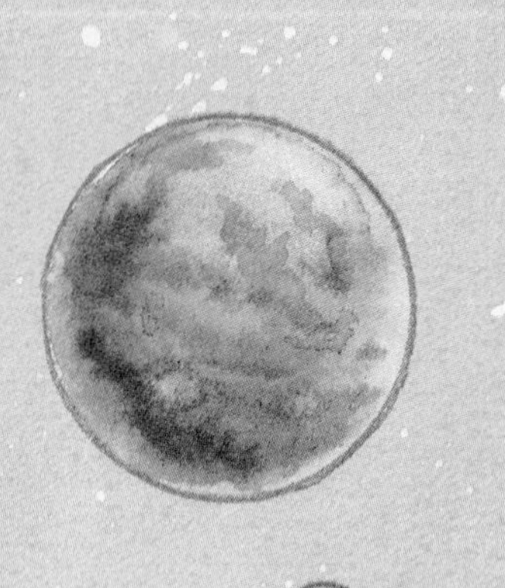

UNIT FIVE

HOME PLANET / 400

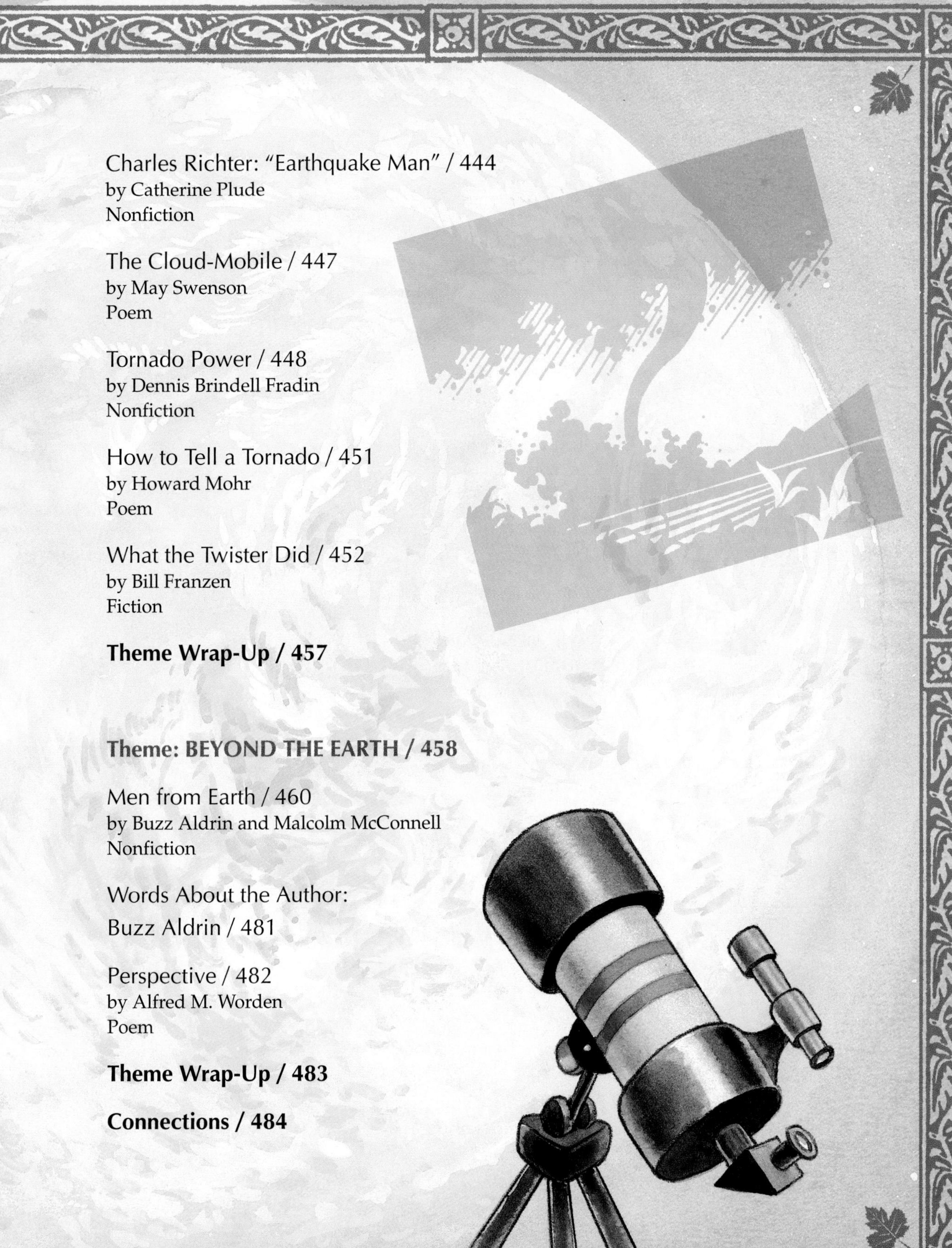

UNIT SIX

INSPIRATIONS / 486

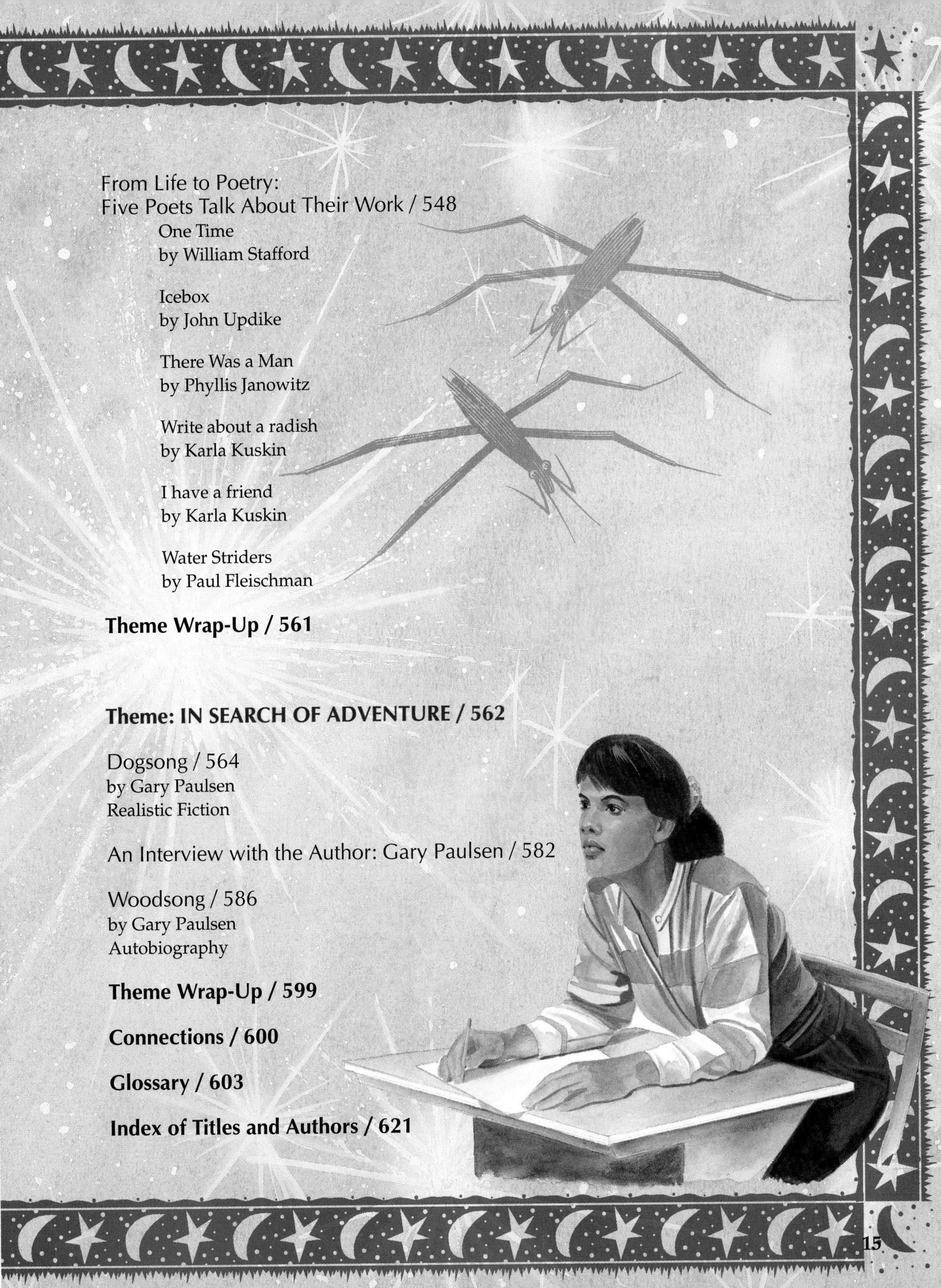

UNIT ONE

INVESTIGATIONS

Exploration and discovery can take place anywhere. On the snows of the Arctic, Matthew Henson and Robert Peary risked their lives in a search for the North Pole. In a science lab in Alabama, George Washington Carver made amazing new products from peanuts. As you share in the investigations in this unit, think about the qualities that make a good investigator: the desire to know the truth, the willingness to have an open mind, the courage to take risks. Think also about the kind of investigation that appeals to you.

THEMES

TALES OF A DEAD KING

BY WALTER DEAN MYERS

John Robie and Karen Lacey travel to Egypt to help John's great-uncle on an archeological dig. Little do they know that mystery and intrigue await them.

HARCOURT BRACE LIBRARY BOOK

WHO PUT THE CANNON IN THE COURTHOUSE SQUARE?

BY KAY COOPER

This how-to book on researching and writing local history has easy-to-follow examples and activities.

The Callender Papers

BY CYNTHIA VOIGT

Jean Wainwright accepts the job of sorting through the family papers of the late Irene Callender Thiel. While doing so, she uncovers some startling information that puts her in danger.

Edgar Allan Poe Award

Marie Curie and the Discovery of Radium

BY ANNE STEINKE

Discover the determination of a true scientist. Marie Curie's dedication to research on radioactive elements is inspiring.

The Drackenberg Adventure

BY LLOYD ALEXANDER

The lively Vesper Holly meets a remarkable assortment of people during her thrilling adventures in Drackenberg.

Children's Choice

THEME

If animals could talk, what would they say about humans? The next selections will take you into a fanciful world where you will see people and events from the point of view of some unusual animals.

CONTENTS

the DOG

Not many years ago there was an old lady living in Washington Square, New York. Her name was Mrs. Logan, and she lived right in the park; she hung her clothes on a tree, on coat hangers, and ate her breakfast sitting on a bench. She lived there with her cab-horse, Murphy—and her cab too, of course.

They are not there now. This is the story of why they lived there, and why they left.

At the time I am speaking of, there was also a poet, called Paul Powdermaker, living in a fourth-floor studio in a house in Twelfth Street, five minutes' walk from Washington Square.

Living with Paul was a Labrador dog called Bayer. Bayer was big, with a thick black shiny coat and thoughtful brown eyes. Paul had taken charge of Bayer when his previous owner moved to Patagonia. Paul was not accustomed to dogs, but he had a very kind nature. Bayer was good-natured too, as black Labradors mostly are, and the two got on well. (Poets and dogs nearly always do get on well; they speak the same language.)

Bayer had only one bad habit: of course he did not consider it bad, but some people might. His previous owner had trained him to howl at the sound of a Salvation Army band—or any music played in the street. At the first sound of a transistor, or people singing, or drums, or guitars, Bayer would start to bark and howl and carry on, making as much noise as he could to drown the music.

Paul had one fault too: he never took Bayer out for a walk. He didn't realize that dogs need adventures.

on the ROOF

by Joan Aiken

Illustrations by Randy Chewning

Luckily in the studio they shared there was a door that led out on to the roof. So, five or six times a day, Bayer would pad over to this door and give a short, polite bark; then Paul would get up, pen in hand, open the door, shut it again behind Bayer, and go on with his writing, which he did for twenty hours a day.

Once outside, Bayer would suddenly change from being a rather fat, slow, sleepy, lazy indoor dog to a keen, alert, active (but still rather fat), outdoor one.

First he would rush to the edge of the roof and look down to see what was going on in Twelfth Street. Then he would bark hard, about twenty times, just to announce that he was observing everybody in the street and keeping an eye on everything. There were trees along each side of the street, and birds in them, and sometimes a cat or two in the front gardens, and pigeons and blue jays on the roofs, and a few people strolling or walking briskly.

Sometimes there would be another dog down in the street; then Bayer would bark extra loud. And Bayer had a friend, called Rackstraw, who lived in the basement area of the house along at the corner; so some of his barks were for Rackstraw, and meant, "Good morning! How are you down there? I'm all right up here. Isn't it hot/cold/fine/rainy/frosty/snowy today?"

We shall come back to Rackstraw later.

When Bayer had finished his barking, he would take off like a champion hurdler and race right along the block all the way from one end to the other and then back, several times. The roofs were not all flat. Some sloped up to parapets; some were two or three feet higher than their neighbors; here and there, studio skylights stuck up like big triangular boxes; or there were clusters of chimneys like giants' fingers, or water tanks on legs which looked like pointed rockets about to take off.

Bayer knew all this landscape of roof as well as most dogs know their backyards, and he went bounding along, clearing the walls like a greyhound, nipping among and through the chimneys like a polo pony, skirting around the water tanks and studio skylights like a St. Bernard on the slopes of the Alps. Bayer had a very good head for heights, and, though he often dashed right to the edge of a roof and barked so hard that he looked as if he were going to bark himself right off, he had never done so yet.

When he had breathed in enough fresh air, he would return to his own door, and let out another short polite bark, and Paul Powdermaker would let him in.

Though he worked so hard at it, Paul did not earn a very good living from his poetry writing. Very few poets do. He wrote hundreds of poems, and sent them to dozens of magazines, but hardly any of his poems were printed. And the payment for those that were printed was not high. So, as well as poetry, Paul wrote fortunes for the fortune cookies used in Chinese restaurants. He was paid for his work not in money but in big boxes of free fortune cookies; and these were what he and Bayer mostly ate. Bayer had become very expert at eating the cookies and spitting out the slips of paper with the fortunes printed on them.

One sharp December evening Paul had just let out Bayer, and was writing a fortune for a cookie: "Never hide inside a teapot. Someone might pour boiling water on you." At this moment he heard Bayer up above on the roof, barking much louder than usual.

Paul opened the window, leaned out, and looked down to see what was causing Bayer's agitation.

Down below on the sidewalk, clustered around a little ginkgo tree, he saw a group of carol singers with two guitars and a drum. They were singing "The Holly and the Ivy" and, up above, Bayer was accompanying them by howling as loudly as he could. They weren't a Salvation Army band but, so far as Bayer was concerned, there wasn't a lot of difference. He stood right on the edge of the roof and made a noise like a police siren with hiccups, jerking himself backward and forward with every bark.

The carol singers didn't mind Bayer; they thought he was joining in out of Christmas spirit; in any case he didn't sound so loud to them, four stories down, because they were making a good deal of noise themselves.

In the midst of all this commotion, old Mrs. Logan drove slowly along the street in her horse-drawn cab. Mrs. Logan was not really driving the cab; she was asleep. Her horse, Murphy, knew the way home perfectly well. So Mrs. Logan was inside the cab, having a nap, while Murphy plodded thoughtfully along, taking his time.

They were returning from their usual day's inactivity, spent outside a big hotel, the Plaza, waiting for customers who might wish to drive around Central Park or along the main shopping streets in an open horse-drawn cab. Very few customers *did* want to at such a cold time of year. And if by any chance they felt like a cab ride, they hardly ever picked Mrs. Logan's cab, because Murphy, a brown horse the color of gingerbread, was so terribly thin that his ribs resembled a rusty radiator; they looked as if you could play a tune by running a stick across them. Murphy looked as if his maximum speed would be about half a mile per hour.

So customers generally picked cabs with fatter, stronger horses. And tonight, as on nearly all other evenings, Murphy and Mrs. Logan were coming home to their sleeping quarters in Washington Square without having had a single fare all day. Mrs. Logan would then wrap Murphy in a lot of old quilts she kept folded up in a cardboard box; and she would wrap herself up in a lot more; and they would share a supper of half-eaten rolls, ends of pretzels, bits of sandwiches, and other food that Mrs. Logan had picked out of garbage cans early that morning. Then they would go to sleep, Murphy standing, Mrs. Logan sleeping in the cab, which would be parked under a big stone arch, the Washington Arch.

No policeman ever bothered Mrs. Logan.

The first time she spent a night in Washington Square a policeman called O'Grady said to her, "Ma'am, you shouldn't be camping here, you know."

"Ah, now, have a heart, dear boy," said Mrs. Logan. "I'm from way back in the country, from the lovely little town of Four Corners, New Hampshire—and the sight of the green leaves and the squirrels in this park will be easing the sadness of my poor

homesick heart. I tell you what, Officer O'Grady," she said, "I'll be singing you a song now."

So she sang him a beautiful song that went:

When an Irish Robin
Hops into your waistcoat pocket
Won't your ould heart shoot up
Like a fine skyrocket?
Remember the nest
In the Isle of the Blest
With four beautiful eggs of blue
Where an Irish Robin
Is waiting and singing
For you!

Officer O'Grady was so charmed by this song, which Mrs. Logan sang in a very sweet voice, thin as a thread but dead on the note, that he immediately gave her leave to stay under the Washington Arch just as long as she liked, and furthermore he told all his friends in the Sixth Precinct office that Mrs. Logan was not to be bothered.

So all that any of the other policemen did was to pass the time of day and keep a friendly eye on her, and sometimes ask her to sing the song about the Irish Robin, which she always did for them.

Just as Mrs. Logan and Murphy drew abreast of the carol singers (who had now got to "The First Noel"), Bayer, up above on the roof, became so overexcited that he did something he never had before: he barked himself right off the roof, and fell like a heavy black plum, down, down, four stories, until, as luck would have it (and very fortunately), he landed on the canvas hood of Mrs. Logan's cab. This worked as well as a trampoline; Bayer bounced on it a couple of times, then he tumbled into the cab itself, not hurt at all, but a trifle surprised.

Mrs. Logan was surprised too.

"Musha!" she said. "Will ye be believing it now, dogs falling from the sky!

What next, at all?"

Bayer politely removed himself from the cab, and jumped to the ground.

"Are you hurt?" inquired Murphy, who was just as surprised as Mrs. Logan, but not given to exclaiming.

"No, thank you, not at all," said Bayer. "I hope I didn't frighten your driver."

"Oh, very little frightens Mrs. Logan. She is quite a calm person," said Murphy, and he went on plodding in the direction of Washington Square.

Bayer felt that, now he was down in the street, he might as well take advantage of the opportunity. It was a long time since he had had the chance to run about and sniff all the delicious smells at ground level, and he was fairly sure that Paul would not begin to worry about him for some time. So he loped along companionably beside Murphy, slowing his pace to the horse's tired, stumbling walk.

When the cab came to a stop under the Washington Arch, and Mrs. Logan wrapped up herself and the horse, and divided a handful of crusts and pretzel-ends between them, Bayer was rather shocked.

"Don't you have a proper stable?" he asked the horse. "And is that *all* you get for supper?"

Compared with this, Bayer's own quarters in the fourth-floor studio and his supper of fortune cookies seemed comfortable, even princely.

"How long have you lived here?" he asked.

"Nine or ten years, I suppose," said Murphy.

"Can't you find anything better?"

"Mrs. Logan hasn't any money," Murphy explained, and then he told the story of how they came to be living under the Washington Arch.

"We come from a little town many hundreds of miles from here," he said, heaving a sigh that went all along his bony ribs, like a finger along the keys of a piano. "It is called Four Corners, New Hampshire, and there *are* only four corners in it—and the train station of course. We used to wait at the station, and as ours was the only cab, we made a good living. Mrs. Logan lived with her brother, who has a farm. But one day four men got off the train and asked if we would take them all the way to New York. They offered eighty dollars for the ride. I've begun to think, lately, that perhaps they were robbers. On the way down (which took several days) they talked a lot about banks, and money, and the police.

"When we reached New York they said they hadn't any cash on them, but if Mrs. Logan would be outside the Plaza Hotel next morning at ten, they would be there to pay her the eighty dollars. So we spent the night here and went to the Plaza next day; but the men never turned up with the money. And, though we have gone back there each morning at ten ever since, we have never seen them again."

"What a set of scoundrels!" exclaimed Bayer. "Maybe they never meant to pay you at all."

"That is what I begin to think," agreed Murphy sadly. "But Mrs. Logan still believes they will turn up one of these days; she thinks they must be having a little difficulty earning the money."

"Why don't you both go back to Four Corners?"

"Oh, Mrs. Logan would never do that. She would think that looked as if she didn't trust the men to keep their promise. But," said Murphy, sighing again, "I am growing very tired of the city—though it is so grand—I often wish I was back in my own stable at Four Corners—especially on a cold night like this one."

That night was bitterly cold; the stars shone bright as flares, and the moon was big as an ice rink. Far away along Fifth Avenue the pointed tower of the Empire State Building glowed pink and green and blue against the night sky. All the squirrels of Washington Square were curled up tight in their nests; the rollerskaters and skateboarders and the Frisbee-slingers had long gone home to bed. Mrs. Logan and Murphy and Bayer were the only live creatures there, standing patiently under the Washington Arch.

"Well, I think it's a shocking shame," said Bayer, and then he trotted away, thinking hard as he went. He was going home, but first he intended to consult another acquaintance of his who lived in the basement area at the end of Twelfth Street.

This was a skunk named Rackstraw. Bayer and Rackstraw often held conversations, from roof to street, but up till now they had never met face to face.

Rackstraw had not been in Twelfth Street very long. He had arrived one day in a Rolls Royce car; Bayer wanted to know more about him.

The basement area of the end house held several trash cans, a box or two, a stone trough containing laurel bushes, and a picnic basket lined with newspaper.

The carolers were now singing "Good King Wenceslas" at the other end of the block, so Bayer went, a little warily, down a couple of the stone steps that led to the basement door, and called, loud enough for the skunk to hear over the music, "Rackstraw? Are you at home?"

Instantly Rackstraw's handsome black and white head poked out of the picnic basket.

"Good heavens, Bayer! Is that you? What in the world are you doing down in the street?"

"Oh, I just jumped down," Bayer said carelessly. "There was no problem about it, I landed on the roof of Mrs. Logan's cab."

"My stars! I wouldn't dare do a thing like that!" said Rackstraw. He spoke with an English accent. Bayer had noticed this before; he recognized the English accent because Paul Powdermaker had an English friend called Lord Donisthorpe.

"Do you come from England?" Bayer inquired. "I didn't know there were English skunks."

"I was born and brought up in an English zoo," explained Rackstraw. "But my mother always told me that I ought to return to the land of my ancestors, if I could. The zoo where I lived was in a large park, where there were a lot of other entertainments as well—outdoor plays, and opera, and circuses. Last month an opera was being performed, and the audience ate picnic suppers by their cars in between the acts. I was hidden in a bush munching a piece of smoked salmon I had managed to pick up when I heard American voices. Somebody said, 'We'll drive the car on board the ship tomorrow.' I thought, Now's my chance! So, while they were eating, I climbed into the luggage compartment of their car (which was a Rolls Royce) and hid under a rug. The next day the car was driven onto a ship, which sailed to New York. The trip took five days."

"And you were in the luggage place all that time?" Bayer was greatly impressed. "Didn't you run out of air and food?"

"There was plenty to eat, because they had left the remains of the picnic—bread and cheese and salmon and fruit and salad and plum cake. And the trunk was a big airy place. When we reached New York and they drove away from the dock I waited for my chance, and as soon as they opened the lid of the trunk I shot out. This was where they stopped, on Twelfth Street, so I have lived here ever since. It isn't bad—the people in the house are quite kind and give me fried potatoes; but in the spring I shall move on."

"Where to?"

"Back to the place my mother and father came from. There are some cousins still living there. It is Mount Mosscrop, a hill in New Hampshire near a little town called Four Corners."

"Why!" exclaimed Bayer, amazed, "that's where Murphy comes from!" and then he told Rackstraw the story of Mrs. Logan.

Rackstraw said thoughtfully, "If only we could persuade Mrs. Logan to go back home, I could ride with her as a passenger."

"You could if you promised—"

"Promised what?"

All this time, Bayer had been keeping at a careful distance from his neighbor. Now he said, rather hesitantly, "Well—er—I was brought up in the city, I never met a skunk before, personally, that is. But, well, I always heard—I was told that skunks—that you were able to—that is to say—"

"Oh," said Rackstraw, "you mean the smell?"

"Well—yes," apologized Bayer, moving back onto a higher step, lest the skunk had taken offense. But Rackstraw did not seem annoyed.

"My mother trained me not to, except in emergencies," he said. "People in England are very polite; they don't like it. And my mother was very particular about manners. 'Never, never do it,' she used to say, 'unless you are in great danger.' So I never have."

"It never happens by accident?"

"I suppose it might—if one were to sneeze violently—but it never has to me. Now, let's think how we can persuade Mrs. Logan to return to Four Corners."

Just then they heard the voice of Paul Powdermaker, who was walking slowly along the street, whistling and calling: "Bayer? Bayer? Where are you?"

"We'll talk about this again," said Bayer hastily. "It's good to have met you. See you soon. Take care!"

"Good night!" called Rackstraw, and he slipped back into his cozy, insulated nest.

Bayer ran along Twelfth Street with his master, and climbed the seventy-four stairs back to their warm studio, where he had a late-night snack of fortune cookies. One of them said: "A bone contains much that is noble. And L is for love."

"Did you write that?" Bayer said to Paul. "I don't think much of it."

"One can't hit top notes all the time," said Paul, who was hard at work on a long poem about the ocean. "Don't distract me now, there's a dear fellow. And, next time you want to go into the street, warn me in advance; I nearly dropped dead of fright when I saw you jump off the roof."

Bayer apologized for causing Paul so much anxiety, and climbed into his basket. But it was a long time before he slept. He kept thinking of Mrs. Logan and Murphy, out in the bitter cold, under the Washington Arch, waiting for morning to come.

After that day, Bayer always kept his ears pricked for the sound of Murphy's hoofs slowly clopping along the street. When he heard them, he would bark to go out on the roof. Mrs. Logan formed the habit of putting up the hood of her cab when she drove along Twelfth Street, and Bayer would jump down onto the hood, bounce once or twice, and then either ride on the box with Mrs. Logan, or run in the street beside Murphy. Paul grew accustomed to this, and stopped worrying. Bayer made himself useful helping Mrs. Logan hunt for edible tidbits in trash cans—he was much better at it than the old lady—and he spent many days in town with the pair, talking to Murphy and keeping an eye out for the four men who owed Mrs. Logan eighty dollars.

"One of them was tall and thin, with glasses," Murphy told Bayer, "one was little and round with a red nose; one was very pale, white-haired and blue-eyed; and one was dotted all over with freckles and had red hair. They rode with us for so many days that I had plenty of time to get to know them."

Mrs. Logan's cab was parked outside the Plaza Hotel. She nodded sleepily in the sunshine, while Bayer and Murphy watched all the well-dressed people pass by. As Christmas was near, there were several men dressed as Santa Claus, ringing bells and collecting money for charity.

Whenever they rang their bells, Bayer barked, but not so loudly as he would have three weeks ago; these days, Bayer didn't bark so loudly or so often, and since he was getting more exercise, he was not so fat.

He found a chunk of pretzel in the gutter and offered it to Murphy.

"How about you?" said the horse. "Wouldn't you like it?"

"Oh, I'll be getting my fortune cookies later on."

"Well—thanks, then."

Paul wrote:

> The ocean, like a great eye
> Stares at the sky.

Then he stopped writing and stared at the dog.

"What's the trouble, Bayer? Do you want another fortune cookie?"

"No," said Bayer, "I need a whole lot of spinach."

"Spinach!" exclaimed Paul, just as Bayer had earlier. "What do you need that for?"

"What's your favorite food?" Bayer asked, as Murphy hungrily chewed the pretzel.

"Spinach," answered Murphy when he had swallowed. "Mrs. Logan always buys me a bag of spinach if we earn any money. Up at Four Corners," he said sighing, "I used to be given as much spinach as I could eat; I had bushels of it. Mrs. Logan's brother grew fields and fields of it, and I used to do the plowing for him."

"Spinach?" cried Bayer. "I never heard of anybody liking *that* stuff!"

That evening, when Bayer was back at home, he sat beside Paul and laid a paw beseechingly on the poet's knee.

"For a friend."

"Spinach—spinach—" Paul began to mumble, coming out of his poem slowly like a mouse out of a cheese. "Now let me think—I read something about spinach in the paper—two or three days ago it was—"

Paul had *The New York Times* delivered every day, and there were piles of newspapers lying about all over the floor. He rummaged around in these untidy heaps, and it took ever so long before he found what he wanted.

"'Load of Spinach Goes Begging,'" he read aloud to Bayer. "'A freighter packed to the portholes with spinach is lying at anchor off the Morton Street pier, waiting

for somebody to buy up her load. The asking price is twenty dollars. The ship met with such severe gales on the way to New York from Florida that the usual two-day run was extended to eight. Consequently the cargo has deteriorated, and New York greengrocers are not keen to buy. The owner will probably accept a giveaway price if anyone is prepared to take his load off his hands. Come along, Popeye, here's your chance!'"

"Twenty dollars," thought Bayer sadly. "That's a terrible lot of money. But a whole load of spinach would certainly set Murphy on his feet again, and make him fit for the trip back to Four Corners."

The next day at seven, Bayer was out on the roof although it was still dark and bitterly cold. The streetlamps down below glimmered like Christmas oranges in the bare trees of Twelfth Street. Bayer heard the slow clip-clop of Murphy's hoofs coming along, and he jumped down as usual, bouncing lightly off the canvas hood onto the road below. He trotted beside the cab, and was about to tell Murphy of the boatload of spinach off the Morton Street pier when a most unexpected thing happened.

Around the corner of the street marched fifty-seven Santa Clauses.

They were wearing Father Christmas costumes. Some carried sacks, and some had bells. Many held Christmas trees. They marched in rows: five rows of ten, and one row of seven.

Mrs. Logan, who had been dozing on the box, woke up and stared with astonishment at the sight.

"Glory be to goodness!" she murmured. "That's enough Santa Clauses for every week in the year, so it is, and five more for luck!"

Then she looked more closely at the last row of Santa Clauses, who were breaking rank to pass the cab, and she cried out, "Divil fly away with me if those aren't the fellas that rode with us down from Four Corners, New Hampshire! Will ye be after giving me my eighty dollars now, if ye please?" she called to them.

Murphy recognized the men at the same instant, and he whinnied loudly; Bayer, catching the general excitement, barked his head off. Rackstraw bounced out of his nest.

Most of the Father Christmases seemed mildly surprised at this; but four of them dropped their Christmas trees and bolted away, as if they had suddenly remembered they had a train to catch.

Murphy did his best to chase them; but he was far too thin and tired to keep up more than a very slow canter for a couple of blocks, and the men easily got away from him; very soon they were out of sight. Bayer and Rackstraw followed a few blocks farther, but they, too, lost the men in the end. One of the men, however, had dropped a wallet in his fright; Bayer pounced on that and carried it back in triumph. Inside were four five-dollar bills. Twenty dollars!

The owner of the freighter anchored off the Morton Street pier was greatly astonished when a shabby old cab, drawn by a skeleton-thin old horse, drew up on the dock by his ship, and an old lady, waving a handful of green paper money, offered to buy his load.

"Certainly you can have it," the owner said. "But where will you put it? The Port Authority won't allow you to leave it on the dock."

"Ah, sure, then, they'll let me keep it there for a night or so," said Mrs. Logan hopefully. "And in the meanwhile old Murphy here will eat a great, great deal of it."

So the load of spinach was dumped out on the dock. It was in a very limp and wilted state, but even so it made a massive pile, twenty feet high and thirty feet long. Murphy gazed as if, even now he saw it, he could hardly believe his eyes.

"Go on then, ye poor ould quadruped," said Mrs. Logan. "Eat your head off, for once."

Murphy didn't wait to be told twice. After ten minutes he had made a hole as big as himself in the green mountain of spinach. Then Mrs. Logan packed as much spinach as she could into the cab.

Murphy reluctantly stopped eating—"Best ye don't gobble too much all at once," Mrs. Logan warned him, "or 'tis desperate heartburn ye'll be getting—" and they started slowly back toward Washington Square.

Lifting the spinach and packing it into the cab had been a hard, heavy job, and it made a heavy load to pull; Bayer could see that Mrs. Logan and Murphy were not going to be able to shift very many loads before nightfall. And a Port Authority inspector was walking up and down, looking disapprovingly at the hill of spinach.

Bayer galloped back to Twelfth Street to consult with Rackstraw.

Greatly to his surprise, when he reached the door of his own house, he saw, parked at the curb, the very same white Rolls Royce that had brought Rackstraw to the city. And on the doorstep Paul Powdermaker was enthusiastically shaking the hand of his English friend, Lord Donisthorpe.

"Oh, please, oh, please, Paul, dear Paul, we need your help and advice very badly!" exclaimed Bayer, bounding all around Paul in his agitation.

Lord Donisthorpe, who was a thin elderly English gentleman with a tuft of gray hair like a secretary-bird and a long nose, and a pair of spectacles which were always halfway down it, gazed with a mild dreamy interest at Bayer. Lord Donisthorpe knew a great deal about animals; in fact he was the owner of the zoo from which Rackstraw had escaped.

"Gracious me, my dear Paul! How very remarkable and touching! You and the dog are in verbal communication! You talk to one another! That is remarkably interesting. I shall certainly write a paper on it, for the Royal Society."

"Oh, it's nothing," said Paul, rather shyly and shortly. "Poets and dogs generally understand one another, I believe. Well, Bayer, what is it? Can't whatever it is wait for a few minutes? Lord Donisthorpe has just arrived from his Mexican trip—"

"Oh, no, Paul, it can't, you see it's that mountain of spinach by the Morton Street pier that Mrs. Logan wants to move to Washington Square—the spinach has to be moved today or the Port Authority will tell the sanitation trucks to take it away. But we need a car or a truck—Mrs. Logan and Murphy can't possibly manage it all on their own."

Paul—whose mind was still half on his ocean poem—could not make head or tail of this at first, and it needed endless repetitions before he managed to understand what Bayer was talking about. By that time Lord Donisthorpe had also grasped the nature of the problem; and the sight of Murphy and Mrs. Logan doggedly plodding along Twelfth Street with another load of spinach finally brought it home to both men.

Lord Donisthorpe ran out into the street and took hold of Murphy's bridle. Murphy came to a relieved stop.

"My dear ma'am! Excuse me—ahem!—I am not usually one to meddle in other people's affairs—but I own a zoo, in England—I do know quite a lot about animals—and that horse, my dear ma'am—really that horse is too thin to be pulling a cab so laden with spinach. What he needs, if you will forgive my saying so, is about twenty square meals."

"Man, dear, don't I know it!" said Mrs. Logan. "And there's about a hundred square meals waiting for the blessed cray-ture; if only we can get the stuff shifted to Washington Square."

The end of it was that Paul Powdermaker and Lord Donisthorpe spent the rest of the day shifting spinach from the dockside to Washington Square in Lord Donisthorpe's Rolls. They had just delivered the last load before darkness fell. In the middle of Washington Square there is a paved area; all the spinach was piled here in a huge mound, the height and shape of an outsize Christmas tree.

Mrs. Logan and Murphy passed the day resting; Mrs. Logan thought long and hard, while Murphy ate. Bayer ran back and forth alongside the Rolls, and greatly enjoyed himself.

Police Officer O'Grady had long ago been moved on from that precinct; but another policeman called O'Brien walked by at dusk and thoughtfully surveyed the huge pile of spinach.

"I doubt ye won't be allowed to keep that there, ma'am," he said mildly.

"Ah, glory be! Where else can I keep it, at all?" said Mrs. Logan.

"Well, maybe it can stay there till just after Christmas," said O'Brien.

"In that case there's no call to worry; Murphy will have ate it all by then."

Indeed, during the next few days Murphy munched so diligently at the great pile that it shrank and shrank, first to the size of an upended bus; then to the size of Lord Donisthorpe's car; and finally to no size at all. Meanwhile, Murphy, from all this good nourishing food, grew bigger and bigger; his coat became thick and glossy; his head, which had hung down like a wet sock, reared up proudly; his mane and tail grew three inches a day, and even his hoofs began to shine. He took to trotting, and then to cantering, around and around Washington Square, among the rollerskaters; he even frisked a little, and kicked up his heels.

During this time Lord Donisthorpe and Paul Powdermaker had many conversa-tions with Mrs. Logan over cups of tea and muffins in a coffee shop in University Place.

"If I were you, ma'am," said Lord Donisthorpe, "I would wait no longer, hoping to get your money back. I fear those wretches who deceived you are gone for good. If I were you, I should take that fine horse of yours, and go back to Four Corners, New Hampshire."

Mrs. Logan needed a lot of convincing. But in the end she did agree. "Isn't it a sad thing there should be so much wickedness in the heart of man?" she said. "'Tis the city folk that are bad, I'm thinking. True enough, I'll be glad to go back to Four Corners."

"What will you do for food along the way?" said Paul. "It's not so easy to pick up broken pretzels and sandwich crusts in the country."

Mrs. Logan had an idea about that.

"Now Murphy's in such grand shape, I reckon we'll be entering for the Christmas Day cab-horse race. If we win, 'tis a five-hundred-dollar prize; that money would buy us journey food back to Four Corners, and leave plenty over a Christmas gift for my brother Sean, who must have thought me dead these ten years."

"Christmas race?" said Lord Donisthorpe. "If Murphy wins that—and I really don't see why he should not—it will be a fine endorsement for my Spinach Diet Plan for horses. I shall write a paper about it for the Royal Society. . . ."

So it was agreed that Murphy and Mrs. Logan should enter for the race.

Paul and Lord Donisthorpe polished up the cab, and the brass bits of Murphy's harness, checked the reins, saddle soaped the leather, and waxed the woodwork, until the cab looked—not new, but a bit better than it had before. And they tied a big red rosette on Murphy's headband.

But meanwhile there was trouble brewing in Twelfth Street.

At this time of year, people had naturally been buying Christmas trees and taking them home, putting them in pots and decorating them with tinsel and lights.

But after a couple of days in warm houses, many of the trees began to smell truly terrible.

A meeting of the Twelfth Street Block Association was held.

"It's that skunk living at the end of the street!" people said. "We always knew that having a skunk in the street would lead to trouble. That skunk has to go."

Paul Powdermaker argued that this was unfair and unreasonable. "That skunk—whose name is Rackstraw, I might inform you—has never been near any of your Christmas trees. He has not touched them. How could he? He lives outside in his picnic basket; the trees are inside. There has been no connection. Furthermore he is a very well-behaved skunk; my dog—who ought to know—informs me that Rackstraw never gives offense, in any possible way."

But just the same, the Block Association decided that Rackstraw must be removed to the Central Park Zoo.

Only, nobody quite knew how to set about this. Whose job is it to remove a skunk? First they called the Sanitation Department and asked them to send a garbage truck. The Sanitation Department said it was no business of theirs. The police said the same thing.

The Central Park Zoo said that they would take Rackstraw, if somebody would deliver him; but they were not prepared to come and fetch him.

"You had better stay in my studio till all this blows over," Paul said to Rackstraw. But Rackstraw said that he was not used to living indoors; he would prefer to spend a few days with Mrs. Logan in her cab. So that is what he did.

On Christmas Day large crowds assembled in Central Park to watch the cab race.

For this event the cabs had to race three times all around the park—a distance of eighteen miles. During the morning no traffic was allowed on the streets alongside the park.

All the contestants lined up outside the Plaza Hotel—there were thirty of them, cabs polished to a brilliant dazzle, and gay with ribbons, tinsel, and holly. The horses were in tiptop condition, bouncing and eager to be off. Mrs. Logan's cab was certainly not the smartest; but no horse looked in better shape than Murphy. His coat gleamed like a newly baked bun; and he was snorting with excitement.

Lord Donisthorpe was staying with the friends with whom he had crossed the Atlantic. They lived in a top-floor apartment overlooking the park, so after he and Paul had wished Mrs. Logan well, they went up to the penthouse garden, where they would have a grandstand view of the whole race.

The starter's gun cracked, and, after a couple of false starts, the competitors clattered off, whips cracking and wheels flashing.

During the first lap, Murphy drew so far ahead of all the others that it hardly seemed like a race at all. Galloping like a Derby winner, with Bayer racing at his side barking ecstatically, he tore up Central Park West, turned east along 110th Street, crossed the north end of the park, and came racing down Fifth Avenue. All the other contestants were at least half a mile behind.

Then, as Murphy approached the Plaza Hotel, ready to turn the corner and begin his second lap, something unexpected happened. There were four men in Santa Claus costumes outside the Plaza, and, as Murphy came racing along, he had a clear view of their faces. With a loud neigh of recognition, he swung off the racecourse, and started chasing the men, who fled down Fifth Avenue with Murphy thundering after them.

"What's got into that horse?" yelled the crowd of watchers. "Has he lost his way? Has he gone mad? Murphy, Murphy, you took a wrong turn!"

Mrs. Logan had also spotted the men in Santa Claus costumes and she was shouting, "Musha, wisha, come back, ye spalpeens! What about my sixty dollars?"

(As they had spent the twenty dollars from the wallet on spinach, she reckoned that the men owed her only sixty.)

Before, the men had easily escaped from Murphy. But now they hadn't a

chance. Mrs. Logan leaned out with her whip and her umbrella, and hooked them into her cab one by one—helped by enthusiastic people along Fifth Avenue.

Just outside the Forty-Second Street library she grabbed the last Santa Claus. The stone lions in front of the library were roaring their heads off, because it was Christmas; and Murphy whinnied joyfully; and Bayer barked his loudest.

Rackstraw, curled up in the back of the cab, had been rather startled when the thieves were hauled in. For a moment, indeed, he felt tempted to disobey his mother's rule. But he restrained himself. "Politeness always pays, Rackstraw," he remembered his mother saying. So he contented himself with biting the swindlers, who seemed to him to have a terrible smell already.

"Now I have the lot of ye!" said Mrs. Logan. "And it's over to the polis I shall be handing ye, for now I see that ye were a lot of promise-breaking raskills who niver intended to pay me back at all."

By now the police had arrived with sirens screeching and were grouped around the cab waiting to handcuff the Father Christmases. It seemed they had reasons of their own for wanting these men.

So, although Mrs. Logan and Murphy didn't win the Central Park cab race, they did earn the gratitude of the State of New Jersey.

Why? Because these men were Christmas tree thieves, who had been cutting down cedars and spruces along the scenic parkways of New Jersey. But the evergreens had been sprayed by the Highways Department with deer-repellant chemicals, which, when the trees were taken into a warm room, began to smell far, far worse than any skunk. So the stolen trees—and the men who had taken them—were easily identified.

And the grateful Highways Department paid Mrs. Logan a handsome reward.

"I knew the smell of the trees had nothing to do with Rackstraw!" said Bayer.

Rackstraw looked very prim. "I never disobey my mother's rule," he said.

The friends were all back in Washington Square, helping Mrs. Logan and Murphy prepare for their journey.

The cab was stuffed with spinach and pretzels, fried potatoes for Rackstraw, and bottles of root beer for Mrs. Logan.

"How about coming along?" said Murphy to Bayer.

Bayer was deeply tempted. But he said, "I can't leave Paul. He has been very kind to me, and he might be lonely, all on his own."

But inside him Bayer thought sadly how much he would miss his three friends. Poets are poor company, even if they do understand dog language.

"Good-bye, then," said Murphy.

"Good-bye! Good-bye!" called Rackstraw and Mrs. Logan. All Mrs. Logan's police friends had come to the square to wave her good-bye—and a big crowd of other people as well. Newspaper cameras flashed. It was a grand send-off. Mrs. Logan sang her Irish Robin song for the last time; then they started.

As Bayer watched the cab roll away, a huge lump swelled up in his throat. In a moment he knew that a terrible anguished howl was going to come out.

Just then Paul Powdermaker pushed his way through the crowd.

"Bayer," he said, "Lord Donisthorpe has invited me to travel to England and spend a year in his castle. I'd like to go—but if I take you, it means you will have to spend six months in quarantine kennels. The English are very strict about that. So I was wondering if you'd care to go to New Hampshire with Mrs. Logan and Murphy—"

Bayer turned his head and saw that the cab was out of sight. Murphy had broken into a gallop and was whirling Mrs. Logan out of New York faster than any crack stagecoach.

"I'd never catch up with them now," said Bayer.

"Nonsense, my dear dog!" exclaimed Lord Donisthorpe. "What's a Rolls for, may I ask? A good goer Murphy may be, but I never yet heard of a horse who could outrun a Rolls Royce. . . . Jump in, and we'll soon be up with them."

Bayer and Paul leaped into the white Rolls—which still had a certain amount of spinach clinging to its gray tweed upholstery—the motor came to life with a soft purr, and the great car lifted away like a helicopter.

Just the same, Murphy had gone forty miles before they caught up with him.

So that is why, if you to go to Washington Square, New York, you won't find Mrs. Logan hanging her dresses on a tree and singing about the Irish Robin, or Murphy the horse standing under the Washington Arch. They are back in Four Corners, New Hampshire, and Bayer the Labrador and Rackstraw the skunk are with them.

What part of the story do you think is the funniest? Explain your choice.

What early clue do you think should have led Mrs. Logan to suspect that the four men she took to New York were robbers?

Do you think this story is more fantasy or mystery? Explain your response.

WRITE Choose four characters from the story. Write a fortune-cookie saying for each character. You may want to give the character advice or a prediction for the future.

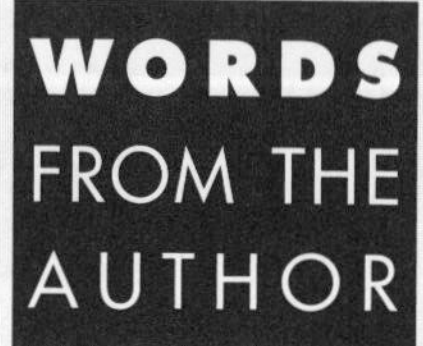

JOAN AIKEN

Joan Aiken is famous for her many novels, short stories, and plays, and for the variety of her writing styles. Here Aiken discusses how she came to write "The Dog on the Roof" and offers some advice to young writers.

AWARD-WINNING AUTHOR

"The Dog on the Roof" was written in New York and put together from a lot of ingredients. First, there really was a dog who used to have daily airings opposite our fifth-floor walk-up apartment on Tenth Street. There was also a skunk, brought back accidentally from Pound Ridge Park in the car trunk of some neighbors of ours on Eleventh Street. Other items in the story were all culled from *The New York Times*—the cab race, the posse of Santa Clauses, the stolen Christmas trees scented with deer repellent, the unwanted shipload of spinach (in fact it was cabbage), and the dog trained to howl at Salvation Army concerts. This is an example of the jigsaw-type story put together from a large number of odd bits.

I do many different kinds of writing — stories for small children, for older children, mysteries, plays, poetry, and serious books for adults. It's hard to say which is my favorite —

If you'd like to write a story, I suggest reading the newspaper carefully every day and chopping out all the interesting, unexpected articles. When you have quite a pile of them, try to assemble them into a story. I have used this process with students in creative-writing courses, and it often produces lively results. After all, this exercise simply speeds up the usual process: A writer collects together in his mind, perhaps over a period of years, all the things that interest and appeal to him; in the end, they form a story.

Another piece of advice for would-be writers: Always carry a small notebook wherever you go; a writer simply cannot be too observant. Lots of ingredients for "The Dog on the Roof" were written in one of my small notebooks.

I began writing when I was five—bought a notebook at the village shop and started right in. My father and stepfather were both writers, and I knew I wanted to be one, too. Mostly at first I wrote poems, or stories that didn't get finished. Then I started telling stories to my younger brother. Then I began writing them down.

I do many different kinds of writing—stories for small children, for older children, mysteries, plays, poetry, and serious books for adults. It's hard to say which is my favorite—I enjoy them all. But perhaps fantasy stories, the kind that are about ten to twelve pages long, are what I like best. I can only write them when they occur to me; they are not planned ahead. So they seem like a kind of gift.

I myself don't enjoy fantasy if it is too far removed from reality. I don't like stories set on some distant planet. I like fantasy to have connections with reality all along the line—like the relation between one's dreaming and daytime lives. So I enjoy constructing a story like "The Dog on the Roof," where a great many of the episodes might happen and some actually have happened—only not in such close juxtaposition. Fiction is like condensing real life—running it extra fast.

Fantasy is our daily life when we are very young. I can see my grandchildren, both under six, instantly turning flowers into fairies' dresses, rabbit holes into huge caves. Their dreams are as important as real events. When we grow up, we stop remembering our dreams; they still happen, only they are shut off from us. I think we miss this without realizing it, which is why so many people have a craving for fantasy fiction.

Macavity: The Mystery Cat

by T. S. Eliot

AWARD-WINNING AUTHOR

Drawings by Edward Gorey

Macavity's a Mystery Cat: he's called the Hidden Paw—
For he's the master criminal who can defy the Law.
He's the bafflement of Scotland Yard,[1] the Flying Squad's
despair:
For when they reach the scene of crime—*Macavity's not there!*

Macavity, Macavity, there's no one like Macavity,
He's broken every human law, he breaks the law of gravity.
His powers of levitation would make a fakir stare,
And when you reach the scene of crime—*Macavity's not there!*
You may seek him in the basement, you may look up in the
air—
But I tell you once and once again, *Macavity's not there!*

Macavity's a ginger cat, he's very tall and thin;
You would know him if you saw him, for his eyes are sunken in.
His brow is deeply lined with thought, his head is highly
domed;
His coat is dusty from neglect, his whiskers are uncombed.
He sways his head from side to side, with movements like a
snake;
And when you think he's half asleep, he's always wide awake.

Macavity, Macavity, there's no one like Macavity,
For he's a fiend in feline shape, a monster of depravity.
You may meet him in a by-street, you may see him in the
square—
But when a crime's discovered, then *Macavity's not there!*

---

[1] Scotland Yard: London police headquarters

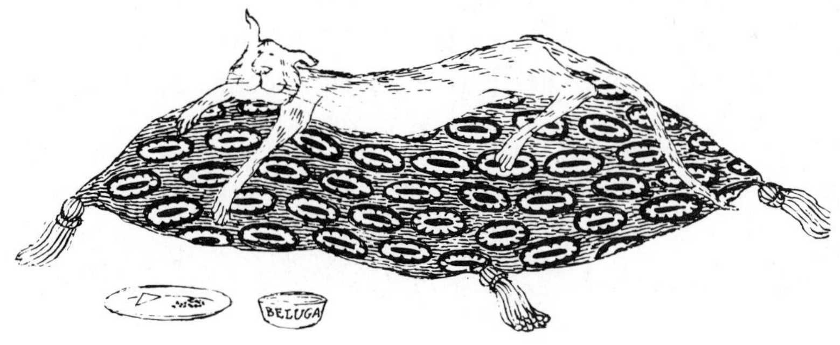

He's outwardly respectable. (They say he cheats at cards.)
And his footprints are not found in any file of Scotland Yard's.
And when the larder's looted, or the jewel-case is rifled,
Or when the milk is missing, or another Peke's[2] been stifled,
Or the greenhouse glass is broken, and the trellis past repair—
Ay, there's the wonder of the thing! *Macavity's not there!*

And when the Foreign Office find a Treaty's gone astray,
Or the Admiralty lose some plans and drawings by the way,
There may be a scrap of paper in the hall or on the stair—
But it's useless to investigate—*Macavity's not there!*
And when the loss has been disclosed, the Secret Service say:
'It *must* have been Macavity!'—but he's a mile away.
You'll be sure to find him resting, or a-licking of his thumbs,
Or engaged in doing complicated long division sums.

Macavity, Macavity, there's no one like Macavity,
There never was a Cat of such deceitfulness and suavity.
He always has an alibi, and one or two to spare:
At whatever time the deed took place—MACAVITY WASN'T THERE!
And they say that all the Cats whose wicked deeds are widely known
(I might mention Mungojerrie, I might mention Griddlebone)[3]
Are nothing more than agents for the Cat who all the time
Just controls their operations: the Napoleon of Crime!

---

[2] Peke: a Pekingese [pē'kə · nēz'], a very small dog originally bred in China

[3] Mungojerrie, Griddlebone: characters in *Old Possum's Book of Practical Cats,* a collection of poems by T. S. Eliot that also includes "Macavity"

Do you think that Macavity would get along with the animals in "The Dog on the Roof"? Explain your opinion.

WRITER'S WORKSHOP

Even though they are animals, Bayer and Macavity seem very much like people. Think about an animal that reminds you of a person. What is special about that animal's looks, actions, or personality? Write a description of the animal.

Writer's Choice What might a clever animal think about people? Choose an animal, and put yourself in its place. Plan a piece of writing that will entertain your readers by showing the animal's point of view. Carry out your plan, and share your writing.

THEME

DETECTIVES AND SCIENTISTS

Mysteries challenge the mental powers of both detectives and scientists and keep them searching as clue leads to clue. See whether these mysteries will challenge you and keep you reading.

CONTENTS

Adapted by Michael and Mollie Hardwick

THE SPECKLED BAND

by **ARTHUR CONAN DOYLE**  illustrated by **SERGIO MARTINEZ**

CHARACTERS

- Sherlock Holmes, a detective residing at 221B Baker Street, London
- Dr. Watson, his friend and associate
- Helen Stoner, a young lady in distress
- Julia Stoner, Helen's twin sister
- Dr. Grimesby Roylott, Helen and Julia's stepfather

WATSON: [*Narrating*] My friend Sherlock Holmes worked rather for the love of his art than for the acquirement of wealth. He refused to associate himself with any investigation which did not tend towards the unusual—even the fantastic. Glancing over my notes of seventy-odd cases, I cannot recall any with more singular features than the Case of the Speckled Band. I might have placed them on record before, but for a promise of secrecy from which I've only been freed in the last month by the untimely death of the lady to whom I gave it. There have been widespread rumors as to what really did happen, so it is perhaps as well to bring the facts to light at once. [*Slight pause*] It began early one morning in April, 1883.

[*Sound of door opening*]

HOLMES: Watson! Wake up, Watson!

WATSON: [*Grunting and yawning*] Eh? What on earth?

HOLMES: Come along, Watson. It's a quarter past seven.

WATSON: Quarter past . . . ! Holmes, you . . .

HOLMES: [*Chuckling*] Yes, I know it's a little before my usual time.

WATSON: A little! What is it? A fire?

HOLMES: No. A client. It seems that a young lady has arrived in a considerable state of excitement.

WATSON: Aha!

HOLMES: Now, when young ladies wander about the Metropolis at this hour of the morning and wake sleepy people up out of their beds, I presume that it is something very pressing which they have to communicate. Should it prove to be an interesting case, I'm sure you would wish to follow it from the outset.

WATSON: My dear fellow, I wouldn't miss it for anything. Young woman, eh? Just give me a few minutes to dress and I'm ready.

[*Fade out. Fade in sitting-room. Sound of door opening*]

HOLMES: Good morning, madam. My name is Sherlock Holmes.

HELEN: Good morning, Mr. Holmes.

HOLMES: This is my intimate friend and associate, Dr. Watson.

WATSON: Good morning, ma'am.

HELEN: Good morning, Doctor.

HOLMES: You may speak as freely before Dr. Watson as before myself. [*Door closes*]

HOLMES: Ah, I'm glad to see Mrs. Hudson has had the good sense to light the fire. Pray draw up to it, madam, and I shall order you a cup of hot coffee. You are shivering.

HELEN: No coffee, thank you, Mr. Holmes. It's not the cold which is making me shiver.

HOLMES: What then?

HELEN: It is fear, Mr. Holmes. It is terror.

WATSON: Good heavens!

HOLMES: You must not fear. We shall soon set matters right.

WATSON: Yes, certainly.

HOLMES: You have come in by train this morning, I see.

HELEN: You know me, then?

HOLMES: No, but I observe the second half of a return ticket in the palm of your left glove. You must have started early, and yet you had a good ride in a dog-cart, along heavy roads, before you reached the station.

HELEN: Mr. Holmes, I don't . . .

HOLMES: There is no mystery, my dear madam. The left arm of your jacket is spattered with mud in no less than seven places. The marks are perfectly fresh. There is no vehicle save a dog-cart which throws up mud in that way, and then it's only when you sit on the left hand side of the driver.

HELEN: Well, you're perfectly right. I started from home before six. I reached Leatherhead at twenty past, and I came in by the first train to Waterloo. Sir, I can stand this strain no longer. I shall go mad if it continues.

WATSON: Calm yourself, dear lady.

HELEN: I have no one to turn to—no one, save the one who cares for me, and he can be of little aid. I have heard of you, Mr. Holmes, from Mrs. Fairintosh.

HOLMES: Fairintosh? Ah, yes, the case was before your time, I think, Watson—concerned with an opal tiara.

WATSON: Certainly don't remember it.

HELEN: Mr. Holmes, do you think you could help me too, at least by throwing a little light through the darkness which surrounds me? At present it's out of my power to reward you for your services, but in a month or two I shall be married and have control of my own income, and then I . . .

HOLMES: Madam, I shall be happy to devote the same care to your case as I did to that of your friend. My profession is its own reward, but you are at liberty to defray what expenses I may be put to whenever it suits you to do so.

HELEN: You are very kind, Mr. Holmes.

HOLMES: Now I beg you to lay before us everything that may help in forming an opinion about this matter.

HELEN: The real horror of my situation seems to be that my fears are so vague, and my suspicions depend so entirely on small points which might seem trivial. You'll probably tell me they are nothing but the fancies of a nervous woman. But I've heard, Mr. Holmes, that you can see deeply into the wickedness of the human heart.

HOLMES: I am all attention, madam.

HELEN: My name is Helen Stoner, and I am living with my stepfather, Dr. Grimesby Roylott, of Stoke Moran, on the western border of Surrey.

WATSON: One of the oldest Saxon families in England, I believe?

HELEN: And at one time amongst the richest, too. But in the last century four successive heirs wasted the fortune. All that was left was a few acres of ground and the two-hundred-year-old house. The last squire dragged out his existence there in the horrible life of an aristocratic pauper. But his only son, my stepfather, saw that he must adapt himself to the new conditions and took a medical degree. Then he went out to Calcutta and established a large practice. However, in a fit of anger after his house had been robbed, he beat his native butler to death.

WATSON: Good heavens!

HELEN: He narrowly escaped a capital sentence. As it was, he suffered a long term of imprisonment, and then returned to England a morose and disappointed man.

HOLMES: When did Dr. Roylott marry your mother, Miss Stoner?

HELEN: While he was in India. My mother was the young widow of Major General Stoner, of the Bengal Artillery. My sister Julia and I were twins, and we were only two years old at the time of my mother's remarriage.

HOLMES: I see.

HELEN: My mother had a considerable sum of money—not less than a thousand a year. She bequeathed it to Dr. Roylott entirely while we resided with him, with a provision that a certain annual sum should be allowed to each of us in the event of our marriage. Shortly after our return to England—that was about eight years ago—my mother was killed in a railway accident near Crewe.

WATSON: [*Sympathetic exclamations*]

HELEN: Dr. Roylott then abandoned his attempts to establish himself in practice in London, and he took us to live with him in the ancestral house at Stoke Moran. [*Slight pause*] About this time, a terrible change came over our stepfather.

HOLMES: A change?

HELEN: Yes. Instead of making friends and exchanging visits with our neighbors, he indulged in ferocious quarrels with anyone crossing his path. There was a series of disgraceful brawls, and two of them ended in the police court. My stepfather became the terror of the village. He's a man of immense strength and absolutely uncontrollable anger.

HOLMES: Is there any history of violence or violence of temper in his family, to your knowledge?

HELEN: There is, indeed. I think in my stepfather's case it's even worse, as he lived so long in the tropics. Only last week he threw the local blacksmith over a parapet into a stream. It was only by paying over all the money I could get together that I was able to avert another public exposure.

WATSON: Terrible, terrible!

HELEN: His only friends now are the wandering gypsies. He gives them leave to camp on what's left of the family estate and sometimes wanders away with them for weeks on end. Oh, and he has his animals.

WATSON: Bit of a farmer, then?

HELEN: Nothing like that, I'm afraid. He has a passion for Indian animals. At this moment he has a cheetah and a baboon wandering quite freely over the grounds. They are feared by the villagers almost as much as their master. But to continue—you can imagine that I and my poor sister Julia had no great pleasure in our lives. No servant would stay with us, and for a long time we did all the house work. She was only thirty at the time of her death, but her hair had already begun to whiten even as mine has.

HOLMES: Your sister is dead, then?

HELEN: She died just two years ago. We had an aunt living near Harrow whom we were occasionally allowed to visit. When Julia went there at Christmas two years ago she met a Marine major and got engaged to him. My stepfather learned of the engagement when my sister returned, and offered no objection to the marriage. But within a fortnight of the day which had been fixed for the wedding, this terrible event occurred.

HOLMES: Miss Stoner, pray be precise as to details at this point.

HELEN: It is easy for me to be so, for every event of that dreadful time is seared into my memory. The Manor house, as I have already said, is very old. Only one wing is now inhabited. The bedrooms are on the ground floor. The first is Dr. Roylott's, the second was my sister's, and the third my own. There's no communication between them, but they all open out into the same corridor. Do I make myself plain?

HOLMES: Perfectly so.

WATSON: Yes, yes.

HELEN: The windows of all three rooms open out upon the lawn. That fatal night Dr. Roylott had gone to his room early, and Julia was troubled by the smell of his strong Indian cigars. She left her room and came into mine, where we sat chatting about her approaching wedding. At eleven o'clock she rose to leave me.

[*Fade out. Fade in voices of two young women*]

JULIA: Helen darling . . .

HELEN: Yes, dear?

JULIA: Tell me, have you ever heard anyone whistle in the dead of night?

HELEN: Whistle? No, never.

JULIA: I suppose you don't whistle in your sleep?

HELEN: Certainly not! But why are you asking?

JULIA: Because during the last two nights, at about three in the morning, I've kept hearing a low clear whistle. It wakes me up. I can't tell where it comes from. It seems to be from the next room, or perhaps from the lawn. I thought I would just ask you whether you had heard it.

HELEN: No, I haven't. It must be those gypsies in the plantation.

JULIA: Yes, very likely. And yet if it were on the lawn I wonder you didn't hear it also.

HELEN: Ah, but I've less on my mind than you. And I sleep more heavily than you.

JULIA: [*Laughing*] Well, I don't suppose it matters. Good night, darling.

HELEN: Good night, Julia, dear.

[*Sounds of door closing, key turning in lock. Fade out on Helen yawning. Fade in conversation in Baker Street sitting-room*]

HOLMES: Just one moment, Miss Stoner. You locked the door after your sister?

HELEN: Yes, I did.

HOLMES: Was it your custom always to lock yourselves in at night?

HELEN: Always.

HOLMES: Why was that?

HELEN: Well, I mentioned that Dr. Roylott keeps a cheetah and a baboon. We wouldn't have felt safe unless our doors were locked.

HOLMES: Ah, quite so. Pray continue, please.

HELEN: Well, I couldn't sleep that night. I had a vague feeling of—impending misfortune. My sister and I were twins, you know, and we seemed to be very closely bound.

WATSON: Yes. Often the case.

HELEN: It was a wild night, with the wind howling and rain beating against the windows. Suddenly, over all the hubbub, I heard the wild screams of a terrified woman. I knew it was my sister's voice. I rushed into the corridor. Just as I opened my door I seemed to hear a low whistle and then a clanging sound, as if a mass of metal had fallen. My sister's door was unlocked and it seemed to swing slowly open upon its hinges. I was rooted to the spot, not knowing what was about to issue from it. Then, by the light of the corridor lamp, I saw my sister coming out, with her face blanched with terror and her hands groping for help.

[*Quick fade out and fade in of young women's voices*]

HELEN: Julia! Julia, my darling!

JULIA: [*Groan*]

HELEN: What is it? What's happened to my darling?

JULIA: Oh, Helen! It was—it was the band! The speckled band!

HELEN: The speckled band?

JULIA: The . . . the . . .

[*She falls, with a choking sob*]

HELEN: Julia! Oh, darling! [*Moving off, calling*] Stepfather! Stepfather, come quickly, please!

[*Fade out. Fade in Baker Street sitting-room*]

HELEN: When he reached my sister's side she was unconscious. She slowly sank and died without recovering consciousness. And that was the dreadful end of my beloved sister.

WATSON: A terrible story, ma'am.

HOLMES: One moment—you are sure about this whistle and the metallic sound? Could you swear to it?

HELEN: That was what the county coroner asked me at the inquiry. It's my strong impression that I heard it.

WATSON: Of course, there was the noise of the gale. I suppose the old house creaked a bit.

HELEN: It's possible that I was deceived. I don't know.

HOLMES: Was your sister dressed?

HELEN: No, she was in her nightdress. In her right hand we found the charred stump of a match, and a matchbox in her left.

HOLMES: Showing that she had struck a light and looked around when she was alarmed. That is important.

WATSON: What conclusions did the coroner come to, Miss Stoner?

HELEN: He was unable to find any satisfactory cause of death. The evidence showed that Julia's door had been fastened on the inside, and the windows were blocked with old-fashioned shutters with broad iron bars. They were fastened every night. The walls were carefully sounded, and they were found to be quite solid all round. The floor was also examined, with the same result.

HOLMES: The chimney?

HELEN: It's wide, but heavily barred.

WATSON: Then your sister was quite alone when she met her end?

HOLMES: Were there any marks of violence on her?

HELEN: None.

HOLMES: How about poison?

HELEN: The doctors examined her for it, but there was nothing.

HOLMES: Miss Stoner, what do *you* think this unfortunate lady died of?

HELEN: It's my belief, Mr. Holmes, she died of pure fear and nervous shock.

HOLMES: And what do you think frightened her?

HELEN: That's what I can't imagine.

WATSON: You said there were gypsies about the place. Were there any at the time?

HELEN: Yes, Dr. Watson. There are nearly always some.

WATSON: Mm!

HOLMES: What did you gather from this allusion to a speckled band?

HELEN: I've thought sometimes it was merely the wild talk of delirium. But it may have referred to some band of people.

WATSON: The gypsies!

HELEN: It had crossed my mind. I don't know whether the spotted handkerchiefs some of them wear over their heads might be described as speckled bands.

HOLMES: These are very deep waters. Pray go on with your narrative.

HELEN: Two years have passed since then, Mr. Holmes. My life has been lonelier than ever, until just lately. However, a dear friend whom I've known for many years has done me the honor to ask me to marry him. His name is Percy Armitage. We're to be married during the next few weeks.

WATSON: If I may offer my congratulations?

HELEN: Thank you, Doctor.

HOLMES: What is your stepfather's view?

HELEN: Oh, he's offered no opposition whatever.

HOLMES: I see.

HELEN: But two days ago some repairs were started in the west wing of the building. My bedroom wall is affected, so I had to move into the room in which my sister died. I'm sleeping in the very bed in which she slept. So you can imagine my terror last night as I lay awake, thinking of her awful fate, when I suddenly heard that same low whistle which had occurred just before her death.

WATSON: Great heavens!

HELEN: I sprang up and lit the lamp, but nothing was to be seen in the room. I was too shaken to go to bed again, though. I got dressed, and as soon as it was daylight I slipped down to the Crown Inn and got a dog cart to drive me to Leatherhead. My one object was to see you, Mr. Holmes, and ask your advice.

HOLMES: You have done wisely, Miss Stoner. But have you told me everything?

HELEN: Yes, I have.

HOLMES: I fancy you have not.

HELEN: Mr. Holmes!

HOLMES: You are shielding your stepfather.

HELEN: I don't understand. What do you mean?

HOLMES: If you will permit me to turn back the fringe of your sleeve—thank you.

WATSON: Great heavens!

HOLMES: You have been cruelly used, madam.

HELEN: [*Flustered*] He—he is a hard man. Perhaps he hardly knows his own strength.

HOLMES: This is very deep business. There are a thousand details I should like to know before I decide on our course of action. But we haven't a moment to lose. Now if we were to come to Stoke Moran today, would it be possible for us to see these rooms without your stepfather's knowledge?

HELEN: Yes. As it happens he was speaking of coming into town today on some important business. He will probably be away all day, and there should be nothing to disturb you. We have a housekeeper now, but she is old and foolish. I could easily get her out of the way.

HOLMES: Excellent! You are not averse to this trip, Watson?

WATSON: By no means, Holmes.

HOLMES: Then we shall both come. What are you going to do yourself, Miss Stoner?

HELEN: Now that I'm in town there are one or two things that I'd like to do. I shall go back by the twelve o'clock train, so as to be there in time for your coming.

HOLMES: Then you may expect us early in the afternoon. I, too, have some small business matters to attend to first. Won't you wait and have breakfast, though?

WATSON: Yes, do.

HELEN: No, thank you. I must go. My heart is lightened already, gentlemen. [*Going*] I shall look forward to seeing you again this afternoon.

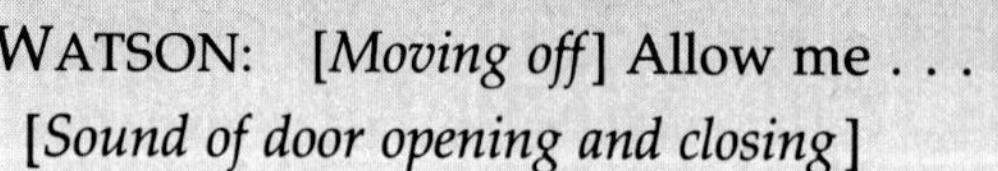

WATSON: [*Moving off*] Allow me . . .
[*Sound of door opening and closing*]

WATSON: Well, Holmes?

HOLMES: And what do you think of it all, Watson?

WATSON: Dark and sinister, that's what I think of it.

HOLMES: Dark enough and sinister enough.

WATSON: But, Holmes—if she's correct in saying the floors and walls are sound, and the door and window and chimney impassable, then her sister must have been absolutely alone when she met her death.

HOLMES: Death in a sealed room, in other words?

WATSON: Then, what about these nocturnal whistles—and what she said about a speckled band?

HOLMES: I was hoping you were going to provide me with those answers, Watson.

WATSON: Well, you'll have to hope again. I haven't a notion.

HOLMES: Dear me!

WATSON: Have you?

HOLMES: We have whistles at night, a band of gypsies on very friendly terms with a doctor who has a financial interest in preventing his stepdaughter's marriage. We have a dying reference to a speckled band, and the fact of a metallic clang which might have been caused by one of those metal bars on the shutters falling back into place. If we combine these ideas I think there is good ground to believe that the mystery may be cleared along those lines.

WATSON: But what did the gypsies do, then?

HOLMES: I cannot imagine.

WATSON: Neither can I. I can see plenty of obstacles to my theory involving them.

HOLMES: And so can I. It's precisely for that reason that we're going to Stoke Moran today. I want to see just how much can be explained away.
[*Disturbance outside door*]

HOLMES: What in the name of the devil . . .
[*Door flung open*]

ROYLOTT: Which of you is Holmes?

HOLMES: My name, sir. But you have the advantage of me.

ROYLOTT: I am Dr. Grimesby Roylott of Stoke Moran.

HOLMES: Indeed, Doctor. Pray take a seat.

ROYLOTT: I will do nothing of the kind. My stepdaughter has been here. I have traced her. What has she been saying to you?

HOLMES: It *is* a little cold for the time of the year.

ROYLOTT: What has she been saying to you?

HOLMES: But I have heard that the crocuses promise well.

ROYLOTT: Ha! You think you can put me off, do you? I know you, you scoundrel! I have heard of you before. You are Holmes the meddler.

HOLMES: [*Chuckles*]

ROYLOTT: Holmes the busybody!

HOLMES: *[Chuckles louder]*

ROYLOTT: Holmes the Scotland Yard troublemaker.

HOLMES: *[Laughs heartily]* Your conversation is most entertaining, Dr. Roylott. When you go out, close the door. There's a decided draft.

ROYLOTT: I will go when I have had my say. Don't you dare to meddle with my affairs. I know the girl has been here. I'm a dangerous man to fall foul of. *[Moving off]* See here.

[Rattle of fire irons]

ROYLOTT: I'll show you how I can bend a poker, and how I could bend you for two pins. *[Grunts with effort]* There!

[Clatter as poker is hurled to floor]

ROYLOTT: That's what I could do to you. See that you keep yourself out of my grip.

[Sound of door slamming]

WATSON: Well, really.

HOLMES: *[Laughing]* He seems a very amiable fellow. *[Moving off]* I'm not quite so bulky myself, but if he'd stayed I might have shown him that my grip is not much more feeble than his own.

[Clatter of poker being retrieved. Holmes grunts with effort]

HOLMES: There you are—quite straight again.

WATSON: I say, Holmes!

HOLMES: And fancy his having the insolence to confuse me with the official detective force! However, the incident gives zest to our investigation.

WATSON: I hope the dear little lady won't suffer from allowing this brute to trace her.

HOLMES: Let's hope not. And now,

Watson, we shall order breakfast. Afterwards I shall walk down to Doctors' Commons, where I hope to get some data which may help us in this matter.

[*Fade out. Fade in Baker Street sitting-room. Sound of door closing*]

WATSON: Ah, Holmes! Wondered if you'd be back for lunch.

HOLMES: Not quite one o'clock, I think.

WATSON: What have you got there?

HOLMES: Some rather interesting notes. I've been examining the will of the deceased wife.

WATSON: Roylott's?

HOLMES: Yes. The total income at the time of his wife's death was little short of eleven hundred pounds. Agricultural prices have fallen since then though, so it's not much more than seven hundred and fifty pounds now. Each daughter could claim an income of two hundred and fifty pounds in case of marriage. So, if both girls had married, our strong man would have had a mere pittance left.

WATSON: I see. Even one marriage would have cut his income by a good third.

HOLMES: Exactly. My morning's work has proved that he has the very strongest motives for standing in the way of anything of the sort. And now, Watson, this is too serious for dawdling, especially as the old man knows that we are interesting ourselves in his affairs. I think we must forgo lunch and take a cab to Waterloo.

WATSON: Very well, if you say so.

HOLMES: I'd be much obliged if you would slip your revolver into your pocket. An Eley's No. 2 is an excellent argument with gentlemen who can twist steel pokers into knots. I think that and a toothbrush are all we shall need.

[*Fade out. Fade in sound of voices*]

HELEN: Mr. Holmes, Dr. Watson—I've been waiting so eagerly for you. It's all turned out splendidly. Dr. Roylott has gone to town, and it's unlikely he'll be back before evening.

HOLMES: We had the pleasure of making the doctor's acquaintance ourselves.

HELEN: Where?

WATSON: He came to our rooms. Threw his weight about a bit too. Trying to warn us off.

HELEN: He followed me, then?

HOLMES: So it appears.

HELEN: What will he say when he returns?

HOLMES: He had better be on his guard. He may find there is someone more cunning than himself on his track. You must lock yourself in safely tonight. If he tries violence, we shall take you away to your aunt's. But now, we must make the best use of our time.

HELEN: Yes, of course.

HOLMES: If you will kindly take us at once to the rooms we are to examine.

HELEN: If you'll follow me, then.

[*Fade out. Fade in sound of steps in hall*]

HOLMES: And this, I take it, is the room in which you are now sleeping?

HELEN: Yes. This is where my sister met her death.

HOLMES: Dr. Roylott's room is on one side of it, and your old room on the other?

HELEN: That's so.

HOLMES: You are sleeping in here only while alterations are going on, I believe you said?

HELEN: Well . . .

WATSON: There doesn't seem much need for those alterations. It's a solid enough wall.

HELEN: There is none. I believe it was simply an excuse to move me from my room.

HOLMES: Ah! Now, if I may examine the room itself.

HELEN: Yes. Please come in.

[*Sound of door opening*]

HOLMES: I see. Now, as both you and your sister locked your doors at night, your rooms were quite unapproachable from the corridor.

HELEN: Yes.

HOLMES: And there are the shutters you close over the windows at night.

WATSON: Strong enough, by the look of them. Solid iron hinges. Nowhere to get a knife through to raise the bar.

HOLMES: I believe you're correct, Watson. [*Moving slightly off*] Well, what else have we? What is that over the bed? A bell-rope?

HELEN: Yes. It rings in the housekeeper's room.

HOLMES: It looks newer than the other things here.

HELEN: Yes. It was only put there a couple of years ago.

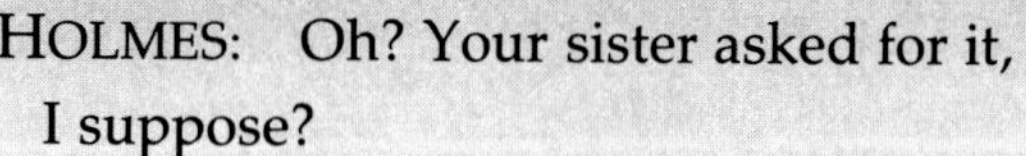

HOLMES: Oh? Your sister asked for it, I suppose?

HELEN: No. I never heard of her using it. We always used to get what we wanted for ourselves.

HOLMES: Indeed! Care to give it a tug, Watson?

WATSON: Certainly. What about the, er, housekeeper?

HELEN: She won't hear it, Dr. Watson. She's in the washhouse, well out of our way this afternoon.

WATSON: [*Moving off*] Right. [*Slight pause*] Hello, that's funny.

HOLMES: What is it, Watson?

WATSON: Doesn't seem to work. No give in it at all.

HOLMES: Let me see. [*Slight pause*] Mm! This bell-rope is a dummy.

HELEN: You mean it won't ring?

HOLMES: No. It is not even attached to a wire.

WATSON: Very strange.

HOLMES: And very interesting. Look—you can see it's fastened to a hook just above the little opening of the ventilator.

HELEN: How very absurd! I never noticed that before.

HOLMES: Hm! There are one or two very singular points about this room. For instance, do you notice that the ventilator connects with the adjoining room?

WATSON: Good heavens!

HOLMES: What a fool a builder must be to ventilate one room from another when he could just as easily have cut the ventilator through the outside wall to the fresh air.

HELEN: The ventilator was quite a recent addition, too.

HOLMES: Done about the same time as the bell-rope, I fancy.

HELEN: Yes. There were several little changes carried out about that time.

HOLMES: They seem to have been of a most interesting character—a dummy bell-rope and a ventilator which doesn't ventilate. With your permission, Miss Stoner, we shall now carry our researches into the next apartment—Dr. Roylott's own room.

[*Sounds of steps as they move to the other room*]

HOLMES: Sparsely furnished, I see.

HELEN: Yes.

HOLMES: And a safe. What's in it?

HELEN: My stepfather's business papers.

HOLMES: Oh! You've seen inside then?

HELEN: Only once, some years ago. It was full of papers.

HOLMES: There isn't a cat in it, for example?

WATSON: Cat in a safe, Holmes?

HELEN: No. Of course not.

HOLMES: Well, look at this. What's a saucer of milk doing here?

HELEN: Well, I don't understand. We don't keep a cat. But there is a cheetah and a baboon.

HOLMES: Well, a cheetah is just a big cat, and yet I dare say a saucer of milk wouldn't go very far in satisfying its wants. There is one point I should like to determine.

WATSON: What's that, Holmes?

HOLMES: The seat of this wooden chair

here. Just get my lens onto it. [*Slight pause*] Hm! That's quite settled, then.

WATSON: What . . .

HOLMES: [*Slightly off*] Hello! Here *is* something interesting.

WATSON: Looks like a dog leash.

HOLMES: Curled upon itself and tied to make a loop of a whipcord. What do you make of that, Watson?

WATSON: Well, it's a common enough object. But I don't know why it should be tied like that.

HOLMES: That isn't quite so common, is it? Ah, me! It's a wicked world, and when a clever man turns his brain to crime it is the worst of all. I think I have seen enough now, Miss Stoner. With your permission we shall walk out upon the lawn.

HELEN: Certainly.

[*Sounds of steps as they leave house*]

HOLMES: It is very essential, Miss Stoner, that you should absolutely follow my advice in every respect. Your life may depend upon your compliance.

HELEN: I assure you I am in your hands.

HOLMES: In the first place, my friend and I must spend the night in your room.

WATSON: Holmes . . .!

HELEN: I don't . . .

HOLMES: Yes, it must be so. Let me explain. I believe that is the village inn over there?

HELEN: Yes, that is the Crown.

HOLMES: Very good. Your windows would be visible from there, I think?

HELEN: Certainly.

HOLMES: You must confine yourself to your room with a headache when your stepfather comes back. When you hear him retire for the night, you must open the shutters on your window, undo the hasp, put your lamp there as a signal to us, and then withdraw from the room with everything you're likely to want. You must go into the room which you used to occupy. I've no doubt that you could manage there for one night?

HELEN: Oh, yes, easily.

HOLMES: The rest you will leave in our hands.

HELEN: But what will you do?

HOLMES: We shall come over from the inn and spend the night in the room you have left, and we shall investigate the cause of this noise which has disturbed you.

HELEN: Mr. Holmes, I believe you have already made up your mind.

HOLMES: Perhaps I have.

HELEN: Then for pity's sake tell me what was the cause of my sister's death.

HOLMES: I should prefer to have clearer proof before I speak. And now, Miss Stoner, we must leave you. If Dr. Roylott returned and saw us, our journey would be in vain. Watson and I must make our way to the Crown and engage a room commanding a view of this part of Stoke Moran Manor House. Goodbye, Miss Stoner. Be brave.

HELEN: Thank you, Mr. Holmes. I have complete faith in you.

[*Fade out. Fade in sound of voices in room at inn*]

WATSON: [*Off*] Now he is shaking his fists at the boy. Didn't open the gates quick enough for him. Ah, there he goes.

[*Distant sound of horsetrap driving away*]

HOLMES: Well, so the good doctor returns.

WATSON: And in a very nasty mood, if you ask me, Holmes.

HOLMES: You know, Watson, I really have some scruples about taking you with me tonight. There is a distinct element of danger.

WATSON: Can I be of assistance?

HOLMES: Your presence might be invaluable.

WATSON: Then I shall certainly come.

HOLMES: It is very kind of you.

WATSON: You speak of danger, Holmes. You've evidently seen more in those rooms than I did.

HOLMES: No. I imagine you saw as much as I. But I fancy I may have deduced a little more.

WATSON: I didn't notice anything remarkable except the bell-rope.

HOLMES: You saw the ventilator, too?

WATSON: Yes. But I don't think it's such a very unusual thing to have a small opening between two rooms. I mean, dash it, it's so small that a rat could hardly get through.

HOLMES: Before we even came to Stoke Moran I knew we should find a ventilator.

WATSON: My dear Holmes!

HOLMES: Oh, yes, I did. You remember in her statement she said that her sister could smell Dr. Roylott's cigar?

WATSON: Yes.

HOLMES: Well, of course, that suggests at once that there must be a communication between the two rooms.

WATSON: Ah!

HOLMES: It could only be a small one, or it would have been remarked on at the coroner's inquiry. Therefore, I deduced a ventilator.

WATSON: Pretty obvious, I suppose.

HOLMES: Oh, yes!

WATSON: But what harm can there be in that?

HOLMES: Well, there is at least a curious coincidence of dates. A ventilator is made, a bell-rope is hung, and a lady who sleeps in the bed dies. Did you observe anything peculiar about that bed?

WATSON: No.

HOLMES: It was clamped to the floor.

WATSON: What?

HOLMES: The lady could not move her bed. It must always be in the same relative position to the ventilator and to the rope.

WATSON: Holmes! Now I'm beginning to see.

HOLMES: Capital!

WATSON: We're only just in time to prevent another horrible crime!

HOLMES: Horrible and subtle. When a doctor does go wrong, he is the first of criminals. He has nerve and he has knowledge. Palmer and Pritchard were among the heads of their profession. This man strikes even deeper, but I think, Watson, that we shall be able to strike deeper still. But we shall have horrors enough before the night is over. For goodness sake, let us turn our minds for a few hours to something more cheerful.

[*Fade out. Fade in*]

WATSON: Holmes! There's the light from the manor house. Her signal.

HOLMES: About eleven o'clock. Come along, then. And keep a sharp lookout for that baboon.

WATSON: And the cheetah! I shall be a good deal happier when we're in that room.

HOLMES: Now come along.

[*Fade out. Fade in sound of wind*]

HOLMES: [*Speaking low*] Now, Watson, there is the window. She has left it open for us. We must get in as quietly as possible and close the shutters without a sound. We must sit without a light. He would see it through the ventilator.

WATSON: Yes. I understand.

HOLMES: Do not go to sleep. Your life may depend on it. Have your pistol ready in case we should need it. I will sit on the side of the bed, and you in the chair.

WATSON: Right.

HOLMES: I've brought a candle and matches with me. We shall have to turn out her lamp as soon as we enter, so that he'll think that she's gone to bed. But if anything happens I have my candle ready to light. Now, my dear Watson, is everything understood?

WATSON: Perfectly.

HOLMES: Good. Let's get in, then. [*Rustle of shrubbery, then slight noises as men climb through window*]

HOLMES: [*Whispers*] Excellent. Now put out the lamp, Watson. Good. Now then, quite still, not a sound.

WATSON: [*Whispers*] Holmes—something's happening. A lantern's been lit in the next room.

HOLMES: Yes, I see. Listen!

[*Slight hissing comes and goes several times*]

WATSON: What is it?

[*Low whistle from next room*]

HOLMES: Right, Watson. Stay where you are.

[*Match struck and candle lit. Holmes leaps to his feet and lashes several times at the bell-rope with his cane*]

HOLMES: [*Shouting*] You see it, Watson? You see it?

WATSON: I can't . . .

HOLMES: Ah! It's getting away!

WATSON: What is it, Holmes? I can't see . . .

ROYLOTT: [*Screams in the next room*]

HOLMES: Quickly, Watson. Into the next room.

[*Sound of running feet*]

WATSON: What does it mean, Holmes?

HOLMES: Get your pistol out, and into Roylott's room quickly.

ROYLOTT: [*Moans with pain as they enter*]

WATSON: Look at him—look at his head! Wrapped around it!

HOLMES: The band—the speckled band!

ROYLOTT: [*Gives a final strangled cry and is silent*]

HOLMES: It's a swamp adder—the deadliest snake in India. He's dead already.

WATSON: Great heavens!

HOLMES: Violence does, in truth, recoil upon the violent. The schemer falls into the pit which he digs for another.

WATSON: Shall I shoot it?

HOLMES: No, this noose in the dog leash will do it. It's obviously intended for this. Just slip it around the reptile's neck—like that—and if you will be so good as to open the safe door a little wider we'll pop it inside—like that. Now close the door quickly.

WATSON: With the greatest pleasure!

[*Clang of door*]

HOLMES: And now we must remove Miss Stoner to some place of shelter and let the county police know what has happened.

[*Fade in conversation in train compartment*]

WATSON: But Holmes, what made you suspect you would find a snake?

HOLMES: When I examined the room, it became clear to me that whatever danger threatened could not come either from the window or the door. The discovery that the bell-rope placed behind the ventilator was a dummy and that the bed was clamped to the floor instantly made me suspicious that the rope was there as a bridge. The idea of a snake occurred to me instantly, and when I coupled it with my knowledge that Dr. Roylott was a fancier of creatures from India, I felt sure I was on the right track.

WATSON: Yes, of course. I see.

HOLMES: The idea of using a form of poison which could not possibly be discovered by any chemical test was just such a one as would occur to a clever and ruthless man who had had an Eastern training. From his point of view, also, the speed with which such a poison would take effect would be an advantage. It would be a sharp-eyed coroner indeed who could distinguish the two little dark punctures which would show where the poison fangs had done their work.

WATSON: That's quite so. Miss Stoner made no mention of anything like that having been discovered.

HOLMES: I'm sure they weren't.

WATSON: Well, what about the whistle?

HOLMES: That was the next thing I thought about. He would put the snake through the ventilator with the certainty that it would crawl down the rope and land on the bed. He couldn't be sure that it would bite the occupant of the bed. She might escape every night for a week before she fell a victim. Therefore, he had to be able to recall the snake before the morning light or she would have seen it. He trained it—probably by the use of the milk which we saw—to come back to him when he whistled to it.

WATSON: Bit of a snake charmer, eh?

HOLMES: Something of the kind. Well, I had come to these conclusions before I had even entered his room. You remember I examined his chair with my lens?

WATSON: What was all that, then?

HOLMES: Simply to confirm to myself he had been in the habit of standing on it in order to reach the ventilator. When I saw the safe, the saucer of milk, and this loop of whipcord, any doubts I might still have had were dispelled.

WATSON: So the metallic clang . . .

HOLMES: Obviously her stepfather hastily closing the door of his safe on its terrible occupant.

WATSON: Holmes . . .

HOLMES: Yes, Watson?

WATSON: I'm just beginning to feel rather thankful that I didn't know any of this before we settled down in that room in the dark. When I think of that creature sliding down the bell-rope towards us . . .

HOLMES: Well, at least I sat on the bed and gave you the chair.

WATSON: So you did. And you knew what to expect too.

HOLMES: As soon as I heard the creature hiss I knew for certain what we were up against. I don't mind admitting I was glad to get that candle lit and use my stick upon the brute.

WATSON: With the result of driving it through the ventilator. Was that what you wanted to do?

HOLMES: No, I wouldn't say that. Some of my blows got home upon it and must have roused its snakish temper. It fled through the ventilator and fastened upon the first person it saw. No doubt I'm indirectly responsible for Dr. Grimesby Roylott's death—but I can't say it's likely to weigh very heavily upon my conscience.

Do you think this mystery is realistic? Explain why or why not.

Sherlock Holmes is famous for his ability to make deductions from the details he observes. Which of his deductions in this play did you find the most impressive?

What qualities does Sherlock Holmes have that make him a good detective?

At the end of the play, what could Dr. Watson conclude about Sherlock Holmes's reasoning?

WRITE List several deductions an investigator like Sherlock Holmes might make about you based upon your appearance today, and explain how he could have arrived at each deduction.

WORDS ABOUT THE AUTHOR: ARTHUR CONAN DOYLE

From childhood Arthur Conan Doyle had a great love for making up exciting tales. He turned this gift to practical advantage at the bleak schools he attended, where the boys were poorly fed. He told adventure stories to his classmates in return for pastries; the cakes had to be handed over before he would end the story. Even at school he was a devoted admirer of chivalry, setting rules for fair fighting and for treating women and girls honorably. This interest, combined with his mother's passion for genealogy, later inspired him to write historical romances, the kind of novel he preferred.

At seventeen Conan Doyle entered medical school. When his practice was new and patients were slow in coming, he used his free time to write the first Sherlock Holmes story, *A Study in Scarlet.* He modeled his detective partly after a former teacher, Joseph Bell, who encouraged his students to track the symptoms of a disease to their source with the same rigorous logic that a detective uses in uncovering a crime.

After writing another Holmes novel, Conan Doyle began to submit shorter "Sherlocks" to the *Strand* magazine, where they were a great success. Holmes's career would have ended after half a dozen of these short cases, but the editors clamored for more. Less than two years later, however, the author decided to rid himself of a subject he no longer wanted to write about and let Holmes plunge into the depths of the Reichenbach Falls, a Swiss tourist attraction that Conan Doyle had visited with his wife. Thousands of readers were so outraged that they canceled their subscriptions to the *Strand,* but it was almost ten years before Holmes's creator was willing to resurrect him. (The London Post Office still receives mail for Holmes from people who do not understand that he is fictional.)

THE COIN EXPERT

by FALCON TRAVIS

Here is a mystery for you to solve. Watch for clues as you read.

Inspector Donna DiAnsa and Sergeant Dunitz turned into a narrow side street and headed toward the little shop of C. J. Silver, buyer and seller of coins and medals. They stood in front of the shop for a few minutes, studying the trays of coins on display. Then, after briefly consulting an inventory of stolen property, the Inspector put the list into her purse and went to the door. As she turned the handle, a young man came to the door and unbolted it.

"You're opening late this morning," said the Inspector, as she walked inside, followed by Sergeant Dunitz. "Is Mr. Silver in?"

"Mr. Silver is my uncle. I'm helping him as much as I can until he can get around again," explained the young man. "He hurt his foot badly a few days ago, but he comes in every day anyway. I couldn't manage this place if he didn't. I don't know anything about coins. He's in his workroom at the back, sorting out a batch of coins. I've just been making us some coffee."

"We know your Uncle George very well," said Inspector DiAnsa. "We're police officers. Sorry to hear about his accident. Our questions won't keep you long. Your uncle is one of the great authorities on rare coins. His own private collection is worth a fortune, as I'm sure you know. I remember him telling me that as an only child and a lifelong bachelor, he's used to being on his own and really prefers his own company, but I'm sure he's glad to have you around at a time like this."

"I hope so," said the young man. "I'm doing my best. Now how can I help you? I hope Uncle hasn't been breaking the law."

"No, nothing like that," said the Inspector. "It's a general query about Roman coins. It cropped up the other day at the station, and I'd like to be sure about it. Will you go ask your uncle whether the date on an early Roman coin has the B.C. in front of it or after it? For example, B.C. 55 or 55 B.C.? I think 55 B.C. is correct."

The young man disappeared into the back of the store and Inspector DiAnsa turned to the Sergeant. "The man's a fraud, Hugh," she said. "When he comes back out here with the answer, if I put my hand up on the counter, grab the man and hold him. Otherwise, leave the next move to me. The real business we came about can wait."

"You were right, Officer," said the man, as he came back into the room, "55 B.C. is correct."

Inspector DiAnsa put her hand on the counter. Sergeant Dunitz grabbed the man in a vise-like hold. The Inspector dashed through to the back room and found Mr. Silver lying bound and gagged and in a dazed state.

"How did you know that fellow was a fraud?" asked Mr. Silver later, after a police van had taken the man away.

"He made three slips, Mr. Silver," answered Donna DiAnsa. "Or rather, I *led* him into making three slips."

"I spotted two of them," said Sergeant Dunitz.

How many did you spot?

CLUES

Clues: Look again at the coin expert's name, the young man's relationship to him, and the date of the coin.

SOLUTION

Solution: Donna DiAnsa tested the young man by referring to Mr. Silver as his Uncle "George," which the man didn't question, although, being "C. J." Silver, he was obviously not a George.

Mr. Silver, being an only child and a lifelong bachelor, could not be anybody's uncle.

No coin could be given a B.C. (Before Christ) date, because nobody knew beforehand how many years later Christ would be born, which showed that the young man had not asked Mr. Silver, who would certainly have known.

DR. GEORGE WASHINGTON CARVER
UNITED STATES POSTAGE
3¢

The Great Peanut Puzzle

by Gail Kay Haines

In A. Conan Doyle's mystery books, desperate people came from all over England to lay their problems before Sherlock Holmes. He always solved his cases by outthinking everyone else.

In "The Great Peanut Puzzle," farmers from all over Alabama brought a life-and-death problem to the smartest man they knew. His ideas often sounded crazy, but they always worked. Until now.

The first mystery George Washington Carver found when he arrived at Tuskegee Institute in 1896 was: where is the laboratory? He had been hired to teach agricultural science at a new Alabama college for black students. There seemed to be plenty of students, but very little college.

George walked around, noting the acres of bare, rutted dirt stretching in all directions, with no grass, no trees, and no crops. He smelled the pigpens and watched the turkey buzzards dive in and out of a huge rubbish heap, but he couldn't find the laboratory. There was no laboratory.

In place of the well-equipped lab and greenhouse at Iowa State Agricultural College, where he had been teaching, Carver acquired one bare room in a dilapidated building—to live in as well as work in—and twenty acres of dirt so poor it could barely grow weeds.

The handful of students assigned to work with Dr. Carver worked under protest. Farming, to them, meant hopeless drudgery. They would rather study almost anything else.

Born a slave, George Carver had been on his own since he was ten years old. He knew how to make do and do without. He

Top: Slater-Armstrong Memorial Trades Building, Tuskegee Institute. Bottom: Students made the brick and constructed the building at Tuskegee Institute in the late 1800s.

also knew how to make the best of almost any situation.

Carver sent his students scouring through the trash heap at school and through dumps all over town. He had them asking at doors for cast-off pans and bottles, wire, string, and can lids, rubber, and glass or almost anything that might possibly be useful. He even sent the boys for armloads of reeds from the swamp.

With this pile of junk in an empty room, Carver solved his first mystery. He "found" a laboratory. One old lamp served to heat and melt samples, to light his microscope (a gift from his friends in Iowa), and as a hand warmer on cold mornings. Broken bottles became test tubes and beakers, once he showed students how to give them a clean edge with a burning string. Stalks of hollow reeds took the place of glass pipettes, and he used an old flatiron to pound chunks of rock and dirt into powder to study.

Working from this cluttered room, Carver started on the second, more confusing mystery: what to do about the overwhelming poverty and ignorance and hopelessness all around him.

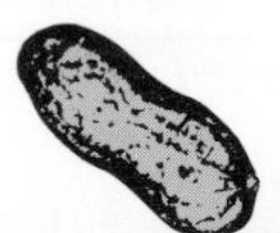

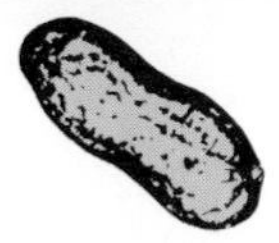

Cotton was king in Alabama, as it was all over the South. Scraggly stalks of cotton grew in almost every field, even up to the walls of the farmers' shacks.

But growing cotton, Carver knew, is hard on the soil. It takes out nutrients and puts nothing back.

Most of the small farm owners, black and white, were too poor to buy fertilizer. They just kept planting cotton, year after year, harvesting smaller and poorer crops each time. But they were not interested in advice from any northern scientist, especially a black northern scientist. What could he know about raising cotton?

So he showed them. On his twenty farmed-out acres, Carver helped his students plant cowpeas, which take nitrogen from the air and put it back into the soil. He had them carry muck from the swamp and spread it as fertilizer over the barren land. And he started a giant compost heap, using every scrap of organic waste he and his students could scrounge for miles around.

Carver and his students raised a crop of cotton on their "hopeless" land that produced five times more cotton fiber per acre than any other farm in the area. Black and white Alabamians came from all over the countryside just to stare at the bushy stalks.

After that, slowly, the people began to listen to and trust the teacher from "up north." They took his advice about everything from eating tomatoes (everyone had thought they were poisonous) to decorating their homes with paint made from Alabama clay.

But almost no one was ready to take his advice about giving up cotton. The more he talked about "resting the fields" and raising other kinds of produce, the more grimly they hung onto the only crop they knew someone would buy.

Disaster changed their minds. Trouble had been creeping up from Texas across the South for several years, and in 1915 it hit Alabama. The boll weevil burrowed its way into the cotton crop and ate its way out, as the stalks of cotton turned yellow, withered, and died. The destructive little beetles had killed the one crop upon which everyone's life depended.

Carver saw the deadly insects coming. He tried to get ready, but there was not much that could be done. The only hope was turning to another crop.

But what? Carver thought of sweet potatoes. Many farmers already grew them in small amounts, but they didn't seem like a cash crop. He experimented with soybeans, from China. They grew well and had plenty of uses, but they were totally strange to the southern farmer. Finally, he settled on the peanut.

Peanuts had been brought to North America by slave traders looking for the cheapest way to feed their victims. Many farmers already had a few vines growing around the house, for their children to pick and eat. It sounded perfect.

Peanuts could be roasted and eaten by the handful, but that was not nearly all. As Carver experimented in the kitchen, he learned more than a hundred ways to cook and eat peanuts. He even engineered a dinner party, cooked by the girls from the Home Economics department. The girls served soup, mock chicken, a creamed vegetable, bread, salad, ice cream, cookies, candy, and coffee. No one guessed that every single dish, including the coffee, was made mostly from peanuts.

People took Carver's advice. Hadn't he always been right before?

Soon the soft-shelled underground nuts (which are really a kind of bean) were growing all through eastern Alabama down to the Florida border. Carver was elated. His plan to save the farmer was working.

But the problems were just beginning. One day in October, an elderly widow knocked timidly on Carver's door. She asked the embarrassing question farmers all over the area were beginning to ask. "Who will buy my peanuts?" The third and deadliest mystery had arrived, and Carver had no ready answer.

The problem was too many peanuts for too small a market. No one bought them for anything but roasting, and there were tons going to waste. What to do was a mystery—and a matter of life and death for the farmers. George Carver knew peanuts were valuable. But how could he prove it?

At first, he was stumped. So he went for a walk.

All his life, George had loved going out into the woods at dawn to look at plants and to talk to God. This time, as the scientist described it years later, he wanted to talk to God about peanuts.

As the story goes, he first asked God to tell him why the universe was made. God answered that he wanted to know too much. So he asked why man was made. That was still too much. Finally, Carver asked, "Mr. Creator, why did you make the peanut?"

"That's better!" the Lord is said to have replied. And, as George Carver always told the story, he and God went into the laboratory together, to get to work.

Professor Carver had a well-equipped laboratory by this time, in a newer and larger building. But most of the old vinegar jars and sawed-off bottles and bent saucepans from that first makeshift lab were still in use. George never threw anything useful away.

Carver locked the door of "God's Little Workshop," as the students had nicknamed the new lab, with several bushels of peanuts inside. The mystery was how to make them valuable.

He thought a minute, first. Every plant is made from chemicals, combined by nature. In a chemical lab those chemicals can be taken apart and put together in new ways. Carver set out to remodel the peanut.

Wearing his old flour-sack apron, Carver shelled a handful of peanuts. His long fingers carefully separated and saved every scrap.

First, he ground the nuts to a fine, floury powder. He heated the powder and

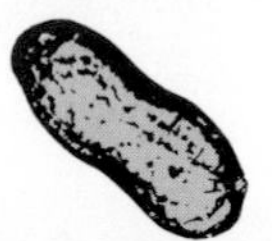

George Washington Carver (second from left) working with students in his laboratory at Tuskegee Institute.

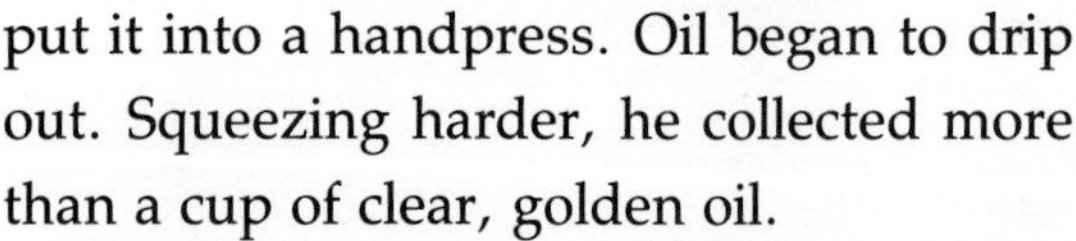

put it into a handpress. Oil began to drip out. Squeezing harder, he collected more than a cup of clear, golden oil.

Carver experimented with the oil until he had separated it into its chemical parts. He felt a thrill of excitement. This oil was special.

Most of the oil in Carver's day came from animal fat. It had a tough, jellylike coating on the oil particles, which made it hard to mix with other things. Peanut oil, without the coating, was smooth and quick-mixing.

Carver began thinking of ways to use the new easy-blending oil. He made soap and a few kinds of cosmetics. He tried rubbing it on his skin. He used it to fry other foods. In every way, it seemed superior to lard or animal tallow. Carver filled a row of little bottles with his new products.

Next, he picked up the cake of leftover peanut meal and rubbed it through his fingers. He blended it with water, warmed it, and cooled it, and flavored it with a little salt and sugar until he had a pitcher of creamy, good-tasting "milk."

The "milk" tasted so delicious he drank about half of the first batch. But Carver was working as a chemist, not a cook. Just tasting good was not enough. He tested the "milk" and all the other food products carefully, to see what they contained. Peanut milk and, in fact, most of the food products turned out to be as wholesome and rich in protein and vitamins as the foods they imitated.

Separating the different chemicals into jars, Carver investigated shoe polish, ink, dye, shaving cream, metal polish, axle grease, and even shampoo.

He made paper from the thin red skin found between a peanut and its hull. And from the broken hulls, he made insulating board, soil conditioner, and even a hard, shiny imitation marble.

For the first few days, George Carver did not leave the laboratory. He opened the door only to take in more peanuts. He refused the meals students set outside his door. When he got hungry, he ate a handful of peanuts or taste-tested one of his edible products.

By the end of the first week, Carver had developed more than a dozen useful, salable products that could be made from peanuts. Over the next few years he brought the list to over three hundred.

Businessmen were quick to make use of his findings. And since Carver refused to patent or take money for any of his discoveries, the ideas could be put into immediate use.

The peanuts were ready, and labor was available. It was not long before factories began to appear, making products from peanuts and making money for the farmers and the manufacturers and the whole South. Carver had solved the mystery in a very profitable way—for everyone but himself. (That didn't matter to George Carver. Most of the time he didn't even bother to cash his paychecks.)

When the U.S. entered World War I and foreign supplies and products became difficult to get, Carver's synthetic

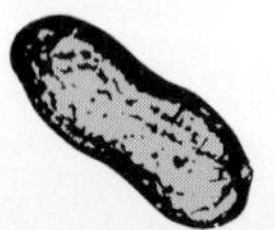

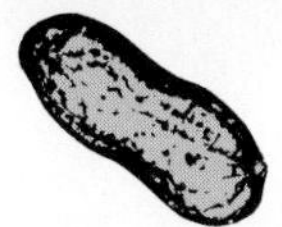

peanut-products became more and more important. Peanuts eventually became the second leading cash crop in the South, and one of the six leading crops in the United States.

In 1919, the people of Alabama built a monument to the boll weevil, in joking appreciation of what it had done for the economy by driving the farmers into raising peanuts. They might also have raised a monument to the small black man who made peanuts worth growing.

But Dr. Carver was already becoming famous around the country and the world for his scientific abilities. In 1923, he received the Spingarn Medal for "highest achievement by a man or woman of African descent," and other medals and honors recognized his contributions.

In a day before the synthetic materials taken for granted today were known, Carver helped to create a new science called chemurgy. Chemurgy is a branch of chemistry dealing with the use of organic products, especially farm products, to manufacture new, non-food items.

Not all the products Carver developed are still being made commercially, and many never were. But Carver's most important "discovery" was the idea that renewable resources can serve as the raw materials of industry. George Washington Carver's answer to "The Great Peanut Puzzle" led to a new branch of science that is becoming more important than ever before, today and for the future.

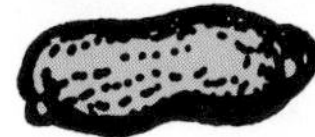

What impressed you most about George Washington Carver?

What details of the selection suggest that Carver did not work for money but for the love of his work?

How was the process of Carver's experiments just as important as the results of his discoveries?

WRITE What do you think it takes to be as good a scientific investigator as George Washington Carver? Write a paragraph explaining two or three important traits that a scientist needs to be successful.

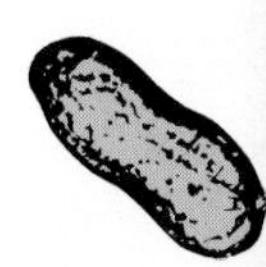

*T*he *G*reat SHUT-EYE *M*ystery

In an average lifetime, you will spend upwards of twenty-five years sleeping. It won't be out of choice, but out of necessity, although no one knows quite why. Every sixteen hours or so, the release of various chemicals in your brain will force you to stop what you are doing and pay your prisoner's debt. And nearly every animal in the world will go right along with you, all members of the mysterious sleep chain gang, from the smallest rodent to the largest elephant. We understand very little about the sleep phenomenon and yet, ironically, it is as essential to us as breathing.

BY JUDITH HERBST

FROM *BIO AMAZING: A CASEBOOK OF UNSOLVED HUMAN MYSTERIES*

ILLUSTRATED BY DAVID GROFF

Through the years, literature has given us several notable sleep champs. In a short story by Washington Irving, Rip van Winkle nods out for twenty years. Sleeping Beauty goes nonstop for a hundred, and according to legend, King Arthur is not really dead, but sleeping. That would make Arthur the longest snoozer in history at about fourteen hundred years and still counting.

Although there is a great range in people's normal sleep periods, sleepathons like these are pure fiction. Some people insist they must get upwards of ten hours of sleep, while others need as little as four. There are even cases of people who seem to be able to condense their sleep and wake up feeling refreshed after a mere two hours. But despite the fact that our parents usually tell us we need eight hours, eight is only an average. A person's body knows instinctively how much sleep it needs, and when it has had enough, it will automatically rouse itself. You can sometimes force more sleep on yourself, but you certainly can't challenge Rip van Winkle. Conversely, you can also force yourself to stay awake for a few hours past your normal bedtime, but again, the body sets strict limits. It will put up with only a short extension—say, nine or ten hours—and if you try to postpone sleep for much longer than that, you will find your sleep center taking over and practically conking you on the head.

"Enough is enough," it seems to be saying. "You've had your fun, but now out you go."

Apparently, this bullying on the part of our sleep center is for our own good. The truth is, if we go without sleep for too long, some very strange things begin to happen, as New York disc jockey Peter Tripp proved in 1959.

Tripp staged a "radiothon" to raise money for the polio fund. His intention was to do his regular three-hour evening show and then remain awake continuously off the air for as long as he could. To encourage donations to the fund, he moved from the broadcasting studio to a glass Armed Services recruiting booth in the middle of Times Square. He had a suite of rooms in a hotel across the street where he washed up, changed his clothes, and ate his meals. A staff of physicians and scientists monitored Tripp's health and administered batteries of tests to measure attention span, reaction time, and so forth.

The first twenty-four hours went fine. The public flocked to the recruiting booth, mostly out of curiosity, and saw a professional radio announcer doing his stuff without the slightest problem. The monsters, however, were waiting in the wings.

Tripp hit his first major snag after about two days. He began to hallucinate. He had been about to change his shoes when he suddenly dropped the one he was holding because he saw cobwebs inside it. Later, in the broadcast booth, Tripp said there were bugs all over the table, and he demanded to know who had put the rabbit in the corner. Meanwhile, his test performance was dropping. The slightest thing broke his concentration, and he had to summon all of his willpower to get it back. He was spending more and more time on each question and not always coming up with the right answer. He had grown nervous and fidgety.

By day five Tripp's hallucinations had taken on a whole new dimension. They were expanding in size and scope, becoming much more threatening. Tripp saw a scientist's tie squirming and jumping around as though it were alive. He recoiled in horror from one of the nurses who he said was leering at him and dripping saliva. A psychiatrist's tweed suit looked to him like a blanket of furry worms. That evening he ran screaming from his hotel room because he thought flames were shooting out of the bureau drawers. He had grown suspicious of everyone and accused the medical staff of plotting against him. Tripp was in bad shape. Continual wakefulness was taking its toll.

Day six—almost one hundred forty hours without sleep, and Tripp was now disoriented. He didn't know where he was or even who he was. He kept staring at a large wall clock in the broadcast booth, imagining it was the face of an actor he knew made up to look like Dracula. After a while, he couldn't tell if he were Peter Tripp or the disembodied Dracula face. The doctors and nurses seemed more menacing than ever. Tripp was convinced they were out to get him, planning something awful, and he had to be constantly reassured.

But what is perhaps the most amazing part of Tripp's ordeal is that the listening public had absolutely no clue that anything was wrong. For a few hours each night, Tripp did his show with astonishing self-control. He played records, read commercials, announced the time, did weather forecasts, chatted with the audience—all without a single blooper, flub, or embarrassing remark. He didn't even sound tired! Tripp seemed to be holding a small section of his mind in reserve. Even though he was actually displaying signs of severe mental illness (paranoia and hallucinations), he was somehow able to override them when he had to.

Tripp's terrifying journey through his sleep-starved mind finally ended on the tenth day. Just prior to his last broadcast, Tripp suffered a grotesque hallucination

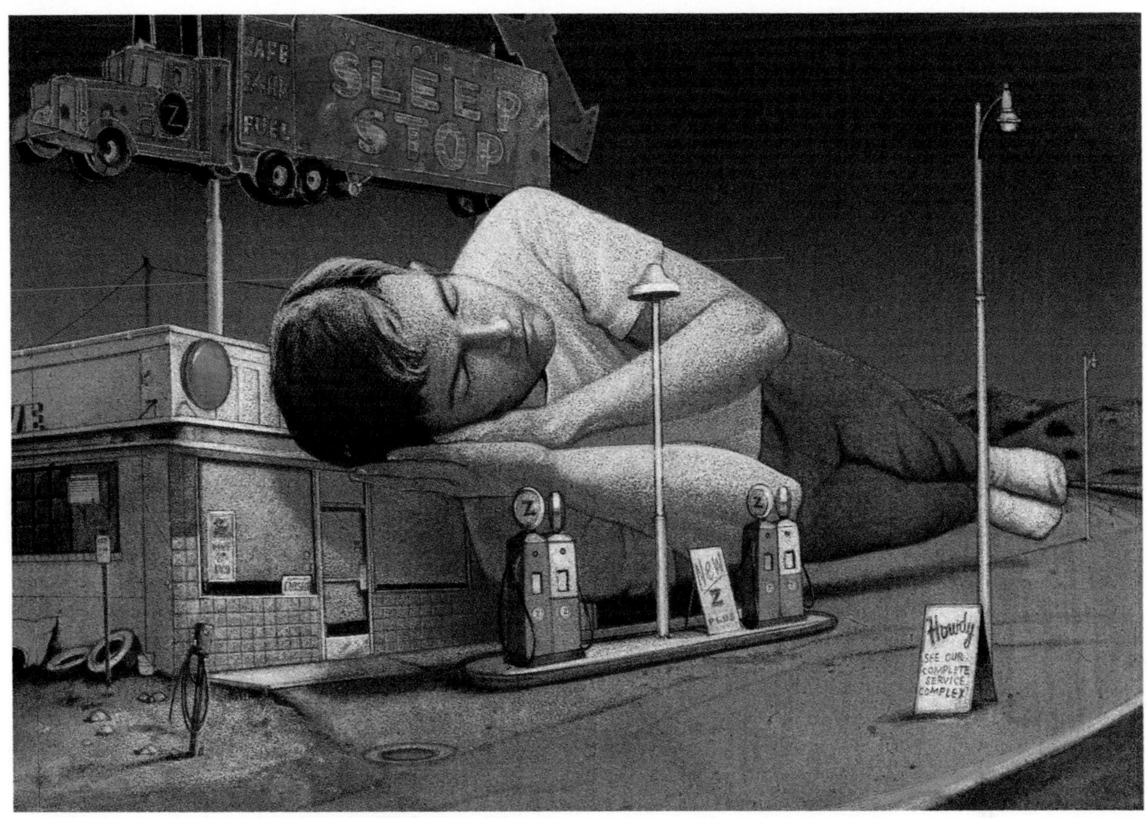

involving a neurologist who had come to examine him. The doctor asked Tripp to lie down, and as he was bending over him, Tripp's paranoia suddenly emerged full-blown. He imagined that the doctor was an undertaker sent by the medical team to bury him alive. Seized by sheer panic, Tripp bolted from the room, screaming hysterically. His eyes were wide and glassy, his heart thundering in his chest. He fought off everyone who tried to contain him. To see him like that, no one would have ever believed him capable of speaking coherently, let alone doing a three-hour radio show for hundreds of thousands of people. But that evening, Tripp was behind the microphone as usual, carrying off what can only be called a bio amazing feat. Then, after one last physical exam and a run-through of the test questions, Tripp let the sandman carry out his assigned orders.

Obviously, something very important had begun to break down inside the body of Peter Tripp. The doctors couldn't detect any physical changes, but there is no doubt that Tripp's mind was short circuiting.

Up to now, it has been assumed that sleep is a little like stopping off at a service station to fill your car with gas. Sleep restores us, revitalizes us, allows our body to replace whatever it is that we use up while we are awake. But while the theory appears to make sense, there are problems with it. First, not everybody needs the same amount of sleep. Second, in many animals, sleep time and waking time seem to be all out of whack. Elephants stomp around the savannah for about twenty-two hours, leaving only two hours to restore themselves through sleep. The opossum is just the opposite. What could it possibly be doing during its six hours of wakefulness that it requires eighteen hours of sleep to counterbalance? Opossums do not lead such hectic lives! And then there are the shrews—a kind of rodent—and some types of fish, which may not even sleep at all!

It has been suggested that sleep may be ridding our body of certain chemicals that build up during the day. If we don't sleep, these mystery chemicals will reach toxic proportions and could eventually kill us. The theory is certainly interesting, but so far, no one has identified these chemicals or explained how sleep might be getting the job done. Nevertheless, whatever sleep is or does, the process is incredibly effective. Disc jockey Peter Tripp was able to repair his eight sleepless nights' worth of damage in just thirteen hours.

We do know that sleep is a general slowing down of bodily functions. Breathing, heart rate, blood pressure, and body temperature all decrease. For approximately eight hours, you are neither hungry nor thirsty. Your sense of sight has been temporarily eliminated. Your senses of taste, touch, smell, and hearing are dulled. You are aware of your immediate environment, but your awareness is limited and selective. You are curiously able to ignore the familiar, such as a clock ticking or traffic sounds, but will often respond to something sudden and unfamiliar—a thunderstorm, for example, or a cold draft in the room.

Scientists have peeked at sleep with a spyglass called an electroencephalograph, or EEG for short. The EEG is a machine that records brain wave patterns, and when we go to sleep, we leave very distinct tracks. Our brain waves change quite dramatically; but they do not match the brain waves of an unconscious person or someone in a coma. Sleep, then, is a unique state, quite different from anything else.

It's awfully boring to watch somebody else sleep, but the scientists and the EEG have discovered that it isn't boring at all to be asleep. Sleep is a roller coaster ride, up and down, and up and down through four levels, or stages, all night long. Stage I is the level closest to consciousness and the level from which it is the easiest to rouse someone. Stages II through IV take you deeper and deeper into the mysterious Land of Nod. You spend about forty minutes in Stage IV and then begin your ascent back to Stage I, making five round trips each night. Every time you hit another level, your brain waves change, which is, of course, how scientists discovered the four levels of sleep.

Without a doubt, dreaming is the

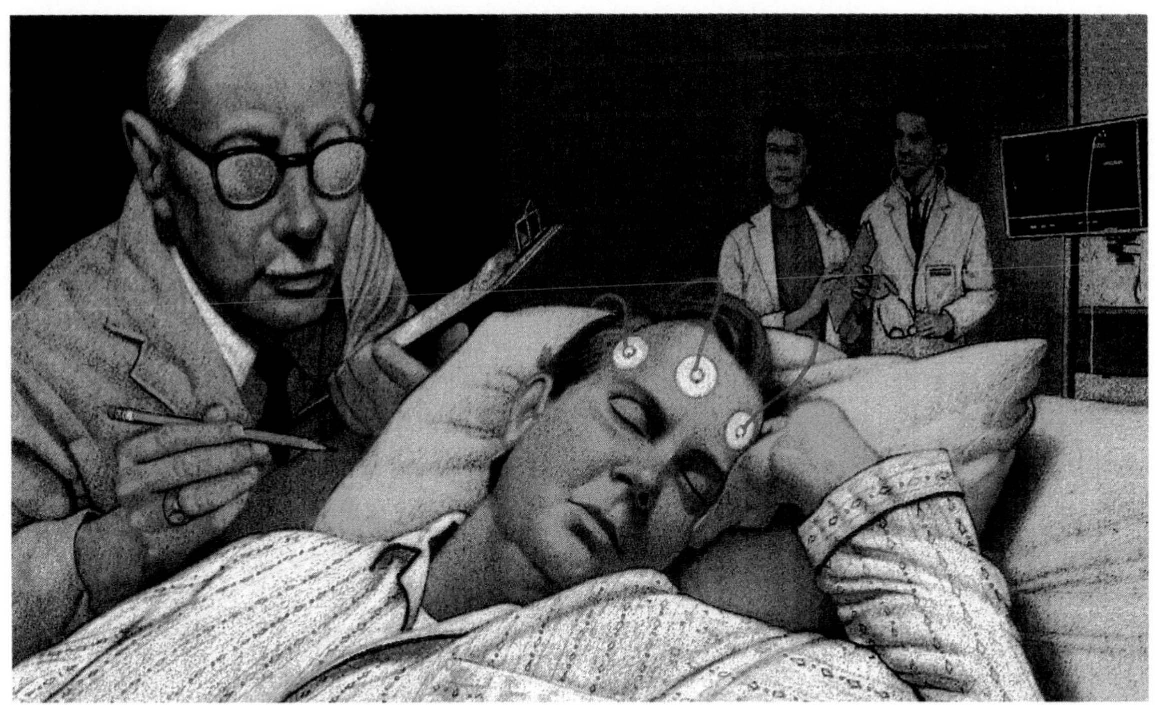

weirdest part of sleep. It occurs almost exclusively in Stage II, and we all do it, whether we are aware of it or not. For some, dreams appear in technicolor, while other people claim they only dream in black and white or grays. Blind people dream just like everybody else, but the form their dreams take depends on when they lost their sight. People who have been blind since birth dream in sounds and textures, while people whose blindness occurred later in life continue to dream in pictures. This suggests that we draw on our experiences and memories to fashion our dreams. That makes us the writer, producer, and director of our dreams. We usually have a starring role and absolute say in who acts out the other parts. We supply the props and the costumes. Five times a night we are creative geniuses without even trying.

MIDNIGHT AT THE MOVIES PRESENTS

DREAMS

ASTOUNDING . . . BAFFLING . . . UNEXPLAINED

Filmed on location with a cast of thousands

FIVE SHOWS NIGHTLY

You have been asleep for perhaps an hour. Your muscles are relaxed. Your chest rises and falls with the slow, even rhythm of your breathing. There is a calm, almost angelic expression on your face. Silence and peace surround you. The clock on your dresser ticks out the minutes to showtime. Four . . . three . . . two . . . one . . .

And suddenly the curtain is up! Your eyes are rolling back and forth, back and forth, back and forth behind your closed lids. This is it! This is REM, the amazing, mysterious Rapid Eye Movement that signals a dream is in progress. You appear to be watching something, but your eyes are not looking at anything at all, because blind people also display REM.

REM begins quite early in our development as human beings. It seems to be controlled by a part of the brain called the pons, which is located in the brain stem. Research has shown that as soon as the brain stem develops in the fetus, there are signs of REM. So it looks as though we all start dreaming even before we're born, but what fetal dreams are like is anybody's guess.

. . . back and forth, back and forth, back and forth . . .

This is the dance of REM. Somewhere deep inside your mind you are creating a little drama for an audience of one. Your story, though, can hardly be called one of the year's ten best. It's almost impossible to follow. The events are confusing and disconnected. The characters come and go for no apparent reason. The dialogue doesn't make any sense. It's a mess, all right, but you don't seem to notice it. On and on you dream, accepting even the most ridiculous situations without question, thoroughly convinced that it's all really happening. Furthermore, you are not just a sleepy member of the audience; you're a participant, and you react to everything that goes on. A frightening dream in particular catches you like a hook, and you actually experience fear.

OH MY GOSH!

You're in the back seat of a speeding car and there's no driver! You try desperately to reach the steering wheel, but you can't move. Crazily, the car swerves off the road. The brake! You've got to reach the brake!

Meanwhile, back in your bedroom, your heart is thundering. Your breath is coming in quick, shallow bursts. Beads of perspiration break out, soaking your pajamas and pasting your hair to your forehead. Your blood pressure has shot up, and the adrenaline is pumping, pumping, pumping.

Suddenly the car is on a high cliff. The speedometer needle is climbing . . . 90 . . . 100 . . . 110 . . . You can see the edge of the cliff just ahead. It's an endless drop to nowhere. Do something! DO SOMETHING!

Your terror in this dream is very real. You are not pretending to be scared; you *are* scared, and all the readouts in the sleep laboratories prove it. The readouts also show something else. You are almost completely paralyzed. With a few exceptions, your muscles have lost so much tone, they are literally immovable.

We do indeed toss and turn and roll around quite a bit while we're sleeping but not during a dream. During a dream we have about as much ability to get up and walk around as our pillow does. Scientists believe the purpose of this strange paralysis is to prevent us from acting out our dreams.

Although sleepwalkers appear to be giving a dream performance, they are not. In fact, sleepwalkers are in an entirely different level of sleep. They are sound asleep but strangely mobile. No one knows why some people—several million in North America alone—sleepwalk. This bizarre activity may begin at any time in a person's life and without any apparent cause. Sleepwalkers are completely unaware of what they are doing and usually remain ignorant unless they are told about it. And even then, they will strenuously deny it. They'll insist they've been asleep all night, as, of course, they have. But while they've been snoozing upright, they have been involved in some very strange activities.

Like fleshy robots, they will suddenly open their eyes, swing their legs over the side of the bed, and head off on some mysterious midnight errand. Talk to them and they won't answer. Wiggle your fingers in front of their eyes and they won't see you. They will, however, steer their way around furniture, take the dog for a walk, do their grocery shopping, and even drive a car.

But sleepwalking is only funny in the cartoons. Scores of people have been injured during a walk because they managed to climb out onto window ledges thinking they were stepping onto their front porch. Members of the family have been taken for intruders and attacked. It is a ridiculous myth that if you awaken a sleepwalker he or she will get lockjaw, die of a heart attack, or become paralyzed. The danger, instead, lies in what the sleepwalker is doing, since these people have been known to get themselves into some pretty scary situations. Unfortunately, sleepwalking is as mysterious as dreaming, and science has not yet come up with a way to prevent a person from going on midnight strolls.

Of course, sleepwalkers dream, just like everybody else, which makes for a pretty active night. They return to bed, settle in, and slip easily into the next level of sleep. Before long, they are involved in more excitement, but this time their muscles are holding them prisoner. Now they have to be content to stay put while a whole series of strange events unfolds before them.

Sleep researcher Stephen La Berge has identified something about our dreams that most of us experience but few of us are aware of. La Berge calls the phenomenon "lucid dreams." A lucid dream is one which you recognize as a dream. You almost say to yourself, "Hey! Hold on, here. This is a dream. All this stuff is fake. I'm dreaming!"

La Berge believes that once we know

we are dreaming, we have the ability to control the outcome of the dream on a conscious level. We can change whatever we don't like. He says he has learned to alter his dreams while he's asleep, and he can teach others to do the same. But if dreams, as they unfold naturally, are important in some way, perhaps we shouldn't be fiddling with them. Perhaps we should let nature take its course. Who knows? Maybe dreams are serving a very definite purpose, whether we remember them or not.

Dreams seem to be speeded-up versions of events, like a movie run in fast forward, but actually, dreamtime parallels realtime quite closely. If it takes you three seconds to open a door in realtime, that's how long it will take you to open a door in your dream. The speed at which you do things in a dream is only an illusion, because you edit the scene. If you begin to walk across a bridge in your dream, each step will match your waking steps, but you get to the other side faster than normal because you have edited out most of the steps. They are not necessary to the plot, so to speak. That's why you are able to be in a wheat field one minute and standing on a street corner the next. You simply eliminate the travel time for the sake of the "real" action.

You are also able to put your dream into slow motion. You can slow down an attacking tiger to keep him from grabbing you. If you're running through deep snow, you can slow down the steps to make the event very frustrating. Why you do this, however, is unclear, although it may have to do with the purpose of the dream itself.

In our lifetime we will crank out 125,000 dreams. No one knows why. Most scientists today admit that dreams are far more complex bits of mind stuff than we ever, well . . . than we ever dreamed. Nature has provided us with a truly bio amazing mechanism. Now, if we could just figure out what it's for. . . .

Do you think scientists will one day understand why sleep and dreams are necessary? Explain your answer.

What conclusions did you draw about sleep after you finished reading the selection?

WRITE In a paragraph, tell what you think is the strangest or most mysterious aspect of sleep.

Nightmares

by Siv Cedering

Nighttime II, Gregory B. Larson

Some say the nightmare is
a horse
that starts to gallop in a dream
and scares the sleeping one awake.

Some say the nightmare is
a sea
where storms have made the waves so big
that they frighten me.

I do not know
what nightmares are,
I only know
they are.

But though the nightmares come
at times,
they do not come as often as
the pretty horse, as often as
the calmer sea, that bring
all other dreams to me.

DETECTIVES AND SCIENTISTS

Detectives and scientists are investigators who examine facts and draw conclusions. How are the questions that detectives and scientists investigate similar? How are they different?

WRITER'S WORKSHOP

The first step in investigating a problem is usually to find its causes. Think of a problem you have read about or tried to solve yourself. In an essay, explain the causes of the problem and tell what the solution turned out or might turn out to be.

Writer's Choice Given what you have learned from these selections, what do you think you would like about scientific or detective work? Share your ideas in a piece of writing such as an essay, a job description, or a word puzzle.

THEME

THE TRUTH REVEALED

Should people always be honest with each other? Is there a difference between lying and just pretending? You will be thinking about questions like these as you read the following stories, in which some very urgent situations force the characters to reveal and confront the truth.

CONTENTS

M.C. HIGGINS, THE GREAT

Mayo Cornelius Higgins lives with his family in the hills a few miles from the Ohio River. Few strangers come into the area, so M.C. is surprised one day to see an unfamiliar girl on the path ahead of him. When M.C. and his mother, Banina, go swimming in the lake the next morning, they see a tent on the shore. M.C. is certain it belongs to the girl. Soon M.C.'s sister and brothers—Macie Pearl, Lennie Pool, and Harper—and his father, Jones, come down to the lake for a swim. Their noise awakens the girl, who finally comes out of her tent when everyone but M.C. has left. She explains that she works after school to save money and travels during the summer, searching for quiet, beautiful places to explore. M.C. enjoys talking to her and is annoyed when his sister and brothers return, but he invites the girl to come into the lake with all of them for a swim.

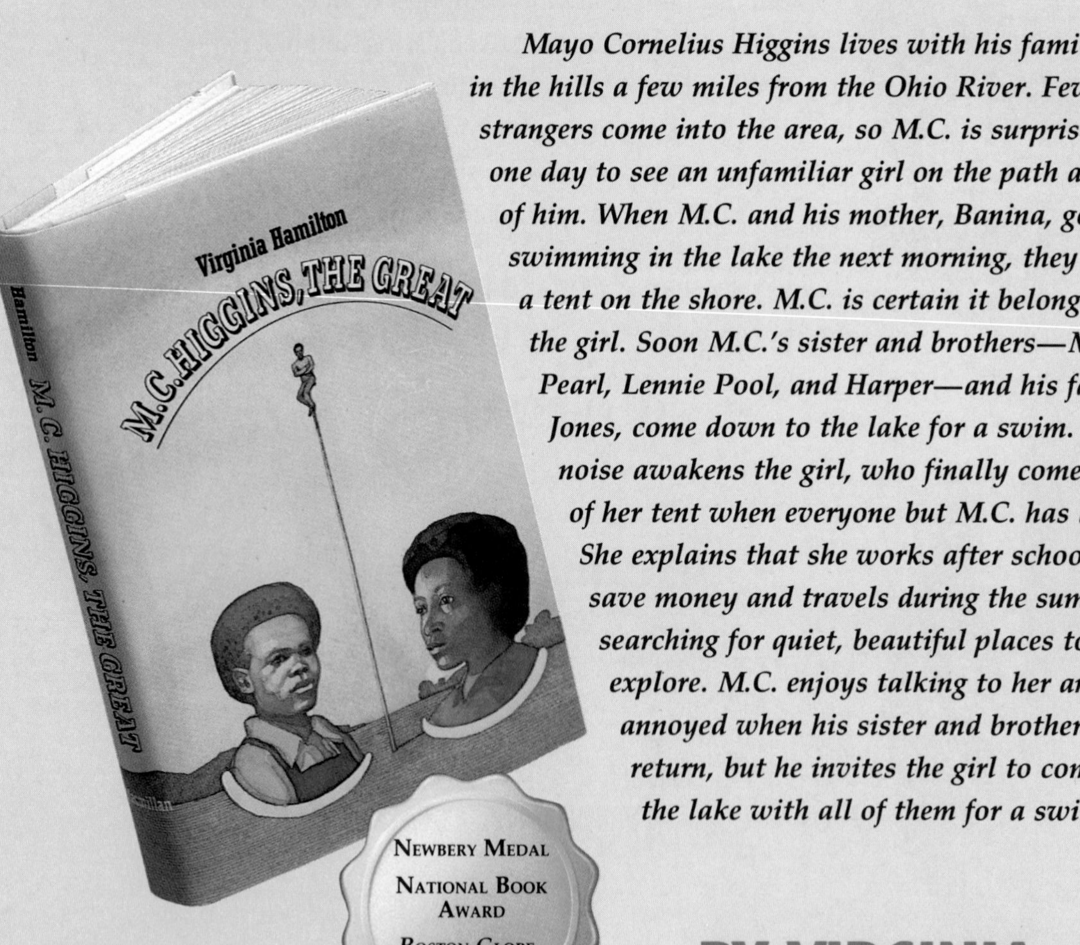

BY VIRGINIA HAMILTON

ILLUSTRATED BY DAVE LAFLEUR

Hemmed in by mountains, surrounded by tall pines, the dark surge of the lake was magical. Fascinated, the girl watched it and the way M.C. cut through it, until she could no longer resist. She backed away, turned and disappeared into her tent. When she came out again, M.C. and the children were down at the far end of the lake.

She wore wrinkled, pink shorts and a faded man's shirt with sleeves cut away. She had tied the shirttails in a knot at her waist. M.C. thought she was about as nice-looking as she could be. But rather than strike out into the water from where she was, she came around the shore.

"Come on in," they shouted to her.

She preferred to walk down to the end of the beach. There she leaned on the rocks and plunged a foot in the water. "That's cold!" she said, looking pleased that they had invited her.

"Not underneath," Macie said. "Just on the top. You get in, and it's real warm."

M.C. said something to his brothers, and then: "Don't let Macie . . . I'm going through."

Head first, he upended himself and vanished beneath the surface. The water grew still again as if he had never been there. Macie rode on Harper's back until he grabbed the rocks and shook her off. Once he had climbed up on them, he gave Macie a hand. Lennie Pool followed.

The girl watched the water but it remained smooth and dark.

"What's your name?" Macie said, curious all of a sudden.

The girl smiled at Macie. But then her eyes flicked back to the lake where M.C. had gone under. She began to walk back and forth, her hands on her hips.

The children watched her.

"What's he doing down there?" she asked them.

They said nothing.

"I don't think he's coming up, you'd better do something."

Macie broke their silence with a giggle. "He's not even down there," she said. "Just over and behind these rocks." She led the way around the edge of the rocks. Harper and Lennie went, too, and cautiously the girl followed.

On the other side lay a surprise. It was an opening in the rocks. No one who didn't know would suspect it was there. The rocks fell back in a small clearing where there was a silent pool with grassy banks.

The children stopped at the edge. Macie turned brightly to the girl and smiled.

M.C. surged up from the center of the pool in a great splash. He sucked in air as though he would never again get enough of it, as the girl covered her mouth to stifle a scream.

The kids laughed at her. "It's a water tunnel," Harper told her in his soft, urgent voice. He told how the tunnel went under the rocks beneath the water at the edge of the lake and ended at the pool.

"Only M.C. can travel it," Macie said. "We ain't allowed. The kids from town don't even know there's a tunnel."

"You wouldn't know it, either, if you hadn't caught me doing it once," M.C. said. "Better keep the sense never to try it, too."

"How do you hold your breath so long?" The girl, talking to M.C. as though he were older, showing respect for him now.

He pulled himself up on the grassy bank and wiped water out of his eyes. He had to smile. She kneeled next to him, her fear of him and the children gone.

Proud he'd done something she never expected he could do. And she had come from somewhere by herself in a car. But he could be by himself, too. He could travel through water like nobody. First he thought of lying, to tell her he could hold his breath longer than anyone. The kids would know.

Finally he said, "It's not so long. I came up before you all ever got here. Hear you coming, and I just went under and waited. Then I splash up like I was out of breath."

She didn't seem to mind he had played a trick. "It's dark in the tunnel?" she asked him. Her face so close, he could see tiny bumps he hadn't noticed before.

Shyly, he looked at his feet hanging in the water. "It's gray light, kind of," he said. "This pool is at the end of the tunnel. Sunlight drifts in and gets faded, I guess. But I see, a little. It's ghostly, though, when fishes slide over your skin."

She cringed with the picture of it. Watching her, Macie shivered with delight.

His eyes on the pool, M.C. sensed the girl watching him. Felt himself reaching out for her, the way he often reached out when he sat next to Jones. His skin itched and came alive with little things he seemed to know about her. She might travel alone, but every minute she was scared

being by herself. The impression came to him, swift and certain.

Already he felt attuned to the girl, less self-conscious at having her so near.

He rubbed his arms and neck until the itching went away. Tiredness settled in the knot on his forehead in a dull ache that came and went. He wasn't feeling quite himself this morning. Yet he didn't want to go and leave her.

"What's your name?" he asked.

She shrugged. "No use of saying names."

"I told you our names," he said.

"I could tell you a name and you wouldn't know if it was really mine."

"Where do you come from then?"

"Same thing," she said. "You wouldn't know if I came from where I said."

"Then why not tell?"

She said nothing. She looked at him and quickly away, as if she wanted to speak out, but couldn't. Soon she was looking from the pool to the rocks and back to the pool.

She did this several times before it came to M.C. what was on her mind.

"A water tunnel won't be like a pool," he told her, "or even a lake."

She nodded, staring at the rocks.

"A pool or even a lake is simple. Water will lift you," he said.

She sat still, with just her head turning to look at him and then away.

"But tunnel is a bottleneck. No place to take off the pressure; or maybe pressure's not the trouble. It's just a tight place without a top, and you can get sick to your stomach."

A long silence in which she said nothing.

"How long can you hold your breath?" M.C. asked her.

"What?"

"If you travel that tunnel," he said. "How long can you go with no breathing?"

Wide-eyed, she stared at him. "As long as anybody." All at once she breathed hugely, holding the air in.

Macie and the boys scrambled close to see. Everything was still. The girl's eyes began to pop and tear. She held out while none of them moved, until at last her breath burst through her teeth. She fell back, panting.

"That was long!" Harper said.

"Maybe forty-five seconds," M.C. said. "Not long enough."

The girl sat up again.

"Try it once more," M.C. said.

"You don't think I can do it," she said.

"I'm not thinking a thing. It just has to be longer," he said. "Long enough to reach the pool."

"Well, I don't know," she said, her voice edgy. She searched M.C.'s face.

"If you're worried, don't try it," he said.

Then she was smirking at him. "Sure think you're something, don't you?" she said. "I saw you on that pole.[1] Not just with the fire, but in the daylight. Sitting up there with nothing to do and no place to do it!"

Her anger shot through him. It hurt him and he didn't know what to say. He hadn't meant anything bad by what he said.

"The tunnel is fun," he said quietly, "but you have to have the lungs to hold out."

The girl sucked in her breath again. M.C. kept his eyes on the pool. He didn't want to be watching her if this time she failed. He tried just to feel when the time was long enough. But in spite of himself, he began counting in his head.

When he knew she would have to breathe, he turned to her. Still she held out. Tendons and veins stood out on her neck. Her eyes were squeezed shut. Her cheeks and mouth were twisted in an awful face.

She exploded, bursting with air and squirming on the ground, trying to breathe again. Uncomfortably, M.C. turned his face away.

"You did it!" Macie yelled. Lennie Pool grinned and Harper clapped his hands.

"M.C., she did it!" Macie screeched. "Didn't she?"

He nodded at Macie to let all of them know. But he was wondering if he had forgotten something he should have remembered to ask.

Never taken someone through that tunnel, he thought. Maybe I shouldn't.

"Are you going to swim it right now?" Macie asked the girl.

But she couldn't answer. She seemed to be having that cold, sickening feeling that came from holding your breath too long. M.C. knew this. Drying sweat caused his skin to itch again.

---

[1] that pole: M.C.'s prize possession, a 40-foot steel pole with a bicycle seat on top

"We maybe can swim it later on," he said. "Give you plenty of time . . ."

The girl shot up from the ground. Even though she looked weak, she stood with her hands firmly on her hips. "You think I can't do it." Her eyes snapped at him.

M.C. couldn't get himself loose from those eyes, they were so pretty. Slowly he got to his feet.

There grew a silence between them that separated them from the children. They stood close together, watching each other.

"You have to do just as I say," M.C. told her.

"Why?"

"'Cause I know how to get through."

She thought a moment. "Okay," she said.

They were in a world all their own, where she was older but he was the leader. He knew why she had to try the tunnel.

Not because I've done it. 'Cause I'm the only one.

He turned and led the way over the rocks to the lake. The girl followed close on his heels.

The lake lay as serene and peaceful as when they had left it. Way down at the other end was the ridge. In between the ridge and the rocky end where now he and the girl crouched was the tent, like an intruder in the sun. All around them were pines, undergrowth, greens and browns closing in the magical shimmer of the lake.

He and the girl hung onto rocks just above the waterline. The children were clinging a foot above them.

"The tunnel's right down there," M.C. told her. "About eight to ten feet down. Maybe twelve feet long and that's a couple of body lengths." He paused, looking out over the lake. "Now I lead," he told her. "I lead and we hold together like this." With his right hand, he took hold of her left arm, forcing her to balance herself with her back against the rocks. "Hold on to my arm just above the wrist."

"Like this?" She grabbed his arm with fingers stronger than he'd expected. So close to her, he felt shy but calm.

"We jump here, we get more power," he told her. "We get down faster but it has to be done just right."

"How?" she said.

M.C. didn't know how. He was figuring it all out as he went along, working fast in his head the best way to jump and the quickest way to get through the tunnel.

"Best way is . . . if I jump backward and you jump frontward." He spoke carefully. "See, I hit and go in facing the tunnel. I have your left arm and you are pulled over. You follow in just in back of me. Now. In the tunnel, you have your right arm free and I have my left." They would use their free arms to push them through if they had to, and they could kick with their feet.

"Tunnel sides are moss," he said. "Push off from them when you bump them. It'll feel slimy but it won't hurt."

"Okay," she said.

"Pay no mind to fishes," he went on. "Most times, they're but just a few. They don't do nothing but get out of your way."

She nodded. M.C. could feel her tension through her arm.

"You all ready?" Macie asked from above them.

M.C. looked at the girl. "I'm ready," she said.

"You have to hold out for most of a minute."

"I can do it," she said.

"If you lose air, just stay calm," M.C. said. "I can get us out."

"I said I can do it!"

Her anger cut through him again, making him ashamed, he didn't know why.

"Macie, you count it off," he said grimly.

"She always get to do something," Harper said.

"He told *me*, now shut," Macie said.

"Stay out of the water. Wait for us at the pool. Now," M.C. said.

"Ready!" Macie yelled. "Get yourself set. . . ."

The girl grew rigid.

"You have to stay calm," M.C. told her. He held her arm as tightly as he could without hurting her. Her fingers dug into his wrist.

"Watch your nails!" he warned. They both sucked in air.

"Go, y'all!"

They leaped out and plunged. They hit the water at the same time, but M.C. went under first because he was heavier. The girl turned facing him before her head went under. That was good, but pulling her after him slowed M.C. It seemed to take forever to get down to the tunnel level. Water closed in on them. Sounds became muffled and then no sound at all. They were alone as never before. And there was nothing for M.C. to do but get it over with.

M.C. liked nothing better than being in the deep, with sunlight

breaking into rays of green and gold. Water was a pressure of delicious weight as he passed through it, down and down. It was as if feeling no longer belonged to him. The water possessed it and touched along every inch of him.

He pulled out of his downward fall at the sight of the gaping tunnel opening. He no longer felt the girl next to him. He knew she was there with him by the impression she made on the deep. And he would remember her presence, her imprint, on this day for weeks.

Bending her wrist forward, he stretched her arm out straight as he kicked hard into the tunnel. Here the water was cooler and cast a gray shimmer that was ghostly. Pressure grew like a ball and chain hanging on his right shoulder. It was the girl like a dead weight.

Kick with your feet!

With a powerful scissoring of his legs, he tried to swim midway between the ceiling and the bottom of the tunnel.

Push off with your hand!

Her dead pressure dragged him down. His knees banged hard against the bottom. His back hit the tunnel side as he realized she was struggling to get away. Fractions of seconds were lost as he tried twisting

her arm to pull her body into line. Fishes slid over his skin, tickling and sending shivers to his toes. They must have touched the girl, for he had no moment to brace himself as she shot up on her back toward the ceiling.

Won't make it.

Horror, outrage stunned him. He had taken for granted the one thing he should have asked her. For the want of a question, the tunnel would be a grave for both of them.

She kicked futilely against the tunnel side and rose above him, twisting his arm straight up.

Yank, like Macie will pull down on a balloon.

If he could get the girl turned over, they might have a chance. But his breath seemed to be gone.

Not a grave, it's a tunnel.

In his lungs, emptiness was pain. But the will not to fail was there in his burning chest, in his free arm pushing hard against the deep. His legs were still loose and working. Then a sudden surge of strength, like a second wind.

Be M.C. Higgins, the Great.

He yanked the balloon down—he mustn't break the string. At the same time he propelled himself forward, knowing she would follow as she turned over.

An awful pounding in his head snapped his brain open. M.C. shot out of the tunnel like a cork from a jug of cider. And arching his back, he swung mightily with his right arm.

Dark balloon to the light above.

He hadn't the strength to hurl her to the surface. But he was right behind her. Before she could struggle down again, he was there, pulling at her. She opened her mouth in a pitiful attempt to breathe. He pounded her back, hoping to dislodge water. And held her close a split second to calm her. She was rigid.

Girl, don't drown.

Swiftly he caught her ankles and tossed her up over his head. She broke the surface. He was there, feeling sweet air just when he would have had to open his mouth or have his lungs collapse.

M.C. fought against dizziness, aware he had his hand on her neck in a bruising clasp to hold her up. He had to let go or break it.

The girl was gagging, trying to breathe. He heard his own breath in a harsh, raw heaving. He was daydreaming a distant cheering. Then he saw the children, feet jumping up and down on the grassy bank. A swirl of rocks before he realized the girl was sinking. He must have let her go. But he had the sense to catch her again around the waist.

Still M.C. Still the leader. He had taken her through the tunnel and they were back in the world together. Still all the blame was his. But he could fix it. Could keep the children from knowing about her.

Moaning cry, coughing, she clung to him.

"No." He knocked her hands away. With just the pressure of his arm and shoulder on her back, he forced her flat out. As though she were dog-paddling, he glided her into the land. The feet jumping on the grassy bank fell back and were still.

Macie stood there on the bank, closest to M.C.'s head.

"She's weak," he said to Macie. "See if you can help pull her some . . . my wind is gone."

Macie clasped the girl's arm. M.C. had her by the waist. Halfway out of the water, she kicked M.C. away. She slithered and kneed her way over the bank. On the grass, she hunched into a ball, and struggling to breathe, closed her eyes.

Dark balloon.

M.C. climbed out and crawled a distance to collapse on his back. He was away from the girl, with the children between them, but he kept his eye on her. They were close together in his mind, where a vision had started. Day after day, they swam the lake. Hour upon hour, they sunned themselves on the shore.

M.C.'s chest wouldn't stop its heave and fall. His mouth watered with stomach bile as the pounding ache spread out across his forehead.

None of them moved. For a long while neither Harper nor Macie asked a single question. Lennie Pool never did say much.

M.C. felt as if every muscle were trying to get out of his skin. He was sick with exhaustion. But light out of the sky bore into him, warming and relaxing him. It was a healing band on his eyelids. As the ache in his forehead moved off, tunnel and water filled his mind. His eyes shot open, blinding the awful memory.

Seeing that M.C. was awake, Macie came over to him. "You did it!" she said happily. "Were you scared?"

He knew he would vomit if he tried to talk. He swallowed hard.

"You sure took your time. Was it any trouble?" Macie asked.

"Just took it easy," he said finally.

The girl brought up pool water she had swallowed. Half an hour later, she sat up shakily on her knees. In a slow, mechanical sweep, she brushed grass and twigs from her drying clothes.

M.C. raised his head. "You all right?" he asked her.

When she stood, the children stood with her. M.C. was on his feet as well, as though he moved only when she moved.

Slowly she seemed to change. He watched her grow stronger, throwing her head back, thrusting out her chin.

"I went all the way through that tunnel," she said, smiling vaguely. "I could have drowned—I can't even swim a lick."

The children gaped at her. Shocked, they turned to M.C.

"And you took her down?" Macie gasped. "You took her clear through . . . you didn't even know!"

The kids began to giggle, jostling one another, with the girl looking solemnly on.

M.C. felt the heat of shame rising in his neck. Only this one secret between them, but the girl wouldn't have it. She made him stand there with the kids laughing at him. He stared at his hands, at the jagged nails which he bit down to the skin while sitting on his pole.

"I can't stand a lying kid," the girl said.

Worse than a slap in the face, but he said evenly, "I'm not any kid. And I didn't lie."

"You told your sister we took it easy," she said, smirking at him.

"*I* took it easy," he said. "If I hadn't, you wouldn't be here, girl."

The children stared at him soberly now. The girl looked uncertain.

"It's no joke not to tell somebody you can't swim," he said.

"Somebody didn't ask me," she said sullenly.

"Didn't need to ask—you should've told me!"

"I just wanted to see it. I didn't know it was going to be so *long*."

"So you want to see something and we almost drown?" He was shaking now with the memory of the tunnel. "Ever think of somebody but yourself?"

The girl shrank back. Uncomfortably, they watched her. M.C. hadn't meant to make her appear stupid. But she was quick to apologize.

"I'm sorry," she said simply. "You told me you were some M.C., the Great. . . ."

The look she gave him, as if she knew only he could have saved her, made him feel proud. He had to smile. "You have some good nerve. A lot of real good nerve," he said at last.

Do you think M.C. lives up to his name "the Great" in this episode from the novel? Explain your answer.

Why do you think the girl wants to go through the water tunnel with M.C.? Why does M.C. want to take her?

What do you think M.C. learns from this experience?

WRITE What does this selection show about the possible consequences of pretending to be something you are not? Explain your answer in a paragraph or two, adding examples from your own experience if you wish.

Words About the Author

Virginia Hamilton

Virginia Hamilton was born in 1936 in Ohio, the same state in which she set her story about M.C. Higgins and his family. Her mother's father, Grandpaw Levi Perry, was born into slavery and later brought to Ohio by his mother, who was a conductor on the Underground Railroad. This brave and generous woman made many trips to rescue her people; she was finally caught and never heard from again, but her legend lives on in the author's family.

Virginia Hamilton's father, a classical mandolinist, had dreams of rising to the height of his profession, but as an African American, he could not belong to the musicians' union. He created his own opportunities, putting together groups and performing in small towns.

Young Virginia had her dreams too and has seen more of them come true than her father did. She left Antioch College to go to New York, where, supporting herself as a bookkeeper, she began writing. It was several years, however, before she saw her first book, *Zeely,* in print. The plot centers around a farm girl, Elizabeth, who imagines that a tall, beautiful woman raising pigs on her uncle's property is really an African princess.

Since that first success, this award-winning author has written more than twenty books for young people, including biographies of famous African American leaders. Her collection of African American folktales, *The People Could Fly,* reflects her admiration for her ancestors, who, she says, "came in from the fields and talked themselves into new states of mind."

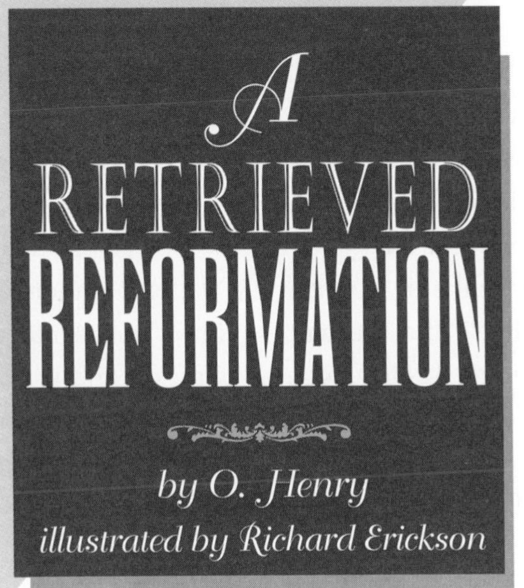

A Retrieved Reformation

by O. Henry

illustrated by Richard Erickson

A guard came to the prison shoe-shop, where Jimmy Valentine was assiduously stitching uppers, and escorted him to the front office. There the warden handed Jimmy his pardon, which had been signed that morning by the governor. Jimmy took it in a tired kind of way. He had served nearly ten months of a four-year sentence. He had expected to stay only about three months, at the longest. When a man with as many friends on the outside as Jimmy Valentine had is received in the "stir" it is hardly worthwhile to cut his hair.

"Now, Valentine," said the warden, "you'll go out in the morning. Brace up, and make a man of yourself. You're not a bad fellow at heart. Stop cracking safes, and live straight."

"Me?" said Jimmy, in surprise. "Why, I never cracked a safe in my life."

"Oh, no," laughed the warden. "Of course not. Let's see, now. How was it you happened to get sent up on that Springfield job? Was it because you wouldn't prove an alibi for fear of compromising somebody in extremely high-toned society? Or was it simply a case of a mean old jury that had it in for you? It's always one or the other with you innocent victims."

"Me?" said Jimmy, still blankly virtuous. "Why, warden, I never was in Springfield in my life!"

"Take him back, Cronin," smiled the warden, "and fix him up with outgoing clothes. Unlock him at seven in the morning, and let him come to the bull-pen. Better think over my advice, Valentine."

At a quarter past seven on the next morning Jimmy stood in the warden's outer office. He had on a suit of the villainously fitting, ready-made clothes and a pair of stiff, squeaky shoes that the state furnishes to its discharged compulsory guests.

The clerk handed him a railroad ticket and the five-dollar bill with which the law expected him to rehabilitate himself into good citizenship and prosperity. The warden gave him a cigar, and shook hands. Valentine, 9762, was chronicled on the books "Pardoned by Governor," and Mr. James Valentine walked out into the sunshine.

Disregarding the song of the birds, the waving green trees, and the smell of the flowers, Jimmy headed straight for a restaurant. There he tasted the first sweet joys of liberty in the shape of a broiled chicken and a bottle of white wine—followed by a cigar a grade better than the one the warden had given him. From there he proceeded leisurely to the depot. He tossed a quarter in the hat of a blind man sitting by the door, and boarded his train. Three hours set him down in a little town near the state line. He went to the café of one Mike Dolan and shook hands with Mike, who was alone behind the bar.

"Sorry we couldn't make it sooner, Jimmy, me boy," said Mike. "But we had that protest from Springfield to buck against, and the governor nearly balked. Feeling all right?"

"Fine," said Jimmy. "Got my key?"

He got his key and went upstairs, unlocking the door of a room at the rear. Everything was just as he had left it. There on the floor was still Ben Price's collar-button that had been torn from that eminent detective's shirt-band when they had overpowered Jimmy to arrest him.

Pulling out from the wall a folding-bed, Jimmy slid back a panel in the wall and dragged out a dust-covered suitcase. He opened this and gazed fondly at the finest set of burglar's tools in the East. It was a complete set, made of specially tempered steel, the latest designs in drills, punches, braces and bits, jimmies, clamps, and augers, with two or three novelties invented by Jimmy himself, in which he took pride. Over nine hundred dollars they had cost him to have made at ———, a place where they make such things for the profession.

In half an hour Jimmy went downstairs and through the café. He was now dressed in tasteful and well-fitting clothes, and carried his dusted and cleaned suitcase in his hand.

"Got anything on?" asked Mike Dolan, genially.

"Me?" said Jimmy, in a puzzled tone. "I don't understand. I'm representing the New York Amalgamated Short Snap Biscuit Cracker and Frazzled Wheat Company."

This statement delighted Mike to such an extent that Jimmy had to take a seltzer-and-milk on the spot. He never touched "hard" drinks.

A week after the release of Valentine, 9762, there was a neat job of safe-burglary done in Richmond, Indiana, with no clue to the author. A scant eight hundred dollars was all that was secured. Two weeks after that a patented, improved, burglar-proof safe in Logansport was opened like a cheese to the tune of fifteen hundred dollars, currency; securities and silver untouched. That began to interest the rogue-catchers. Then an old-fashioned bank-safe in Jefferson City became active and threw out of its crater an eruption of bank-notes, amounting to five thousand dollars. The losses were now high enough to bring the matter up into Ben Price's class of work. By comparing notes, a remarkable similarity in the methods of the burglaries was noticed. Ben Price investigated the scenes of the robberies, and was heard to remark:

"That's Dandy Jim Valentine's autograph. He's resumed business. Look at that combination knob—jerked out as easy as pulling up a radish in wet weather. He's got the only clamps that can do it. And look how clean those tumblers were punched out! Jimmy never has to drill but one hole. Yes, I guess I want Mr. Valentine. He'll do his bit next time without any short-time or clemency foolishness."

Ben Price knew Jimmy's habits. He had learned them while working up the Springfield case. Long jumps, quick get-aways, no confederates, and a taste for good society—these ways had helped Mr. Valentine to become noted as a successful dodger of retribution. It was given out that Ben Price had taken up the trail of the elusive cracksman, and other people with burglar-proof safes felt more at ease.

One afternoon Jimmy Valentine and his suitcase climbed out of the mail-hack in Elmore, a little town five miles off the railroad down in the black-jack country of Arkansas. Jimmy, looking like an athletic young senior just home from college, went down the board sidewalk toward the hotel.

A young lady crossed the street, passed him at the corner, and entered a door over which was the sign "The Elmore Bank." Jimmy Valentine looked into her eyes, forgot what he was, and became another man. She lowered her eyes and colored slightly. Young men of Jimmy's style and looks were scarce in Elmore.

Jimmy collared a boy that was loafing on the steps of the bank as if he were one of the stock-holders, and began to ask him questions about the town, feeding him dimes at intervals. By and by the young lady came out, looking royally unconscious of the young man with the suitcase, and went her way.

"Isn't that young lady Miss Polly Simpson?" asked Jimmy, with specious guile.

"Naw," said the boy. "She's Annabel Adams. Her pa owns this bank. What'd you come to Elmore for? Is that a gold watch-chain? I'm going to get a bulldog. Got any more dimes?"

Jimmy went to the Planter's Hotel, registered as Ralph D. Spencer, and engaged a room. He leaned on the desk and declared his platform to the clerk. He said he had come to Elmore to look for a location to go into business. How was the shoe business, now, in the town? He had thought of the shoe business. Was there an opening?

The clerk was impressed by the clothes and manner of Jimmy. He, himself, was something of a pattern of fashion to the thinly gilded youth of Elmore, but he now perceived his shortcomings. While trying to figure out Jimmy's manner of tying his four-in-hand he cordially gave information.

Yes, there ought to be a good opening in the shoe line. There wasn't an exclusive shoe-store in the place. The dry-goods and general stores handled them. Business in all lines was fairly good. Hoped Mr. Spencer would decide to locate in Elmore. He would find it a pleasant town to live in, and the people very sociable.

Mr. Spencer thought he would stop over in the town a few days and look over the situation. No, the clerk needn't call the boy. He would carry up his suitcase, himself; it was rather heavy.

Mr. Ralph Spencer, the phoenix that arose from Jimmy Valentine's ashes—ashes left by the flame of a sudden and alternative attack of love—remained in Elmore, and prospered. He opened a shoe-store and secured a good run of trade.

Socially he was also a success, and made many friends. And he accomplished the wish of his heart. He met Miss Annabel Adams, and became more and more captivated by her charms.

At the end of a year the situation of Mr. Ralph Spencer was this: he had won the respect of the community, his shoe-store was flourishing, and he and Annabel were engaged to be married in two weeks. Mr. Adams, the typical, plodding, country banker, approved of Spencer. Annabel's pride in him almost equalled her affection. He was as much at home in the family of Mr. Adams and that of Annabel's married sister as if he were already a member.

One day Jimmy sat down in his room and wrote this letter, which he mailed to the safe address of one of his old friends in St. Louis:

Dear Old Pal:

I want you to be at Sullivan's place, in Little Rock, next Wednesday night at nine o'clock. I want you to wind up some little matters for me. And, also, I want to make you a present of my kit of tools. I know you'll be glad to get them—you couldn't duplicate the lot for a thousand dollars. Say, Billy, I've quit the old business—a year ago. I've got a nice store. I'm making an honest living, and I'm going to marry the finest girl on earth two weeks from now. It's the only life, Billy—the straight one. I wouldn't touch a dollar of another man's money now for a million. After I get married I'm going to sell out and go West, where there won't be so much danger of having old scores brought up against me. I tell you, Billy, she's an angel. She believes in me; and I wouldn't do another crooked thing for the whole world. Be sure to be at Sully's, for I must see you. I'll bring along the tools with me.

Your old friend,
Jimmy

On the Monday night after Jimmy wrote this letter, Ben Price jogged unobtrusively into Elmore in a livery buggy. He lounged about town in his quiet way until he found out what he wanted to know. From the drug-store across the street from Spencer's shoe-store he got a good look at Ralph D. Spencer.

"Going to marry the banker's daughter are you, Jimmy?" said Ben to himself, softly. "Well, I don't know!"

The next morning Jimmy took breakfast at the Adamses. He was going to Little Rock that day to order his wedding-suit and buy something nice for Annabel. That would be the first time he had left town since he came to Elmore. It had been more than a year now since those last professional "jobs," and he thought he could safely venture out.

After breakfast quite a family party went down town together—Mr. Adams, Annabel, Jimmy, and Annabel's married sister with her two little girls, aged five and nine. They came by the hotel where Jimmy still boarded, and he ran up to his room and brought along his suitcase. Then they went on to the bank. There stood Jimmy's horse and buggy and Dolph Gibson, who was going to drive him over to the railroad station.

All went inside the high, carved oak railings into the banking-room—Jimmy included, for Mr. Adams's future son-in-law was welcome anywhere. The clerks were pleased to be greeted by the good-looking, agreeable young man who was going to marry Miss Annabel. Jimmy set his suitcase down. Annabel, whose heart was bubbling with happiness and lively youth, put on Jimmy's hat and picked up the suitcase. "Wouldn't I make a nice drummer?" said Annabel. "My! Ralph, how heavy it is. Feels like it was full of gold bricks."

"Lot of nickel-plated shoe-horns in there," said Jimmy, coolly, "that I'm going to return. Thought I'd save express charges by taking them up. I'm getting awfully economical."

The Elmore Bank had just put in a new safe and vault. Mr. Adams was very proud of it, and insisted on an inspection by every one. The vault was a small one, but it had a new patented door. It fastened with three solid steel bolts thrown simultaneously with a single handle, and had a time-lock. Mr. Adams beamingly explained its workings to Mr. Spencer, who showed a courteous but not too intelligent interest. The two children, May and Agatha, were delighted by the shining metal and funny clock and knobs.

While they were thus engaged Ben Price sauntered in and leaned on his elbow, looking casually inside between the railings. He told the teller that he didn't want anything; he was just waiting for a man he knew.

Suddenly there was a scream or two

ELMORE BANK

from the women, and a commotion. Unperceived by the elders, May, the nine-year-old girl, in a spirt of play, had shut Agatha in the vault. She had then shot the bolts and turned the knob of the combination as she had seen Mr. Adams do.

The old banker sprang to the handle and tugged at it for a moment. "The door can't be opened," he groaned. "The clock hasn't been wound nor the combination set."

Agatha's mother screamed again, hysterically.

"Hush!" said Mr. Adams, raising his trembling hand. "All be quiet for a moment. Agatha!" he called as loudly as he could. "Listen to me." During the following silence they could just hear the faint sound of the child wildly shrieking in the dark vault in a panic of terror.

"My precious darling!" wailed the mother. "She will die of fright! Open the door! Oh, break it open! Can't you men do something?"

"There isn't a man nearer than Little Rock who can open that door," said Mr. Adams, in a shaky voice. "My God! Spencer, what shall we do? That child—she can't stand it long in there. There isn't enough air, and, besides, she'll go into convulsions from fright."

Agatha's mother, frantic now, beat the door of the vault with her hands. Somebody wildly suggested dynamite. Annabel turned to Jimmy, her large eyes full of anguish, but not yet despairing. To a woman nothing seems quite impossible to the powers of the man she worships.

"Can't you do something, Ralph—*try*, won't you?"

He looked at her with a queer, soft smile on his lips and in his keen eyes.

"Annabel," he said, "give me that rose you are wearing, will you?"

Hardly believing that she heard him aright, she unpinned the bud from the bosom of her dress, and placed it in his hand. Jimmy stuffed it into his vest-pocket, threw off his coat, and pulled up his shirt-sleeves. With that act Ralph D. Spencer passed away and Jimmy Valentine took his place.

"Get away from the door, all of you," he commanded, shortly.

He set his suitcase on the table, and opened it out flat. From that time on he seemed to be unconscious of the presence of anyone else. He laid out the shining, queer implements swiftly and orderly, whistling softly to himself as he always did when at work. In a deep silence and immovable, the others watched him as if under a spell.

In a minute Jimmy's pet drill was biting smoothly into the steel door. In ten minutes—breaking his own burglarious record—he threw back the bolts and opened the door.

Agatha, almost collapsed, but safe, was gathered into her mother's arms. Jimmy

Valentine put on his coat, and walked outside the railings toward the front door. As he went he thought he heard a far-away voice that he once knew call "Ralph!" But he never hesitated.

At the door a big man stood somewhat in his way.

"Hello, Ben!" said Jimmy, still with his strange smile. "Got around at last, have you? Well, let's go. I don't know that it makes much difference, now."

And then Ben Price acted rather strangely.

"Guess you're mistaken, Mr. Spencer," he said. "Don't believe I recognize you. Your buggy's waiting for you, ain't it?"

And Ben Price turned and strolled down the street.

What is the most suspenseful part of the story? Explain what makes this part suspenseful.

Which do you think was harder for Jimmy Valentine—his reformation or his decision to rescue the little girl trapped in the safe? Explain your answer.

Why do you think Ben Price said that he did not recognize Jimmy?

WRITE In your opinion, has Jimmy Valentine truly reformed by the end of the story, or might he someday turn back to a life of crime? Write a paragraph in which you support your opinion with details from the story.

THE TRUTH REVEALED

Compare the endings of "M. C. Higgins, the Great" and "A Retrieved Reformation." In which selection do you think the main characters learn more of the truth about each other? Explain.

WRITER'S WORKSHOP

M. C. Higgins is surprised to find out that his diving partner can't swim. The Adamses are surprised to find out that "Ralph" can break into a safe. Imagine that you find out someone you know is different from what he or she has led you to believe. Write a story about finding out the truth. Depict realistic events and feelings.

Writer's Choice Sometimes a truth is revealed through a discovery. Think about the word *discovery.* What writing ideas does the word bring to mind? Choose one idea, and write about it in your own way. Then think of a way to share your writing.

CONNECTIONS

MULTICULTURAL CONNECTION

FRIGID FINDINGS

One of the great explorers of the twentieth century was Robert E. Peary, who led several expeditions in the Arctic and is generally credited with discovering the North Pole. But it was actually his African American partner, Matthew Henson, who first reached the point they believed to be the Pole.

Henson was born in 1866 in Maryland. His parents died while he was young, and he became a cabin boy on a cargo ship. In 1887 he joined Peary on a journey to Central America. Later, when the eyes of explorers turned northward toward the Arctic, Peary and Henson made several attempts to reach the North Pole. Henson became a favorite among the Eskimos and was the only member of Peary's team to learn the Inuit language.

In 1909 Peary and Henson set out by dogsled through blinding snow and temperatures of sixty degrees below zero. Peary fell behind, but Henson pushed on to arrive first at the North Pole. Years later, Henson received a congressional medal for his achievement.

Find out more about Matthew Henson and other twentieth-century explorers. Have a class discussion on the explorers, and compare their achievements.

SOCIAL STUDIES CONNECTION

ARCTIC VS. TROPICAL EXPLORATION

Matthew Henson explored two very different parts of the world: the rain forests of Central America and the ice fields of the Arctic. Find out how conditions affected travel in each place in 1900. Then compare and contrast the two areas by writing a paragraph about each area or by making a chart. Topics you might compare and contrast include land, climate, transportation, animals, people, and problems.

SCIENCE CONNECTION

POLAR INVESTIGATION

In their journeys to the Arctic, Peary and Henson gathered scientific data and carried out experiments. Scientists today continue to study the Arctic and the Antarctic (the region around the South Pole) as well. Read about the scientific research that is going on in the polar regions. Write about one of the studies that interests you. Explain what the scientists are trying to learn and what they have found out so far. Share your information with your classmates.

Clockwise from upper left: Matthew Henson, Arctic explorer; Matthew Henson beside one of the sledges used on the successful expedition to the North Pole; Henson receiving the gold medal of the National Geographic Society

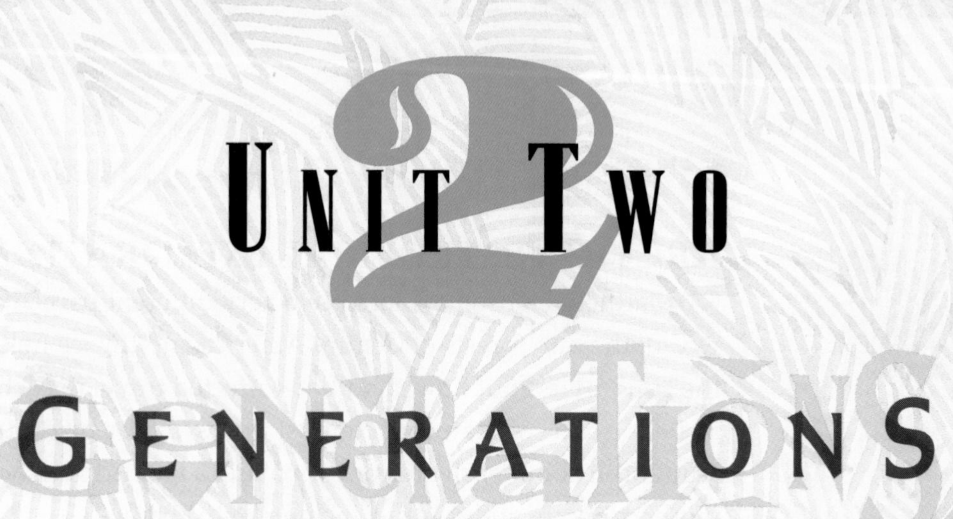

UNIT TWO

GENERATIONS

And remembering . . .
Remembering, with twinklings and
twinges, . . .
Gwendolyn Brooks

Family memories of special occasions, of holidays, and even of tragedies will stay with you throughout your life. In this unit you will explore the importance of family ties and memories as you share in the experiences of famous writers such as Gary Soto, Russell Baker, and Gwendolyn Brooks. You will also consider how knowledge of the past can lead to an understanding of the present and to a clearer focus on the future. As you read, think of what you appreciate about your own family and its history.

THEMES

BOOKSHELF

ONE-EYED CAT

BY PAULA FOX

A stray cat mysteriously enters Ned's life. What does the cat want with Ned, and why does Ned feel so guilty about disobeying his father?

Newbery Honor Book, Notable Children's Trade Book in the Field of Social Studies

HARCOURT BRACE LIBRARY BOOK

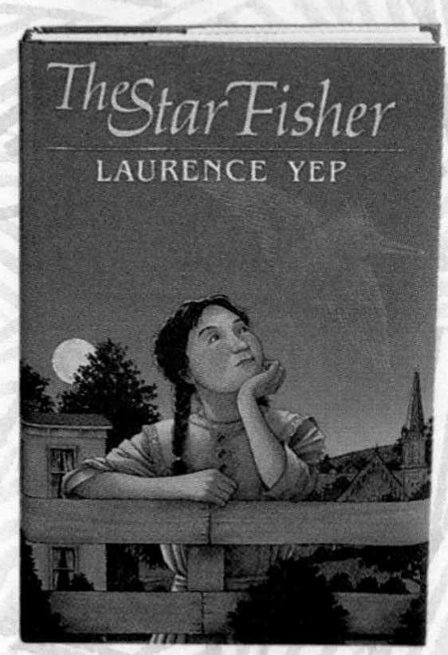

THE STAR FISHER

BY LAURENCE YEP

Chinese American Joan Lee and her family move from Ohio to West Virginia to open a new laundry business and are shunned by the townspeople. At school, however, Joan finds an extraordinary friend.

Christopher Award, IRA Teachers' Choice, Notable Children's Trade Book in the Field of Social Studies

Taking Sides

BY GARY SOTO

Lincoln's move from the barrio to a white suburb presents new problems. How can he play basketball against his former teammates in the big game?

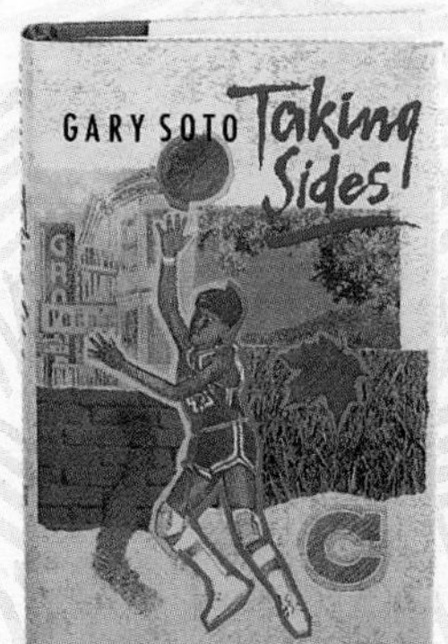

Black Star, Bright Dawn

BY SCOTT O'DELL

When her father, an Eskimo hunter, is injured, Bright Dawn takes his place in the Iditarod, a grueling and dangerous dogsled race.

Notable Children's Trade Book in the Field of Social Studies

The Trouble with Gramary

BY BETTY LEVIN

Newcomers to a small coastal town think the welding business run by Merkka's grandmother is an eyesore. Merkka loves her grandmother but is torn by her own wishes for a new home.

THEME

FAMILY TIES

Differences in outlook between parents and children may lead to a generation gap in families. Yet family ties are usually stronger than such differences. In the next selections, you will explore the importance of family ties and go ancestor hunting to find out more about generations of families.

CONTENTS

M·O·T·H·E·R and Daughter

ALA Best Book for Young Adults

by Gary Soto

Illustration by Stephanie Garcia

Yollie's mother, Mrs. Moreno, was a large woman who wore a muumuu and butterfly-shaped glasses. She liked to water her lawn in the evening and wave at low-riders, who would stare at her behind their smoky sunglasses and laugh. Now and then a low-rider from Belmont Avenue would make his car jump and shout *"Mamacita!"* But most of the time they just stared and wondered how she got so large.

Mrs. Moreno had a strange sense of humor. Once, Yollie and her mother were watching a late-night movie called "They Came to Look." It was about creatures from the underworld who had climbed through molten lava to walk the earth. But Yollie, who had played soccer all day with the kids next door, was too tired to be scared. Her eyes closed but sprang open when her mother screamed, "Look, Yollie! Oh, you missed a scary part. The guy's face was all ugly!"

But Yollie couldn't keep her eyes open. They fell shut again and stayed shut, even when her mother screamed and slammed a heavy palm on the arm of her chair.

"Mom, wake me up when the movie's over so I can go to bed," mumbled Yollie.

"OK, Yollie, I wake you," said her mother through a mouthful of popcorn.

But after the movie ended, instead of waking her daughter, Mrs. Moreno laughed under her breath, turned the TV and lights off, and tiptoed to bed. Yollie woke up in the middle of the night and didn't know where she was. For a moment she thought she was dead. Maybe something from the underworld had lifted her from her house and carried her into the earth's belly. She blinked her sleepy eyes, looked around at the darkness, and called, "Mom? Mom, where are you?" But there was no answer, just the throbbing hum of the refrigerator.

Finally, Yollie's grogginess cleared and she realized her mother had gone to bed, leaving her on the couch. Another of her little jokes.

But Yollie wasn't laughing. She tiptoed into her mother's bedroom with a glass of water and set it on the nightstand next to the alarm clock. The next morning, Yollie woke to screams. When her mother reached to turn off the alarm, she had overturned the glass of water.

Yollie burned her mother's morning toast and gloated. "Ha! Ha! I got you back. Why did you leave me on the couch when I told you to wake me up?"

Despite their jokes, mother and daughter usually got along. They watched bargain matinees together, and played croquet in the summer and checkers in the winter. Mrs. Moreno encouraged Yollie to study hard because she wanted her daughter to be a doctor. She bought Yollie a desk, a typewriter, and a lamp that cut glare so her eyes would not grow tired from hours of studying.

Yollie was slender as a tulip, pretty, and one of the smartest kids at Saint Theresa's. She was captain of crossing guards, an altar girl, and a whiz in the school's monthly spelling bees.

"Tienes que estudiar mucho," Mrs. Moreno said every time she propped her work-weary feet on the hassock. "You have to study a lot, then you can get a good job and take care of me."

"Yes, Mama," Yollie would respond, her face buried in a book. If she gave her mother any sympathy, she would begin her stories about how she had come with her family from Mexico with nothing on her back but a sack with three skirts, all of which were too large by the time she crossed the border because she had lost weight from not having enough to eat.

Everyone thought Yollie's mother was a riot. Even the nuns laughed at her antics. Her brother Raul, a nightclub owner, thought she was funny enough to go into show business.

But there was nothing funny about Yollie needing a new outfit for the eighth-grade fall dance. "We don't have the money," said her mother, genuinely sad because they couldn't buy the outfit, even though there was a little money stashed away for college. Mrs. Moreno remembered her teenage years and her hardworking parents, who picked grapes and oranges, and chopped beets and cotton for meager pay around Kerman. Those were the days when "new clothes" meant limp and out-of-style dresses from Saint Vincent de Paul.

The best Mrs. Moreno could do was buy Yollie a pair of black shoes with velvet bows and fabric dye to color her white summer dress black.

"We can color your dress so it will look brand-new," her mother said brightly, shaking the bottle of dye as she ran hot water into a plastic dish tub. She poured the black liquid into the tub and stirred it with a pencil. Then, slowly and carefully, she lowered the dress into the tub.

Yollie couldn't stand to watch. She *knew* it wouldn't work. It would be like the time her mother stirred up a batch of molasses for candy apples on Yollie's birthday. She'd dipped the apples into the goo and swirled them and seemed to taunt Yollie by singing "*Las Mañanitas*" to her. When she was through, she set the apples on wax paper. They were hard as rocks and hurt the kids' teeth. Finally they had a contest to see who could break the apples open by throwing them against the side of the house. The apples shattered like grenades, sending the kids scurrying for cover, and in an odd way the birthday party turned out to be a success. At least everyone went home happy.

To Yollie's surprise, the dress came out shiny black. It looked brand-new and sophisticated, like what people in New York wear. She beamed at her mother, who hugged Yollie and said, "See, what did I tell you?"

The dance was important to Yollie because she was in love with Ernie Castillo, the third-best speller in the class. She bathed, dressed, did her hair and nails, and primped until her mother yelled, "All right already." Yollie sprayed her neck and wrists with Mrs. Moreno's perfume and bounced into the car.

Mrs. Moreno let Yollie out in front of the school. She waved and told her to have a good time but behave herself, then roared off.

Yollie ran into her best friend, Janice. They didn't say it, but each thought the other was the most beautiful girl at the dance; the boys would fall over themselves asking them to dance.

The evening was warm but thick with clouds. Gusts of wind picked up the paper lanterns hanging in the trees and swung them, blurring the night with reds and yellows. The lanterns made the evening seem romantic, like a scene from a movie. Everyone danced, sipped punch, and stood in knots of threes and fours, talking. Sister Kelly got up and jitterbugged with some kid's father. When the record ended, students broke into applause.

Janice had her eye on Frankie Ledesma, and Yollie, who kept smoothing her dress down when the wind picked up, had her eye on Ernie. It turned out that Ernie had his mind on Yollie, too. He ate a handful of cookies nervously, then asked her for a dance.

"Sure," she said, nearly throwing herself into his arms.

They danced two fast ones before they got a slow one. As they circled

under the lanterns, rain began falling, lightly at first. Yollie loved the sound of the raindrops ticking against the leaves. She leaned her head on Ernie's shoulder, though his sweater was scratchy. He felt warm and tender. Yollie could tell that he was in love, and with her, of course. The dance continued successfully, romantically, until it began to pour.

"Everyone, let's go inside—and, boys, carry in the table and the record player," Sister Kelly commanded.

The girls and boys raced into the cafeteria. Inside, the girls, drenched to the bone, hurried to the restrooms to brush their hair and dry themselves. One girl cried because her velvet dress was ruined. Yollie felt sorry for her and helped her dry the dress off with paper towels, but it was no use. The dress was ruined.

Yollie went to a mirror. She looked a little gray now that her mother's makeup had washed away but not as bad as some of the other girls. She combed her damp hair, careful not to pull too hard. She couldn't wait to get back to Ernie.

Yollie bent over to pick up a bobby pin, and shame spread across her face. A black puddle was forming at her feet. Drip, black drip. Drip, black drip. The dye was falling from her dress like black tears. Yollie stood up. Her dress was now the color of ash. She looked around the room. The other girls, unaware of Yollie's problem, were busy grooming themselves. What could she do? Everyone would laugh. They would know she dyed an old dress because she couldn't afford a new one. She hurried from the restroom with her head down, across the cafeteria floor and out the door. She raced through the storm, crying as the rain mixed with her tears and ran into twig-choked gutters.

When she arrived home, her mother was on the couch eating cookies and watching TV.

"How was the dance, *m'ija*?[1] Come watch the show with me. It's really good."

Yollie stomped, head down, to her bedroom. She undressed and threw the dress on the floor.

Her mother came into the room. "What's going on? What's all this racket, baby?"

"The dress. It's cheap! It's no good!" Yollie kicked the dress at her mother and watched it land in her hands. Mrs. Moreno studied it closely but couldn't see what was wrong. "What's the matter? It's just little bit wet."

"The dye came out, that's what."

Mrs. Moreno looked at her hands and saw the grayish dye puddling in the shallow lines of her palms. Poor baby, she thought, her brow darkening as she made a sad face. She wanted to tell her daughter how sorry she was, but she knew it wouldn't help. She walked back to the living room and cried.

The next morning, mother and daughter stayed away from each other. Yollie sat in her room while her mother watered her plants.

"Drink, my children," she said loud enough for Yollie to hear. She let the water slurp into pots of coleus and cacti. "Water is all you need. My daughter needs clothes, but I don't have no money."

Yollie was embarrassed at last night's tirade. It wasn't her mother's fault that they were poor.

When they sat down together for lunch, they felt awkward about the night before. But Mrs. Moreno had made a fresh stack of tortillas and cooked up a pan of *chile verde,* and that broke the ice. She licked her thumb and smacked her lips.

"You know, honey, we gotta figure a way to make money," Yollie's mother said. "You and me. We don't have to be poor. Remember the Garcias. They made this stupid little tool that fixes cars. They moved away because they're rich. That's

---

[1] *m'ija* [mē´hä]: contraction of *mi hija;* Spanish for "my daughter"

why we don't see them no more."

"What can we make?" asked Yollie. She took another tortilla and tore it in half.

"Maybe a screwdriver that works on both ends? Something like that." The mother looked around the room for ideas, but then shrugged. "Let's forget it. It's better to get an education. If you get a good job and have spare time then maybe you can invent something." She rolled her tongue over her lips and cleared her throat. "The county fair hires people. We can get a job there. It will be here next week."

Yollie hated the idea. What would Ernie say if he saw her pitching hay at the cows? How could she go to school smelling like an armful of chickens? "No, they wouldn't hire us," she said.

The phone rang. Yollie lurched from her chair to answer it, thinking it would be Janice wanting to know why she had left. But it was Ernie wondering the same thing. When he found out she wasn't mad at him, he asked if she would like to go to a movie.

"I'll ask," Yollie said, smiling. She covered the phone with her hand and counted to ten. She uncovered the receiver and said, "My mom says it's OK. What are we going to see?"

After Yollie hung up, her mother climbed, grunting, onto a chair to reach the top shelf in the hall closet. She wondered why she hadn't done it earlier. She reached behind a stack of towels and pushed her chubby hand into the cigar box where she kept her secret stash of money.

"I've been saving a little every month," said Mrs. Moreno. "For you, *m'ija.*" Her mother held up five twenties, a blossom of green that smelled sweeter than flowers on that Saturday. They bought a blouse, shoes, and a skirt that would not bleed in rain or any other kind of weather.

Explain whether you sympathize with Yollie or feel she is too self-conscious about her appearance.

Do you think Yollie and her mother have a good relationship? Explain your response.

Think about the fairy tale "Cinderella." How are "Cinderella" and "Mother and Daughter" similar? How are they different?

At the end of the story, Mrs. Moreno decides to spend some of the money she has saved for Yollie's education. Why do you think she does so?

WRITE Do you think this story is realistic? Support your written response with at least two reasons for your opinion.

Gary Soto, a Mexican American educator and poet, was born in Fresno, California. His heritage influences his writing and gives it a unique regional flavor. Here Soto explains how his background and experiences work together to help him create award-winning pieces.

I came from a family of Chicano field workers. My mother peeled potatoes for a living. My uncles tossed buckets of raisins into big vats to be washed. After doing that all day, you don't want to come home and talk about poetry. Even though you want your child to advance, it's a question of how do you do it. How do you make this person move on? For me, most of my motivation came from the absolute desire to make it as a writer. Of course, I started as a poet, a seemingly unmarketable occupation.

After a number of years as a poet, I shifted genres, mostly out of curiosity. My poetry tends to be narrative anyway, so it was easy to slip into writing recollections, which my stories are. I wanted to paint a portrait of growing up in San Joaquin Valley, where I came from. After my first book came out, I got letters, lots of them from throughout the Southwest. They were so touching because people were seeing themselves in what I was writing.

AWARD-WINNING AUTHOR

My book *Baseball in April,* from which this story comes, was rejected everywhere when I first started sending it around. I believe in a regional literature, but the publishers wanted more generic writing. I wanted to write about a real place and real characters. That's what mature writers like William Faulkner and Eudora Welty do; they set their stories in one region and don't go beyond it. So I worked with that premise. Still, these stories are fiction. Though people who have floated through my life sometimes provide the kernels for my characters, much of my writing comes from the imagination.

FoxTrot

by Bill Amend

A Mother in Mannville

by Marjorie Kinnan Rawlings

• • •

The orphanage is high in the Carolina mountains. Sometimes in winter the snowdrifts are so deep that the institution is cut off from the village below, from all the world. Fog hides the mountain peaks, the snow swirls down the valleys, and a wind blows so bitterly that the orphanage boys who take the milk twice daily to the baby cottage reach the door with fingers stiff in an agony of numbness.

Award-Winning Author

illustrated by Byron Gin

"Or when we carry trays from the cookhouse for the ones that are sick," Jerry said, "we get our faces frostbit, because we can't put our hands over them. I have gloves," he added. "Some of the boys don't have any."

He liked the late spring, he said. The rhododendron was in bloom, a carpet of color, across the mountainsides, soft as the May winds that stirred the hemlocks. He called it laurel.

"It's pretty when the laurel blooms," he said. "Some of it's pink and some of it's white."

I was there in the autumn. I wanted quiet, isolation, to do some troublesome writing. I wanted mountain air to blow out the malaria from too long a time in the subtropics. I was homesick, too, for the flaming of maples in October, and for corn shocks and pumpkins and black-walnut trees and the lift of hills. I found them all, living in a cabin that belonged to the orphanage, half a mile beyond the orphanage farm. When I took the cabin, I asked for a boy or man to come and chop wood for the fireplace. The first few days were warm, I found what wood I needed about the cabin, no one came, and I forgot the order.

I looked up from my typewriter one late afternoon, a little startled. A boy stood at the door, and my pointer dog, my companion, was at his side and had not barked to warn me. The boy was probably twelve years old, but undersized. He wore overalls and a torn shirt, and was barefooted.

He said, "I can chop some wood today."

I said, "But I have a boy coming from the orphanage."

"I'm the boy."

"You? But you're small."

"Size don't matter, chopping wood," he said. "Some of the big boys don't chop good. I've been chopping wood at the orphanage a long time."

I visualized mangled and inadequate branches for my fires. I was well into my work and not inclined to conversation. I was a little blunt.

"Very well. There's the ax. Go ahead and see what you can do."

I went back to work, closing the door. At first the sound of the boy dragging brush annoyed me. Then he began to chop. The blows were rhythmic and steady, and shortly I had forgotten him, the sound no more of an interruption than a consistent rain. I suppose an hour and a half passed, for when I stopped and stretched, and heard the boy's steps on the cabin stoop, the sun was dropping behind the farthest mountain, and the valleys were purple with something deeper than the asters.

The boy said, "I have to go to supper now. I can come again tomorrow evening."

I said, "I'll pay you now for what you've done," thinking I should probably have to insist on an older boy. "Ten cents an hour?"

"Anything is all right."

We went together back of the cabin. An astonishing amount of solid wood had been cut. There were cherry logs and heavy roots of rhododendron, and blocks from the waste pine and oak left from the building of the cabin.

"But you've done as much as a man," I said. "This is a splendid pile."

I looked at him, actually, for the first time. His hair was the color of the corn shocks and his eyes, very direct, were like the mountain sky when rain is pending—gray, with a shadowing of that miraculous blue. As I spoke, a light came over him, as though the setting sun had touched him with the same suffused glory with which it touched the mountains. I gave him a quarter.

"You may come tomorrow," I said, "and thank you very much."

He looked at me, and at the coin, and seemed to want to speak, but could not, and turned away.

"I'll split kindling tomorrow," he said over his thin ragged shoulder. "You'll need kindling and medium wood and logs and backlogs."

At daylight I was half wakened by the sound of chopping. Again it was so even in texture that I went back to sleep. When I left my bed in the cool morning, the boy had come and gone, and a stack of kindling was neat against the cabin wall. He came again after school in the afternoon and worked until time to return to the orphanage. His name was Jerry; he was twelve years old, and he had been at the orphanage since he was four. I could picture him at four, with the same grave gray-blue eyes and the same—independence? No, the word that comes to me is "integrity."

The word means something very special to me, and the quality for which I use it is a rare one. My father had it—there is another of whom I am almost sure—but almost no man of my acquaintance possesses it with the clarity, the purity, the simplicity of a mountain stream. But the boy Jerry had it. It is bedded on courage, but it is more than brave. It is honest, but it is more than honesty. The ax handle broke one day. Jerry said the woodshop at the orphanage would repair it. I brought money to pay for the job and he refused it.

"I'll pay for it," he said. "I broke it. I brought the ax down careless."

"But no one hits accurately every time," I told him. "The fault was in the wood of the handle. I'll see the man from whom I bought it."

It was only then that he would take the money. He was standing back of his own carelessness. He was a free-will agent and he chose to do careful work, and if he failed, he took the responsibility without subterfuge.

And he did for me the unnecessary thing, the gracious thing, that we find done only by the great of heart. Things no training can teach, for they are done on the instant, with no predicated experience. He found a cubbyhole beside the fireplace that I had not noticed. There, of his own accord, he put kindling and "medium" wood, so that I might always have dry fire material ready in case of sudden wet weather. A stone was loose in the rough walk to the cabin. He dug a deeper hole and steadied it, although he came, himself, by a short cut over the bank. I found that when I tried to return his thoughtfulness with such things as candy and apples, he was wordless. "Thank you" was, perhaps, an expression for which he had had no use, for his courtesy was instinctive. He only looked at the gift and at me, and a curtain lifted, so that I saw deep into the clear well of his eyes, and gratitude was there, and affection, soft over the firm granite of his character.

He made simple excuses to come and sit with me. I could no more have turned him away than if he had been physically hungry. I suggested once that the best time for us to visit was just before supper, when I left off my writing. After that, he waited always until my typewriter had been some time quiet. One day I worked until nearly dark. I went outside the cabin, having forgotten him. I saw him going up over the hill in the twilight toward the orphanage. When I sat down on my stoop, a place was warm from his body where he had been sitting.

He became intimate, of course, with my pointer, Pat. There is a strange communion between a boy and a dog. Perhaps they possess the same singleness of spirit, the same kind of wisdom. It is difficult to explain, but it exists. When I went across the state for a weekend, I left the dog in Jerry's charge. I gave him the dog whistle and the key to the cabin, and left sufficient food. He was to come two or three times a day and let out the dog, and feed and exercise him. I should return Sunday night, and Jerry would take out the dog for the last time Sunday afternoon and then leave the key under an agreed hiding place.

My return was belated and fog filled the mountain passes so treacherously that I dared not drive at night. The fog held the next morning, and it was Monday noon before I reached the cabin. The dog had been fed and cared for that morning. Jerry came early in the afternoon, anxious.

"The superintendent said nobody would drive in the fog," he said. "I came just before bedtime last night and you hadn't come. So I brought Pat some of my breakfast this morning. I wouldn't have let anything happen to him."

"I was sure of that. I didn't worry."

"When I heard about the fog, I thought you'd know."

He was needed for work at the orphanage and he had to return at once. I gave him a dollar in payment, and he looked at it and went away. But that night he came in the darkness and knocked at the door.

"Come in, Jerry," I said, "if you're allowed to be away this late."

"I told maybe a story," he said. "I told them I thought you would want to see me."

"That's true," I assured him, and I saw his relief. "I want to hear about how you managed with the dog."

He sat by the fire with me, with no other light, and told me of their two days together. The dog lay close to him and found a comfort there that I did not have for him. And it seemed to me that being with my dog, and caring for him, had brought the boy and me, too, together, so that he felt that he belonged to me as well as to the animal.

"He stayed right with me," he told me, "except when he ran in the laurel. He likes the laurel. I took him up over the hill and we both ran fast. There was a place where the grass was high and I lay down in it and hid. I could hear Pat hunting for me. He found my trail and he barked. When he found me, he acted crazy, and he ran around and around me, in circles."

We watched the flames.

"That's an apple log," he said. "It burns the prettiest of any wood."

We were very close.

He was suddenly impelled to speak of things he had not spoken of before, nor had I cared to ask him.

"You look a little bit like my mother," he said. "Especially in the dark, by the fire."

"But you were only four, Jerry, when you came here. You have remembered how she looked, all these years?"

"My mother lives in Mannville," he said.

For a moment, finding that he had a mother shocked me as greatly as anything in my life has ever done, and I did not know why it disturbed me. Then I understood my distress. I was filled with a passionate resentment that any woman should go away and leave her son. A fresh anger added itself. A son like this one— The orphanage was a wholesome place, the executives were kind, good people, the food was more than adequate, the boys were healthy, a ragged shirt was no hardship, nor the doing of clean labor. Granted, perhaps, that the boy felt no lack, what blood fed the bowels of a woman who did not yearn over this child's lean body that had come in parturition out of her own? At four he would have looked the same as now. Nothing, I thought, nothing in life could change those eyes. His quality must be apparent to an idiot, a fool. I burned with questions I could not ask. In any, I was afraid, there would be pain.

"Have you seen her, Jerry—lately?"

"I see her every summer. She sends for me."

I wanted to cry out, "Why are you not with her? How can she let you go away again?"

He said, "She comes up here from Mannville whenever she can. She doesn't have a job now."

His face shone in the firelight.

"She wanted to give me a puppy, but they can't let any one boy keep a puppy. You remember the suit I had on last Sunday?" He was plainly proud. "She sent me that for Christmas. The Christmas before that"—he drew a long breath, savoring the memory—"she sent me a pair of skates."

"Roller skates?"

My mind was busy, making pictures of her, trying to understand her. She had not, then, entirely deserted or forgotten him. But why, then—I thought, "I must not condemn her without knowing."

"Roller skates. I let the other boys use them. They're always borrowing them. But they're careful of them."

What circumstance other than poverty—

"I'm going to take the dollar you gave me for taking care of Pat," he said, "and buy her a pair of gloves."

I could only say, "That will be nice. Do you know her size?"

"I think it's 8 1/2," he said.

He looked at my hands.

"Do you wear 8 1/2?" he asked.

"No. I wear a smaller size, a 6."

"Oh! Then I guess her hands are bigger than yours."

I hated her. Poverty or no, there was other food than bread, and the soul could starve as quickly as the body. He was taking his dollar to buy gloves for her big stupid hands, and she lived away from him, in Mannville, and contented herself with sending him skates.

"She likes white gloves," he said. "Do you think I can get them for a dollar?"

"I think so," I said.

I decided that I should not leave the mountains without seeing her and knowing for myself why she had done this thing.

The human mind scatters its interests as though made of thistledown, and every wind stirs and moves it. I finished my work. It did not please me, and I gave my thoughts to another field. I should need some Mexican material.

I made arrangements to close my Florida place. Mexico immediately, and doing the writing there, if conditions were favorable. Then, Alaska with my brother. After that, heaven knew what or where.

I did not take time to go to Mannville to see Jerry's mother, nor even to talk with the orphanage officials about her. I was a trifle abstracted about the boy, because of my work and plans. And after my first fury at her—we did not speak of her again—his having a mother, any sort at all, not far away, in Mannville, relieved me of the ache I had had about him. He did not question the anomalous relation. He was not lonely. It was none of my concern.

He came every day and cut my wood and did small helpful favors and stayed to talk. The days had become cold, and often I let him come inside the cabin. He would lie on the floor in front of the fire, with one arm across the pointer, and they would both doze and wait quietly for me. Other days they ran with a common ecstasy through the laurel,

and since the asters were now gone, he brought me back vermilion maple leaves, and chestnut boughs dripping with imperial yellow. I was ready to go.

I said to him, "You have been my good friend, Jerry. I shall often think of you and miss you. Pat will miss you too. I am leaving tomorrow."

He did not answer. When he went away, I remember that a new moon hung over the mountains, and I watched him go in silence up the hill. I expected him the next day, but he did not come. The details of packing my personal belongings, loading my car, arranging the bed over the seat, where the dog would ride, occupied me until late in the day. I closed the cabin and started the car, noticing that the sun was in the west and I should do well to be out of the mountains by nightfall. I stopped by the orphanage and left the cabin key and money for my light bill with Miss Clark.

"And will you call Jerry for me to say good-by to him?"

"I don't know where he is," she said. "I'm afraid he's not well. He didn't eat his dinner this noon. One of the other boys saw him going over the hill into the laurel. He was supposed to fire the boiler this afternoon. It's not like him; he's unusually reliable."

I was almost relieved, for I knew I should never see him again, and it would be easier not to say good-by to him.

I said, "I wanted to talk with you about his mother—why he's here—but I'm in more of a hurry than I expected to be. It's out of the question for me to see her now too. But here's some money I'd like to leave with you to buy things for him at Christmas and on his birthday. It will be better than for me to try to send things. I could so easily duplicate—skates, for instance."

She blinked her honest spinster's eyes.

"There's not much use for skates here," she said.

Her stupidity annoyed me.

"What I mean," I said, "is that I don't want to duplicate things his mother sends him. I might have chosen skates if I didn't know she had already given them to him."

She stared at me.

"I don't understand," she said. "He has no mother. He has no skates."

How did you feel at the end of the story? Why?

Why do you think Jerry pretends to have a mother?

Why do you think Jerry is not at the orphanage when the narrator comes to say good-by?

As the narrator looks back on her time in the mountains, do you think she has any regrets about the way she treated Jerry? Explain.

WRITE In a letter to either Jerry or the narrator, explain how his or her situation made you feel.

September

(BINI´ANT´AATSOH)

by Ramona Maher

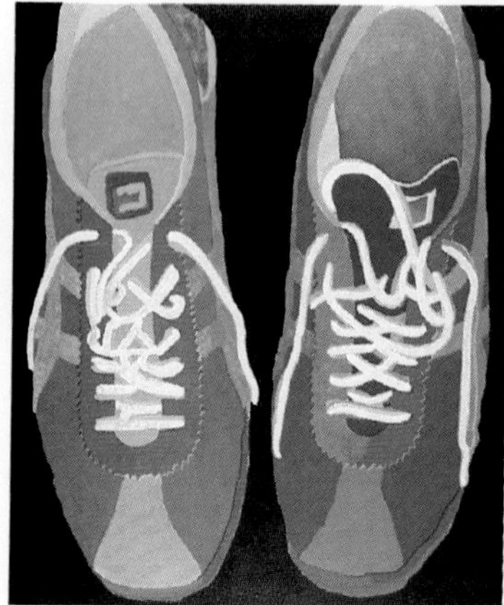

Shoe Series 3
by Marilee Whitehouse-Holm
Private Collection

Alice pulls her hair back into one long braid.
Last year's gym shorts are too short. She's grown.
Her toes won't even wiggle
in last year's tennies.
It's a mile through the dust
to the yellow bus stop. In winter: through mud.
The pup seems to beg with his eyes:
"Stay home. Let's us play, Alice Yazzie.
The two of us."

Grandfather frowns.
"We do what we must.
I see you must go to school. This year—
not so many hot dogs in the cafeteria.
More books in the learning center.
We'll see to that."
Grandfather sits on the school board
and helps decide about classes and buildings.
The oldest school board man, he sees change happening.
He says it must come.
He even voted for girls to play football
if they want to. And study mechanical drawing.

Alice starts off in her tie-dyed T-shirt
and a denim skirt faded canyon blue.
Grandfather calls. He gives Alice a ride
behind him, on his horse,
to the bus stop shelter.
Alice is surprised.
"Remember," says Grandfather,
nudging the old mare until she faces around.
"You don't have to take mechanical drawing
if you don't want to."

"Thank you, Grandfather."
As they move off, old man on old horse,
Alice feels winter coming.

Bus Depot Reunion

by David Allen Evans

Just over the edge
of my *Life* a young sailor
bounds from a Greyhound's
hiss into his mother's hug,
steps back, trades hands
with his father, then turns
to an old, hunched man
maybe his grandfather—

no hand, no word goes out,
they regard each other,

waiting for something, and
now their hands cup,

they begin to crouch
and spar, the old man

coming on like a pro,
snuffling, weaving,

circling, flicks
out a hook like a lizard's tongue,

the boy ducking, countering,
moving with his moves,

biffing at the bobbing
yellow grin, the clever

head, never landing a real
punch, never taking one

until suddenly, exactly
together they quit,

throw an arm around each other
and walk away laughing

Anticamente by G.G. Kopilak,
Private Collection

LILA PERL
The Great Ancestor Hunt
THE FUN OF FINDING OUT WHO YOU ARE

The GREAT ANCESTOR HUNT

BY LILA PERL

We come across an old family photograph. The photo is in black and white, and it's faded and cracked. The person in the picture stands stiffly against a real or painted background of draperies, foliage, and elaborate furnishings.

This old-fashioned studio portrait was taken in the early 1900s. At that time, posing for one's photograph was a serious business. It meant "freezing" in front of the big, bulky studio camera for many seconds or even minutes. The quick, informal snapshots of today were still a rarity because small hand-held cameras had only recently been invented.

But who is this person in the picture? Is it your great-grandfather's brother, the first member of the family to become a famous brain surgeon, fondly and respectfully known to all as Great-Uncle Edgar? Or is it your great-grandfather himself, the most studious boy in his class, who sadly had to drop out of school to go to work and never fulfilled his dream of becoming a brilliant district attorney?

Here's another photo. Who are the two little girls, aged eight and ten, in their hair bows, sailor dresses, dark cotton stockings, and high-laced shoes? Would you be surprised to learn that they are your great-grandmother and her sister?

Can you see any family resemblance between you and the child your great-grandmother once was? Do you think your ambition to become a doctor or lawyer might have anything to do with the careers dreamed of by relatives who were growing up years ago?

Possibly you don't see any connection at all, and you're wondering why we should even care about our ancestors. Your great-grandparents may have died before you were born. Or, if they are alive, they may live in a distant place. The same may be true of your grandparents.

These days, it's easy to lose touch even with our own parents. They may have separated or divorced. One or both of them may have remarried, and we may find ourselves part of a step-family, with a whole new set of relatives. Or possibly we are being raised by just one parent. Many young Americans today can't even *name* all four of their parents' parents.

Yet, whether we know our ancestors or not, we are each a link in a human chain. We share our genes—the tiny units in our body cells that are responsible for inherited traits—with our forebears. And we'll pass on new combinations of these traits to our children and our children's children.

Could one of these two little girls in hair bows and high-laced shoes have been your great-grandmother?

The word *genealogy*, which means the study of family lines of descent, is related to *gene*. Our genes are what determine the color of our eyes and hair, the shape of our bodies, the special workings of our brains. They are what give us our inborn talent for music, science, or sports. Even certain diseases, how long we will live, and what we will eventually die of may be traceable to our genes.

Scientists believe that there may be as many as thirty-five hundred inherited, or genetic, diseases. Some are as mild as a mere tendency toward hay fever. Others are as serious as hemophilia, in which the blood's failure to clot can lead to uncontrollable bleeding from even a tiny cut or scrape. In many cases, healthy parents are the carriers of the disease-causing genes. Some inherited illnesses are found in specific racial groups. Sickle-cell anemia strikes children of black families, while Tay-Sachs disease attacks Jewish infants of eastern European ancestry. Death in infancy or early childhood can result from such abnormalities of the genes.

On a happier note, we can also inherit a trait such as great musical talent from our ancestors. An amazing example

Great-great-grandparents seem easier to reach when we remember that they are our grandparents' grandparents. Here they pose in a 1904 photograph with their three young daughters, one of whom could have been your grandmother's mother.

is found in the family of the famous composer Johann Sebastian Bach. Bach's earliest-known musical ancestor was born in the late 1500s. Forty out of sixty of this ancestor's descendants, many of whom lived during the 1700s, became accomplished and even outstanding musicians!

Heredity—the Bach "bloodline"—was an important factor in producing so much musical talent. But was it the only reason? The various Bach-family children all grew up in strongly disciplined, music-centered households. Their surroundings helped their inborn abilities to blossom. Similar abilities in children who were not exposed to music may have withered because their talents were never encouraged.

In other words, our home, our schooling, the time and place in which we live are all important influences on how we develop. They form part of what we call our environment. It isn't merely sharing certain genes that accounts for similarities among family members. We often are alike because of our shared experiences.

Adopted children, for example, may be closer in mannerisms, attitudes, and even appearance to their adoptive family than to their natural, or biological, family. They "take after" their adoptive parents—to whom they have no "blood" ties—because of close family ties, or environment.

Heredity or environment, which links us more closely to our living, and even dead, ancestors? The answer is probably a combination of the two. You may grow up to have the tall, broad-shouldered build

Right: *A great-great-grandmother who fled her tiny Russian village for America.* Left: *A great-grandmother—her daughter—as a young woman posing for her engagement photograph.*

and prematurely white hair of your great-great-grandfather. That's heredity.

If, on the other hand, your great-great-grandfather hadn't courageously crossed the Atlantic as a young man nearly one hundred years ago—and soon sent for your great-great-grandmother and their two-year-old daughter (your great-grandmother)—would you be living in America today? In having left the poverty and fearful uncertainties of life in a tiny European village, your great-great-grandparents changed not only their own environment. They changed yours as well.

Who were the very first people to keep records of their family lines and why? People have been searching for their "roots," constructing their "family trees" ever since earliest times. They have done so out of curiosity, a sense of family pride, and often, too, to establish inheritance claims. For, by tradition, rights of rulership, land holdings, and other possessions have been handed down from parent to child.

Even before they kept written records, many peoples relied on oral history to recall their ancestors. This was true among the ancient Scandinavians, Irish, Scots, and Welsh. Storytellers and poet-singers known as bards passed on the names and heroic deeds of dozens of earlier generations to younger members of the clan or tribe, to be memorized for safekeeping. We think of a generation as the time span between *our* being born and the birth of our children—usually twenty-five to thirty years. But there have been—and still are—peoples among whom a new generation was produced as often as every fifteen to twenty years.

Among certain Africans, Indonesians, and Pacific islanders, oral history is still very much alive. In recent times, a chieftain of the Maori, the Polynesian people native to New Zealand, recited a thirty-four-generation history of his people as a claim to the inheritance of a certain piece of territory in that country. His recital was said to have taken three days!

The children of a Kiowan Indian chief of long ago, two sisters and a baby in a cradleboard. Native American families were among those who recalled their ancestors through oral history.

The lengthiest oral history ever delivered is reported to have covered *seventy* generations. It was offered by an old man on a small Indonesian island off the coast of Sumatra, in the Indian Ocean. Island people are among the most likely to have spoken records that go back so far. One reason is that it's easier to keep track of one's family history in a confined area. Another is that land is in short supply on an island, so the inheritance rights passed (in most cases) from father to son have to be clearly spelled out.

By contrast, the Native Americans of the territory that is today the United States and Canada were few in number compared with the large land mass they occupied. They didn't think in terms of land ownership. And so, although American Indians recalled their ancestry through oral history, they seldom went back more than five or six generations.

Oral history endures, of course, only as long as it is both remembered and retold. Otherwise it dies. In 1966, a group of high school English students in Rabun Gap, Georgia, began to interview the Appalachian mountain people among whom they lived. Many, in fact, were elderly members of the students' own families. Under the guidance of their teacher, Eliot Wigginton, the students published a magazine called *Foxfire*. It contained the spoken rememberings of the mountain dwellers.

As the wealth of material grew, the magazine developed into a numbered series of best-selling *Foxfire* books, covering traditional crafts and skills—

from banjo making to bear hunting—stories, songs, and other mountain lore. *Foxfire* not only preserved the rich heritage of a fast-disappearing segment of American life. It also enriched the young people who collected the folkways of the southern Appalachians. And it gave rise to many similar projects throughout the country.

Probably the most famous personal experience with oral history in our time is the one that Alex Haley wrote about in his book *Roots: The Saga of an American Family*. Haley's story, which was published in 1976, described what he learned as a result of his amazingly successful search for his African ancestry.

Haley's first slave ancestor, as revealed in *Roots*, was a man named Kunta Kinte, who had been brought to America in the 1760s. During Haley's childhood years, his grandmother had told him stories she had heard as a child about a man called "Kintay" who'd been kidnapped by slavers near the "Kamby Bolongo" in Africa and taken by ship to a place called "Naplis" in the United States. There he was sold to a plantation owner who brought him to work in Virginia, under the slave name of Toby.

The spoken memories of Haley's grandmother made a deep impression on him. As a grown man, he began a twelve-year search for his roots. "Naplis," he discovered, was Annapolis, a port city in Maryland, while the "Kamby Bolongo" was the Gambia River in the West African country of Gambia. Learning that there

A black settler family in front of their sod house on the Nebraska plains

A covered-wagon family pauses as it crosses the inhospitable plains on the journey westward.

were tribal historians in Gambia known as *griots,* Haley traveled to that country. There, a *griot* recited for Haley the history of his family, the Kinte clan, tracing the line all the way back to the time of Kunta Kinte's grandfather in the early 1700s.

The people who kept the first *written* records of their ancestry were probably the ancient Egyptians and the Chinese. Such records were especially important to the wealthier classes in these civilizations because they had the most to gain through inheritance. At the very top of the heap were the royal families, known as dynasties, that ruled in both Egypt and China for thousands of years. Enormous power and untold wealth were bestowed on the members of those noble family lines.

Among the Chinese, the common people, too, kept detailed family records. This was because the devotion of sons to fathers and the worship of ancestors were important parts of the teachings of Confucius, a Chinese philosopher who lived twenty-five hundred years ago. Confucianism spread through all levels of Chinese society. Even the poorest homes had altars inscribed with the names of ancestors. It was the duty of the eldest son in the family to burn incense and make offerings at the altar.

In religions like those of ancient Greece and Rome, the gods themselves had complete family trees. In fact, they were much like earthly royal families, to whom they were sometimes "related." Romulus and Remus, the founders of Rome, were said to be the twin sons of Mars, the Roman god of war. While the story of Rome's founding is a legend, many *real* earthly rulers, over the centuries, have claimed godly or other kinds of glorious ancestors.

In this century, an African monarch, Emperor Haile Selassie of Ethiopia, claimed to trace *his* ancestry all the way back to the Old Testament, which is also called the Hebrew Bible. When he was crowned in 1930, Haile Selassie declared himself to be the 225th ruler of the hereditary line that started with the union of King Solomon and the Queen of Sheba.

The Bible itself, beginning with Adam and Eve, often reads like a vast family history. The words *bore* and *begot* spring from many of its pages, as the family lines of biblical characters are described along with their deeds and teachings.

An Italian family arriving in America during the great wave of immigration that took place between 1880 and 1920

As European society developed, from the Middle Ages onward, members of the upper classes often referred to their family history as their "pedigree." Today this word makes us think of some prize-winning animal, like a carefully bred racehorse, a blue-ribbon bull, or a fancy show poodle. Actually, the word *pedigree* comes from the Middle French *pie de grue,* meaning "foot of a crane." This is because, on old genealogy charts, the lines showing who was descended from whom formed a pattern resembling the shape of a crane's foot.

In America, searching for an illustrious ancestor didn't become fashionable until the 1800s. Once the Revolutionary War period was over, some Americans who had begun to enjoy increased wealth started to look around for a way to add to their family's dignity. One mark of distinction was to be able to say that you were descended from a passenger who had arrived on the *Mayflower,* the ship that carried the first Pilgrims to America in 1620. Another was to trace your roots to one of the "first families of Virginia," which became a colony of the English king in 1624.

Being related to a signer of the Declaration of Independence or to someone who fought in the American Revolution was also a great honor for a family to claim. Some of the tracings of wealthy Americans seeking a glorious past tended to be a little fuzzy, though. And a few individuals made real blunders. Imagine trying to get anyone to believe that you were a direct descendant of George Washington. History tells us that the famous "father of his country" never had any children of his own!

— ❖ —

An event that helped change the way ordinary, everyday Americans thought about their family backgrounds was the 1976 Bicentennial. This two hundredth anniversary of the signing of the Declaration of Independence celebrated the birth of the United States.

People from other lands had been arriving on America's shores even before the time of the *Mayflower*. But the greatest flow of immigrants to the United States had taken place in the years between 1880 and 1920. A large percentage of Americans in the Bicentennial birthday period were the children, grandchildren, and great-grandchildren of those immigrants. They felt that this was a time for looking back as well as ahead, for tracing the way they had come. Others, whose families had been in America longer—as well as those who had arrived more recently—were also caught up in the great ground swell of interest in family origins.

Americans began to realize that everyone—not just people who were trying to come up with a notable pedigree—had a family history. Alex Haley's discovery of his African ancestors served as a perfect example. And, by happy coincidence, his book *Roots* was published in the very year of America's Bicentennial. Soon afterward, Haley's story was presented as a TV miniseries that was seen by a vast audience, and the book itself was translated into more than forty languages.

Today most of us go ancestor hunting because we both appreciate and are proud of the struggles and achievements of the earlier generations of our family. At the same time, getting to know our origins gives us a sense of stability in an uncertain and rapidly changing world. Finding out where we came from can help to explain and clarify the present, and may make it easier to focus on the future.

How important is it to you to know your origins? Explain.

What does Johann Sebastian Bach's family teach us about heredity and environment?

Why did some people keep extensive oral histories, while other people kept track of only a few generations?

What did America's Bicentennial and Alex Haley's book *Roots* help people to realize about family histories?

WRITE Write a paragraph explaining what you would like to find out about your ancestors.

FOXTROT
by Bill Amend
FOURTH AND GOAL. TWO SECONDS LEFT ON THE CLOCK. CAN PETER FOX PULL OFF A MIRACLE?

FOR THE ANSWER, LET'S CHECK IN WITH OUR HEAD STATISTICIAN...

PETER FOX TAKES THE SNAP...

HE LOOKS LEFT... HE LOOKS RIGHT...

HE PASSES TO HIM-SELF... THE DEFENSE IS STUNNED...

HE SPOTS HIS CHANCE... HE LEAPS OVER THE CHARGING LINEBACKERS...

TOUCHDOWN! THE CHEERLEADERS SWARM THEIR HERO...
TO THINK I SHARE HIS GENES.
TO THINK I SHARE BOTH YOUR GENES.
TO THINK I HELPED GIVE HIM THOSE GENES.
YO, PETE! I'M OPEN!
AMEND 11-18

Which story or poem in this group gave you the greatest sense of the importance of family ties? Explain your answer.

WRITER'S WORKSHOP

Two people in a family are never exactly alike, but they can be similar in many ways. Write an essay that compares and contrasts two members of a family. Describe traits they share as well as the things that make each person unique.

Writer's Choice The family relationships in this theme may have given you new ideas about families. Maybe you'd like to express your thoughts in a children's book, a cartoon strip, or a collection of photos and captions. Carry out your own writing project, to plan and share your work.

THEME

MEMORIES

When you think back to experiences you and your family have had together, which ones stand out in your mind? Holiday memories and family traditions are the focus of the next selections.

CONTENTS

Growing Up

by Russell Baker

Russell Baker, a Pulitzer Prize–winning journalist, grew up during the Great Depression. Times were hard, but Baker's autobiography tells about the good times as well as the bad.

I was often astonished when my mother did me some deed of generosity, as when she bought me my first Sunday suit with long pants. The changeover from knickers to long pants was the ritual recognition that a boy had reached adolescence, or "the awkward age," as everybody called it. The "teenager," like the atomic bomb, was still uninvented, and there were few concessions to adolescence, but the change to long pants was a ritual of recognition. There was no ceremony about it. You were taken downtown one day and your escort—my mother in my case—casually said to the suit salesman, "Let's see what you've got in long pants."

For me the ritual was performed in the glossy, mirrored splendor of Bond's clothing store on Liberty Street. She had taken me for a Sunday suit and, having decided I looked too gawky in knickers, said, "Let's see what you've got in long pants." My physique at this time was described by relatives and friends with such irritating words as "beanpole," "skinny," and "all bones." My mother, seeing me through eyes that loved, chose to call me "a tall man."

The suit salesman displayed a dazzling assortment of garments. Suit designers made no concessions to youth; suits for boys were just like suits for men, only smaller. My mother expressed a preference for something with the double-breasted cut. "A tall man looks good in a double-breasted suit," she said.

The salesman agreed. Gary Cooper, he said, looked especially good in double-breasted suits. He produced one. I tried it on. It was a hard fabric, built to endure. The color was green, not the green of new grass in spring, but the green of copper patina on old statues. The green was relieved by thin, light gray stripes, as though the designer had started to create cloth for a bunco artist, then changed his mind and decided to appeal to bankers.

"Well, I just don't know," my mother said.

Her taste in clothes was sound rather than flamboyant, but I considered the suit smashing, and would have nothing else. The price was $20, which was expensive even though it came with two pairs of pants, and upon hearing it I said, "We can't afford it."

"That's what you think, mister," she said to me. "It's worth a little money to have the man of the house look like a gentleman."

In conference with the salesman, it was agreed that she would pay three dollars down and three dollars a month until the cost was amortized. On my attenuated physique, this magnificent, striped, green, double-breasted suit hung like window drapes on a scarecrow. My mother could imagine Gary Cooper's shoulders gradually filling out the jacket, but she insisted that Bond's do something about the voluminous excesses of the pants, which in the seat area could have accommodated both me and a watermelon. The salesman assured her that Bond's famous tailors would adjust the trousers without difficulty. They did so. When finally I had the suit home and put it on for its first trip to church, so much fabric had been removed from the seat that the two hip pockets were located with seams kissing right over my spine.

My mother was dazzled. With visions of a budding Gary Cooper under her wing, she said, "Now you look like somebody I can be proud of," and off to church we went.

She was a magician at stretching a dollar. That December, with Christmas approaching, she was out at work and Doris was in the kitchen when I barged into her bedroom one afternoon in search of a safety pin. Since her bedroom opened onto a community hallway, she kept the door locked, but needing the pin, I took the key from its hiding place, unlocked the door, and stepped in. Standing against the wall was a big, black bicycle with balloon tires. I recognized it instantly. It was the same second-hand bike I'd been admiring in a Baltimore Street shop window. I'd even asked about the price. It was horrendous. Something like $15. Somehow my mother had scraped together enough for a down payment and meant to surprise me with the bicycle on Christmas morning.

I was overwhelmed by the discovery that she had squandered such money on me and sickened by the knowledge that, bursting into her room like this, I had robbed her of the pleasure of seeing me astonished and delighted on Christmas day. I hadn't wanted to know her lovely secret; still, stumbling upon it like this made me feel as though I'd struck a blow against her happiness. I backed out, put the key back in its hiding place, and brooded privately.

I resolved that between now and Christmas I must do nothing, absolutely nothing, to reveal the slightest hint of my terrible knowledge. I must avoid the least word, the faintest intonation, the weakest gesture that might reveal my possession of her secret. Nothing must deny her the happiness of seeing me stunned with amazement on Christmas day.

In the privacy of my bedroom I began composing and testing exclamations of delight: "Wow!" "A bike with balloon tires! I don't believe it!" "I'm the luckiest boy alive!" And so on. They all owed a lot to movies in which boys like Mickey Rooney had seen their wildest dreams come true, and I realized that, with my lack of acting talent, all of them were going to sound false at the critical moment when I wanted to cry out my love spontaneously from the heart. Maybe it would be better to say nothing but appear to be shocked into such deep pleasure that speech had escaped me. I wasn't sure, though. I'd seen speechless gratitude in the movies too, and it never really worked until the actors managed to cry a few quiet tears. I doubted I could cry on cue, so I began thinking about other expressions of speechless amazement. In front of a hand-held mirror in my bedroom I tried the whole range of expressions: mouth agape and eyes wide; hands slapped firmly against both cheeks to keep the jaw from falling off; ear-to-ear grin with all teeth fully exposed while hugging the torso with both arms. These and more I practiced for several days without acquiring confidence in any of them. I decided to wait until Christmas morning and see if anything came naturally.

Christmas was the one occasion on which my mother surrendered to unabashed sentimentality. A week beforehand she always concocted homemade root beer, sealed it in canning jars, and stored it in the bathroom for the yeast to ferment. Now and then, sitting in the adjoining kitchen, we heard a loud thump from the bathroom and knew one of the jars had exploded, but she always made enough to allow for breakage. She took girlish delight in keeping her brightly wrapped gifts hidden in closets. Christmas Eve she spent in frenzies of baking—cakes, pies, gingerbread cookies cut and decorated to look like miniature brown pine trees and Santa Clauses. In the afternoon she took Doris and me to the street corner where trees were piled high and searched through them until she found one that satisfied our taste for fullness and symmetry. It was my job and Doris's to set the tree up in the parlor and weight it with ornaments, lights, and silver icicles, while she prepared Christmas Eve dinner. This was a ritual meal at which the centerpiece was always oysters. She disliked oysters but always ate them on Christmas Eve. Oysters were the centerpiece of the traditional Christmas Eve supper she remembered from her girlhood in Virginia. By serving them she perpetuated the customs of Papa's household.

She did not place her gifts under the tree that night until Doris and I had gone to bed. We were far beyond believing in Santa Claus, but she insisted on preserving the forms of the childhood myth that these were presents from some divine philanthropist. She planned all year for this annual orgy of spending and girded for it by putting small deposits month after month into her Christmas Club account at the bank.

That Christmas morning she roused us early, "to see what Santa Claus brought," she said with just the right tone of irony to indicate we were all old enough to know who Santa Claus was. I came out of my bedroom with my presents for her and Doris, and Doris came with hers. My mother's had been placed under the tree during the night. There were a few small glittering packages, a big doll for Doris, but no bicycle. I must have looked disappointed.

"It looks like Santa Claus didn't do too well by you this year, Buddy," she said, as I opened packages. A shirt. A necktie. I said something halfhearted like, "It's the thought that counts," but what I felt was bitter disappointment. I supposed she'd found the bike intolerably expensive and sent it back.

"Wait a minute!" she cried, snapping her fingers. "There's something in my bedroom I forgot all about."

She beckoned to Doris, the two of them went out, and a moment later came back wheeling between them the big black two-wheeler with balloon tires. I didn't have to fake my delight, after all. The three of us—Doris, my mother, and I—were people bred to repress the emotional expressions of love, but I did something that startled both my mother and me. I threw my arms around her spontaneously and kissed her.

"All right now, don't carry on about it. It's only a bicycle," she said.

Still, I knew that she was as happy as I was to see her so happy.

Russell Baker attempts to entertain as well as move readers with his story. What details do you find especially entertaining or touching?

Do you think Mrs. Baker knew that Russell had peeked at his Christmas gift? Explain your answer.

Explain why shopping for pants and being surprised on Christmas were such important memories for Russell Baker.

WRITE Can you recall a "deed of generosity" in your own life? Write about a time when someone was generous toward you or when you acted in a generous way.

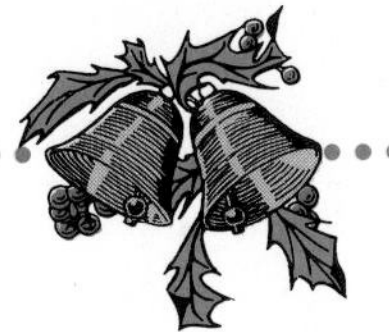

REPORT from Part One

by Gwendolyn Brooks

Gwendolyn Brooks, one of America's most famous poets, grew up in the 1920s in Chicago, Illinois. In this excerpt from her autobiography, she shares some of her childhood memories and tells how she began writing.

illustrated by Greg King

Home always warmly awaited me. Welcoming, enveloping. Home meant a quick-walking, careful, Duty-Loving mother, who played the piano, made fudge, made cocoa and prune whip and apricot pie, drew tidy cows and trees and expert houses with chimneys and chimney smoke, who helped her children with arithmetic homework, and who sang in a high soprano:

"Brighten the corner where you are!—
Br-rrr-righten the corner where you are!—
Some one far from harbor you may guide
    across the bar—
Brigh-TEN the cor-nerr—
    where
        you
            are."

Home meant my father, with kind eyes, songs, and tense recitations for my brother and myself. A favorite of his, a wonderful poem about a pie-making lady. Along had come a man, weary, worn, to beg of the lady a pie. Those already baked, she informed him, were too large for the likes of him. She said she would bake another. It, too, was "large." And the next was large. And the next, and the next. Finally the traveler, completely out of patience, berated her and exclaimed that henceforth she should draw her own sustenance from the bark of trees. And she became, *mirabile dictu*,[1] a woodpecker and flew off. We never tired of that.

My father seemed to Gwendolyn and Raymond a figure of power. He had those rich Artistic Abilities, but he had more. He could fix anything that broke or stopped. He could build long-lasting fires in the ancient furnace below. He could paint the house, inside and out, and could whitewash the basement. He could spread the American Flag in wide loud magic across the front of our house on the Fourth of July and Decoration Day. He could chuckle. No one has ever had, no one will ever have, a chuckle exactly like my father's. It was gentle, it was warmly happy, it was heavyish but not hard. It was secure, and seemed to us an assistant to the Power that registered with his children. My father, too, was almost our family doctor. We had Dr. Carter, of course, precise and semi-twinkly and effective—but it was not always necessary to call him. My father had wanted to be a doctor. Thwarted, he read every "doctor book" (and he remembered much from a black tradition) he could reach, learning fine secrets and curing us with steams, and fruit compotes, and dexterous rubs, and, above all, with bedside compassion. "Well, there, young lady! How's that

---

[1] *mirabile dictu* [mə · rä′bə · lē dik′to͞o]: amazing to say

throat now?" "Well, let's see now. This salve will take care of that bruise! Now, we're going to be all right." In illness there was an advantage: the invalid was royalty for the run of the seizure.

And of course my father furnished All the Money. The "all" was inadequate, felt Keziah Wims Brooks: could he not leave the McKinley Music Publishing Company, which was paying him about twenty-five dollars a week (from thirty to thirty-five when he worked overtime)? Uncle Paul, her sister Gertrude's husband, worked at City Hall—had a "snap" job—made *fifty* dollars a week. . . . True, during the bad times, during the Depression, when McKinley, itself stricken, could pay my father only in part—sometimes eighteen dollars, sometimes ten dollars—our family ate beans. But children dread, often above all else, dissension in the house, and we would have been quite content to entertain a beany diet every day, if necessary, and *not* live in Lilydale as did bungalow-owning Aunt Gertrude and Uncle Paul, if only there could be, continuously, the almost musical Peace that we had most of the time.

Home. Checker games. Dominoes. Radio (Jack Benny, Ben Bernie, and Kate Smith; "Amos and Andy"; Major Bowes' "Amateur Hour"; Wayne King, the Waltz King; and "Ladies and Gentlemen: Easy Aces"). Christmases. I shall stop right here to tell about those. They were important.

The world of Christmas was firm. Certain things were done. Certain things were not done.

We did not put Christmas trees outdoors.

We did not open Christmas presents on Christmas Eve.

And we had *not* made fruitcakes two or three months ahead of time.

A Christmas tree, we felt—my mother, my father, my brother, and I—belonged in the living room. Green, never silver or gold or pink. Full-branched and aspiring to the ceiling.

Christmas presents were wrapped and hidden on Christmas Eve. Oh, the sly winks and grins. The furtive rustle of tissue, the whip of ribbon off the spool, semiheard. The trippings here and there in search of secure hiding places. Our house had nooks and crannies, a closet, a pantry, alcoves, "the little room," an extensive basement: There were hiding places aplenty.

Fruitcakes were made about a week before Christmas. We didn't care what the recipe books said. We liked having all the Christmas joy as close together as possible. Mama went downtown, as a rule, for the very freshest supplies. Candied cherries and pineapple but no citron. Mama didn't like citron (*I* did and do), so that was out. Candied orange and lemon, however. Figs galore. Dates galore. Raisins, raisins, raisins.

We children had the bake-eve fun of

cutting up the candied fruit, shelling and chopping the nuts, and mixing everything together. Our fingers got tired, our teeth and tongues never. We tasted and tasted and took gay tummy aches to bed. Next day, the house was rich with the aroma of fruit and spice. How wonderful. How happy I was.

It was the baking of the fruitcakes that opened our Christmas season. After that, there was the merriest playing of Christmas carols on the piano by my mother and me, with everybody singing; mysterious shopping jaunts; the lingering, careful purchase of Christmas cards; the visit to Santa Claus; the desperately scrupulous housecleaning; for my mother and myself, the calls at the beauty shop for Christmas hairdos (you had to look your very best on Christmas Day); the Christmas hunt, undertaken by all, with the marvelous pungent symbol *found* and borne back triumphantly through the dusk of the third or fourth day before Christmas.

All this. So much more that fades, and fades. I almost forgot the high, high angel-food cake, made a day or two before Christmas. We were, somehow, not great Christmas-cookie advocates, but there would be a few frosted cookies about. We had Christmas candy. And filled candies and Christmas mints. Some of those dates, too, were stuffed with nuts and sugared over, to make another sort of confection.

On Christmas Eve we decorated the Christmas tree. So much silver tinsel. And ropes of fringed gold, and red, silver, blue, and gold balls, and a star on top. We children hung our stockings on the mantel—in the morning they would ache with apples, oranges, nuts, and tiny toys—over our, yes, *real* fireplace! That night we were allowed to "sample the sample"—that is, "test" fruitcake that my mother always made in a shallow pan, along with the proper proud giants—and with it we had eggnog with nutmeg on top.

Next day it was so hard to wait for the sky to turn on its light. As soon as it did, out of bed we children threw ourselves and rushed into the living room. There we found, always, that Papa had turned on the Christmas-tree lights, and under the tree shone *just about* everything we had asked of Santa Claus. (Of course, Mama *always* "helped" us with our letters to Santa Claus.) My brother remembers trains and tracks, baseball equipment, wagons, skates, games. Various Christmases brought me dishes, a rocking chair, a doll house, paper dolls which I liked better than hard dolls because so much more could be done with the paper ones. My most delicate and exquisite Christmas-gift memory is of a little glass deer, dainty-antlered, slender-legged, and filled with perfume.

Of course, there were clothes—"secondary" gifts.

And BOOKS.

About books. My "book Christmas" had already begun, on Christmas Eve, soon after the Christmas tree was strung with lights. It was for long my own personal tradition to sit behind the tree and read a paper book I still own: *The Cherry Orchard,* by Marie Battelle Schilling, and published by the David C. Cook Publishing Company. It had been given me by Kayola Moore, my Sunday school teacher. I don't know why I enjoyed reading that book, Christmas Eve after Christmas Eve, to the tune of black-walnut candy crunching.

And back I went—to the back of the Christmas tree—with my new books. Late, late. After the relatives, after the Christmas turkey, after the cranberries—fresh!—none of your canned cranberries for us—and the mashed potatoes and gravy and baked macaroni and celery and candied sweet potatoes and peas-and-carrots, and the fruitcake and angel cake and eggnog. Back, while the rest of the family forgot it all in bed, to the else-dark room. The silence. The black-walnut candy. And the books that began the giving again.

•••

Dreamed a lot. As a little girl I dreamed freely, often on the top step of the back porch—morning, noon, sunset, deep twilight. I loved clouds, I loved red streaks in the sky. I loved the gold worlds I saw in the sky. Gods and little girls, angels and heroes and future lovers labored there, in misty glory or sharp grandeur.

I was writing all the time. My mother says I began rhyming at seven—but my notebooks date back to my eleventh year only. Careful rhymes. Lofty meditations.

FORGIVE AND FORGET

If others neglect you,
Forget; do not sigh,
For, after all, they'll select you,
In times by and by.
If their taunts cut and hurt you,
They are sure to regret.
And, if in time, they desert you,
Forgive and forget.

THE BUSY CLOCK

Clock, clock, tell the time,
Tell the time to me.
Magic, patient instrument,
That is never free.

Tick, tock, busy clock!
You've no time to play!
Bustling men and women
Need you all the day.

When I was thirteen I met, somehow, *Writer's Digest.* A milestone. Why, there were *oodles of other* writers! They, too, suffered, and had suffered. They, too,

ached for the want of the right word—reckoned with mean nouns, virtueless adjectives. They, too, sent Things out, got Things back. They, too, knew the coldness of editors, spent much money on stamps, waited, loud-hearted, for the postman.

My father provided me with a desk, an old desk given him "at McKinley's," a desk with many little compartments, with long drawers at the bottom, and a removable glass-protected shelf at the top, for books. Certainly up there, holding special delights for a writing-girl, were the Emily books, L. M. Montgomery's books about a Canadian girl who wrote, kept notebooks even as I kept notebooks, dreamed, reached. I loved the little adventures—yearning to meet their splendid creator. But who ever met an Author? Certainly there, also, to look down at me whenever I sat at the desk, was Paul Laurence Dunbar. *"You,"* my mother had early announced, "are going to be the *lady* Paul Laurence Dunbar." I still own the Emily books and the "Complete Paul Laurence Dunbar."

Of course I would be a poet! *Was* a poet! Didn't I write a poem every day? Sometimes *two* poems?

How would you describe a happy family? In what ways does Gwendolyn Brooks's family fit your description?

Family traditions are often handed down for many generations. What Christmas traditions do you think Gwendolyn Brooks might have shared with her own children?

Gwendolyn Brooks was sure she would become a poet. What influences in her home life might have encouraged her in this ambition?

WRITE Look at the way Gwendolyn Brooks uses details to describe her father in the second paragraph. Write a character sketch of someone you know, using details to show what the person is like.

"When Handed A Lemon, Make Lemonade"

AWARD-WINNING AUTHOR

by Gwendolyn Brooks

(title by Anonymous)

Still Life with Flowers and Fruit
by Emile Renard (1850-1930)

I've lived through lemons,
sugaring them.
"When handed a lemon,
make lemonade."
That is what
some sage has said.
"When handed a lemon,
make lemonade."

There is always a use
for lemon juice.

Do you know what to do with
trouble, children?
Make lemonade. Make lemonade.
"Handed a lemon, make lemonade."

The Bean Eaters

AWARD-WINNING AUTHOR

by Gwendolyn Brooks

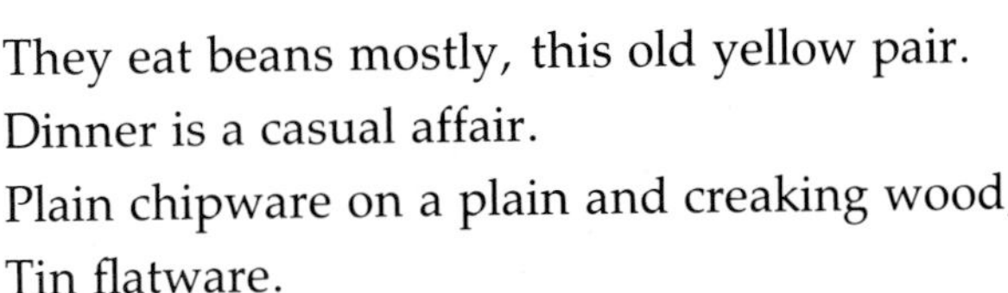

They eat beans mostly, this old yellow pair.
Dinner is a casual affair.
Plain chipware on a plain and creaking wood,
Tin flatware.

Two who are Mostly Good.
Two who have lived their day,
But keep on putting on their clothes
And putting things away.

And remembering . . .
Remembering, with twinklings and twinges,
As they lean over the beans in their rented back room that
is full of beads and receipts and dolls and cloths,
tobacco crumbs, vases and fringes.

The Banjo Lesson by Henry Ossawa Tanner, Hampton Institute

The Parakeet Named Dreidel

Award-Winning Author

It happened about ten years ago in Brooklyn, New York. All day long a heavy snow was falling. Toward evening the sky cleared and a few stars appeared. A frost set in. It was the eighth day of Hanukkah, and my silver Hanukkah lamp stood on the windowsill with all candles burning. It was mirrored in the windowpane, and I imagined another lamp outside.

My wife, Esther, was frying potato pancakes. I sat with my son, David, at a table and played dreidel with him. Suddenly David cried out, "Papa, look!" And he pointed to the window.

I looked up and saw something that seemed unbelievable. Outside on the windowsill stood a yellow-green bird watching the candles. In a moment I understood what had happened. A parakeet had escaped from its home somewhere, had flown out into the cold street and landed on my windowsill, perhaps attracted by the light.

A parakeet is native to a warm climate, and it cannot stand the cold and frost for very long. I immediately took steps to save the bird from freezing. First I carried away the Hanukkah lamp so that the bird would not burn itself when entering. Then I opened the window and with a quick wave of my hand shooed the parakeet inside. The whole thing took only a few seconds.

by Isaac Bashevis Singer

Illustrated by Doug Knutson

In the beginning the frightened bird flew from wall to wall. It hit itself against the ceiling and for a while hung from a crystal prism on the chandelier. David tried to calm it: "Don't be afraid, little bird, we are your friends." Presently the bird flew toward David and landed on his head, as though it had been trained and was accustomed to people. David began to dance and laugh with joy. My wife, in the kitchen, heard the noise and came out to see what had happened. When she saw the bird on David's head, she asked, "Where did you get a bird all of a sudden?"

"Mama, it just came to our window."

"To the window in the middle of the winter?"

"Papa saved its life."

The bird was not afraid of us. David lifted his hand to his forehead and the bird settled on his finger. Esther placed a saucer of millet and a dish of water on the table, and the parakeet ate and drank. It saw the dreidel and began to push it with its beak. David exclaimed, "Look, the bird plays dreidel."

David soon began to talk about buying a cage for the bird and also about giving it a name, but Esther and I reminded him that the bird was not ours. We would try to find the owners, who probably missed their pet and were worried about what had happened to it in the icy weather. David said, "Meanwhile, let's call it Dreidel."

That night Dreidel slept on a picture frame and woke us in the morning with its singing. The bird stood on the frame, its plumage brilliant in the purple light of the rising sun, shaking as in prayer, whistling, twittering, and talking all at the same time. The parakeet must have belonged to a house where Yiddish was spoken, because we heard it say *"Zeldele, geh schlofen"* (Zeldele, go to sleep), and these simple words uttered by the tiny creature filled us with wonder and delight.

The next day I posted a notice in the elevators of the neighborhood houses. It said that we had found a Yiddish-speaking parakeet. When a few days passed and no one called, I advertised in the newspaper for which I wrote, but a week went by and no one claimed the bird. Only then did Dreidel become ours. We bought a large cage with all the fittings and toys that a bird might want, but because Hanukkah is a festival of freedom, we resolved never to lock the cage. Dreidel was free to fly around the house whenever he pleased. (The man at the pet shop had told us that the bird was a male.)

Nine years passed and Dreidel remained with us. We became more attached to him from day to day. In our house Dreidel learned scores of Yiddish, English, and Hebrew words. David taught him to sing a Hanukkah song, and there was always a wooden dreidel in the cage for him to play with. When I wrote on my Yiddish typewriter, Dreidel would cling to the index finger of either my right or my left hand, jumping acrobatically with every letter I wrote. Esther often joked that Dreidel was helping me write and that he was entitled to half my earnings.

Our son, David, grew up and entered college. One winter night he went to a Hanukkah party. He told us that he would be home late, and Esther and I went to bed early. We had just fallen asleep when the telephone rang. It was David. As a rule he is a quiet and composed young man. This time he spoke so excitedly that we could barely understand what he was saying. It seemed that David had told the story of our parakeet to his fellow students at the party, and a girl named Zelda Rosen had exclaimed, "I am this Zeldele! We lost our parakeet nine years ago." Zelda and her parents lived not far from us, but they had never seen the notice in the newspaper or the ones posted in elevators. Zelda was now a student and a friend of David's. She had never visited us before, although our son often spoke about her to his mother.

We slept little that night. The next day Zelda and her parents came to see their long-lost pet. Zelda was a beautiful and gifted girl. David often took her to the theater and to museums. Not only did the Rosens recognize their bird, but the bird seemed to recognize his former owners. The Rosens used to call him Tsip-Tsip, and when the parakeet heard them say "Tsip-Tsip," he became flustered and started to fly from one member of the family to the other, screeching and flapping his wings. Both Zelda and her mother cried when they saw their beloved bird alive. The

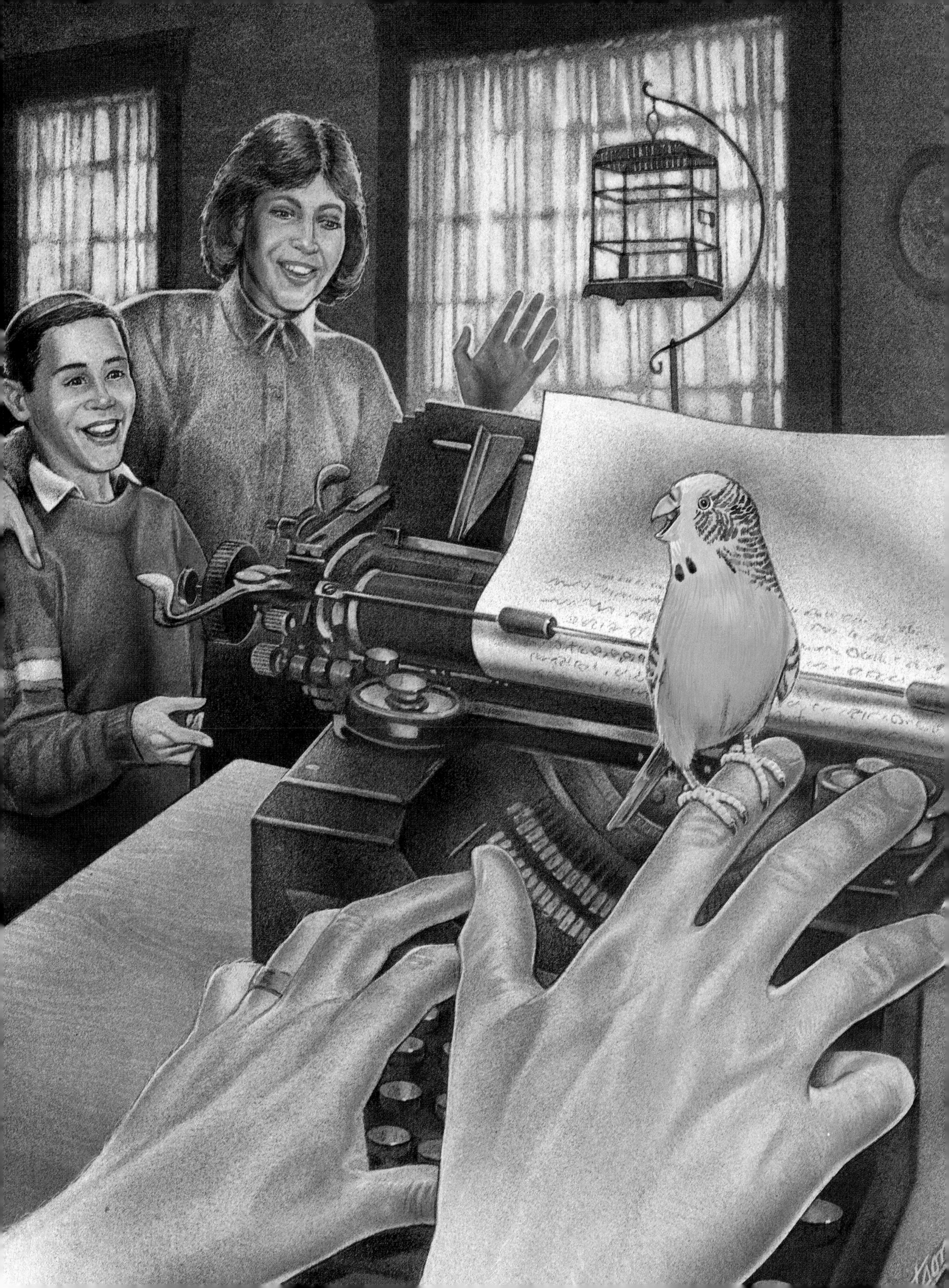

father stared silently. Then he said, "We have never forgotten our Tsip-Tsip."

I was ready to return the parakeet to his original owners, but Esther and David argued that they could never part with Dreidel. It was also not necessary, because that day David and Zelda decided to get married after their graduation from college. So Dreidel is still with us, always eager to learn new words and new games. When David and Zelda marry, they will take Dreidel to their new home. Zelda has often said, "Dreidel was our matchmaker."

On Hanukkah he always gets a gift—a mirror, a ladder, a bathtub, a swing, or a jingle bell. He has even developed a taste for potato pancakes, as befits a parakeet named Dreidel.

Do you think Dreidel is a lucky bird? Explain your answer.

Why do you think the narrator and his family become so attached to Dreidel?

Why does Zelda think Dreidel was a matchmaker?

WRITE Write about an episode in your own life in which an animal played an important part.

WORDS • ABOUT

• ISAAC • BASHEVIS •

SINGER

Isaac Bashevis Singer narrowly escaped dying young. Born in Poland in 1904, he came to New York in his early thirties to visit his brother, Israel Joshua, also a writer. In this way he avoided the Nazi Holocaust that in a few years would destroy not only millions of European Jews but also their ancient ways of living, studying, and praying.

Fortunately Singer carried that whole society with him in his head and heart. In earlier years, he had lived in the town of Bilgoray, a place untouched by the twentieth century, which he called a "spiritual treasure trove." It gave Singer a chance to see "our past as it really was," a past that would find immortality in his stories.

Persecutions that had happened hundreds of years before he was born were as vivid to him as the events of the preceding day. His first novel is set in the seventeenth century, when the cruelties of the Russian Cossacks were most severe. His compassion is also well represented in his book *The Power of Light*, a collection of eight Hanukkah tales, (including "The Parakeet Named Dreidel"). In these stories, boys and girls and men and women love each other tenderly and faithfully in times of peace and in times of trial.

Singer believed in the value of Yiddish, a German dialect that was the mother tongue of European Jews. After his relocation to the United States, where relatively few people spoke his language, he was not able to publish his writing for over five years. He then made up for that period of silence by becoming a prolific and distinguished author. He won many American literary awards and in 1978 was granted a Nobel prize. He died in 1991.

My Mother Pieced Quilts

by Teresa Palomo Acosta

Femme Cousant, c. 1886: by Mary Cassatt (1844–1926), Musée d'Orsay, Paris

they were just meant as covers
in winters
as weapons
against pounding january winds

but it was just that every morning I awoke to these
october ripened canvases
passed my hand across their cloth faces
and began to wonder how you pieced
all these together
these strips of gentle communion cotton and flannel nightgowns
wedding organdies
dime store velvets

how you shaped patterns square and oblong and round
positioned
balanced
then cemented them
with your thread
a steel needle
a thimble

how the thread darted in and out
galloping along the frayed edges, tucking them in
as you did us at night
oh how you stretched and turned and rearranged
your michigan spring faded curtain pieces
my father's santa fe work shirt
the summer denims, the tweeds of fall

in the evening you sat at your canvas
—our cracked linoleum floor the drawing board
me lounging on your arm
and you staking out the plan:
whether to put the lilac purple of easter against the red plaid of
winter-going-
into-spring

whether to mix a yellow with blue and white and paint the
corpus christi noon when my father held your hand
whether to shape a five-point star from the
somber black silk you wore to grandmother's funeral

you were the river current
carrying the roaring notes . . .
forming them into pictures of a little boy reclining
a swallow flying
you were the caravan master at the reins
driving your threaded needle artillery across the mosaic cloth
    bridges
delivering yourself in separate testimonies

oh mother you plunged me sobbing and laughing
into our past
into the river crossing at five
into the spinach fields
into the plainview cotton rows
into tuberculosis wards
into braids and muslin dresses
sewn hard and taut to withstand the thrashings of twenty-five
    years

stretched out they lay
armed/ready/shouting/celebrating

knotted with love
the quilts sing on

Theme Wrap-Up

MEMORIES

What similarities do you see in the values that authors Russell Baker, Gwendolyn Brooks, and Isaac Bashevis Singer express through their narratives about holiday traditions?

WRITER'S WORKSHOP

What holidays do you and your family celebrate? Write a narrative of a holiday memory of your own. Use descriptive details to make your story vivid.

Writer's Choice Sharing memories can help people understand each other. Ask an older relative or family member to share some memories with you. Write about some of those memories or your thoughts about them. You may wish to write a family anecdote, a conversation, or a family fact book. Plan to share your writing.

a
b
c
d
e

THEME

THE FUTURE

What if you could find out about your future? Would you want to know what you are going to do when you grow up? Reading the next selections may give you some insight into your dreams and expectations.

CONTENTS

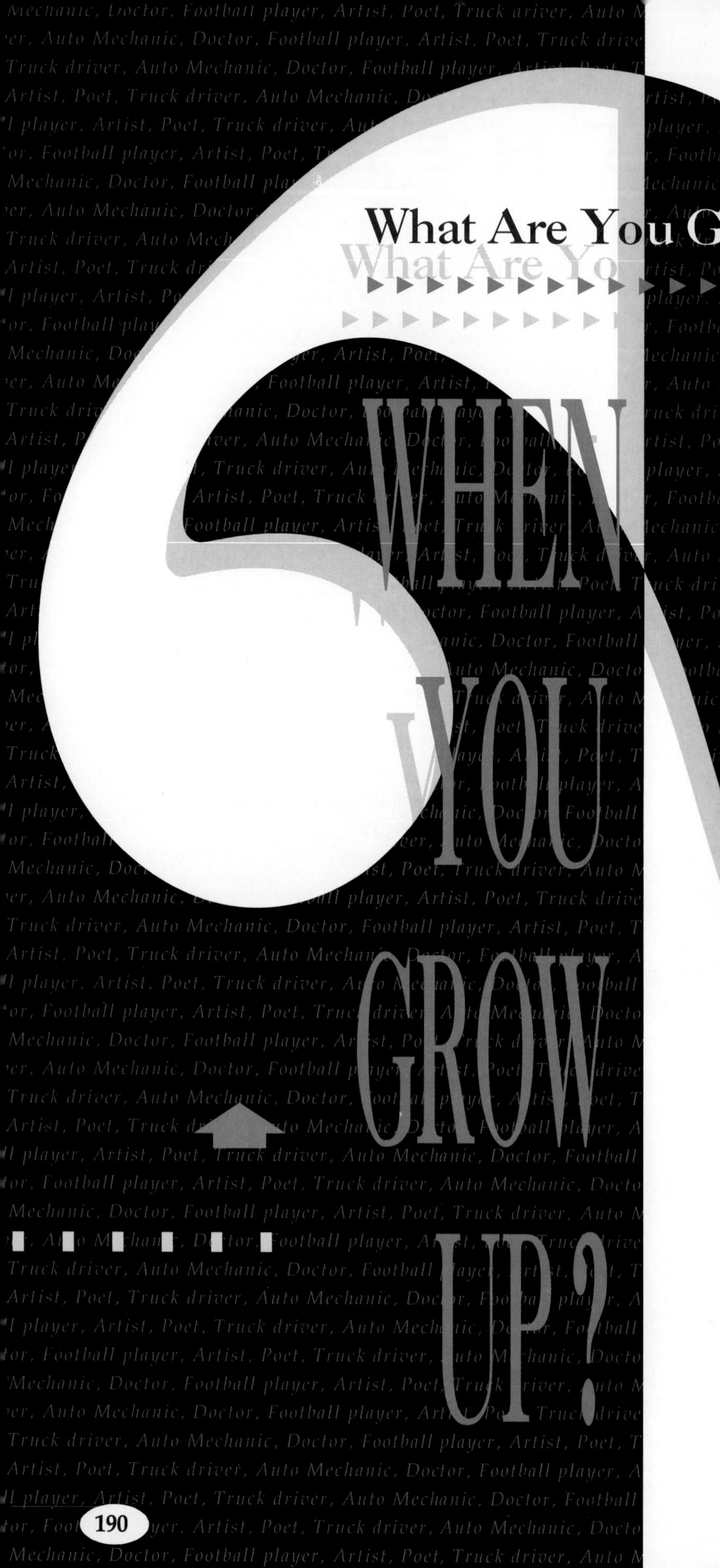

What Are You Going to Be WHEN YOU GROW UP?

by Gregory Benford

At dinner his sister asked the question that had been bothering Mark all day.

"What are *you* going to be when you grow up, Mark?" Claire asked. She had been talking all through dinner about Jobs Week at their school. It was a series of films and talks about what adults did at work. All Mark's friends had been talking about it too.

"I don't know," Mark said irritably. "Maybe a cowboy."

Claire laughed along with Mark's father and mother. "There aren't cowboys anymore," she said.

"Sure there are!" Mark said. "On TV."

"Those are actors," his father said quietly.

Mark had been feeling more and more uncomfortable all week. All his friends at school seemed to know what they were going to be as adults. But until Jobs Week started, Mark hadn't even thought about having to hold a job. It suddenly seemed as though he was far behind everybody else.

"Well," he said, searching for something to say, "I like developing pictures in Photography Club."

"Machines develop film now," Claire said haughtily. "I saw some on a field trip." She was two years older than Mark and liked to remind everybody.

Mark pressed his lips together and decided not to get into an argument with his sister. It never paid off. "Dad," he said, "what's your job like?"

His father looked startled. Usually his father never talked about work while he was at home. "I'm a scientist, and I do a lot of complicated things," he said vaguely.

"We *know* that, Daddy," Claire said. "You're impossibly brilliant, *every*body agrees."

They all laughed. Mark's father smiled and said, "I think about problems, mostly."

"Very *com*plicated problems," Claire said in a hollow, joking voice.

"Don't you use your hands?" Mark asked.

"Sure. Sometimes I build electronics instruments."

Mark considered this, nodding his head in approval. He liked the concrete feel of making things. Fixing them was good too. He enjoyed tinkering with the engines of his father's power tools. "Is it fun?"

"Why not come see?" his father asked.

"Could I?"

"I think it could be arranged," his father said, as he spooned out some red sherbet dessert for them all. "I can show you my big surprise."

Mark had been thinking about what it would be like to fix cars, or maybe airplanes. "Huh? What, Dad?"

Mom said, "Your father has been working on a time machine."

Claire looked puzzled. "You mean a clock? There are lots of clocks already."

"No, dummy," Mark said. It felt good to call her a name, but his mother frowned at him, and Mark started again. "No, Claire. Clocks just *measure* time. A time machine lets you *travel* in time."

"Travel?" Claire raised her eyebrows.

"To go into the past," Mother explained. "Or into the future."

"You mean I could visit last week?" Claire asked, staring off into space with a vacant look.

"In a way," Dad said. He handed around dessert. There was a silence while everyone started eating.

Mark wanted to ask more questions. But after dessert there were dishes for him and Claire to do, and then homework. He decided to wait until tomorrow, when he could talk to his father alone. Then he could see the time machine itself.

■ ■ ■

Mark had visited his father's laboratory before, but somehow today it seemed different. For one thing, his father didn't just show him the offices in the front of the building. Instead, he took Mark back through the offices filled with clattering computer printers and people making big drawings. They pushed open a tall, heavy door. Beyond were the big, open rooms where the experiments were done. This was the heart of the laboratory.

There were rows of computers and electrical power devices. Thick wires—colored orange, or yellow, or red—seemed to wind their way all over the big rooms. Mark nearly tripped on one.

His father led him among humming machinery. Men and women were repairing complex electronics instruments. People peered at television screens that were filled with numbers and printing.

"Wow," Mark said, "making a time machine is a lot of work."

"Yes, it is," his father said. "And this is the very first time machine ever invented. We're still just learning how to use it."

"Dad, where *is* the time machine?"

"What?" His father looked around

at Mark in surprise. "Why, all around us. Everything you see is part of the machine." He waved a hand to take in all the laboratory.

"I thought it would be something like . . . well . . . like a car."

"Maybe someday it will be, Mark. But for now— Come, I'll show you."

His father led Mark into a small room. Lights winked and flickered on one wall.

It looked interesting, but Mark couldn't help but think that even time travel seemed a little dull. The laboratory was mostly gray cabinets and workbenches.

He had seen a television show about time travel once. The people in the show wore bright red uniforms. They went back in time to hunt dinosaurs with laser pistols. It was very exciting. Of course, Mark knew his father wasn't doing anything like that. But still . . .

"This is the heart of the time machine," Dad said.

"It looks like a telephone booth," Mark said.

And it did. Mark could see through the sides of the little booth. There was an ordinary wooden chair inside.

"Not very impressive," Mark said.

His father nodded. "I agree, it's not. But it works."

"How?"

"I'll show you."

Dad led him over to a small table near the booth. "Let me have your hand," he said.

Mark's father took his hand and stuck one finger into a tube. "Hold still." Mark felt the jab of a needle.

"What's that?" Mark said, startled.

"The tracer," Dad said. "It takes a little piece of your skin. A sample. Then it looks at the molecules in your body."

"It hurts," Mark said, taking his finger out of the tube. "Not much, though."

"The machine memorizes the special molecules you have in you. Your DNA molecules, we call them. Then it can find you in the future."

"Find me?"

"Yes, that's right." Dad looked at him. "There's a Mark in the future. He's not the same as you are now, of course. He's older, and different. But he has the same basic molecules in him that you do."

"So this machine finds him?"

"That's it. The time machine can take you into the future—*your* future. Not your body, though. Just your, well, a piece of your mind."

"What piece?"

"Well, suppose you went into the future. You would see things as though you were the Mark at that time. The future Mark."

"Oh . . ." Mark studied the booth, thinking.

"The machine follows what we call your space-time track. That's the path you follow both in space and in time. The machine finds you in the future. And *only* you. That way, you can't interfere with anybody else's future."

"I see," said Mark. He was beginning to think of a plan.

"Say—" Dad glanced at his watch. "Time waits for no man, as the poet said. I have to check on some things."

"I'll wait here, Dad."

"Good. I'll be right back."

"See you, Dad."

When the door closed Mark suddenly felt very alone. He had thought of an idea, and if he dared . . .

Mark studied the dials and switches beside the booth. Above two of the dials was printed FUTURE DATE.

Each dial was like a clock. One was marked with years. Mark used a knob beside the clock to set it for fifteen years in the future.

The other clocklike dial showed months. Mark set it for October. He had always liked the fall.

Without giving himself time to think about his plan, he stepped into the booth and closed the door. It clicked shut.

The booth was completely quiet. There were buttons on the booth's wall.

A light winked on red. Then it turned green.

Mark sat down and studied the control panel inside the booth. There was another dial like a clock. Under it was printed LENGTH OF TRIP.

Mark turned the knob beside the clock until it read 45 MINUTES. That seemed like long enough to visit the future.

The clock buzzed.

Suddenly a tiny television screen on the control panel flickered into life. A word flashed onto the screen: READY.

The booth hummed. Mark looked out at the laboratory clock on the far wall. It read 4:36 P.M.

The humming got louder. The lights dimmed.

Well, Mark thought, *if I want to find out what I'll be when I grow up, this is the way to do it.*

He clenched his teeth.

Something screeched. The lights went out.

Pop.

■ ■ ■

Pop.

The laboratory was gone.

The booth was gone.

Mark looked around. He was standing in a big, cold room. A steady *bang bang bang* came from nearby.

He turned. A man in a cap was hammering on the front of a car. The car was bent and broken in several places. It must have been in a wreck. *Bang clang crash.*

"Hey!" The man in a cap looked up at Mark. "Come here and hold this for me."

Mark walked over. There were other cars here. Men were working on them. He tripped over a rubber car tire lying on the concrete floor.

"Come on!" the man called out. Mark hurried.

"Here." The man pointed at the front of the car. "Hold it."

The car had a kind of grill on its front.

Mark had never seen anything like it. He bent over and held the metal grill at the edge, away from the big dent in the center.

The man frowned. "No, higher." Mark put his hands further up. "Okay."

The man adjusted his cap and began hitting the grill. He used a big hammer that had a rubber head on it. *Bang bang clang.* The noise hurt Mark's ears.

He gritted his teeth and looked at the car. It was small and funny-shaped. The back was narrow and it didn't stand very high off the floor. The car looked hard to get into. Suddenly Mark realized that this was the way cars would look fifteen years from his time. He couldn't tell if this one was better than the cars he was used to, but it certainly *looked* uncomfortable.

Bang clang. The man stopped. The dent was straight now.

He noticed the way Mark was studying the car. "Some baby, huh?" he asked.

"What?" Mark said.

"Some fancy car, isn't it? Costs a lot."

"This?" Mark was surprised.

"Why, sure." The man looked at Mark. "It'll be a long time before you or I can afford to buy one of these jobs."

"Oh. I see." He didn't really see at all, but Mark nodded anyway. He stood up. He felt an ache in his back.

Now that he thought about it, his body seemed different. Mark looked down. His blue coveralls could not hide the bulging muscles in his arms and legs.

He was a *man.* He brought up a big hand and stared at the thick ridges of callus on it. Mark felt his cheek. A light beard rasped against his fingers. It felt so strange to be grown up. . . .

Mark walked over to a grimy window. His body felt heavier and more solid than when he had been a boy.

Rain spattered on the window. This didn't look like a very pretty part of town. He could make out a gray factory across the street. A short truck rumbled by. It had a strange machine with funny arms and levers riding in the back.

Mark moved over to the next window. His boots made a *clump clump* sound. When he peered out the window he had to blink twice to be sure he was seeing things correctly.

A crew of workers were fixing part of the street. They were digging a hole. Some others were mixing black, sticky tar in a big bucket. But the repairmen weren't men at all—they were chimpanzees!

The chimpanzees wore yellow uniforms with long sleeves. A man worked with them, showing them what to do. The chimpanzees could shovel dirt out of the hole very fast. They carried buckets of tar—far more than a man could.

Somehow these chimpanzees looked different from the ones Mark had seen in the zoo. They tilted back their furry heads and listened when the man spoke to them. Could they understand English?

Mark wondered if something had been done to the chimpanzees to make

them smarter. They looked so odd, all bent over and digging with their long arms. . . .

"Hey! Mark! Get back to work!"

Mark looked around to see who had shouted at him. A short man had an angry expression on his face and was pointing at a repair bench nearby.

"No time to daydream, lookin' out the window," the man yelled harshly.

Mark nodded. He sat down at the workbench. Somehow he knew which tools to pick out and what to do with them. He took a socket wrench over to the nearest car and opened the car's hood. He remembered that he was supposed to fix the engine.

Mark worked steadily for several minutes. It was hard to concentrate with all the noise in the garage. His feet were cold. He stamped them on the concrete to warm them.

Still, it felt good to have a job to do, and to know how to do it. There was something fun about taking an engine that didn't work and making it run again.

Mark felt a bit strange in this older body. He could remember, in the back of his mind, other things about his job. He had done these same repairs earlier in the day, and in the days before, too.

One part of him was bored because he had repeated this same job so many times before, on other cars. But another part of him liked the feel of doing it, of putting things right.

Mark shook his head. It was confusing. Did he like this work, or not? He wasn't sure.

He reached for a screwdriver and wiped his brow. Then the clatter of the garage work began to fade. He looked up. The lights were getting pale.

Pop.

Pop.

Stillness.

Mark opened his eyes. Neon light came flooding in. He was back in the booth.

He looked at the clock on the far wall. It read 4:36 P.M.

Mark blinked. He had spent forty-five minutes in the future. But the time machine had returned him to exactly the moment when he left!

Quickly he stepped out of the booth and clicked the door shut. His head was swimming with all the things that he'd seen, but Mark wanted to be sure he didn't get caught using the machine. His father was sure to be angry.

Mark returned all the dials on the front of the booth to where they had been before his trip. He spun the last one into place with a clicking sound. Behind him he could hear a door open.

"Well," his father said, "anything more you want to see?"

Mark held his breath, thinking of all the things he had seen in the last forty-five minutes. Then he said, "No, not really, Dad."

Mark's father looked at his wrist watch. "Almost five o'clock. Let's go home early. Time flies by, doesn't it?"

"Yes," said Mark. "Time flies."

■ ■ ■

On the bus going home Dad talked about the laboratory. Mark tried to listen, but he couldn't. He kept trying to figure out everything that had happened in the future.

He was going to become a garage mechanic, that was clear. It had been fun part of the time too. But other parts weren't fun. Did he really want to spend all his life in that garage?

"Dad," Mark said over the rumble of the bus, "people have used your time machine, haven't they?"

"Of course," his father answered. "A few have gone into the future so far—*their* futures, I mean."

"So they know how their lives are going to turn out?"

"No, not exactly."

"Why not?"

"Well, they saw what will happen *if* they keep on the way they are. That is, keep doing the things they already are doing."

"Then the future really isn't the way they saw it?" Mark asked.

"Well . . ." Mark's father wrinkled his brow, thinking. "What they saw is something we call a probability set."

"What's that?"

"Well, Mark, let's say *you* had gone into the future. Your future."

"Okay." Mark smiled a little. Did Dad suspect?

"Then you saw what will become of you. If you liked what you saw, fine. Just keep on doing what you were doing already, and your future will turn out the way you saw it."

"What if I didn't like it?"

"Ummm . . ." Mark's father frowned again and rubbed his jaw. "Then I guess you could change things. Stop doing what you were doing. We haven't tried anything like that using the machine yet, though."

Dad looked at Mark as their bus slowed at their stop. "That's a very interesting question, Mark. Asking the right questions is the most important part of science. Maybe you should be a scientist."

"Maybe so," Mark said. "Come on, Dad, let's get home. I've got to help make supper."

■ ■ ■

At supper that evening Claire talked a lot about her friends. They were all interested in playing football on the school team. The girls had a team as well as the boys.

"Why you spend your time on that photography stuff I'll never know, Mark," Claire said. "Not when you could be playing football. You used to be good at it."

She leaned forward, expecting an argument. Mark and Claire nearly always disagreed about something over supper. They enjoyed the chance to match wits.

But tonight Mark said simply, "Maybe you're right," and kept on eating his supper.

For the next two months Mark's world was football, and only football.

For a moment Claire was speechless. Then she said, "You mean you'll start going to the football tryouts every afternoon?"

"Yes," Mark said, and kept eating.

Dad looked at Mark and smiled. "That sounds like a good idea. You can get outside and have some exercise."

"That's not why I'm doing it, though, Dad," Mark said.

"Well then," Mark's mother said warmly, "why are you? You'll have to give up the Photography Club for football."

"I know," Mark said. "But I've been thinking. I'd like to play football for one of the big teams."

"You mean play on the school team when you get to high school?" Claire asked.

"No. A *professional* team."

"You mean the ones on television?" Dad asked.

"Yes."

They all looked at Mark, surprised.

"That's *hard,*" Claire said. "Really, Mark, you have no idea how hard. It's *impossible.*"

"Claire, it isn't impossible," Mom said. "But it is difficult." She looked at Mark, concerned. "You know, dear, I don't want you to get hurt. Football is a rough game."

"Then I suppose I had better find out if I can take it," Mark said seriously.

"It seems awfully ambitious," Mom said slowly.

"I think we have an ambitious son,"

Dad said. Dad glanced at Mom, and Mark could see him give her a wink.

■ ■ ■

For the next two months Mark's world was football, and only football. He practiced each school day. He met friends for games in a vacant lot on Saturday and Sunday afternoons. He read books about football tactics. In his dreams he would see himself carrying the ball down the field, puffing as he ran over the green grass, the crowd cheering. Or else he was the one who threw the ball for a winning touchdown.

At supper he talked about football constantly. He asked Dad what position he should play.

"Play whatever your coach says," Mark's father answered.

Mark nodded. He knew his father was right. The coach knew best. But deep inside, Mark wanted to be the quarterback. That way he would get to throw the passes. There was something about seeing the ball fly through the air and land in exactly the right spot that thrilled Mark. He couldn't put it into words, but he knew that was what he wanted to do.

One afternoon, after practice, Mark's friend Anna was watching as he came off the field. She held a camera.

Mark's football cleats rasped against the concrete walkway as he stopped beside her. He rubbed a sore leg muscle.

"You're getting to be a good player, Mark," she said. "I was watching."

"I'm okay," Mark said. "Getting better."

"Your sister, Claire, told me you want to be a football player when you grow up," Anna said.

"Not *want* to be. *Will* be," Mark said.

"You've changed, Mark," Anna said.

"Oh? How?"

"Well, you seem so determined now."

"Playing football for a living will be a lot more fun than being a garage mechanic," Mark said. "That's what I want."

"I suppose so," Anna said slowly, studying him. "What position do you play now?"

"I'm a lineman," Mark said. It was late fall now, and his breath made little puffs of smoke in the chilled air. "But I'm going to learn to throw passes pretty soon." He scraped his cleats against the walkway to underline what he said.

"That will be nice," Anna said. "I'll take some pictures of you. I've already got some from today's practice." She showed him her camera.

"I thought you were going to start making your own movies by now," Mark said.

"I *will,*" Anna said, "as soon as I can save up the money for a motion picture camera."

"Well, it looks as though we're both sure of what we're going to be when we grow up," Mark said, smiling.

He waved good-bye to Anna and started toward the showers. He felt good. A few months ago he had been confused when Anna and the rest of the gang asked him about his future. Now he knew.

■ ■ ■

But was he *sure*?

One night, just as he was putting away a book about football, a thought struck him.

Mark knew he was good at playing football. After all, the coach had just put him on the second team. The second team members got to play if someone on the school's first team got tired or hurt. Getting on the second team already meant Mark was doing very well for his age, since this was just his first year.

But . . . did that mean he would ever get to be a quarterback?

Mark frowned. He didn't know. The future was hard to figure out.

"Mark! Come to supper," his mother called.

"Hurry up, superstar!" Claire shouted, laughing.

Mark walked in to supper, thinking.

"Dad?" he said after the meal had begun. "Can I go see your laboratory again tomorrow?"

His father looked up, surprised. "Well, I don't know. I'll be kind of busy tomorrow."

"Let him come," Mom said, serving vegetables. "Not every boy's father has a time machine to look at."

Dad beamed. "You're right about that. Okay, Mark. Be at the laboratory tomorrow afternoon."

■ ■ ■

Mark didn't like the idea of sneaking another trip on his father's time machine. But his curiosity got the better of him. He wanted to *know* about the future, not just guess about it.

The laboratory was the same as before—gray cabinets and a bustle of activity. His father showed him some new equipment. The scientists were going to send several people into the future—*their* futures. That way they could piece together a picture of what the future would be like.

Of course, people who traveled forward in time might not like what they saw. They might decide to change their futures by doing things differently. But even so, the basic things about the future should remain the same. That would be useful for the scientists to know.

Dad was showing Mark a new piece of equipment when someone called him away. Mark was interested in the instrument. It ticked and buzzed so hard he thought it might fall apart. But when his father started to leave, Mark saw his chance.

"I'll look around while you're gone, Dad," Mark called. His father nodded absentmindedly as he left.

Mark quickly made his way to the small booth. No one was working in the room. The lights on the control panel glowed.

He set the dials exactly the way he had before. He got in the booth and sat down. In the silence of the booth Mark could hear his pulse thumping in his ears. His hands felt cold and wet.

What would his future be like this time? It *had* to be different. He had stopped tinkering with engines, after all. That should change the future. He was sure now he wouldn't become a garage mechanic.

Now he was playing football. What would that lead to?

The booth hummed. Mark checked the laboratory clock.

2:26 P.M.

A buzz. Something clicked.

A sharp screech—

Pop.

■ ■ ■

Pop.

The booth was gone.

A distant buzz . . . cold air . . .

Clunk!

Something big hit him. Hard.

He tumbled over. His face slammed into the earth. He tasted mud.

Someone was lying on top of him. A shrill whistle blew in the chilly air.

"Hey!" Mark cried out.

"Okay, okay," came a gruff voice. "I hit you a little hard that time."

The weight lifted. Mark stared up into the face of a huge man in the pads and helmet of a football uniform.

I made it! Mark thought. *I'm a football player!*

A light rain drifted in the air. Mark could hear the distant *smack* and *thud* of bodies running into each other. He recognized them as the sounds of a football scrimmage. This was a practice session.

"C'mon, c'mon, on your feet." A big man in a coaching uniform moved into view. He stood over Mark, his hands on his hips.

Mark rolled over and stood up. He felt bulky in the uniform. He looked down. He wore an orange uniform. It was smeared with brown mud.

"Get in the line!" the coach yelled. "Move it!"

Mark glanced around. He was in a big stadium. The stands were empty. Men in football uniforms were practicing passing and kicking beneath a sky of smoky gray. A strange, blue, banana-shaped helicopter clattered by overhead.

"Hey! Mark!" the coach shouted. "You're not getting paid to daydream."

Mark shook his head to clear it and trotted over to the scrimmage line. His side had the ball. There was an empty space in the line between two bulky players.

Mark guessed that was his position. But the men were so big!

He dropped down into his playing crouch between the two men. Facing him was the defense. A huge man opposite Mark scowled at him and then hunched down, settling into the earth. On his helmet was his name—Owens.

Mark got into position too. When he glanced down, his own hands looked enormous. His legs were thick and they bulged with muscles. Mark felt a surge of pride. He was a big, powerful man, just like the others on the team.

The quarterback called out, "Thirty-seven, forty-two, six—hike!"

The center snapped the ball back to the quarterback.

Mark charged forward. Owens smacked into him.

Whoosh—the air rushed out of his lungs. Mark toppled backward.

Owens rolled over him and was through the tumbling pile of men before Mark could do anything. Owens dove forward and tackled the quarterback. They crashed to the ground. The ball popped out. It rolled away.

"Ball! Fumble!" somebody shouted.

One of Mark's teammates fell on it. Mark sucked in air. He was relieved that his side had kept the ball. He got to his feet, panting.

"What *happened* in there?" came the rough voice of the coach. Some of the team turned and looked at Mark.

"I missed him," Mark said simply. He was embarrassed. He noticed that his voice was deep. It seemed to come from farther down inside his chest.

"Okay," the coach said. "Let's try that play again. Quarterback, check your signals first."

Mark hunched down in the line again. He breathed deeply. He was determined to do better.

And he did. On the next play he stopped Owens with a solid block. The collision knocked the wind out of Mark

again, but otherwise he was all right.

The afternoon went on. Mark hit the scrimmage line time and time again. He protected the quarterback while the quarterback threw pass after pass.

Mark's shoulders and knees and hips began to ache where he had been hit. He got used to tasting the muddy field. His orange uniform got so spattered with mud that he had to remember it had been orange before.

Mark grew tired. His eyes began to sting from sweat dripping down into them. He watched the quarterback make beautiful passes to other players down the field. But Mark was a replacement lineman, not a pass receiver. He was there to block, and that was all.

The rain fell harder. Mark slipped in the mud. Getting up from a scrimmage, he said to the coach, "Do we have to practice in a downpour?"

"What'll you do if it rains in a game," the coach said sarcastically, "carry an umbrella to stay dry?"

Mark gritted his teeth and stood, hands on hips, waiting for the next play. Somehow this wasn't going the way he had thought it would. The sports stories he had read were different. They described how the hero made the crucial pass at the very end of the game and won the championship for his team. There wasn't anything at all in those stories about the guys who played in the line.

Mark wasn't sure he liked this part of football. Playing in the line was hard, and he never got to carry the ball. He was a replacement lineman, too, so he wasn't on the starting team. He would play in the game next Saturday only if somebody got injured.

Puffing, he gazed up at the buildings near the stadium. They didn't have very many windows. Mark wondered if that was to save energy. Probably people would have to save more energy in the future. Fewer windows meant less heat was lost in winter.

This was a strange world. Little things were different, like the tiny radio sets in the football helmets. Using the radios, a coach could talk to a player all the way across the field. It seemed like a good idea to Mark.

He peered up into the gray sky. The rain clouds were blowing away. The sky slowly cleared. Mark thought about Anna. He wondered if she was making movies somewhere in this future.

A glimmer caught his eye. Far up in the sky he could see something twinkling. It was too big to be a star. A plane? No, it wasn't moving.

Mark suddenly realized he was seeing a space station. The silvery dot must be in orbit around the Earth!

Mark squinted to see. It was a tiny circle. *A spinning wheel in the sky,* Mark thought. *It must be huge! Wait until I tell Dad about this!*

But then Mark remembered that he couldn't tell Dad anything. He was sneaking this time-travel trip behind Dad's back.

"Get back in that line, you guys!" the coach called.

Mark nodded. His body felt heavy as he walked through the mud. *Squish squish,* his steps sounded. His left side was sore where he had fallen on it.

He saw Owens squatting down in the line. Mark made a sour grin at him and bent over. He wasn't looking forward to smashing into Owens again.

He crouched down in the mud and listened to the count. The pads on his shoulders rubbed against his wet skin.

"Six, seventeen . . ." the quarterback called out.

Mark squeezed his eyes tight.

"Hike!"

Pop.

■ ■ ■

Pop.

Nothing happened.

Owens didn't come crashing into him.

Mark opened his eyes.

The stadium was gone.

The lights of the laboratory beamed down. Mark felt warmer. He reached down and rubbed his legs. They seemed thin and small. But they weren't sore. And his shoulders didn't ache either.

A wave of relief washed over Mark. It felt wonderful to be back in a place he knew, and in a body that wasn't tired and hurt. He sat in the chair for a moment and enjoyed the feeling.

The clock on the wall said 2:27 P.M.

The laboratory door opened.

Mark's father walked in.

Mark jumped up. He stepped out of the time-travel booth.

"Trying it on for size?" Dad said.

"Well . . ." Mark didn't know what to say next.

"Wait a minute." His father frowned. Dad studied the dials on the front of the booth. Mark had not reset them.

"You've been on a time trip," his father said, surprised.

"Well, yes . . . I have."

His father scowled. "That was a very bad thing to do, Mark. It could be dangerous," he said in a serious tone.

"How?"

"Suppose the machine failed? Suppose it broke? Suppose you got stuck up there in the future and couldn't get back?"

"Well . . . it didn't break," Mark said.

His father's mouth pressed into a thin line. "If the time machine didn't bring you back, we would have no way to get you," he said.

Mark had never seen his father so angry. He looked down at his feet and tried to think of something to say.

"We are very careful here in the lab," his father said. "When we use this time machine we have many people standing by in case something goes wrong."

"Uh-huh," Mark muttered.

"You're a very lucky boy to be back here at all."

"I'm sorry, Dad. It seemed like a good idea."

"Well, it wasn't." His father's face

relaxed a little. "Mark, I'll talk to you about this tonight, at home. Right now I want to check out the machine. Your trip may have damaged it."

"Okay, Dad."

"I'm disappointed in you, Mark."

Mark's face felt hot. "G'bye, Dad," he mumbled.

He left the laboratory, walking slowly. His eyes stung, but he blinked back the tears.

■ ■ ■

On the bus Mark watched the houses go by outside. Everything felt comfortable and familiar. The two different futures he had visited weren't like this. They felt strange, in a way he couldn't quite describe.

Inside himself Mark felt confused and sad. He didn't want to go home right away. The bus rumbled by his school. Classes were just ending. He saw some of his friends—Ron, Vanessa and Anna.

Mark suddenly got up and pulled the signal cord to stop the bus. At the next corner the bus wheezed to a stop. Mark got off. He walked back to the school and went inside.

Photography Club was beginning. It was the only place Mark felt like going. He made his way to the darkroom and rapped on the door. A voice called from inside, "Hold on a minute."

Mark paced back and forth outside. When Anna opened the door he asked, "Need any help?"

"Sure," Anna said. She looked glad to see him. "My pictures aren't coming out right. I don't understand what I'm doing wrong."

"Let me see."

Mark worked for a while with the film Anna was trying to develop.

"You have some interesting pictures here," Mark said. "But they're not clear."

He showed Anna how to put the sheets of developing paper in the trays. After waiting a few minutes he fished them out. The pictures were sharp and clear.

"That's great," Anna said happily.

It lifted Mark's spirits to be doing something he enjoyed. In the back of his mind was the memory of that football practice in the future. Before his time-travel trips Mark had been sure he would like to be a garage mechanic or a football player. But they hadn't turned out the way he expected. . . .

Mark pushed these thoughts aside. "Let's try this one," he said. He rolled more of Anna's film on a projector. He clicked a switch. "That's an important step," he said. "The projector puts the picture onto this developing paper."

"That's easy," Anna said. "I can do that. But getting them developed . . ."

Mark swirled the developing fluid around in the tray. Anna's photograph showed a tree with lacy clouds above it. The picture slowly cleared. Mark studied it in the dim, red light of the darkroom. Something about the shadows among the tree limbs caught his eye. He took the photo out of the tray.

"Hey!" Anna cried out. "My picture isn't sharp yet!"

Mark hung it up to dry. "I know. It looks better this way."

"I thought we were always supposed to get our pictures as clear as possible," Anna said.

"I don't think so," Mark said. He pointed at the dripping sheet. "See these fuzzy branches. They're more interesting to look at than ordinary tree branches. And see those clouds? They look like cotton."

"Ummmmmm," Anna said, squinting at the photograph. "I . . . I think I see what you mean. It's *prettier* this way."

She turned to Mark. "You should do this when you grow up, Mark. You're really *good* at seeing interesting things in pictures."

"But my sister said machines develop all the pictures," Mark said.

"Did she?" Anna tossed her head to dismiss the idea. Her pigtails bounced. "Well, she doesn't know about *artistic* pictures, dummy. You could develop the artistic movies I'm going to make."

Mark smiled. One of the things he liked about Anna was how she was so sure of everything she said. It made her funny sometimes, too.

■ ■ ■

That evening his father asked Mark to go for a walk before supper. They puffed as they climbed to the top of a hill near their house. Then they stood looking out over their town. The sun was a dim, orange glow in the west.

"I talked to your mother," Dad said. "We think we know why you used the time machine."

"I wanted to find out what I'd be when I grew up," Mark said quietly.

"Right." Dad nodded.

"I certainly did find out," Mark said, and sighed. He felt tired. A lot had happened that day.

"You found out what you *could* become, Mark. Not what you *must* become."

"But Dad—" Then Mark told his father about the garage and why he didn't like working there. Dad just nodded. He was interested when Mark described the chimpanzees and how they worked.

When his father asked about the second time trip, Mark described the stadium and what it felt like to work as a football player. Mark mentioned the space station and how it looked like a giant wheel in the sky.

"How big did it seem?" his father asked.

"Oh . . . about as big as a dime held at arm's length," Mark said.

"Good grief. That's *enormous.*"

"Maybe I should be a scientist like you, Dad. That way I could get to work on that space station when I grow up. Then I could—"

He stopped, because Dad was chuckling. "You made those kind of plans about playing football when you grew up, too," Dad said.

"Well, gee, I was wrong about football, Dad. That doesn't mean I'm wrong about being a scientist."

"Son, there are good things and bad things about every job. Being a garage mechanic isn't always fun. Neither is being a football player. Or a scientist."

"Well . . . yes . . . I guess."

"You can't just take the good parts and leave the bad ones."

Mark frowned. "Dad? You *invented* the time machine. Have you gone on a time trip yourself?"

"No."

"Why not?"

His father put his hands in his pockets and kicked a rock down the hillside. It thumped and bounced from view. "I'm interested in the future, sure," Mark's father said. "Everybody is. But it isn't so important to me what I'll be doing in fifteen years. What's important is what my life is like *now*. The present is interesting enough."

Mark remembered Anna's photograph. Sometimes things were better if they weren't sharp and clear.

"Dad, I'm sorry about sneaking trips in your time machine. It's . . . it's just that everybody was asking me what I wanted to be, and . . ." Mark stopped, blinking. Below, the yellow lights of the town were winking on.

"Son, never mind how things will turn out. The question to ask yourself is, what do you like doing right now?"

Mark smiled, thinking about all that had happened since that day in the schoolyard, with Anna and her movies and all the rest of the gang. Mark realized that he had never really asked himself Dad's question. Instead, he had tried to guarantee his future. He wanted to "program" his future like a computer.

"I think you'll find one step at a time is quite enough," Dad said quietly.

"One step in *this* time," Mark said, smiling. "And let the future take care of itself."

Do you agree or disagree with Mark's conclusion that sometimes things are better if they aren't sharp and clear? Explain your answer.

At the beginning of the story, why does Mark feel it is so important for him to know what he is going to be as an adult?

Why does Mark feel confused and sad after visiting the two futures?

In the end, what does Mark decide about his future and himself?

WRITE What do you think would be the advantages and disadvantages of a time machine that could take you into your future? Make a list that includes both.

WORDS ABOUT THE AUTHOR

Gregory Benford

Gregory Benford and his twin brother, James, were born in Mobile, Alabama, in 1941. Gregory grew up with an interest in science that would one day bring him international recognition. After he received his doctorate in physics from the University of California at Irvine, he joined the faculty there. He has also held visiting professorships at Cambridge University in England.

Since 1965, Benford has written more than a dozen books of science fiction, some of them co-authored with other well-known writers. In addition to writing short stories and novels, he has written articles on physics and astrophysics for the *Encyclopedia Britannica*. He is also a contributor to the *Smithsonian* and *Natural History* magazines.

Several of Benford's major themes are evident in "What Are You Going to Be When You Grow Up?" Among them is his belief that wisdom is more precious than all the inventions that the scientific imagination can devise. He focuses not on superheroes but on ordinary people, like Mark and his family, who are trying to use technological breakthroughs to improve their daily lives.

Although many social problems of the past and the present have found their way into Benford's fiction, he once wrote, "Writers get boring when they preach." He makes it clear that his interests are in people and scientific landscapes, not in sermonizing. The attitude that comes through to his readers is very much like the attitude of Mark's father: Love the present, nurture your dreams, and fulfill your responsibilities, and the future will take care of itself.

Dreams

by Langston Hughes

Award-Winning Author

Hold fast to dreams
For if dreams die
Life is a broken-winged bird
That cannot fly.

Hold fast to dreams
For when dreams go
Life is a barren field
Frozen with snow.

Crowd 2 by Diana Ong, Private Collection

The Dream Keeper

by Langston Hughes

Bring me all of your dreams,
You dreamers,
Bring me all of your
Heart melodies
That I may wrap them
In a blue cloud-cloth
Away from the too-rough fingers
Of the world.

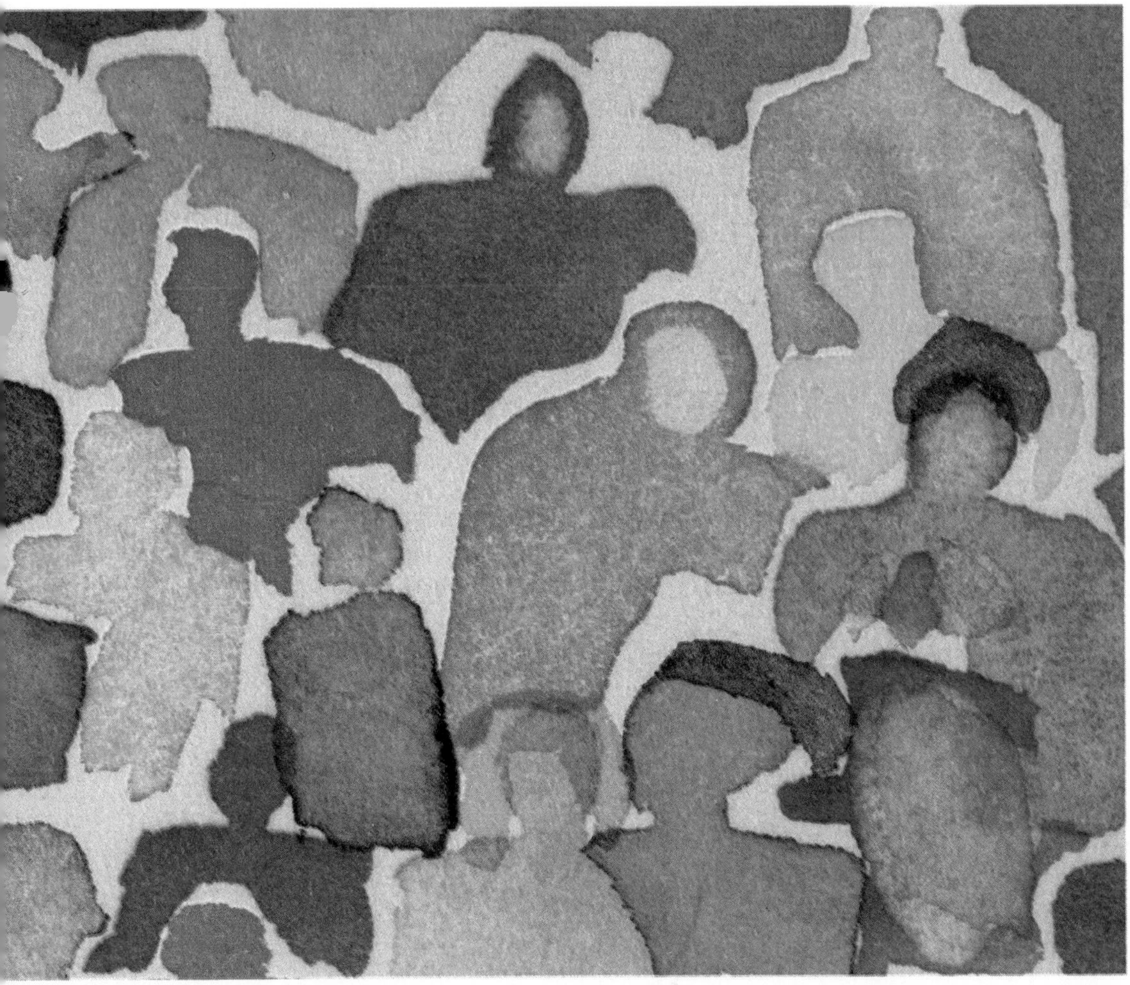

LANGSTON HUGHES

Words About the Poet

What were the dreams of the man who wrote "Dreams" and "The Dream Keeper"? Langston Hughes longed to live in a world where the rights of all human beings would be honored, and any differences between people of black race and white race would be respected. At the time of his birth in 1902, his father, an attorney, was forbidden to take the bar exam in Missouri because he was black. James Hughes moved to Mexico, where he could practice law, but his wife, Carrie Hughes, took their son to Kansas. There, because of her race, she could find only low-paying jobs in spite of her university education. Young Langston was cared for by his widowed grandmother, Mary Langston. Her husband, a freed slave, had been shot during the antislavery attack on Harper's Ferry, led by John Brown. His grandfather's bullet-torn clothing, kept in her home, was one of the poet's earliest memories.

When Langston Hughes graduated from high school, World War I had just ended, and jobs for African Americans were harder to find than ever. While traveling to Mexico to live briefly with his father, he wrote the first of his favorite poems, "The Negro Speaks of Rivers." In the last line, "My soul has grown deep like the rivers," he used the word *soul* as later black artists would use it, as a symbol of the deep feeling and spiritual connectedness that belong to all people descended from the first Africans forced into slavery.

AWARD-WINNING AUTHOR

After taking a job on a freighter bound for Africa and then living for a while in Paris, he settled in New York and became a leading figure in the literary movement called the Harlem Renaissance. His poetry was immediately popular, because he chose ordinary people as his subjects, those "to whom life is least kind"—the laundresses and dayworkers, the porters and dishwashers and doormen. When Hughes died in 1967, he was mourned by thousands of admirers.

THE FUTURE

Both "What Are You Going to Be When You Grow Up?" and the poems by Langston Hughes deal with attitudes about the future. Do you see the messages of the story and the poems as similar or different? What do you think Mark might say after reading "Dreams" and "The Dream Keeper"?

WRITER'S WORKSHOP

Do adults put too much pressure on young people to make decisions about their future, or is it important to start planning for the future as early as possible? Express your opinion in a persuasive letter to the editor that could be published in a school newspaper.

Writer's Choice Did the selections in this theme make you think about your future in a new way? Explore what interests you the most about the future. You may want to share your ideas in a poster, in a futuristic news report, or in some other way.

CONNECTIONS

MULTICULTURAL CONNECTION

GENERATION GAPS

Most Japanese Americans belong to one of three generations: the Issei, the Nisei, or the Sansei.

The Issei are first-generation immigrants who came during the main wave of Japanese immigration, from 1890 to 1924. They faced discrimination in American society but worked hard to make life better for their children.

Their children, the Nisei, were born in this country and mixed their Japanese heritage with American customs. During World War II, many Japanese Americans—including Nisei, who were American citizens—were forced into internment camps, where they suffered severe hardships. Others joined the first all-Nisei combat group, which became the most decorated army unit in United States history. Daniel Inouye was part of that unit. After the war, he entered politics and, as a senator from Hawaii, became the first Japanese American to serve in Congress.

The third generation, the Sansei, retain less of their Japanese heritage but show the same energy and will to succeed that distinguished their parents and grandparents.

In class, discuss how the customs and values of your generation compare with those of your parents and grandparents. Do you think there is usually a generation gap, even in families with no recent immigrant background?

ART CONNECTION

FAMILY QUILT

On paper, design a quilt that has special meaning for you and your family. Your quilt should have three sections: Past, for images relating to past generations; Present, for images relating to your generation; and Future, for images relating to future generations. Explain your quilt in class.

SOCIAL STUDIES CONNECTION

RESEARCHING ANCESTORS

Find out about one of your distant ancestors, someone who came from another land or whose customs were different from your own. If you can't identify a specific ancestor, you may choose a culture that is part of your ancestry. Research that culture and its customs; then compare them with your own culture and customs. Take notes, and share your findings with a small group.

Inset: A Nisei Week celebration is held in Los Angeles, California; inset left: Japanese immigrants as they arrive in San Francisco, California

UNIT THREE

A NEW COUNTRY

The history of every country begins in the heart of a man or a woman.

Willa Cather

As novelist Willa Cather suggests, there is a close connection between personal life and history. Many men and women have put their hearts and souls into the quest for freedom that has helped our country develop. James Forten, Paul Revere, Thomas Jefferson, Harriet Tubman, and Martin Luther King, Jr., are some of the courageous people you will meet in this unit. As you read, decide what freedom means to you, and think about what you can do to help maintain and advance our country's freedom.

THEMES

BOOKSHELF

PHILLIS WHEATLEY

BY MERLE RICHMOND

Brought to Boston on a slave ship at the age of seven, Phillis Wheatley became famous as a poet during the years immediately preceding the War for Independence. This biography weaves the story of Wheatley's unusual life into the story of the American Revolution.

HARCOURT BRACE LIBRARY BOOK

JOHNNY TREMAIN

BY ESTHER FORBES

In this story set in colonial Boston, Johnny Tremain overcomes obstacles and grows from a cocky boy into a responsible man willing to do what he must to preserve his beliefs.

Newbery Medal, ALA Notable Book

The Fifth of March

BY ANN RINALDI

This fictional account of the events that led up to the Boston Massacre is presented through the eyes of Rachel Marsh, indentured servant to John and Abigail Adams. Unexpectedly involved in the tragic events, Rachel makes a difficult and courageous choice.

Black Heroes of the American Revolution

BY BURKE DAVIS

This account of the contributions of African Americans to the American Revolution includes many examples of heroes who fought for the cause of liberty.

Notable Children's Trade Book in the Field of Social Studies

The Great Little Madison

BY JEAN FRITZ

The life of James Madison, the fourth President of the United States and the father of the Constitution, is recounted in this biography.

ALA Notable Book, *Boston Globe*–Horn Book Award, Notable Children's Trade Book in the Field of Social Studies

THEME

THE EARLY SOUTHWEST

The history of the Southwest has excited the imaginations of both explorers and storytellers. In the following selections, you will travel to Colorado as you read about the first discovery of the ancient ruins of a great civilization. Then you will journey to New Mexico to see how a personal story is surrounded by history.

CONTENTS

THE SEARCH FOR EARLY AMERICANS

by Sheila Cowing
Painting by H. Tom Hall

Long before Europeans came to America, great civilizations flourished and disappeared. We know about these early Americans from the ruins they left behind.

In the late 1800s, a cowboy named Richard Wetherill stumbled upon ancient ruins in Mesa Verde, Colorado. The ruins were like apartment houses carved into a cliff, and Richard named the place Cliff Palace. He went on to explore even older ruins, at a place called Grand Gulch.

Richard called the older race the Basket Makers. He sent his field notes to the American Museum of Natural History in New York with the mummies and their sandals and baskets. He did not write well, but a scientist friend wrote an article in *Harper's Monthly*, a popular magazine, using the notes and the photographs.

Other scientists did not believe Richard. Because he had no scientific training, they insisted he was a fraud. At Harvard University, an archeology professor told his students that Richard had invented a new people in order to sell more artifacts. This criticism did not deter Richard. He kept on exploring, because he was so fascinated he couldn't stop. He loved exploring more than anything else.

During the summer of 1895, Mr. and Mrs. Sidney Palmer and their three children, Marietta, Edna, and LaVern, set up camp near Richard's ranch. Richard showed them the cave dwellings at Mesa Verde. That fall, Richard and the Palmers traveled south one hundred fifty miles to see a big ruin they'd heard about called Pueblo Bonito, in the Navajo reservation in northern New Mexico.

For six days they followed a wheel-rut road. The desert was high and flat with no trees and little grass, and the wind blew constantly. The wagon wheels slipped and dragged in the sand.

When the road turned east through a wide canyon wash where once the Chaco River had flowed, they rode past the ruins of a small pueblo. Soon they saw more tumbled walls. Then, to their left, curved against the dark sandstone mesa,[1] lay a ruin that was larger than anything Richard had ever imagined.

Behind the ruin, he found holes in the cliff face, stairs the ancient pueblo dwellers had chipped with stone tools. Climbing, he stepped out on the mesa top overlooking the wide canyon.

Below him, Pueblo Bonito glowed red in the afternoon sun, spread out like a huge half-moon. The whole of Mesa Verde's Cliff Palace would be lost in one small section.

But that was not all. To the east he could see another great ruin. Across Chaco Canyon he could see mounds where several smaller pueblos might be buried. He might be looking down on an enormous city-state, like Rome or Athens!

Why had this civilization died? Where had all its people gone?

With Mr. Palmer, Richard rode across the northern mesa looking for Navajos who might have some of the answers. In the smoky light of hogans Wetherill spoke to the Navajos in their own language. The older Indian men all gave him the same answer. The great walls looked exactly the same as they had many generations before, when the Navajos first came to the area. At that time more cedar trees and more grass grew on

---

[1] mesa [mā'sə]: a small, high, flat-topped area

Above: Chaco Canyon National Historical Park spans thirty-two square miles in northern New Mexico. Right: At Mesa Verde, Richard Wetherill sits on a windowsill of a beautifully made building now called Balcony House.

the mesa. The Chaco Wash had water in it and the stream flowed at the surface of the canyon floor, not far down between the eroded banks of an arroyo.[2] But the ancient ones were gone, and no one knew who they were. *Anasazi,* the people called them, which meant "ancient enemy."

Richard and the Palmers explored for a month. They found eleven large pueblos with over one hundred rooms each, and more than one hundred smaller pueblos. Pueblo Bonito alone had more than six hundred rooms. It covered three acres and in some places rose five stories tall.

---

[2] arroyo [ə · roi′ō]: a gully cut out by a creek, often dry

Cliff Palace was discovered by Wetherill and Mason in December 1889 at Mesa Verde. It is believed to have had twenty-three ceremonial chambers and 200 other rooms.

After they returned to Mancos, Richard could not stop thinking about Chaco Canyon. At one time thousands of people must have lived there. Could the Navajos, poor, wandering sheepherders, have destroyed so great a city? He did not think so. He knew that answers must lie beneath the piles of rubble inside the walls.

Soon after their visit to Chaco, Richard married Marietta Palmer. They tried to settle down to ranch life, but Richard was too restless. He was so fascinated with the Anasazi that he decided to move to Chaco Canyon. He and Marietta opened a trading post for the Navajos, which Richard hoped would support his family.

The Hyde brothers,[3] who had helped finance the Grand Gulch exploration, agreed to send Richard money to excavate in Chaco Canyon. Richard would again give what he found to the American Museum of Natural History in New York City. The first organized search in Chaco Canyon began in 1896.

Over the next four years, Richard dug out nearly two hundred rooms in Pueblo Bonito. Soon he realized that this pueblo had been built differently than those at Mesa Verde. There, rooms were built as people moved in, with the beautiful towers added. But this huge, horseshoe-shaped pueblo had been designed ahead of time to meet a society's needs.

Some rooms were built of thin, flat rocks, others of large stones and mortar. Such different building methods suggested that the rooms had been built at different times and over many years. Walls in Pueblo Bonito lay twelve feet, or two stories, below the level of the main court and rose five stories above.

Rooms were laid over rooms, with huge pine timber ceilings between. The pine trees grew thirty miles away from the canyon. Traveling by foot, how long had it taken these people to haul pine trunks—thousands of them—to Pueblo Bonito? Construction of the pueblo must have taken a long time.

Richard had no way of knowing how long, or when the pueblo had been started. Years later another searcher, A. E. Douglass, discovered a way to find out. He counted the annual growth rings in the ceiling timbers. Then he compared those rings to many other pine timbers. Pueblo Bonito, he discovered, was begun around A.D. 950. That was five hundred fifty years before Columbus discovered America. Douglass decided that people had lived in Pueblo Bonito until after A.D. 1300. The Mesa Verde cliff dwellings were built later than the main section of Pueblo Bonito and were inhabited a shorter time.

How could people have grown enough food in the open, hot desert

---

[3] Hyde brothers: two wealthy brothers whom Richard met when he exhibited some of his finds at the Chicago World's Fair in 1893

for so long with so little rain? The Chaco River bed was hard, dry sand. When he was digging, Richard found only bitter springs.

Then, in July, it rained almost every day for two weeks. Walls of muddy water swept the wash, flooding ditches that Richard hadn't noticed. On the mesas, rainwater channeled into streams that fell over cliffs into shaded rock pools.

Recent research suggests that the Chaco River once flowed in the wash, flooding its banks each spring the way the Nile River did, watering Egyptian crops in ancient times. Did more rain fall in Anasazi times? Did the cliff pools store enough water for drinking and washing all year around? No one knows. People are still searching for answers in Chaco Canyon.

Not only could the Anasazi feed thousands in desert soil, but they also had time to build the largest city in the desert and to become master artists. Richard found pottery and jewelry more beautiful than any he had ever seen. He found hundreds of jars, many like those he'd found at Mesa Verde, but others painted with intricate designs or encrusted with chunks of turquoise. He found necklaces, pendants, bracelets, and carvings, many inlaid with turquoise or made of abalone shell, which shimmered like pearl in the sunlight.

The nearest turquoise mines were two hundred miles away. The nearest abalone lived in the ocean along the California coast, nearly one thousand miles away. Then Richard found the skeletons of fourteen macaws, large parrots with blue, red, yellow, or green feathers. Parrots live in the western Mexican highlands. These people must have traveled great distances!

Perhaps some of these people had moved to Chaco from the cliff houses at Mesa Verde, but Richard knew now that at Chaco the culture was much more advanced. High on the mesas north and west of Chaco were other ruins that looked similar. Could they have been part of Chaco?

Chaco Canyon was a great center, as Richard had suspected. When modern archeologists looked down on the canyon from the air, they discovered that it was connected to at least seventy-five outlying towns by almost five hundred miles of straight roads. Even though they had no wagons or cars, so many people traveled that the Anasazi dug roads thirty feet wide. In some places, low walls or ledges can still be seen edging the road's shallow depression.

Top: Map of Chaco Canyon and surrounding areas; Bottom: The walls of all structures in Pueblo Bonito were built without mortar. Top inset: A close-up view of a mortarless structure; Bottom inset: A series of doorways shows a different construction seen in Mesa Verde.

A collection of Anasazi kivas from Pueblo Bonito shows the design of the ruins.

Chaco has been called the greatest archeological ruin north of Mexico. An estimated five thousand people lived in four hundred settlements in and around the canyon, dependent on food grown in desert soil. These prehistoric people developed new building techniques. They watched the seasons change with a kind of solar observatory only recently discovered. They were skilled artists. They traded with people over a thousand miles away.

Why did they leave Chaco? Where did they go? Richard found no evidence of terrible battles as he had at Grand Gulch. Later searchers believe that groups of people moved all over the desert, as Mesa Verde people had moved into Chaco Canyon. They probably moved in search of water.

When the trees in the forest thirty miles away were cut for ceiling timbers, the underground water those roots drew to the surface may have sunk. Then when the seasonal rains fell, the thirsty desert absorbed the water too fast for the people to catch and store it. The Chaco people, archeologists believe, wandered east to the Rio Grande, where the river flowed all year around, or south to Acoma and Zuñi, or west to Oraibi, home of the Hopis.

All over the southwestern desert, searchers have found abandoned cliff and mesa houses. Some are still unexplored, their floors littered with miniature corn cobs and shards of pottery. Since the ancient ones had no written language, people are still searching for clues to their history.

In the open desert south of Phoenix, Arizona, an ancient people archeologists call the Hohokam, ancestors of the Pima and the Papago, played an Aztec ball game in walled courts. They used a process of etching with acid cactus sap to decorate seashells, five hundred years before European artists "discovered" the method. The Hohokam did not build great adobe or stone cities.

Another ancient people, the Mogollan Mimbres in southwest New Mexico, were the first Americans to decorate pottery with animal, bird, and geometric designs. Their artistic abilities were unknown for centuries because they drilled holes in their pots and jugs and buried them with their dead.

In 1910 Richard Wetherill was shot and killed by a Navajo man, after an argument over a horse. Richard was fifty-two years old. Seven years earlier, archeologists, insisting that he was vandalizing Pueblo Bonito, convinced the federal government to stop his search. For many years, his collection lay in a storeroom at the American Museum of Natural History in New York City. In the summer of 1987, however, the results of Richard Wetherill's searches, the artifacts of the Hyde Expeditions, were displayed in a show at the museum.

Because Richard had no training, scientists did not afford him the recognition he deserved. But Richard's search laid a cornerstone for the science that became American Southwestern archeology. In 1914, when Alfred Kidder and S. J. Guernsey discovered in northeastern Arizona the same kind of remains that Richard had described at Grand Gulch, archeologists acknowledged Richard's discovery of the Basket Maker civilization. Another archeologist, John C. McGregor, pointed out in his book that when Richard dug beneath the cliff dwellers' floor and concluded that the graves were those of an older people, he was the first to use the principle of stratigraphy, which teaches that what is buried deeper is older. Above all, Richard is remembered as one of the first Americans to prove that a great civilization existed in the desert long before Europeans settled there.

What have you learned about early American civilizations that you did not know before?

Find several details in the selection that show the accomplishments of the people who lived in Chaco Canyon.

Why, according to some modern-day archeologists, did the Anasazi leave Chaco Canyon? Do you find this explanation sufficient? Explain.

What are some of the questions about the Anasazi that are still unanswered?

WRITE In a paragraph, tell what kinds of things you would want to observe if you could visit the ruins of Pueblo Bonito.

THE BELLS OF SANTA CRUZ

by Nina Otero

illustrated by Leslie Wu

During the sixteenth century, Spain sent several expeditions to the New World, and Spanish explorers made their way through what is now the American Southwest. By the eighteenth century, Spanish ranchers and farmers had settled large areas of this land.

This story is set partly in Spain and partly in what is now New Mexico.

In the ancient village of Santa Cruz there is an old saying—"The toll of the bell is not for the dead, but to remind us that we, too, may die tomorrow."

María Concepción told this story to me as we sat under the roof of her *portal*[1] and watched the spring mist drift down the *mesas.*

Two hundred and thirty-nine years have passed since Don Diego de Vargas refounded this little village. It is recorded that the church was built in 1733. But it was of the bells of this church that María Concepción told—bells, rich not alone in metal, but in memories, memories so old, so beautiful.

"That is the Angelus[2] ringing, Doña Concepción."

---

[1] portal [pōr · täl′]: porch

[2] Angelus: a bell rung to call people to prayer

"Ah, little one. Those bells tell of the loves of Castile[3] and of the sorrows that all great loves bring. I will tell you a story that you may repeat it to your nieces and nephews, for perhaps some day they will come here as you have come."

Drawing her shawl more tightly around her, she began:

"Many years ago, many more years than I can count, preparations were under way for the departure from Spain, from Castile, of three priests and a little band of soldiers. It must have been a wonderful sight, for it was a brave undertaking. Don Ángel, a young nobleman and a soldier, a nephew of Father Antonio Moreno who headed the missionary priests, was among those selected with other brave youths to undertake this perilous journey. Don Ángel wished to serve his God and his king! Short service he thought he would have, for, you know, youth feels it can conquer the world within a certain time.

"On his return, Don Ángel was to marry the beautiful noblewoman, Doña Teresa. Oh, they say that her beauty was the talk of the kingdom. She was like the flowers of Castile. Even heaven would rejoice in this union.

"The gaiety of the farewell gathering, where gifts of gold and offerings of value were made to the members of the small band of loyal men, had but one sad note—the parting of the two lovers. Doña Teresa's laugh was her way of weeping to hide her sorrow. Don Ángel gave her a ring for her slender finger, and a chain and cross of gold. He kissed her hand. He waved a farewell to his friends and joined his companions.

"First they crossed the ocean. They tell me it was like flying in the blue sky. They crossed high mountains where unknown animals roamed and where unknown savages lived. Slowly and carefully this small band entered this country. At first the priests spoke to the Indians in symbols, and then instructed them and converted them to the Christian faith. In time Father Moreno started the building of a church. The church we now have is not the first one built, for that was destroyed when the Indians tired of the domination of the Spaniards, whose religion and form of government they did not understand. But this church was built by

---

[3] Castile [käs · tēl′]: a region of Spain

Father Moreno and his men in 1733 with the help of the converted Indians, and it is there in that tower that the bells hang which are so rich in memories. You know, Santa Cruz was the second big Catholic mission built; the first was but a few miles north of here at San Juan of the Gentlemen.

"Time passed, and it was necessary for Father Moreno to return to old Spain, to report to his superiors the progress he had made in the establishment of churches, the number of converts to the Christian religion, and, important too, he must of necessity raise funds for further work in this New Spain, for the erection of churches to house his increasing flock. Don Ángel having proved his ability as a soldier, his loyalty as a Spanish subject, was to accompany his uncle. Don Ángel, sleepless with anticipation and restless under delays, wrote Doña Teresa that he was returning to claim her love.

"But a few days before they were to start, the Indians made a surprise attack. At dawn, as the light made objects distinguishable, loud yells and shrill cries rent the air. The sound of war drums mingled with the war song of the Indian high priest. Arrows shot in every direction. Father Moreno entered the conflict, cross in hand. The young warriors of his band had a hand-to-hand encounter with the Indians whose yells grew louder and more fierce. The sound was as that of coyotes howling after a kill. A loyal Indian runner was sent to San Juan for reinforcements. Father Moreno was the target, and as young Don Ángel rushed to the aid of his uncle, an arrow whirled by the Padre and struck the young man. Don Ángel staggered forward and back and fell to the ground, the arrow deep in his side. Father Moreno ran and knelt to give absolution to the brave youth whose last words were: '*Tío,*[4] tell Teresa that my love was as great as my sacrifice!'

"Soldiers came from San Juan and they assisted in quieting the Indians. Since that time the Indians are our best neighbors. And why not? This ground was watered with the blood of martyrs and Indian braves and by tears of heaven which we call rain. This hallowed ground is also the resting place of the brave Castilian, Don Ángel.

---

[4] *Tío* [tē′ō]: Uncle

"In Spain little was known of the struggle of this band of brave priests and soldiers. When the letters from her beloved stopped coming, Doña Teresa became anxious, but she kept her fear in her heart. If he was brave she, too, must show courage.

"Time passed; word came again from across the sea. A message for Doña Teresa from Padre Moreno:

"'Gracious and courageous young lady:

"'No words of grief and affection can express to you what my heart feels. As a brave and valiant soldier, Don Ángel has not to my knowledge been surpassed. God loved him even more than we, for He has called him to rest in the New World in the shadow of the *Sangre de Cristo* Mountains and the valley of the Holy Cross.'

"Doña Teresa received the news in silence. For her no longer did snows have power to chill, nor the bright rays of the sun to warm. She walked alone in her garden crushing underfoot the new sprouts in flower. There was a smell of earth, that earth which held her beloved gave forth of fragrance; it was the perfume of her heart in sorrow.

"For twelve years the Indians of the Río Grande del Norte had claimed the lovely valley of Santa Cruz. But after the conquest De Vargas sent new settlers and this soon became the largest community in this part of New Spain. Then Spanish people again knelt in peace before the altar of their holy religion.

"The beautiful church took years to build; thousands of *adobes* are in those thick walls. The roof beams came from those *Sangre de Cristo* Mountains. It took several hundred men to put them in place. Oh, it was a labor of love, but when it was completed there were no bells to summon the people to Mass, no bells to announce the baptism of the Indians, or marriages according to the rites of our church. No bells to toll a benediction over their dead. So the priests sent to the Mother Country and there in Spain they held a celebration.

"People were invited to a great ceremony. Bells were to be molded to be sent to the New World. Friends and relatives of warriors and priests gathered in old Castile. A great fire was lighted, over which a huge caldron rested. A long pole was handled by one of the men in the crowd whose body became shiny from the sweat on his back, so hot was the fire that was to melt the metals.

"There was much merrymaking. It was the natural delight for a gift of such significance. And besides there was an opportunity for young people to meet and not be so closely guarded by their parents.

"Word reached Doña Teresa of the occasion for the celebration. Since the death of Don Ángel she had never left her father's palace except to attend Holy Mass. She had been ill with a fever, a long illness which left her weak and frail, but she insisted on taking part in this special celebration, much to the delight of her aged father.

"As young men linked their arms in those of young girls and danced around the caldron, the man stirred the molten metal, keeping time to the rhythm of the music. The fire was crackling. A lovely high coach driven by a team of sleek black horses drove up to the dancing group. It was like encountering the unknown dead when Doña Teresa, with the same charm but with the air of one tired and living in the past, stepped from the coach, accompanied by her father. A hush went over the crowd; a silence which not even the crackling of the burning wood seemed to shatter. Slowly they walked toward the great caldron. With a fixed melancholy expression Doña Teresa watched the seething mass. Ah, faces we see, hearts we do not know! Slowly she removed from her finger a gold ring, and over her head she slipped a gold chain on which hung a cross of gold. She pressed these, the parting gifts of Don Ángel to her bosom for a minute and then threw them into the boiling metal, there to whisper a deeper note of melody and of love.

"A respect for those who mourn and a reverence for the dead you well know is the natural feeling of our old and of our young people. On seeing this act of courage and devotion, even the happy ones turned serious, and in a frenzy of awakened memories they all cast their jewels, silver and gold into the great caldron.

"What wonder that these bells have a different sound from all bells!

"A strange thing—those bells arrived here and were blessed on the day Doña Teresa died in Castile!

"When the Angelus rings, as we hear it now, and the streaks of rain sweep down from the *Sangre de Cristo* Mountains, there, in the mist, maybe the lovers meet—who knows?"

Do you think the story of Don Ángel and Doña Teresa would have been as memorable if it had had a happy ending? Explain your response.

Why did Doña Teresa throw her ring and necklace into the caldron?

What do you think Doña Concepción means when she says that the bells of Santa Cruz have "a different sound from all bells"?

WRITE In a paragraph, summarize what you learned about New Mexico's history from this story.

Words About the Author:

NINA OTERO

Nina Otero wrote "The Bells of Santa Cruz" in her small adobe house twelve miles from Santa Fe, the capital of New Mexico. The story of the bells was included in her book *Old Spain in Our Southwest.* She took advantage of the beauty and solitude of the land she homesteaded there to record her memories of growing up in New Mexico.

Maria Adelina Emelia (Nina) Otero was born into a distinguished family with its origins dating back to eleventh-century Spain. A strong leader like her intrepid ancestors, who helped shape the history of the New World, she worked to improve the status of women and upgrade the educational system in New Mexico. She was a persuasive and effective activist for women's voting rights from 1915 to 1920 and was the first woman in New Mexico to run for the United States Congress. She was Superintendent of Public Schools for Santa Fe County for twelve years, and worked with the Works Projects Administration (WPA) in the 1930s to establish adult literacy programs in New Mexico and Puerto Rico.

Nina Otero's achievements as an educator are remarkable considering that her only formal education consisted of two years at Maryville College of the Sacred Heart in Saint Louis, Missouri. Because of her political and social activism during years when most women were expected to devote their energies to marriage, home, and motherhood, Nina Otero was indeed a woman ahead of her time.

THE EARLY SOUTHWEST

Consider how Richard Wetherill and Nina Otero learned about the history of the Southwest. What are several ways of learning about the history of a region?

WRITER'S WORKSHOP

Why did the Anasazi disappear? How did Spanish settlers in the Southwest live? Write an informational essay that answers one of these questions or explores another historical question that interests you. Do some research to find the facts you need. Then present the information in a clear and interesting way.

Writer's Choice Much food, fashion, and furniture shows a Southwestern influence. Choose an object that makes you think of the Southwest, and plan your own way of writing about it—perhaps a description or a story. Then share your writing with a classmate.

REVOLUTIONARY TIMES

As the American colonies grew and prospered, many colonists began thinking of themselves as Americans rather than as British subjects. Before and during the Revolutionary War, ideas of liberty and equality excited and inspired people in all walks of life, including the people you will read about in the following selections.

CONTENTS

Touchmark

by Mildred Lawrence

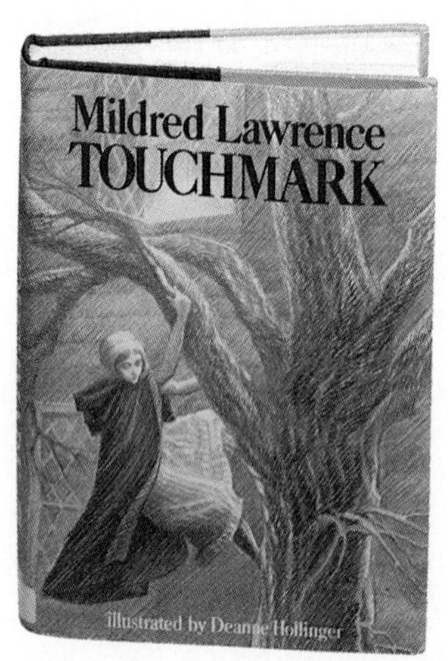

In 1773, Boston is in an uproar over British taxes and the presence of British soldiers. In the midst of this conflict, Abigail Jonas, known as Nabby, has problems of her own. Nabby wants to become a pewterer—her most precious possession is a pewter porringer that her father, who was lost at sea, had brought her from England. But no pewterer in Boston will take a girl as an apprentice. Left homeless by the death of her mother, Nabby becomes a servant in the household of Tobias Butler, a pewterer with an incompetent apprentice named Lonzo. She is a welcome companion for the Butlers' daughter, Emily, who has lost the use of her legs after an illness. Not the type to sit by the fire, Nabby keeps up with the political happenings in Boston through her friend Will Truax, a printer's apprentice who nails up many broadsides, or news sheets, for the Sons of Liberty. One evening Master Butler gives instructions that no one in the house is to cross the threshold that night. In the following chapter from the novel, Nabby finds that strange events are taking place.

Illustrations by Mark Elliott

Nabby threw open the casement window, heedless of the blast of cold air that swept through the room. By leaning out perilously far and craning her neck almost out of joint, she could see dark figures rushing down Milk Street from the direction of the Old South Meeting House, whooping as they went.

"Whoever they are, they are bound for the harbor," she said, "mayhap down Hutchinson Street to Griffin's Wharf." She snatched up her hooded cloak. "Pretend to be sleeping, Emily, in case your mother comes to inquire." She hastily stuffed two of the cushions from Emily's chair under her own bedcover. "There, is it not a fair likeness of me asleep?" She blew out the candle and tiptoed to the door. "Why, 'tis locked!"

"Then you must stay here," Emily said in a relieved voice.

"So it seems, unless—" Nabby looked speculatively at the tree just outside the window. "Emily, if you can close the window behind me to keep out the cold and open it again when I return, I can easily climb down the tree and see what betides."

"Pray, Nabby, do not go." Emily's voice was pleading. "My father —"

"Your father will know naught of it, I promise you, unless you tell."

"I would never tell, but you might fall, and then no one would need to tell."

"I will not fall. I have balanced myself many a time on the deck of the *Boston Traveller* tossing at anchor just opposite our door. Besides, think of what I will be able to tell you—exciting things for your sketches."

"Y-yes." Emily struggled out of bed and reached for her crutches. "You will take care, lest—"

"Lest a wandering bear devour me. Indeed, Emily, I shall skulk from shadow to shadow in my dark cloak, and no one will know I am there."

Through the window and down the tree—it was only a few moments until she was standing on the ground looking up at the white blur of Emily's face. The window closed with the faintest click of the latch. Nabby crept toward the street, keeping close to the wall of the house. No light shone from Master Butler's workroom now. He and his mysterious visitors must have fared forth to see what befell in the street, still noisy with whoops, yells, and whistles.

"Let me out! Let me out!"

Nabby shrank against the wall as Lonzo's muffled voice came to her from the shed room. So he, too, was locked in, but if he had not wit enough to climb out of his own window, he deserved to stay there. She hoped that he, of all people, had not seen her but was only calling out to anybody who might hear. She shivered from cold and excitement but not at all from fear. She was tall and strong and fleet of foot, and she knew every turn of the streets hereabouts.

She peered cautiously around the corner of the house. She was just in time to see, by the pale light of the waning moon, an apprentice climbing down from a nearby roof, apparently smearing soot from the chimney on his face as he went—a strange thing to do, but there had been many strange happenings in Boston of late.

Trying to be invisible, Nabby dodged along the darkest part of the street toward Fort Hill, where the shouts seemed loudest. There a squad of men, ghostly in the shadows, marched smartly past, to be joined by clumps of hurrying stragglers from the lanes and byways. Nabby followed to Griffin's Wharf, aswarm with indistinct figures milling around the tea ships—three of them, now that *Beaver* had been moved out of quarantine to join *Dartmouth* and *Eleanor*. Nabby melted into the shadow of a warehouse to watch in silence with a gathering crowd of men, women, and a few children.

By the flare of scattered torches, whose flames flickered in the wind, Nabby could see that men in outlandish attire were clambering aboard the tea ships. Bandannas, hoods, mufflers, and knit caps were pulled well down to disguise grim faces striped and smeared in black, red, and various shades between. Master Butler would have used charcoal from the forge or the red ocher with which he prepared his molds, if indeed he were here at all. Somehow Nabby could not imagine him whooping like an Indian, with his face streaked with war paint. The light caught the shine of hatchets, and an occasional pistol was stuck pirate-style in a sash or belt. Nabby edged to leeward of a large woman whose bulk would shelter her from a freshening breeze with a feel of icicles in it.

"Hast heard, maid, that the fourth tea ship, the brig *William,* is aground on Cape Cod in a gale?" an old man leaning on a blackthorn stick muttered in Nabby's ear. "One less batch of tea for our stalwart lads to deal with!"

Nabby had not long to wait to see how the stalwart lads were planning to deal with the tea. Clearly in undisputed possession of the ships, men were hauling the tea chests up from the holds by slings and cranes. Hatchets flashed as the chests with their burlap coverings were ripped open and the tea flung overboard.

"At 'em, boys! Leave never a leaf!" the old man cackled gleefully. "Tea and sea water will make a brew fit for a king—King George himself!"

The whole operation, guided by quiet orders from the men on shipboard, was as precise as though each man had been drilled in what he was expected to do. Plainly, this was no sudden outburst of anger like some of the riots of recent weeks.

On the deck of the *Dartmouth,* Nabby caught a flash of red hair straying from under a bandanna with a turkey feather stuck jauntily through the knot. Will Truax, neatly striped with printer's ink, was busily flinging the shattered chests into the sea, where they bobbed on the water like wrecks of children's playboats. Nabby's father had once told her that, while Long Wharf could handle the largest seagoing vessels, the harbor at Griffin's Wharf was never more than a few feet deep. Now, with the tide near its lowest ebb, the three ships looked to be almost aground. As the tea was tossed over the side, it began to build up like beehives in the shallow water.

"You, there, boy! Find some of your fellows and make sure the tea is well awash."

Nabby stared, wide-eyed. It was the unmistakable voice of Master Butler, whose face was decorated with slashes of red ocher under a sloppy turban remarkably like the patched old apron that Mistress Butler wore when she scrubbed the wide boards of the kitchen floor. He and his mysterious visitors must have been busy in the workroom the whole time disguising themselves for this foray.

"'Tis ill that it must be done at low tide," the gaffer with the blackthorn stick gabbled on, "but all must be finished by midnight, they say, else the customs men will take possession."

Nabby nodded impatiently at news she already knew. She edged closer to the plump woman, pleasantly scented with cinnamon, while the old man smelled only of tobacco and stale beer. The dim little moon had set by now, and some of the flares were burning out. Still, Nabby could see a group of boys jumping with joyous whoops onto

the piled-up tea in the water and tossing it to the wind. There would be many a case of chills and fever tomorrow, but who paid heed to that on such a night?

In the confusing swirl of motion ashore, on deck, and asea, Nabby lost track of Master Butler and Will Truax. A few men swept the decks, and others saw that the last broken tea chests were pushed well away from the shallows. A brief uproar arose on the wharf as three men wrestled another to the ground, removed his coat, and emptied something out of his pockets into the water.

"Be off with you!" one of them shouted. "And think yourself lucky that we do not replace your coat with one of tar and feathers!"

"A fair return for filling his pockets with tea!" the old man murmured.

Someone called the apprentices in from their chore of drowning the tea in sea water. The "Indians" began to leave, some forming into groups and others slipping away by twos and threes into the darkness.

"A good night's work! December 16, 1773, will be long remembered." The cinnamon-scented woman spoke her first words of the evening and turned to lumber away, leaving Nabby exposed to a wind that was colder than ever. "No doubt we will pay dearly for it, too, but methinks it will be worth the price."

To Nabby's experienced eye, the tide was on the turn now, washing the tea closer to shore—no matter now, though, since it was well soaked with salt water. Enthralled with the scene, Nabby had quite forgotten that time was passing and that Master Butler might already have left for home. Whether or no, she must rush away at once. If she hurried, she would have time to climb safely into bed before he could remove his war paint and come abovestairs to check on his presumably sleeping household.

She ran at top speed through the lanes to Milk Street, hiding in the shadows from any other night travelers, although all seemed as anxious as she not to be seen. She clambered up the tree like a cat, tapped ever so softly on the window, and tumbled breathlessly into the room the moment the waiting Emily flung open the casement window.

"Safe," Nabby whispered, "thanks to you!" She rubbed Emily's cold hands with her own icy ones. "You have not caught a chill waiting for me? I will tuck you warm in your bed again and perch alongside wrapped in my quilt, for what a tale I have to tell!"

She should almost have thought her tale was merely a dream that had vanished with the day except that Master Butler, eating his mush and milk in gloomy silence the next morning, had a small smear of red at the edge of his hair and a pair of damp boots drying by the fire. Lonzo, sullen-faced, sat picking at a torn pocket of his coat, a much-darned castoff.

"Off with your coat," Mistress Butler said in a resigned voice, "and Nabby will mend the pocket for you."

Lonzo muttered something about having a candlestick to deliver.

"You took that yesterday." Master Butler roused himself from a brown study.

Lonzo angrily passed the coat to Nabby.

"I will wait, then, while you stitch it up."

"You will not wait," said Master Butler. "You will go at once and make up the fire in the forge. You will not need a coat for that or for aught else today. We have the final buffing to do on a pair of mugs, after which I will go to the brass founders to inspect some new molds."

"Molds for what, sir?" Nabby could not resist asking.

"A dram bottle for use," Master Butler said with a wry face, "and a pear-shaped teapot for beauty."

"More teapot molds?" Mistress Butler ventured. "With not a leaf of honest tea to be had in all of Boston?"

"And a pot-bellied creamer," he went on.

So it was going to be business as usual, as though last night had never been.

"Do not fear," Master Butler told his wife. "If I cannot come by some tin soon, I will be making nothing either for use or beauty." He halted Nabby as, with Lonzo's coat tucked under her arm, she prepared to go abovestairs for needle and thread. "How long before we may expect the *Boston Traveller* to return to port?"

Nabby shrugged. "Wind and weather play a part, sir." This was a fact of which Master Butler and everybody else in Boston were well aware. "The ship is not a fast one, she must often wait long in port for a return cargo, and the winter storms are to be feared." She counted

on her fingers. "She left Long Wharf the second week in November, and 'tis now December 17. Oh, sir, she can hardly return before the last of January."

He nodded gloomily. "So I feared. Well, we must still make do with pewter melted down from old pieces and hope to improve the alloy by adding small bits of this and that. The Worshipful Company of Pewterers in London is happy to ship chests of completed pewter pieces to the colonies to be sold, but they make sure that local craftsmen do not have the raw materials needed to make their own—another grievance to add to the ones we already have."

"Pray, sir," Nabby said demurely, "have you news of what befell last night? There was a great whooping and shouting in the street."

Master Butler gave her a sharp look. "The talk is that a tribe of Indians boarded the tea ships and threw all the tea into Boston Harbor."

Mistress Butler gave a little shriek. "Indians? Oh, Tobias, 'tis well that you forbade us to stir across the threshold."

And locked them in, to make doubly sure. Nabby let her glance stray thoughtfully to Master Butler's face.

"Sir, I fear you have hurt yourself. There is a red streak just—"

Mistress Butler fluttered to him. "Oh, Tobias, shall I fetch a cobweb to draw out the soreness?"

"No, woman, no!" Master Butler roared his way to the door. "I mislike this fretting and fussing over nothing—a brier scratch, at worst."

Nabby slid behind his back and abovestairs. What ever had possessed her to bait him in that fashion? Curiosity as to what he might reply was part of it, but also a wish to hear his version of last night's adventures. The only thing she had found out was that he did not intend to reveal his presence at the Boston Tea Party.

She sat down on the bed and sewed up Lonzo's pocket, taking care to reinforce the cloth underneath, which had been torn, too, as though caught on a splinter. She also checked the condition of the other pocket, not because she wished to oblige Lonzo but because care on this chore might convince Master Butler that she was a girl who could do painstaking work of other kinds as well.

As she turned the coat about, a sprinkling of something fell to the floor—a few leaves of tea, as she lived and breathed! So Lonzo had attended the tea party last night, too, ripping his coat as he broke out of his room. Nabby frowned. The tea leaves could mean that he had tried to make off with a whole pocketful of the stuff but had hastily disposed of it when he saw what befell the man who had been threatened with a coat of tar and feathers. Why, then, his reluctance to hand over the coat to be mended?

Nabby laid it out flat on the floor and felt over every inch of it. Not much to her surprise, a flat cloth-wrapped packet tied with twine was thrust deep into the ripped lining of the sleeve. She turned the package over and over in her hand, but curiosity was too much for her. She hurriedly undid the packet, which contained more tea, enough for many a cheering cup for those who could stomach the brew these days, mayhap the wives of British officials in town or of officers stationed at Castle William. Nabby stirred the leaves with her finger—bohea, the black tea much favored in Boston before true patriots gave up drinking it entirely.

So now what? In her hand Nabby held the means of ridding the household of Lonzo. Master Butler might overlook his sneaking out to attend the tea party, but he would never forgive his scooping up some of the hated tea and, Nabby felt sure, selling it wherever he might. With Lonzo gone, Nabby might have a chance to take his place, except— Except that she was a girl, and Master Butler was not yet ready to accept a girl as an apprentice, if indeed he ever would be.

Nabby picked up her little porringer, shimmering in the sun, and turned it over to admire the touchmark. Unwillingly she remembered Master Butler's words: "The touchmark is a pledge of my skill and my honor." Of skill Nabby had none, but honor— Her face clouded. Eager as she was to become a pewterer some day, she would never be able to look with pride at the touchmark she had chosen for herself, the sturdy sailing ship, if she got her start by bearing tales against even the shiftless Lonzo.

All the same, she would make sure that he did not profit from his pilfering. She opened the window and tossed the tea into a brisk breeze that scattered it over three rooftops. Then she tiptoed down the stairs, making sure to skip the step that creaked, and peered into the kitchen, where Emily sat alone.

With a finger at her lips, Nabby climbed onto the settle and took down one of the bunches of parsley that Mistress Butler had hung from the rafters to dry, along with various other herbs for medicinal tea and flavoring. Nabby darted back upstairs, rubbed the dark dried parsley between her hands to the consistency of tea leaves, and tied it up in the packet, which she put back into Lonzo's sleeve lining.

"Here is your coat, as good as new!" she announced cheerily at the doorway to the workroom. "You will hardly know it was torn."

Lonzo, turning the wheel for Master Butler, gave her a suspicious look and no thanks.

"Lay it on the bench there," he said.

"Mind your manners!" Master Butler was stern. "A word of thanks ne'er comes amiss."

Nabby did not wait to hear it but went back to whisper the whole story to Emily in the chimney corner, while Mistress Butler, back from a gossip with the neighbors, tended the shop, now more scantily stocked than ever. Master Butler had paid dearly for the hours he had spent at meetings, where Nabby was sure that every detail of the tea party had been readied for use in case the negotiations among the governor, the tea consignees, and the town meeting came to naught. Now, he must devote himself to pewtering again to make up for lost time.

Will Truax came with spare broadsides for Emily's drawings and paused to warm himself by the kitchen fire and relay the latest news.

"Master Butler has told you what befell the tea? This morning 'tis a strange sight indeed, for the high tide has washed it down the shore like drifts of seaweed."

Emily smiled. "I shall draw it so, then, as well as making a sketch of you, Will Truax, standing on the deck of the *Dartmouth* tossing the tea chests over the side." She clapped her hands over her mouth and gave Nabby a horrified look. "Oh, Nabby, pray forgive my careless tongue. I forgot that—"

"No matter," said Nabby. "Will will tell no tales, any more than he will reveal who else was there, lest the British take their revenge against all who—"

"What's this?" Nabby turned to see Master Butler, in heavy coat and cocked hat, standing in the doorway. "Methinks, Nabby, you

know a great deal about last night's events for a young maid presumed to be at home asleep." His voice turned cold. "Did I not give orders that none in this household were to cross the threshold last night?"

"Sir, those were your very words, repeated to us by Mistress Butler herself."

Master Butler turned as red as the wattles of a turkey cock. "Do you deny that you were at Griffin's Wharf last night?"

Nabby put on her meekest expression. "Oh, no, sir. I was there. Pray do not think me pert, but I did not cross the threshold. I climbed down the tree beside our window."

Do you think Master Butler should accept Nabby as an apprentice? Why or why not?

What kind of person is Nabby? Use details from the selection to support your response.

Why does Nabby decide not to reveal what she found in Lonzo's coat? Do you agree with her idea of honor?

Why do you think Master Butler refuses to reveal his presence at the Boston Tea Party to his family?

WRITE Do you prefer to read fictional or factual accounts of historical events? Write a paragraph or two telling the kinds of things you can learn from each type of account and explaining your preference.

Paul Revere's Ride

by Henry Wadsworth Longfellow

Paul Revere Painted from life by Gilbert Stuart

Listen, my children, and you shall hear
Of the midnight ride of Paul Revere,
On the eighteenth of April, in Seventy-five;
Hardly a man is now alive
Who remembers that famous day and year.
He said to his friend, "If the British march
By land or sea from the town to-night,
Hang a lantern aloft in the belfry arch
Of the North Church tower as a signal light,—
One, if by land, and two, if by sea;
And I on the opposite shore will be,
Ready to ride and spread the alarm
Through every Middlesex village and farm,
For the country folk to be up and to arm."

Then he said, "Good night!" and with muffled oar
Silently rowed to the Charlestown shore,
Just as the moon rose over the bay,
Where swinging wide at her moorings lay
The Somerset, British man-of-war;
A phantom ship, with each mast and spar
Across the moon like a prison bar,
And a huge black hulk, that was magnified
By its own reflection in the tide.

Meanwhile, his friend, through alley and street,
Wanders and watches with eager ears,
Till in the silence around him he hears
The muster of men at the barrack door,
The sound of arms, and the tramp of feet,

And the measured tread of the grenadiers,
Marching down to their boats on the shore.

Then he climbed the tower of the Old North Church,
By the wooden stairs, with stealthy tread,
To the belfry-chamber overhead,
And startled the pigeons from their perch
On the sombre rafters, that round him made
Masses and moving shapes of shade,—
By the trembling ladder, steep and tall,
To the highest window in the wall,
Where he paused to listen and look down
A moment on the roofs of the town,
And the moonlight flowing over all.

Paul Revere's Ride
Hy Hintermeister, 1897–1970

Beneath, in the churchyard, lay the dead,
In their night-encampment on the hill,
Wrapped in silence so deep and still
That he could hear, like a sentinel's tread,
The watchful night-wind, as it went
Creeping along from tent to tent,
And seeming to whisper, "All is well!"
A moment only he feels the spell
Of the place and the hour, and the secret dread
Of the lonely belfry and the dead;
For suddenly all his thoughts are bent
On a shadowy something far away,
Where the river widens to meet the bay,—
A line of black that bends and floats
On the rising tide, like a bridge of boats.

Meanwhile, impatient to mount and ride,
Booted and spurred, with a heavy stride
On the opposite shore walked Paul Revere.
Now he patted his horse's side,
Now gazed at the landscape far and near,
Then, impetuous, stamped the earth,
And turned and tightened his saddle-girth;

But mostly he watched with eager search
The belfry-tower of the Old North Church,
As it rose above the graves on the hill,
Lonely and spectral and sombre and still.
And lo! as he looks, on the belfry's height
A glimmer, and then a gleam of light!
He springs to the saddle, the bridle he turns,
But lingers and gazes, till full on his sight
A second lamp in the belfry burns!

Paul Revere's ride from Boston to Lexington Colored engraving, 19th century

A hurry of hoofs in a village street,
A shape in the moonlight, a bulk in the dark,
And beneath, from the pebbles, in passing, a spark
Struck out by a steed flying fearless and fleet:
That was all! And yet, through the gloom and the light,
The fate of a nation was riding that night;
And the spark struck out by that steed, in his flight,
Kindled the land into flame with its heat.

He has left the village and mounted the steep,
And beneath him, tranquil and broad and deep,
Is the Mystic, meeting the ocean tides;
And under the alders that skirt its edge,
Now soft on the sand, now loud on the ledge,
Is heard the tramp of his steed as he rides.

It was twelve by the village clock,
When he crossed the bridge into Medford town.
He heard the crowing of the cock,
And the barking of the farmer's dog,
And felt the damp of the river fog,
That rises after the sun goes down.

It was one by the village clock,
When he galloped into Lexington.
He saw the gilded weathercock
Swim in the moonlight as he passed,
And the meeting-house windows, blank and bare,

The Midnight Ride of Paul Revere Grant Wood, 1931, Metropolitan Museum of Art

Gaze at him with a spectral glare,
As if they already stood aghast
At the bloody work they would look upon.

It was two by the village clock,
When he came to the bridge in Concord town.
He heard the bleating of the flock,
And the twitter of birds among the trees,
And felt the breath of the morning breeze
Blowing over the meadows brown.
And one was safe and asleep in his bed
Who at the bridge would be first to fall,
Who that day would be lying dead,
Pierced by a British musket-ball.

You know the rest. In the books you have read,
How the British Regulars fired and fled,—
How the farmers gave them ball for ball,
From behind each fence and farm-yard wall,
Chasing the red-coats down the lane,
Then crossing the fields to emerge again
Under the trees at the turn of the road,
And only pausing to fire and load.

Paul Revere's ride from Boston to Lexington Colored engraving, 19th century

So through the night rode Paul Revere;
And so through the night went his cry of alarm
To every Middlesex village and farm,—
A cry of defiance and not of fear,
A voice in the darkness, a knock at the door,
And a word that shall echo forevermore!
For, borne on the night-wind of the Past,
Through all our history, to the last,
In the hour of darkness and peril and need,
The people will waken and listen to hear
The hurrying hoof-beats of that steed,
And the midnight message of Paul Revere.

Why do you think this poem has always been so popular with Americans?

A narrative poem is able to use language that makes events seem especially dramatic and important. Find several examples of such language in "Paul Revere's Ride."

Write What do you think is the "midnight message" that echoes "through all our history"? Is this still an important message today, or did Longfellow exaggerate? Write a paragraph explaining your thoughts.

Concord Hymn

by Ralph Waldo Emerson

SUNG AT THE COMPLETION
OF THE BATTLE MONUMENT,
JULY 4, 1837

Skirmishes at Lexington and Concord on April 19, 1775, marked the beginning of the Revolutionary War. Emerson wrote this poem for the dedication of a monument to the minutemen, who fought the British in these battles.

By the rude bridge that arched the flood,
    Their flag to April's breeze unfurled,
Here once the embattled farmers stood
    And fired the shot heard round the world.

The foe long since in silence slept;
    Alike the conqueror silent sleeps;
And Time the ruined bridge has swept
    Down the dark stream which seaward creeps.

On this green bank, by this soft stream,
    We set today a votive[1] stone;
That memory may their deed redeem,
    When, like our sires, our sons are gone.

Spirit, that made those heroes dare
    To die, and leave their children free,
Bid Time and Nature gently spare
    The shaft we raise to them and thee.

---

[1] votive: given or made as an act of devotion

James Forten

Illustrations by Lonnie Knabel

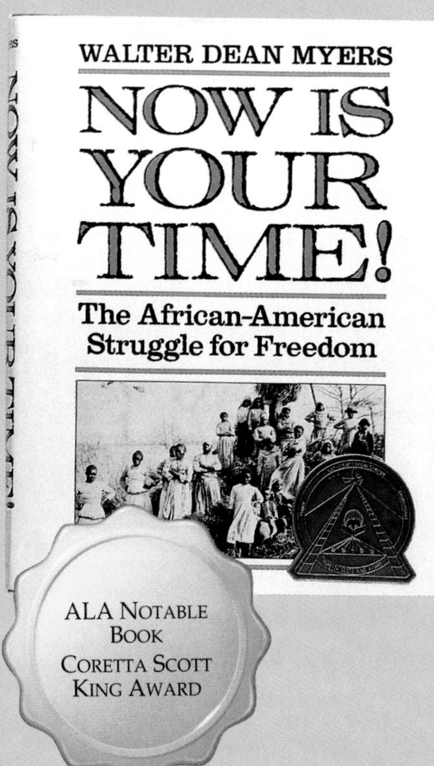

In *Now Is Your Time!* Walter Dean Myers presents the history of African Americans in North America from 1619, when the first African captives were brought to Virginia, to the present day. Myers points out that the labor of enslaved Africans helped to create the prosperity that enabled the American colonies to break away from England. By the time of the Revolutionary War, a number of Africans had obtained their freedom, and some of these joined the fight for independence. The following chapter from the book tells the story of the young African sailor James Forten.

by Walter Dean Myers

Not all Africans were being held on plantations. Some had bought their own freedom; others had been given it by the whites who held them. And when the Africans became free, they did what other Americans were doing. Some worked their own farms; many worked on ships; others started their own business ventures. In Ellicott Mills, Maryland, a free African man named Benjamin Banneker began publishing his almanac and corresponded with Thomas Jefferson. In New York a free African named Samuel Fraunces owned a famous tavern in which George Washington as well as all the leading New Yorkers would eat. An escaped African, Crispus Attucks, was one of five protesters killed when the British fired on a group of colonists in Boston. Hundreds of Africans joined the fight against the British as sailors and soldiers. One of those was James Forten.

It was early morning on Tuesday, September 2, 1766, in the city of Philadelphia. The roads into the city were already filling with farmers bringing in produce to sell. Windows in the city were coming alive with the glow of lamplight. Small factory owners trudged through the winding streets to small shops. Printers, shoemakers, blacksmiths, candle makers, bakers—all began the business of the day. For Philadelphia was indeed a city of business.

As day broke over the harbor, the masts of the ships loomed against the gray skies. The ships rocked at their moorings as if they, too, were ready for the new day.

Hundreds of free men of African descent lived in Philadelphia. The city was the home of a number of noted abolitionists—people who wanted to abolish, or do away with, the practice of slavery—including the Quakers, a powerful and influential religious group. More important was the fact that Africans could find work in Philadelphia.

Many of the Africans worked the docks, loading and unloading the ships that brought products to the colonies from all over the world. Others were tradesmen and seamstresses, cooks, barbers, and common laborers. All along the eastern seaboard, from Baltimore to New England, free Africans worked on boats, hauling loads, carrying passengers, and fishing. Many opened restaurants. Others bought their own boats and tried their luck on the brisk waterfronts.

Thomas Forten, a free African, was employed by Robert Bridges, a sailmaker in Philadelphia. Sail making was a profitable but difficult job. Sewing the coarse cloth was brutal on the hands. The heavy thread had to be waxed and handled with dexterity. A person trying to break the thread with his hands could see it cut through his flesh like a knife. But Forten appreciated his job. It paid reasonably well and the work was steady.

Forten helped in all aspects of sail making and assisted in installing the sails on the ships the firm serviced. With the income from his work he had purchased his wife's freedom. Now, on this early Tuesday morning, a new baby was due. The baby, born later that day, was James Forten.

Young James Forten's early life was not that different from that of other poor children living in Philadelphia. He played marbles and blindman's buff, and he raced in the streets. When he was old enough, he would go down to the docks to see the ships.

Sometimes James went to the shop where his father worked and did odd jobs. Bridges liked him and let him work as much as he could, but he also encouraged Thomas Forten to make sure that his son learned to read and write.

The Fortens sent their son to the small school that had been created for African children by a Quaker, Anthony Benezet. He believed that the only way the Africans would ever take a meaningful place in the colonies would be through education.

Thomas Forten was working on a ship when he fell to his death. James Forten was only seven at the time. His mother was devastated, but still insisted that her son continue school. He did so for two more years, after which he took a job working in a small store.

What James wanted to do was to go to sea. He was fourteen in 1781 when his mother finally relented and gave her permission. America was fighting for its freedom, and James Forten would be fighting, too.

He knew about the difficulties between the British and the American colonists. He had seen first British soldiers and then American soldiers marching through the streets of Philadelphia. Among the American soldiers were men of color.

A black child in Philadelphia in the 1700's had to be careful. There were stories of free Africans being kidnaped and sold into slavery. He had seen the captives on the ships. They looked like him: the same dark skin, the same wide nose; but there was a sadness about them that both touched his heart and frightened him. He had seen Africans in chains being marched through the streets, on their way to the South. He never forgot the sight of his people in bondage, or accepted it as natural that black people should be slaves.

But the black soldiers Forten saw were something special. Marching with muskets on their shoulders, they seemed taller and blacker than any men he had ever seen. And there were African sailors, too. He knew some of these men. They had been fishermen and haulers before the conflict with Great Britain; now they worked on privateers and navy ships. Sometimes he heard talk about naval battles, and he tried to imagine what they must have been like.

In the summer of 1781, James Forten signed onto the privateer *Royal Louis,* commanded by Stephen Decatur, Sr. The colonies had few ships of their own to fight against the powerful British navy and issued "letters of marque" to private parties. These allowed the ships, under the flag of the United States, to attack British ships and to profit from the sale of any vessel captured.

The *Royal Louis* sailed out of Philadelphia in August and was quickly engaged by the British vessel *Active,* a heavily armed brig sent from England to protect its trade ships.

The *Royal Louis*'s guns were loaded with gunpowder that was tamped down by an assistant gunner. Then the cannonball was put into the barrel and pushed against the powder. Then the powder would be ignited. The powder had to be kept belowdecks in case of a hit by an enemy ship. "Powder monkeys," usually young boys between ten and fifteen, carried the powder from below to the guns.

Forten was a powder monkey. Up and down the stairs he raced with the powder as shots from the British ship whistled overhead. There were large holes in the sails and men screaming as they were hit with grapeshot that splintered the sides of the ship. The smell of gunpowder filled the air as Captain Decatur turned his ship to keep his broadside guns trained on the *Active*. Sailors all about Forten were falling, some dying even as others cried for more powder.

Again he went belowdecks, knowing that if a shot ripped through to the powder kegs, or if any of the burning planks fell down into the hold, he would be killed instantly in the explosion. Up he came again with as much powder as he could carry.

After what must have seemed forever with the two ships tacking about each other like angry cats, the *Active* lowered its flag. It had surrendered!

Decatur brought his ship into Philadelphia, its guns still trained on the limping *Active*.

Battle Between John Paul Jones's Bonhomme Richard *and Richard Pearson's* Serapis by B.F. Leizalt, about 1781

The crowd on the dock cheered wildly as they recognized the American flag on the *Royal Louis*. On board the victorious ship James Forten had mixed feelings as he saw so many of his comrades wounded, some mortally.

The *Royal Louis* turned its prisoners over to military authorities. On the 27th of September, the *Active* was sold; the proceeds were split among the owners of the *Royal Louis* and the crew.

The sailors with the worst wounds were sent off to be cared for. The others, their own wounds treated, were soon about the business of repairing the ship. Forten must have been excited. Once the fear of the battle had subsided and the wounded were taken off, it was easy to think about the dangerous encounter in terms of adventure. And they had won.

The missing crew was replaced. The ship was checked carefully by its captain and found to be in fine fighting condition. The crew carried more ammunition aboard, more powder, and fresh provisions. Once more they sailed for open waters.

On the 16th of October, 1781, they sighted a ship, recognized it as British, and made for it instantly. As they neared, a second ship was spotted, and then a third. Decatur turned to escape the trap, but it was already too late. The three British ships, the *Amphyon*, the *Nymph*, and the sloop *Pomona*, closed in. It was soon clear that the *Royal Louis* had two choices: to surrender or to be sunk.

The *Royal Louis* lowered its flag. It had surrendered, and its crew were now prisoners. Forten was terrified. He had heard the stories of the British sending captured Africans to the West Indies to be sold into slavery. He knew the *Pomona* had sailed back and forth from the colonies to the island of Barbados, where many Africans already languished in bondage. It was a time for dread.

James was taken aboard the *Amphyon* with others from his crew. On board the British ship Captain Beasley inspected the prisoners. There were several boys among the American crew, and he separated them from the older men.

Captain Beasley's son looked over the boys who had been captured. Many of them were younger than he was. Although still prisoners, the boys were given more freedom than the men, and Beasley's son saw the Americans playing marbles. He joined in the game, and it was during this playing that he befriended Forten.

The result of this tentative friendship was that Captain Beasley did not, as he might have done, send Forten to a ship bound for the West Indies and slavery. Instead he was treated as a regular prisoner of war and sent to the prison ship the *Jersey*.

Dark and forbidding, the *Jersey* was a sixty-gunner anchored off Long Island, in New York. It had been too old to use in the war and had been refitted first as a hospital ship and then as a ship for

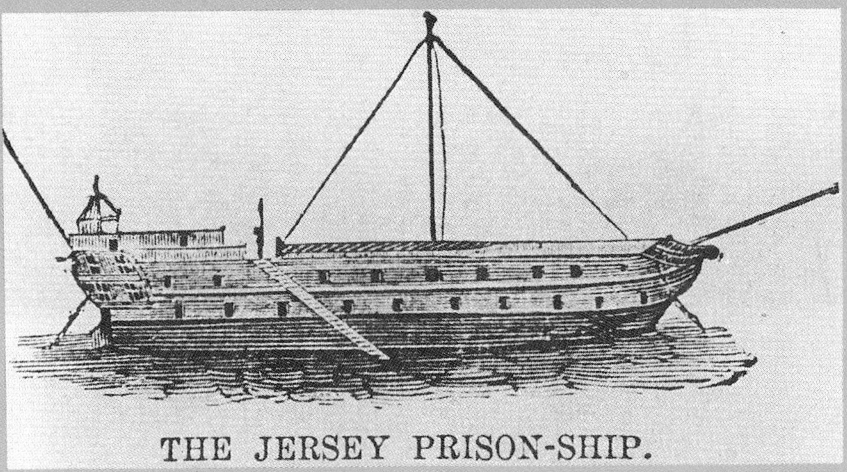
THE JERSEY PRISON-SHIP.

prisoners. The portholes had been sealed and twenty-inch squares carved into her sides. Across these squares iron bars were placed.

The captain of the *Jersey* greeted the prisoners with a sneer. All were searched under the watchful eyes of British marines. The wounded were unattended, the sick ignored. The pitiful cries of other prisoners came from belowdecks. A few pale, sickly prisoners, covered with sores, were huddled around a water cask. Then came the cry that some would hear for months, others for years.

"Down, Rebels, down!"

They were rebels against the king, to be despised, perhaps to be hanged. Traitors, they were being called, not soldiers of America. James was pushed into a line on deck. The line shuffled toward the water cask, where each man could fill a canteen with a pint of water. Then they were pushed roughly belowdecks.

The hold of the ship was dark. What little light there was came from the small squares along the hull. The air was dank as men relieved themselves where they lay. Some of the prisoners were moaning. Others manned pumps to remove the water from the bottom of the boat.

Philadelphia in the 18th Century

Sleep was hard coming, and James wasn't sure if he wouldn't still be sold into slavery. Beasley's son had liked him, he remembered, and the boy had offered to persuade his father to take James to England. It would have been better than the hold of the *Jersey*.

In the morning the first thing the crew did was to check to see how many prisoners had died during the night. Many of the prisoners were sick with yellow fever. For these death would be just a matter of time.

Forten later claimed that the game of marbles with Beasley's son had saved him from a life of slavery in the West Indies. But on November 1, two weeks after the capture of the *Royal Louis*, the news reached New York that Brigadier General Charles Cornwallis, commander of the British army in Virginia, had surrendered to George Washington. Washington had strongly protested the British practice of sending prisoners to the West Indies. It was probably the news of his victory, more than the game of marbles, that saved the young sailor.

James Forten was not a hero. He did not single-handedly defeat the British, or sink a ship. But he fought, like so many other Africans, for the freedom of America, and he fought well. He was only one of thousands of Africans who helped to create the country known as the United States of America.

In Philadelphia, after the war, James Forten became an apprentice to the man his father had worked for, Robert Bridges. Like his father, James was a hard worker. Eventually he would run the business for Robert Bridges, and by 1798 he owned it. At its height the business employed forty workers, both black and white. Forten became one of the wealthiest men in Philadelphia. He married and raised a family, passing on to them the values of hard work he had learned from his father. Forten made several major contributions to the sail-making business, among them a method of handling the huge sails in a shop, which allowed sails to be repaired much faster and saved precious time for shipowners. In the coming years he would use his great wealth to support both antislavery groups and the right of women to vote—at a time when over 90 percent of all Africans in America were still in a state of enslavement.

James Forten became one of the most influential of the African abolitionists. He spent much of his life pleading for the freedom of his people in the country his people had helped to create.

Do you agree with the author that James Forten was not a hero? Do you feel that his life is worth remembering? Explain.

What early home influences probably contributed to James Forten's success later in life?

What special dangers did James Forten face because he was black?

WRITE List several reasons free African Americans might have had for fighting in the Revolutionary War. Then list reasons some might have had for not fighting.

Words About the Author

WALTER DEAN MYERS

Walter Dean Myers may be best known for his fiction books, such as *Fast Sam, Cool Clyde, and Stuff; Mojo and the Russians;* and *The Mouse Rap.* But Myers enjoys writing nonfiction too. "I love doing the research," Myers says. "I enjoy assembling all the pieces of information I find and turning them into a book."

It's not always easy for nonfiction writers to make the various facts they find fit together. Sometimes reference books differ in the dates or places they give for an event. Myers says this was a problem as he was writing *Now Is Your Time!* "I first read about Forten in a book about African American patriots, and it discussed events in Forten's life that happened in 1780. When I tried to verify these facts, I couldn't find anything anywhere to corroborate the material. I was in the library for hours and hours. Finally, I went through newspaper accounts from 1781, and that's where I found the material. The writer was a year off."

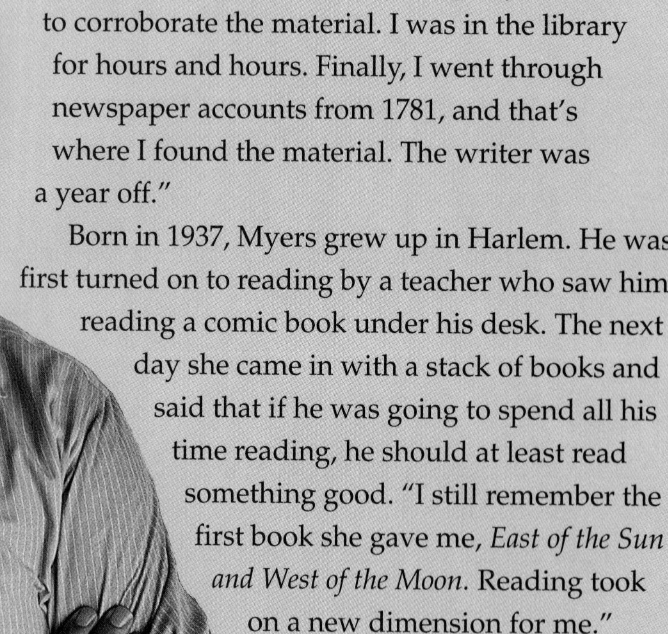

Born in 1937, Myers grew up in Harlem. He was first turned on to reading by a teacher who saw him reading a comic book under his desk. The next day she came in with a stack of books and said that if he was going to spend all his time reading, he should at least read something good. "I still remember the first book she gave me, *East of the Sun and West of the Moon.* Reading took on a new dimension for me."

Revolutionary Times

Abigail Jonas, Paul Revere, and James Forten all believed in the Revolutionary cause. How did each contribute, according to his or her opportunities, to the cause of freedom and independence?

Writer's Workshop

These selections tell about a few of the exciting events that occurred during the American Revolution. Write your own story about an event that takes place during the Revolutionary period. You may portray a historical character such as Paul Revere or a character of your own creation. Do research as necessary to check the historical facts that relate to your story.

Writer's Choice If you could go back in time to a period of United States history, which would you choose? Why? Plan a piece of writing about what you might learn from such a trip. For example, you might want to write a play or a travel journal. Think of a way to share your writing.

IN CONGRESS, JULY

The unanimous Declaration of the thirteen united States

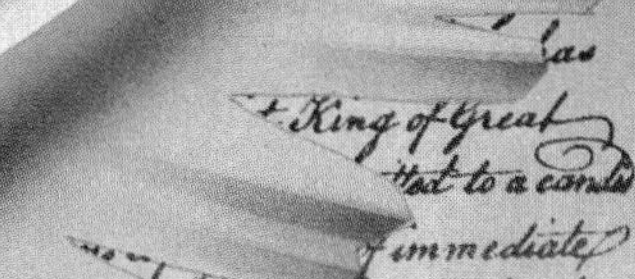

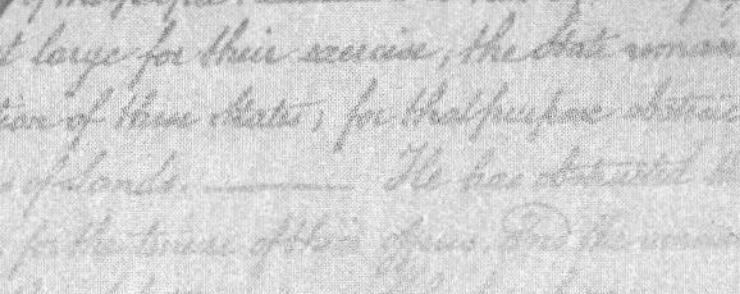

THEME

AMERICAN IDEALS

The United States was founded on the principles and ideals set down in the Declaration of Independence and in the Constitution. As you read about the making of these documents and learn what various people have had to say about the American ideals, you will have the opportunity to examine what these ideals mean to you.

CONTENTS

FROM THE AMERICAN REVOLUTIONARIES:
A HISTORY IN THEIR OWN WORDS, 1750–1800

EDITED BY MILTON MELTZER

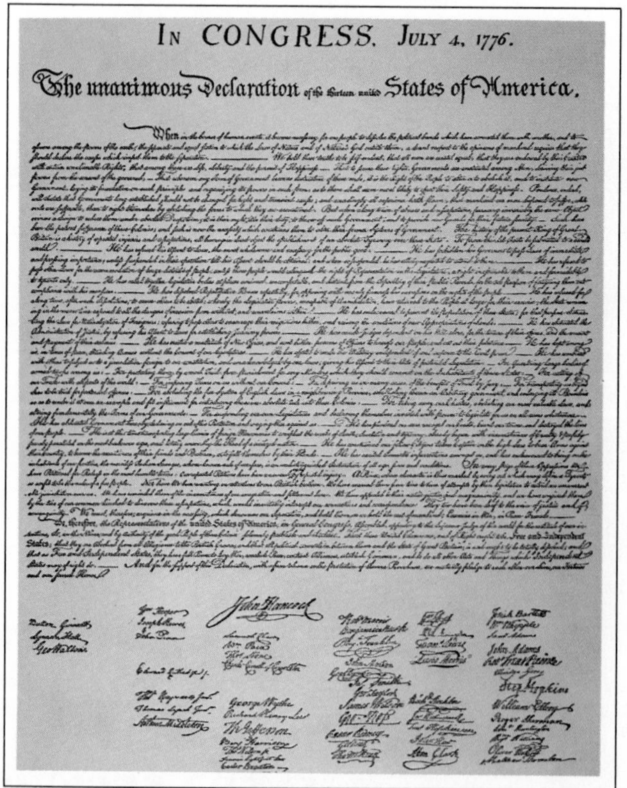

In March 1776 the British shipped out of Boston, taking about a thousand loyalists with them. By May the Continental Congress was using the term "states," not "colonies," and advising the states to establish governments independent of Britain. On June 7, a Virginia delegate introduced an independence resolution in Congress. The delegates debated it for several days, meanwhile appointing a committee to draft a declaration of independence, just in case. On July 2, the Congress resolved "that these United Colonies are, and of right ought to be free and independent states."

It was Thomas Jefferson of Virginia, only thirty-three, who was asked to draft the Declaration of Independence with the helping hands of committee members Benjamin Franklin and John Adams. Jefferson was tall, slender, and red-haired. His shyness made him seem stiff to strangers. He was a brilliant student with an extraordinary range of interests and skills in the arts and sciences. A competent lawyer, he served in the Virginian legislature and the Continental Congress. At this time he was a rising star in Virginia's ruling class. Congress made some further changes in Jefferson's draft, taking out most importantly an attack upon the slave trade, for which the king had been blamed. This deletion was made, said Jefferson at the time, upon the request of South Carolina and Georgia, "who had never attempted to restrain the importation of slaves, and who on the contrary still wished to continue it. Our northern brethren also I believe felt a little tender under those censures, for though their people had very few slaves themselves yet they had been pretty considerable carriers of them to others."

Th Jefferson

On July 4, the Declaration was adopted, and then printed. The text was read aloud to jubilant crowds throughout the states. A year later the country began the now hallowed tradition of celebrating the Fourth of July as Independence Day.

The aim of the Declaration, Jefferson wrote later, was not to say something new. Rather, it was "to place before mankind the common sense of the subject, in terms so plain and firm as to command their assent. . . . Neither aiming at originality of principles nor sentiments, nor yet copied from any particular and previous writing, it was intended to be an expression of the American mind."

The Declaration has a preamble stating the rights at issue, followed by a list of grievances about the infringements upon those rights, and it closes with a mutual pledge to support the steps taken to independence. Here is the text, minus the specific charges against Britain and the king:

When in the course of human events, it becomes necessary for one people to dissolve the political bands which have connected them with another, and to assume among the powers of the earth, the separate

The committee to draw up a Declaration of Independence presents it to the Second Continental Congress in Philadelphia in 1776. In rear center is Thomas Jefferson, handing the draft to John Hancock, seated in the back. Seated in front center is Benjamin Franklin. Standing at left center of the group is John Adams.

and equal station to which the laws of nature and of nature's God entitle them, a decent respect to the opinions of mankind requires that they should declare the causes which impel them to the separation.

The Day We Celebrate (The Fourth of July): American Engraving, 1875

We hold these truths to be self-evident, that all men are created equal, that they are endowed by their Creator with certain unalienable rights, that among these are life, liberty, and the pursuit of happiness.

That to secure these rights, governments are instituted among men, deriving their just powers from the consent of the governed, that whenever any form of government becomes destructive of these ends, it is the right of the people to alter or to abolish it, and to institute new government, laying its foundation on such principles and organizing its powers in such form, as to them shall seem most likely to effect their safety and happiness. Prudence, indeed, will dictate that governments long established should not be changed for light and transient causes; and accordingly, all experience hath shown, that mankind are more disposed to suffer, while evils are sufferable, than to right themselves by abolishing the forms to which they are accustomed. But when a long train of abuses and usurpations, pursuing invariably the same object evinces a design to reduce them under absolute despotism, it is their right, it is their duty, to throw off such government, and to provide new guards for their future security.

Such has been the patient sufferance of these colonies; and such is now the necessity which constrains them to alter their former systems of government. The history of the present king of Great Britain is a history of repeated injuries and usurpations, all having in direct object the establishment of an absolute tyranny over these states. To prove this, let facts be submitted to a candid world. . . .

We, therefore, the representatives of the United States of America, in General Congress, Assembled, appealing to the Supreme Judge of the world for the rectitude of our intentions, do, in the name and by authority of the good people of these colonies, solemnly publish and declare, that these united colonies are, and of right ought to be free and independent states; that they are absolved from all allegiance to the British Crown, and that all political connection between them and the state of Great Britain, is and ought to be totally dissolved; and that as free and independent states, they have full power to levy war, conclude peace, contract alliances, establish commerce, and to do all other acts and things which independent states may of right do. And for the support of this declaration, with a firm reliance on the protection of Divine Providence, we mutually pledge to each other our lives, our fortunes and our sacred honor.

Through this selection, what did you learn about the Declaration of Independence that you did not know before?

Thomas Jefferson described the Declaration of Independence as "an expression of the American mind." Do you think this description still applies today? Explain your response.

Summarize the main argument of the Declaration of Independence.

Write Write a letter to a real or imaginary friend in another country explaining why the Declaration of Independence is such an important document for Americans.

REMEMBER THE LADIES

NOTABLE CHILDREN'S TRADE BOOK IN THE FIELD OF SOCIAL STUDIES

FROM AMERICAN WOMEN: THEIR LIVES IN THEIR WORDS

EDITED BY DOREEN RAPPAPORT

It was the beginning of the American Revolution, and the colonists were challenging the authority of the king of England and fighting for the right to make their own decisions about their lives. Though everyone understood that politics was the business of men, many women, fired by patriotism, rallied to the cause. Banding together, women refused to buy English goods until the Townshend Act of 1767, with its excessive taxes, was repealed. Women joined the "home manufacture" movement, weaving their own cloth, sewing their own clothes, and concocting home brews to replace the "illegally" taxed tea.

When war came, hundreds of women followed their husbands to battle, serving as cooks, bakers, laundresses, and nurses. The women at home kept the farms and businesses going, took care of the children, and worked for the war effort. They collected money for new recruits, sewed clothing for the army, and nursed the sick and wounded. When storekeepers tried to take advantage of the shortage of goods by selling what they had at higher prices, women organized committees to pressure merchants to set fixed prices for all goods. In Boston when a greedy merchant didn't cooperate, the women wheeled him through town, took his keys, and hoisted barrels of coffee out of his warehouse.

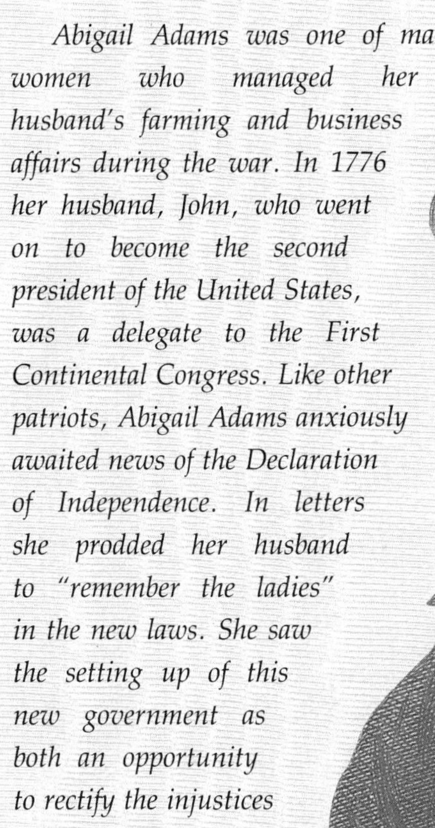

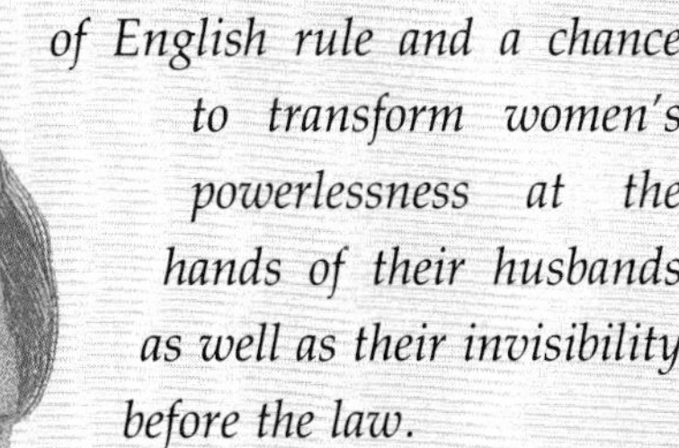

Abigail Adams was one of many women who managed her husband's farming and business affairs during the war. In 1776 her husband, John, who went on to become the second president of the United States, was a delegate to the First Continental Congress. Like other patriots, Abigail Adams anxiously awaited news of the Declaration of Independence. In letters she prodded her husband to "remember the ladies" in the new laws. She saw the setting up of this new government as both an opportunity to rectify the injustices of English rule and a chance to transform women's powerlessness at the hands of their husbands as well as their invisibility before the law.

Molly Pitcher took her husband's place beside the cannon after he suffered heat stroke during the Battle of Monmouth, 28 June 1778.

Braintree, 31 March, 1776

I long to hear that you have declared an independency. And, by the way, in the new code of laws which I suppose it will be necessary for you to make, I desire you would remember the ladies and be more generous and favorable to them than your ancestors. Do not put such unlimited power into the hands of the husbands. Remember, all men would be tyrants if they could. If particular care and attention is not paid to the ladies, we are determined to foment a rebellion, and will not hold ourselves bound by any laws in which we have no voice or representation.

That your sex are naturally tyrannical is a truth so thoroughly established as to admit of no dispute; but such of you as wish to be happy willingly give up the harsh title of master for the more tender and endearing one of friend. Why, then, not put it out of the power of the vicious and the lawless to use us with cruelty and indignity with impunity? Men of sense in all ages abhor those customs which treat us only as the [servants] of your sex; regard us then as being placed by Providence under your protection, and in imitation of the Supreme Being make use of that power only for our happiness.

From John Adams to Abigail Adams, April 14, 1776

As to your extraordinary code of laws, I cannot but laugh. We have been told that our struggle has loosened the bonds of government everywhere; that children and apprentices were disobedient; that schools and colleges were grown turbulent; that Indians slighted their guardians, and negroes grew insolent to their masters. But your letter was the first intimation that another tribe, more numerous and powerful than all the rest, were grown discontented. This is rather too coarse a compliment, but you are so saucy, I won't blot it out. Depend upon it, we know better than to repeal our masculine systems. Although they are in full force, you know they are little more than theory. We dare not exert our power in its full latitude. We are obliged to go fair and softly, and, in practice, you know we are the subjects. We have only the name of masters, and rather than give up this, which would completely subject us to the despotism of the petticoat, I hope General Washington and all our brave heroes would fight.

From Abigail Adams to John Adams, Braintree, 7 May 1776

I cannot say that I think you are very generous to the ladies; for, whilst you are proclaiming peace and good-will to men, emancipating all nations, you insist upon retaining an absolute power over wives. But you must remember that arbitrary power is like most other things which are very hard, very liable to be broken; and, notwithstanding all your wise laws and maxims, we have it in our power, not only to free ourselves, but to subdue our masters, and without violence, throw both your natural and legal authority at our feet.

No one remembered the ladies. The new Constitution [eleven years later] simply ignored them. They remained without public or political power, still legally subject to their husbands. Blacks, Native Americans, and white men who did not own property also were given no rights of citizenship.

Which argument do you find more reasonable, Abigail's or John's? Explain.

Why do you think no one "remembered the ladies" when the Declaration of Independence and the Constitution were written?

How would you describe John Adams's attitude toward his wife's request?

WRITE Would you call the new United States proclaimed by the Declaration of Independence a free country? In a paragraph, explain why or why not.

In May of 1787, Jared Mifflin, a young Philadelphian, is looking forward to a leisurely summer before entering college in the fall. When the Constitutional Convention convenes in Philadelphia's State House, Jared's uncle Thomas Mifflin, one of the delegates, arranges for him to be James Madison's aide. Jared is kept so busy serving Mr. Madison, running errands for the delegates, and trying to keep spectators away from the meetings that he barely has time for courting Hetty Morris, a lovely and talented artist.

Through his work he makes two new friends who open his eyes to other ways of life less fortunate than his own. Henry Blair is a slave who has come with one of the delegates from Georgia and has been working at an inn. William Ellsworth is a British immigrant who arrived in America only to find his uncle in jail for debt. Penniless, he took a job as houseboy for Benjamin Franklin and came to Philadelphia with Dr. Franklin for the Convention. Now, at Jared's suggestion, William plans to work as a courier, distributing copies of the Constitution to the colonies.

After sixteen weeks of deliberation and debate, the Constitution is presented to the delegates for approval. This excerpt from the novel describes the historic occasion.

We, the People of the United States, in order to form a more perfect Union, establish Justice, insure domestic Tranquillity, provide for the common defense, promote the general Welfare, and secure the Blessings of Liberty to ourselves and our Posterity, do ordain and establish this Constitution for the United States of America. . . .

As Secretary Jackson continued to read, Jared stood in the back of the East Room gazing upon the delegates, none of whom moved a hair as they listened to the words they had labored so hard to formulate into a sturdy document. *Another hour or so, and the whole thing will be over,* Jared thought, a tinge of sadness stirring his soul as he realized his unique experience was coming to an end.

The windows of the East Room had finally been opened, allowing an unfamiliar cool breeze to descend upon the delegates at this, their last official meeting.

1787

by Joan Anderson

Jared could hear the stirrings of the crowd now gathering outside. William would be among the crowd, packed and ready to depart, he supposed, the moment he was given copies of the Constitution to deliver. Jared wondered if Hetty was about, ready as ever to capture the departure scene on her sketch pad. Henry had given notice at the Indian Queen a week ago in order to spend his last week of "freedom," as he put it, drinking up city life before returning to Abraham Baldwin's plantation.

"And so, let it be Done," General Jackson began the final phrase that now was familiar to Jared because he had read and reread Uncle Thomas's first draft, ". . . in convention by the unanimous consent of the states present, the seventeenth day of September in the year of our Lord, One Thousand Seven Hundred and Eighty Seven and of the Independence of the United States of America the Twelfth. In witness whereof we have hereunto subscribed our names."

Jared gazed about the room, wondering what would happen next. He focused on General Washington, assuming that he would make the next move. There were some stirrings from the Virginians. *They're probably thinking up last-minute suggestions,* Jared surmised. Suddenly, George Mason asked for the floor. Everyone was sitting on the edge of their chairs.

"Gentlemen," he said in a strong, bold tone, "after much soul-searching I must inform you that since this Constitution does not yet contain a Bill of Rights I cannot, in all good conscience, subscribe to the document that lays waiting."

Jared was stunned. Mr. Mason's attendance during the summer had been almost perfect, and he'd sat on many committees. How could he not sign? No sooner had he taken his seat than Virginia's Governor Randolph rose—to agree with George Mason. "I will gladly present this Constitution to the legislature in Virginia but cannot, at this time, find it in my heart to put name to paper."

Now the room was full of rumblings. Governor Randolph had been one of the early arrivals and the first to speak at the opening of the Convention. He was the one who presented the Virginia Plan, Jared recalled—the paper from which the new Constitution drew some of its ideas! The various states were now huddled together in discussion and General Washington had to bang the gavel several times to bring order to the room. *How many others would follow suit?* Jared wondered.

"I must inform my colleagues that I, too, will not sign this Constitution in its present form," Elbridge Gerry of Massachusetts announced from his seat at the back of the room.

Here we go, Jared thought. *Divisiveness spreading once again from state to state.*

"Mr. President," the voice of Alexander Hamilton rose from the other side of the room. "May I speak?"

Washington nodded, not a trace of emotion on his stoic face.

Jared turned to look at Mr. Hamilton, the man responsible for calling the meeting at Annapolis, where the writing of a Constitution was first discussed. More than anyone else, it seemed that Alexander Hamilton cared about nationhood. He had written numerous articles and papers advocating a strong federal government. Ironically he'd had to endure a delegation that completely disagreed with him throughout this Convention.

"I must express my deepest anxiety that every member should sign," he said with an urgency in his voice. "If a few characters of consequence refuse to sign, their actions could do infinite mischief by kindling latent sparks which lurk under the general enthusiasm for this Constitution." He sat down, but did not take his eyes off Governor Randolph, to whom he was obviously delivering these brief but firmly stated remarks.

There was momentary silence. Jared wished that General Washington would rise and simply commence the signing. Instead, yet another delegate took the floor. *Oh, no,* Jared thought, *another Massachusetts man. Will he also dissent?*

Nathaniel Gorham instead moved that the stipulation for representation in the House be changed from one representative per forty thousand citizens to one per thirty thousand. *How could they change anything now?* Jared wondered, as he gazed over at the beautifully printed pieces of parchment that were spread out on the table. *With this latest diversion, the Convention will surely trail on for days,* he sighed. Knowing how meticulously these men had worked over this document, clause by clause, article by article, Jared resigned himself to the delay and took a seat on the stool provided for him by the door.

Rufus King seconded the motion, and Jared got set to watch yet another debate on representation. But instead, General Washington rose from his seat to make a statement. "Being the presiding member," he informed the group, "I know I am not at liberty to comment one way or

another and have not done so until this moment. However, I must agree with my colleagues," he continued. "It has always appeared to me that an exceptional plan would be to have one representative for every thirty thousand citizens, and it would give me much satisfaction to see it adopted."

That did it. Everyone agreed to vote with the man considered to be the foremost of all Americans. With the representation issue finally put to rest and no one else jumping up with final objections, Dr. Franklin asked for the floor.

Finally! Jared said to himself. *Not many men here are going to disagree with Benjamin Franklin, no matter what he says.*

"Due to a weakened voice, gentlemen," he began, "I have asked my friend James Wilson to read you my sentiments on this momentous day." He nodded for Wilson to begin:

> "Mr. President, I confess that there are several parts of this Constitution which I do not at present approve, but I am not sure I shall never approve them. For having lived a long time, I have experienced many instances of being obliged by better information or fuller consideration to change opinions even on important subjects which I once thought right, but found to be otherwise.
>
> It is, therefore, that the older I grow, the more apt I am to doubt my own judgment, and to pay more respect to the judgment of others.
>
> In these sentiments, sir, I agree to this Constitution with all its faults, if they are such. . . . I doubt, too, whether any other convention we can obtain, may be able to make a better Constitution.
>
> For when you assemble a number of men to have the advantage of their joint wisdom, you inevitably assemble with those men all their prejudices, their passions, their errors of opinion, their local interest, and their selfish views. From such an assembly can a perfect production be expected?
>
> It, therefore, astonishes me, sir, to find this system approaching so near to perfection as it does; and I think it will astonish our enemies. . . .
>
> Thus I consent, sir. I cannot help expressing a wish that every member of the Convention who may still have objections to it, would with me, on this occasion, doubt a little of his own infallibility, and to make manifest our unanimity, put his name to this instrument."

Good old Dr. Franklin! Jared felt like running down the center aisle and giving the man a pat on the back. *No one will dare raise another issue,* he thought, and he was right. General Washington rose almost on cue to suggest that the signing commence.

Jared could hear a pin drop as George Washington stepped slowly off the balcony, where he had been perched for the last one hundred days, and strode toward the table upon which the Constitution lay. "Every king looks like a valet next to Washington," Jared recalled someone saying, *and whoever had said it was right!* he thought as he watched the general cross the room.

The five magnificently printed pieces of parchment had been laid out in a perfect row, their cream color glowing as they rested on the green baize that covered the tabletop.

Shining brightly in the center of the table and casting an occasional reflection about the room was Philip Syng's pen and ink holder. Probably the finest silversmith in all of the thirteen colonies, Mr. Syng had designed the set especially for the signing of the Declaration of Independence. Now, once again, his beautiful piece of craftsmanship would be used to help cement the fate of the new nation.

Jared could hear the scratchy sound of quill sliding across paper as General Washington signed his name.

His signature affixed, the general returned to his seat. *He must feel relief,* Jared thought. *He's been imploring these men to do something to create a stronger government for years.*

Thereafter, each state delegation followed suit. A feeling of utter peace descended on the East Room. Yet, Jared noticed, there seemed to be a sense of sadness registering on many of the faces. Most turned and nodded at Benjamin Franklin before walking back to their respective seats. Perhaps many of the delegates knew they would never again serve with this beloved citizen. Jared also thought that perhaps many realized that this particular group would never again have an opportunity to work together—at least not with the same intensity and certainly not for a cause as worthy as this one.

Over the past one hundred days, Jared had gotten to know these men. He was well aware how important the nation was to each of them. Some had fought in the Revolution, others helped draw up the Articles of Confederation, and still others sat on the Continental Congress. Tom Paine's words came flashing through Jared's head as he watched each

man take his turn signing the document: "Those who expect to reap the blessings of freedom must undergo the fatigue of supporting them."

As the powder was sprinkled over the thirty-ninth signature, the clock struck four o'clock. General Washington exited first as usual, and by the time he reached the Chestnut Street doorway the roar of the crowd had become deafening. It was done.

"Mr. Madison," Jared said, racing down the aisle. He could stay silent no longer. "Congratulations!" he called, interrupting several other well-wishers.

"We did it, my boy, we did it!" Mr. Madison exclaimed with uncharacteristic enthusiasm, clasping Jared's arms as the two shook hands.

"I beg your pardon," Jared said, "but I believe that it is *you*, sir, who did it."

"With your help and the help of those around me. It has been a long summer, Jared, but one I feel this nation shall never forget. And as for you, my boy, I plan to see quite a bit of you in the future, perhaps in our new Congress . . . yes?" he questioned.

"It would be my honor, sir," Jared responded.

"Well, here you go, Jared," Mr. Madison said, lifting the heavy pile of documents that lay on his desk and handing them to Jared. "You know where they must go. It's up to the people now," he said. Jared walked slowly up the aisle. *In my arms I carry the future,* he thought as he reached the familiar East Room doors.

He stopped briefly for one last look, and as he turned to leave bumped straight into William Ellsworth.

"What have you been doing?" William asked. "My horse is getting restless, and so am I for that matter. I want to be the first courier to reach New England, Jared. Hand them over," he said, reaching out for his copies of the Constitution.

"Come on, Jared," he heard Uncle Thomas say. "We've been here long enough, don't you think?" He gave his nephew a customary slap on the back. "I've got to come back here tomorrow and read the thing to the Pennsylvania legislature. Can you believe that?"

"Sorry I won't be here to listen, Uncle," Jared answered, honestly feeling regret. "I'm already two days late for university, you know, and for a few uncertain moments today, I thought I'd be even later. I'd say that was a pretty close call—the signing, I mean."

New York City celebrated the ratification of the Constitution with this parade on July 26, 1788.

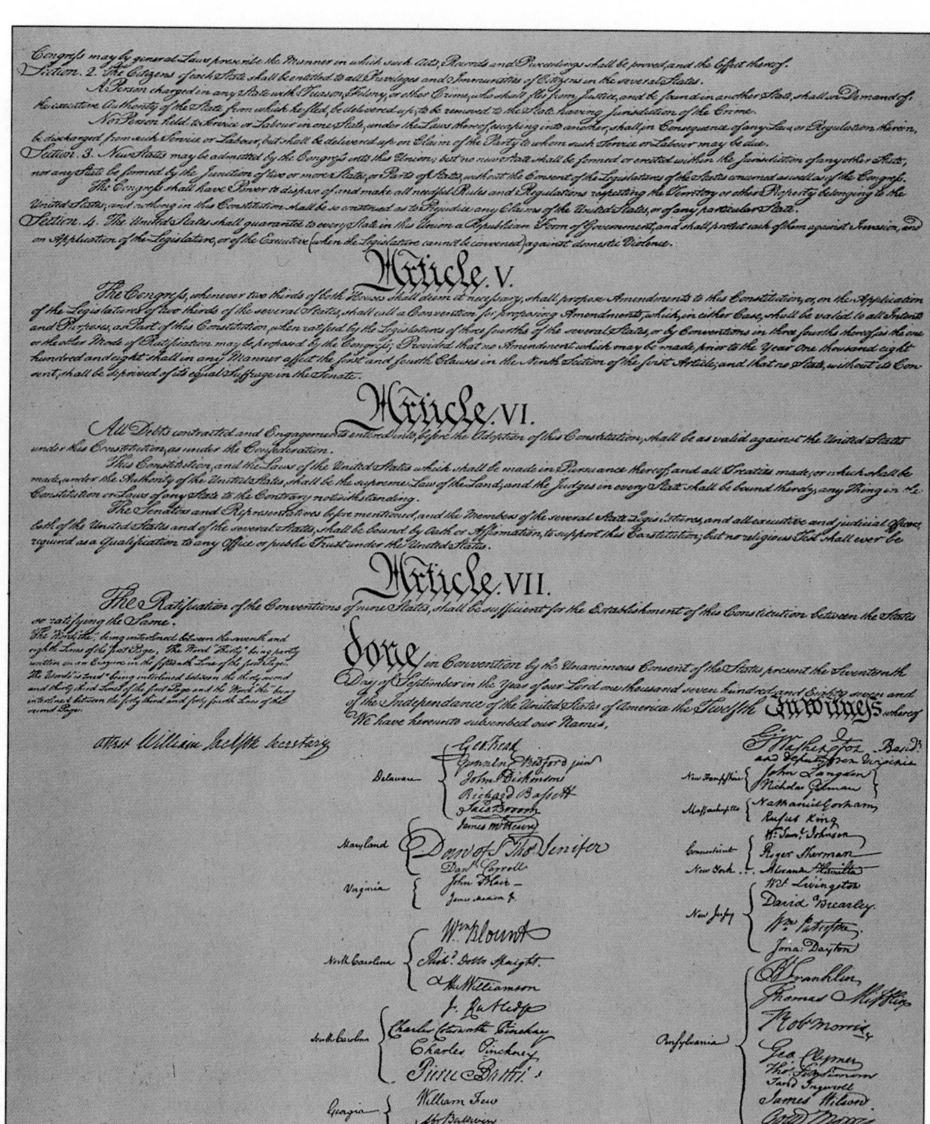

Congress may by general Laws prescribe the Manner in which such Acts, Records and Proceedings shall be proved, and the Effect thereof.

Section. 2. The Citizens of each State shall be entitled to all Privileges and Immunities of Citizens in the several States.

A Person charged in any State with Treason, Felony, or other Crime, who shall flee from Justice, and be found in another State, shall on Demand of the executive Authority of the State from which he fled, be delivered up, to be removed to the State having Jurisdiction of the Crime.

No Person held to Service or Labour in one State, under the Laws thereof, escaping into another, shall, in Consequence of any Law or Regulation therein, be discharged from such Service or Labour, but shall be delivered up on Claim of the Party to whom such Service or Labour may be due.

Section. 3. New States may be admitted by the Congress into this Union; but no new State shall be formed or erected within the Jurisdiction of any other State; nor any State be formed by the Junction of two or more States, or Parts of States, without the Consent of the Legislatures of the States concerned as well as of the Congress.

The Congress shall have Power to dispose of and make all needful Rules and Regulations respecting the Territory or other Property belonging to the United States; and nothing in this Constitution shall be so construed as to Prejudice any Claims of the United States, or of any particular State.

Section. 4. The United States shall guarantee to every State in this Union a Republican Form of Government, and shall protect each of them against Invasion; and on Application of the Legislature, or of the Executive (when the Legislature cannot be convened) against domestic Violence.

Article. V.

The Congress, whenever two thirds of both Houses shall deem it necessary, shall propose Amendments to this Constitution, or, on the Application of the Legislatures of two thirds of the several States, shall call a Convention for proposing Amendments, which, in either Case, shall be valid to all Intents and Purposes, as Part of this Constitution, when ratified by the Legislatures of three fourths of the several States, or by Conventions in three fourths thereof, as the one or the other Mode of Ratification may be proposed by the Congress; Provided that no Amendment which may be made prior to the Year One thousand eight hundred and eight shall in any Manner affect the first and fourth Clauses in the Ninth Section of the first Article; and that no State, without its Consent, shall be deprived of its equal Suffrage in the Senate.

Article. VI.

All Debts contracted and Engagements entered into, before the Adoption of this Constitution, shall be as valid against the United States under this Constitution, as under the Confederation.

This Constitution, and the Laws of the United States which shall be made in Pursuance thereof; and all Treaties made, or which shall be made, under the Authority of the United States, shall be the supreme Law of the Land; and the Judges in every State shall be bound thereby, any Thing in the Constitution or Laws of any State to the Contrary notwithstanding.

The Senators and Representatives before mentioned, and the Members of the several State Legislatures, and all executive and judicial Officers, both of the United States and of the several States, shall be bound by Oath or Affirmation, to support this Constitution; but no religious Test shall ever be required as a Qualification to any Office or public Trust under the United States.

Article. VII.

The Ratification of the Conventions of nine States, shall be sufficient for the Establishment of this Constitution between the States so ratifying the Same.

The Word, "the," being interlined between the seventh and eighth Lines of the first Page, The Word "Thirty" being partly written on an Erazure in the fifteenth Line of the first Page, The Words "is tried" being interlined between the thirty second and thirty third Lines of the first Page and the Word "the" being interlined between the forty third and forty fourth Lines of the second Page.

done in Convention by the Unanimous Consent of the States present the Seventeenth Day of September in the Year of our Lord one thousand seven hundred and Eighty seven and of the Independance of the United States of America the Twelfth In witness whereof We have hereunto subscribed our Names,

Attest William Jackson Secretary

Go. Washington—Presidt. and deputy from Virginia

Delaware: Geo: Read, Gunning Bedford jun, John Dickinson, Richard Bassett, Jaco: Broom

Maryland: James McHenry, Dan of St Thos. Jenifer, Danl Carroll

Virginia: John Blair—, James Madison Jr.

North Carolina: Wm. Blount, Richd. Dobbs Spaight, Hu Williamson

South Carolina: J. Rutledge, Charles Cotesworth Pinckney, Charles Pinckney, Pierce Butler

Georgia: William Few, Abr Baldwin

New Hampshire: John Langdon, Nicholas Gilman

Massachusetts: Nathaniel Gorham, Rufus King

Connecticut: Wm. Saml. Johnson, Roger Sherman

New York: Alexander Hamilton

New Jersey: Wil: Livingston, David Brearley, Wm. Paterson, Jona: Dayton

Pennsylvania: B Franklin, Thomas Mifflin, Robt Morris, Geo. Clymer, Thos. FitzSimons, Jared Ingersoll, James Wilson, Gouv Morris

Page four of the Constitution, 1787

"We knew there would be a few who held back. The way I look at it, it's their loss. It's a good Constitution, my boy, wouldn't you agree?"

Jared nodded as they walked into the bright sunlight. He spotted Hetty and Henry almost immediately. They stood apart from the expectant crowd in the southwest corner.

"Excuse me, Uncle. I have some business to attend to." He bolted through the groups of amassed people just as William was about to mount his horse. "Oh, no you don't," Jared said, grabbing William's arm and dragging him along to see Hetty and Henry.

"Well, it's over. I listened as best I could through the window," Hetty said, pointing to the only window under which there was a stump to stand upon. "By the way, I didn't hear one thing mentioned about the ladies. Did they or did they not talk about the fairer sex in our new Constitution?"

Jared hated to answer her. "I'm afraid I heard nothing," he admitted.

"I thought as much," she replied, a tone of resignation in her voice. "Well, I suppose it gives us something to work for."

"And work you will," William chimed in. "I've met few people with your determination. Jared, I would say you have yourself a mighty strong lady here. You'd best hold on to her—if you can, that is!"

Everyone laughed, including Hetty.

"And Henry, before you even ask," Jared said, "I'm ashamed to say that the delegates devoted only a few lines to the issue of slavery. You opened my eyes to a lot of injustices. All I can say is that if I ever make it to Congress, I hope to change things where your people are concerned. We can't rejoice about liberty and justice, it seems, until those values are granted to every citizen."

What did you learn from this selection about the process of setting up the government for a new country?

How is Jared's observation of the signing of the Constitution different from the account you might read in a history book?

Why do you think Benjamin Franklin's words about the Constitution had such a powerful effect on the delegates?

Do you think the author made Jared be ahead of his time in recognizing certain lacks in the Constitution? Explain your response.

WRITE In a paragraph, explain how the meaning of the opening words of the Constitution—"We, the people"—has changed since the Constitution was adopted.

I HAVE A DREAM

BY MARTIN LUTHER KING, JR.
EXCERPT FROM THE SPEECH GIVEN IN WASHINGTON, D.C.
ON AUGUST 28, 1963

. . . I say to you today, my friends, so even though we face the difficulties of today and tomorrow, I still have a dream. It is a dream deeply rooted in the American dream.

I have a dream that one day this nation will rise up and live out the true meaning of its creed: "We hold these truths to be self-evident; that all men are created equal."

I have a dream that one day, on the red hills of Georgia, sons of former slaves and the sons of former slaveowners will be able to sit down together at the table of brotherhood.

I have a dream that one day even the state of Mississippi, a state sweltering with the heat of injustice, sweltering with the heat of oppression, will be transformed into an oasis of freedom and justice.

I have a dream that my four little children will one day live in a nation where they will not be judged by the color of their skin but by the content of their character.

I have a dream today.

I have a dream that one day, down in Alabama, . . . right there in Alabama, little black boys and black girls will be able to join hands with little white boys and white girls and walk together as sisters and brothers.

I have a dream today.

I have a dream that one day "every valley shall be exalted, every hill and mountain shall be made low, the rough places will be made plains, and the crooked places will be made straight, and the glory of the Lord shall be revealed, and all flesh shall see it together."

This is our hope. This is the faith that I go back to the South with. With this faith we will be able to hew out of the mountain of despair a stone of hope. With this faith we will be able to transform the jangling discords of our nation into a beautiful symphony of brotherhood. With this faith we will be able to work together, to pray together, to struggle together, to stand up for freedom together, knowing that we will be free one day.

And this will be the day. This will be the day when all of God's children will be able to sing with new meaning "My country 'tis of thee, sweet land of liberty, of thee I sing. Land where my fathers died, land of the pilgrim's pride, from every mountainside, let freedom ring."

And if America is to be a great nation this must become true. So let freedom ring from the prodigious hilltops of New Hampshire. Let freedom ring from the mighty mountains of New York. Let freedom ring from the heightening Alleghenies of Pennsylvania!

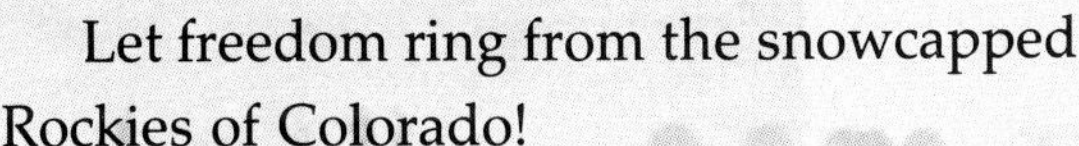

Let freedom ring from the snowcapped Rockies of Colorado!

Let freedom ring from the curvaceous slopes of California!

But not only that; let freedom ring from Stone Mountain of Georgia! Let freedom ring from Lookout Mountain of Tennessee.

Let freedom ring from every hill and molehill of Mississippi. From every mountainside, let freedom ring.

And when this happens, and when we allow freedom to ring, when we let it ring from every village and every hamlet, from every state and every city, we will be able to speed up that day when all of God's children, black men and white men, Jews and Gentiles, Protestants and Catholics, will be able to join hands and sing in the words of that old Negro spiritual, "Free at last! Free at last! Thank God almighty, we are free at last!"

Ever a Seeker

by Carl Sandburg

The fingers turn the pages.
The pages unfold as a scroll.
There was the time there was no America.
Then came on the scroll an early
America, a land of beginnings,
an American being born.
Then came a later America, seeker
and finder, yet ever more seeker
than finder, ever seeking its way
amid storm and dream.

Twilight in the Wilderness 1860, Frederic Edwin Church, 1826–1900, Museum of Art, Cleveland, Ohio

What message about American ideals does Carl Sandburg convey in "Ever a Seeker"? How do you think this message relates to other selections in this section?

WRITER'S WORKSHOP

In "I Have a Dream," Dr. Martin Luther King, Jr., tried to persuade his audience that his dreams for the future could come true. Think about the kind of country in which you can best pursue your dreams for the future. Choose one way in which you would like to see American society change, and write a persuasive essay explaining why this change is needed.

Writer's Choice The word *ideal* implies perfection. Complete the phrase *the ideal* _____ (for example, *sandwich, vacation, friend*); then use your phrase to create a piece of writing. Your writing may be either serious or humorous.

CONNECTIONS

MULTICULTURAL CONNECTION

HARRIET TUBMAN

No ideals were more important in the founding of this nation than those of freedom and equality. And no one fought harder for these ideals than Harriet Tubman.

Tubman was born into slavery on a Maryland plantation about 1821. When she was twenty-eight, she escaped to Philadelphia. At that point, she could simply have enjoyed her newfound freedom. Instead, she dedicated her life to helping other slaves escape.

Tubman became a guide in the Underground Railroad and personally helped more than 300 slaves escape. She once said, "On my Underground Railroad, I never ran my train off the track. And I never lost a passenger."

During the Civil War, Tubman served the Union army as a spy, a scout, and a nurse. She was also the first woman to lead American forces in combat.

Throughout her life, Tubman worked to help African Americans and women achieve equality. By the time of her death at ninety-two, she was known as "the Moses of her People."

Imagine that you are a guide on the Underground Railroad. In a small group, discuss how you would carry out your mission.

Clockwise from top: The Underground Railroad *painted by Charles T. Weber (1825-1911); Harriet Ross Tubman, photo taken by H. B. Lindsley; postage stamp issued in 1978 in honor of Harriet Tubman, designed by artist Jerry Pinkney*

ART CONNECTION

ANALYZE A PAINTING

The painting *The Underground Railroad* shows a scene in which slaves arrive at a farm in Indiana. Examine the painting carefully. Then write a description of what is happening in the painting, telling what each part shows. Finally, tell what thoughts and feelings you have in response to the painting.

LANGUAGE ARTS CONNECTION

WRITE A SCREENPLAY

With a partner, think up a story about the Underground Railroad that would make a good movie. Write down the major events, characters, and settings of your story. Then write one scene for a screenplay of your story, using the format of a play. Include actions and dialogue that will make your scene exciting or emotional. When you've finished, you might enjoy acting out your scene for classmates.

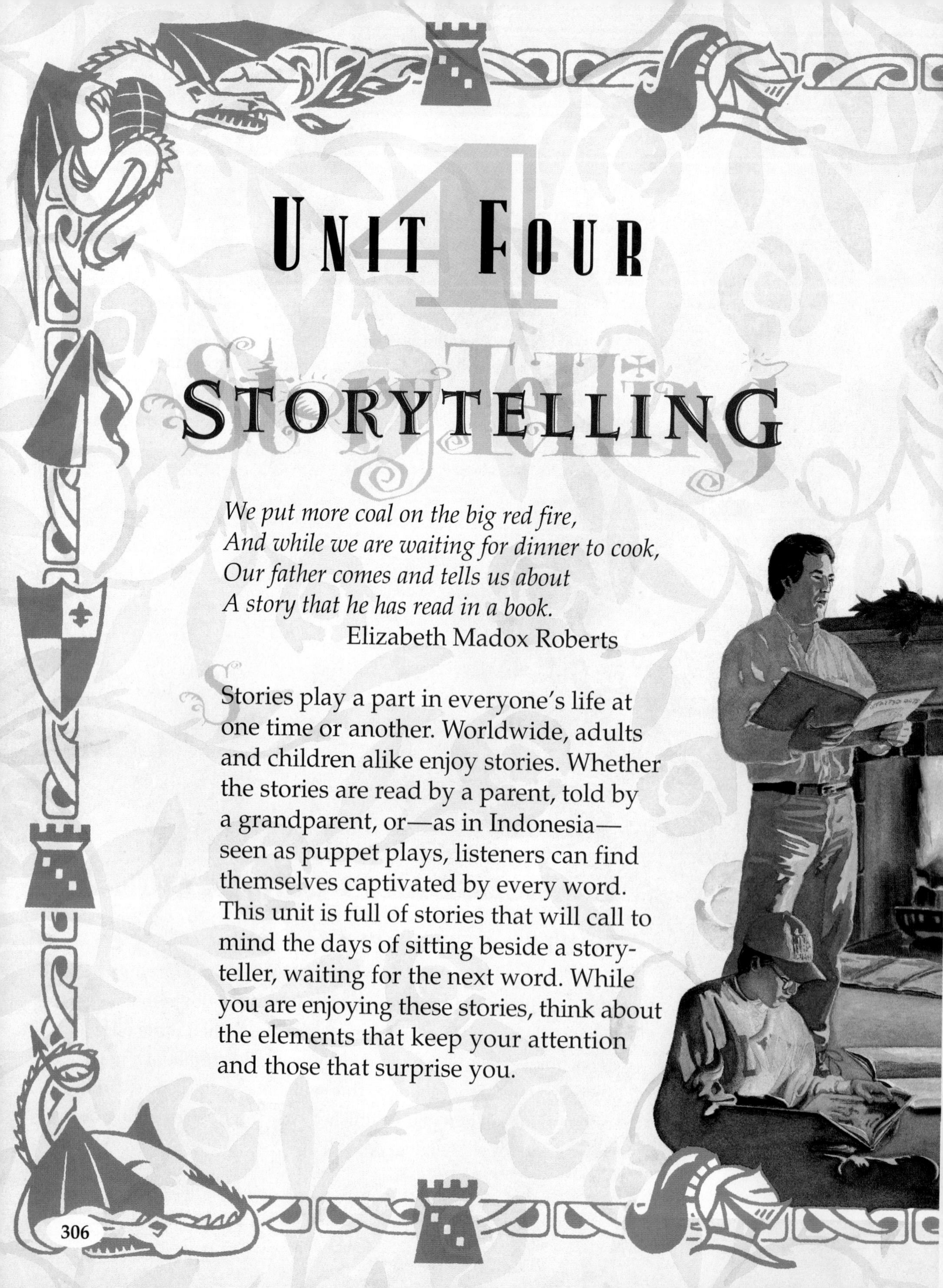

UNIT FOUR

STORYTELLING

We put more coal on the big red fire,
And while we are waiting for dinner to cook,
Our father comes and tells us about
A story that he has read in a book.
Elizabeth Madox Roberts

Stories play a part in everyone's life at one time or another. Worldwide, adults and children alike enjoy stories. Whether the stories are read by a parent, told by a grandparent, or—as in Indonesia—seen as puppet plays, listeners can find themselves captivated by every word. This unit is full of stories that will call to mind the days of sitting beside a storyteller, waiting for the next word. While you are enjoying these stories, think about the elements that keep your attention and those that surprise you.

THEMES

BOOKSHELF

SONG OF THE GARGOYLE

BY ZILPHA KEATLEY SNYDER

After Tymmon's father is abducted, Tymmon is forced to run for his life. Along the way, he meets Troff, who is either a very unusual dog or a gargoyle. Troff's special talents help Tymmon in his adventures.

HARCOURT BRACE LIBRARY BOOK

DEALING WITH DRAGONS

BY PATRICIA C. WREDE

Cimorene, a princess, is bored with her proper and traditional life. She decides to run away and become the princess of a dragon. In the dragon's kingdom, she finds the adventures she longs for.

School Library Journal Best Books of the Year

The Hobbit

BY J. R. R. TOLKIEN

When Bilbo Baggins is chosen by the wizard Gandalf to take part in an adventure, his life changes. In this classic fantasy, Bilbo meets elves, goblins, and dragons as he travels to faraway places.

A Telling of the Tales

BY WILLIAM J. BROOKE

When Paul Bunyan meets Johnny Appleseed, the results are completely unexpected. Familiar tales take odd twists in this wonderful collection.

ALA Notable Book, Children's Choice

Where the Leopard Passes

BY GERALDINE ELLIOT

In these East African folktales, animals such as Nyalugwe the leopard, Kalulu the rabbit, and Njobvu the elephant become involved in some very amusing predicaments and learn some useful lessons.

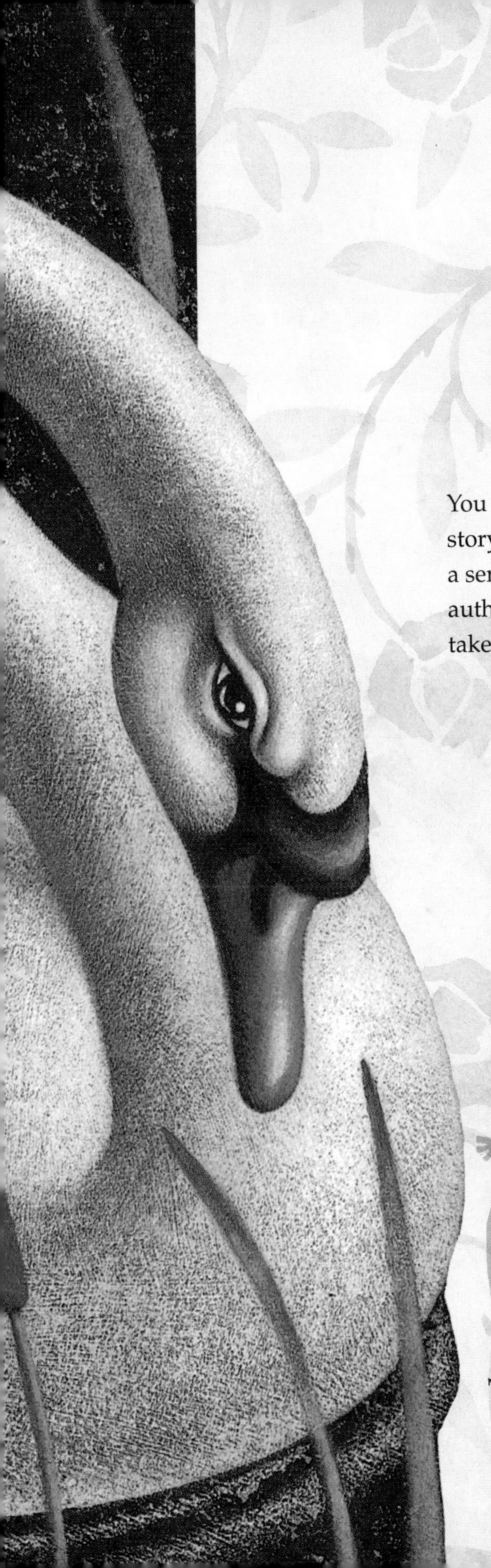

THEME

ONCE UPON A TIME

You would probably agree that the purpose of a story is to give enjoyment, even when the story has a serious meaning. In the following fantasy stories, author Jane Yolen and even some of her characters take a special delight in storytelling.

CONTENTS

Great-Grandfather DRAGON'S TALE

by Jane Yolen

AWARD-WINNING AUTHOR

Illustrated by Martin Springett

— 1 —

"Long, long ago," said the old dragon, and the gray smoke curled around his whiskers in thin, tired wisps, "in the time of the Great-Grandfather of All Dragons, there was no Thanksgiving."

The five little dragons looked at one another in alarm. The boldest of them, Sskar, said, "No Thanksgiving? No feasting? No chestnuts on the fire? Hasn't there always *been a Thanksgiving?"*

The old dragon wheezed. The smoke came out in huge, alarming puffs. Then he started speaking, and the smoke resumed its wispy rounds. "For other animals, perhaps. For rabbits or lions or deer. Perhaps for them there has always been a Thanksgiving."

"Rabbits and lions and deer!" The little dragons said the names with disdain. And Sskar added, "Who cares about rabbits and lions and deer. We want to know about dragons!"

"Then listen well, young saurs. For what was once could come again. What was then could be now. And once there was no Dragons' Thanksgiving."

The little dragons drew closer, testing their claws against the stone floor of the cave, and listened.

Long, long ago *began the old dragon* the world was ice and fire, fire and ice. In the south, great mountains rained smoke and spat flame. In the north, glaciers like beasts crept down upon the land and devoured it.

It was then that the Great-Grandfather of All Dragons lived.

He was five hundred slithes from tip to tail. His scales shimmered like the moon on waves. His eyes were as black as shrouds. He breathed fire storms, which he could fan to flame with his mighty wings. And his feet were broad enough to carry him over the thundering miles. All who saw him were afraid.

And the Great-Grandfather of All Dragons ate up the shaking fear of the little animals. He lived on it and thrived. He would roar and claw and snatch and hit about with his tail just to watch fear leap into the eyes of the watchers. He was mighty, yet he was just one of many, for in those days dragons ruled the earth.

One day, up from the south, from the grassy lands, from the sweet lands, where the red sun pulls new life from the abundant soil, a new creature came. He was smaller than the least of the dragons, not even a slithe and a half high. He had no claws. His teeth were puny and blunt. He could breathe neither fire nor smoke, and he had neither armor to protect himself nor fur to keep himself warm. His legs could only carry him from here—to there. *And the old dragon drew a small line on the rockface with his littlest toenail.*

But when he opened his mouth, the sounds of all beasts, both large and small, of the air and the sea and the sky came out. It was this gift of sound that would make him the new king.

"Fah!" said little Sskar. "How could something that puny be a king? The only sound worth making more than once or twice is this." And he put his head back and roared. It was a small roar for he was still a small dragon, but little as it was, it echoed for miles and caused three trees to wither on the mountain's face. True, they were stunted trees that had weathered too many storms and were above the main tree line. But they shivered at the sound, dropped all their remaining leaves, and died where they stood.

The other little dragons applauded the roar, their claws clacketting together. And one of them, Sskitter, laughed. Her laugh was delicate and high pitched, but she could roar as loudly as Sskar.

"Do not laugh at what you do not understand," said the old dragon. "Look around. What do you see? We are few, yet this new creature is many. We live only in this hidden mountain wilderness while he and his children roam the rest of the world. We glide on shrunken wings over our shrunken kingdom while he flies in great silver birds all over the earth."

"Was it not always so?" asked the smallest dragon, Sskarma. She was shaken by the old one's words.

"No, it was not always so," said the old dragon.

"Bedtime," came a soft voice from the corner. Out from behind a large rock slithered Mother Dragon. "Settle down, my little fire tongues. And you, Grandfather, no more of that story for this night."

"Tomorrow?" begged Sskarma, looking at the old one.

He nodded his mighty head, and the smoke made familiar patterns around his horns.

As they settled down, the little dragons listened while their mother and the old one sang them a lullaby.

"Firelight and firebright,
Bank your dragon flames tonight.
Close your eyes and still your roar,
Sleep is here, my little saur.
Hiss, hiss, hush."

By the time the song was over, all but little Sskar had dropped off. He turned around and around on the cave floor, trying to get settled. "Fah!" he muttered to himself. "What kind of king is that?" But at last he, too, was asleep, dreaming of bones and fire.

"Do not fill their heads with nonsense," said Mother Dragon when the hatchlings were quiet.

"It is not nonsense," said the old dragon. "It is history."

"It is dreams," she retorted. In her anger, fire shot out of her nostrils and singed the old one's nose. "If it cannot feed their bellies, it is worthless. Good night, Grandfather." She circled her body around the five little dragons and, covering them, slept.

The old dragon looked at the six of them long after the cave was silent. Then he lay down with his mouth open facing the cave entrance as he had done ever since he had taken a mate. He hardly slept at all.

— 2 —

In the morning, the five little dragons were up first, yawning and hissing and stretching. They sharpened their claws on the stone walls, and Sskar practiced breathing smoke. None of the others was even close to smoke yet. Most were barely trickling straggles through their nose slits.

It was midmorning before Grandfather Dragon moved. He had been up most of the night thinking, checking the wind currents for scents, keeping alert for dangerous sounds carried on the air. When morning had come, he had moved away from the cave mouth and fallen asleep. When Grandfather awoke it was in sections. First his right foreleg moved, in short hesitations as if testing its flexibility. Then his left. Then his massive head moved from side to side. At last he thumped his tail against the far rocks of the cave. It was a signal the little dragons loved.

Sskarma was first to shout it out. "The story! He is going to tell us the story!" She ran quickly to her grandfather and curled around his front leg, sticking her tail into her mouth. The others took up their own special positions and waited for him to begin.

"And what good was this gift of sound?" asked the old dragon at last, picking up the tale as if a night and half a day had not come between tellings.

"What good?" asked the little dragons. Sskar muttered, "What good indeed?" over and over until Sskitter hit him on the tip of the nose with a claw.

This gift of sound *said Grandfather Dragon* that made the creature king could be used in many ways. He could coax the birds and beasts into his nets by making the sound of a hen calling the cock or a lioness seeking the lion or a bull elk spoiling for a fight. And so cock and lion and bull elk came. They came at this mighty hunter's calling, and they died at his hand.

Then the hunter learned the sounds that a dragon makes when he is hungry. He learned the sounds that a dragon makes when he is sleepy, when he looks for shelter, calls out warning, seeks a mate. All these great sounds of power the hunter learned—and more. And so one by one the lesser dragons came at his calling; one by one they came—and were killed.

The little dragons stirred uneasily at this. Sskarma shivered and put her tail into her mouth once more.

So we dragons named him *Ssgefah,* which, in the old tongue, means enemy. But he called himself Man.

"Man," they all said to one another. "Ssgefah. Man."

At last one day the Great-Grandfather of All Dragons looked around and saw that there were only two dragons left in the whole world—he and his mate. The two of them had been very cunning and had hidden themselves away in a mountain fastness, never answering any call but a special signal that they had planned between themselves.

"I know that signal," interrupted Sskitter. She gave a shuddering, hissing fall of sound.

The old dragon smiled at her, showing 147 of his secondary teeth. "You have learned it well, child. But do not use it in fun. It is the most powerful sound of all."

The little dragons all practiced the sound under their breaths while the old dragon stretched and rubbed an itchy place under his wing.

"Supper!" hissed Mother Dragon, landing on the stone outcropping by the cave mouth. She carried a mountain goat in her teeth. But the little dragons ignored her.

"Tell the rest," pleaded Sskarma.

"Not the rest," said the old dragon, "but I will tell you the next part."

— 3 —

"We must find a young Man who is unarmed," said the Great-Grandfather of All Dragons. "One who has neither net nor spear."

"And *eat* him!" said his mate. "It has been such a long time since we have had any red meat. Only such grasses and small birds as populate tops of mountains. It is dry, ribey fare at best." She yawned prettily and showed her sharp primary teeth.

"No," said the Great-Grandfather of All Dragons. "We shall capture him and learn his tongue. And then we will seal a bargain between us."

His mate looked shocked. Her wings arched up, great ribbed wings they were, too, with the skin between the ribbings as bright as blood. "A bargain? With such a puny thing as Man?"

The Great-Grandfather of All Dragons laughed sadly then. It was a dry, deep, sorrowful chuckle. "Puny?" he said, as quietly as smoke. "And what are we?"

"Great!" she replied, staring black eye into black eye. "Magnificent. Tremendous. Awe inspiring." She stood and stretched to her fullest, which was 450 slithes in length. The mountaintop trembled underneath her magnificently ponderous legs. "You and I," said the Great-Grandfather of All Dragons, "and who else?"

She looked around, saw no other dragons, and was still.

"Why, that's just what you said last night, Grandfather," said little Sskitter.

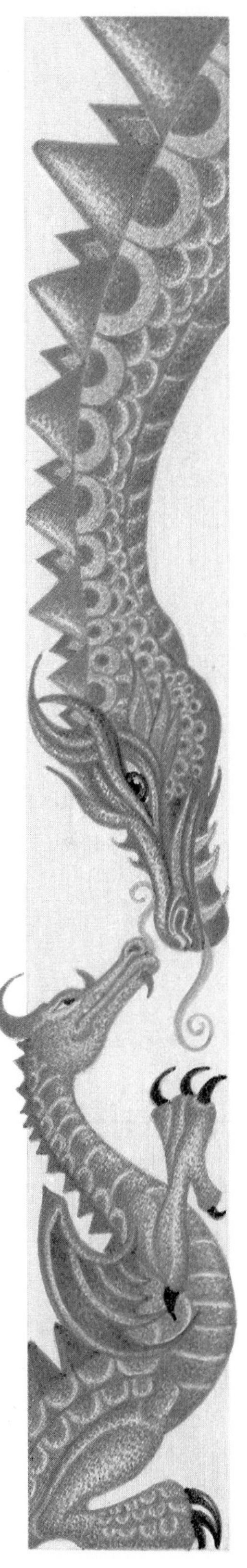

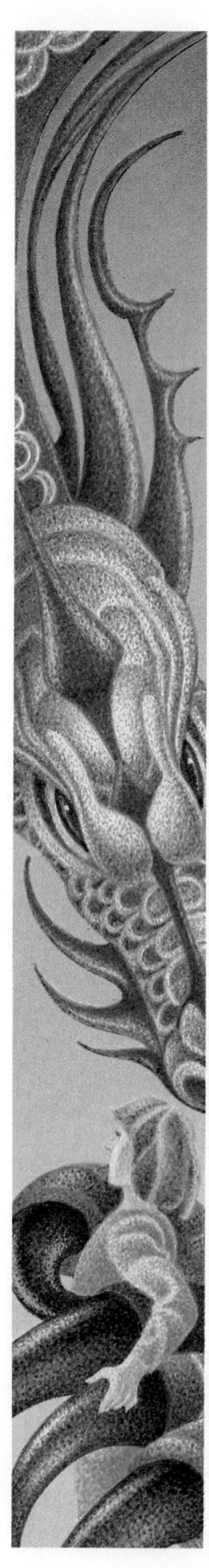

Grandfather Dragon patted her on the head. "Good girl. Bright girl. Perceptive girl."

Sskar drew his claws lazily over the floor of the cave, making awful squeaks and leaving scratches in the stone. "I knew that," he said. Then he blew smoke rings to show he did not care that his sister had been praised.

But the other dragons were not afraid to show they cared. "I remember," said Ssgrum.

"Me, too," said Sstok.

They both came in for their share of praises.

Sskarma was quiet and stared. Then she said, "But more story, Grandfather."

"First comes supper," said Mother Dragon. "Growing bodies need to eat."

This time they all listened.

But when there was not even a smidgeon of meat left, and only the bones to gnaw and crack, Mother Dragon relented.

"Go ahead now," she said. "Tell them a story. But no nonsense."

"This is True History," said Sskitter.

"It's dumb!" said Sskar. He roared his roar again. "How could there be us if they were the last of the dragons?"

"It's a story," said Sskarma. "And a story should be its own reward. I want to hear the rest."

The others agreed. They settled down again around Grandfather Dragon's legs, except for Sskar, who put his back against the old dragon's tail. That way he could listen to the story but pretend not to be interested.

— 4 —

So the Great-Grandfather of All Dragons *began the story once more* flew that very night on silent wings, setting them so that he could glide and catch the currents of air. And he was careful not to roar or to breathe fire or to singe a single tree.

He quartered town after town, village after village, farm after farm all fitted together as carefully as puzzles. And at last he came to a young shepherd boy asleep beside his flock out in a lonely field.

The Great-Grandfather of All Dragons dropped silently down at the edge of the field, holding his smoke so that the sheep—silly creatures—would not catch the scent of him. For dragons, as you know, have no odor other than the brimstone smell of their breath. The black-and-white sheepdog with the long hair twitched once, as if the sound of the Great-Grandfather's alighting had jarred his sleep, but he did not awaken.

Then the Great-Grandfather of All Dragons crept forward slowly, trying to sort out the sight and sound and smell of the youngling. He seemed to be about twelve Man years old and unarmed except for his shepherd's staff. He was fair haired and had a sprinkling of spots over the bridge of his nose that Men call freckles. He wore no shoes and smelled of cheese and bread, slightly moldy. There was also a green smell coming from his clothes, a tree and grass and rain and sun smell, which the Great-Grandfather of All Dragons liked.

The boy slept a very deep sleep. He slept so deeply because he thought that the world was rid of dragons, that all he had to worry about were wolves and bears and the sharp knife of hunger. Yes, he believed that dragons were no more until he dreamed them and screamed—and woke up, still screaming, in a dragon's claw.

Sskar applauded. "I like the part about the dragon's claw," he said, looking down at his own golden nails.

Sskitter poked him with her tail, and he lashed back. They rolled over and over until the old dragon separated them with his own great claws. They settled down to listen.

But when he saw that screaming would not help, the young Man stopped screaming, for he was very brave for all that he was very young.

And when he was set down in the lair and saw he could not run off because the dragon's mate had blocked the door, the young Man made a sign against his body with his hand and said, "Be gone, Worm." For that is how Man speaks.

"Be gone, Worm," Sskitter whispered under her breath.

And Sskarma made the Man sign against her own body, head to heart, shoulder to shoulder. It did not make sense to her, but she tried it anyway.

Sskar managed to look amused, and the two younger dragons shuddered.

"Be gone, Worm," the Manling said again. Then he sat down on his haunches and cried, for he was a very young Man after all. And the sound of his weeping was not unlike the sound of a baby dragon calling for its food.

At that, the Great-Grandmother of All Dragons moved away from the cave mouth and curled herself around the Man and tried to comfort him, for she had no hatchlings of her own yet, though she had wished many years for them. But the Man buffeted her with his fist on the tender part of her nose, and she cried out in surprise—and in pain. Her roar filled the cave. Even the Great-Grandfather closed his earflaps. And the young Man held his hands up over the sides of his face and screamed back. It was not a good beginning.

But at last they both quieted down, and the Manling stretched out his hand toward the tender spot and touched it lightly. And the Great-Grandmother of All Dragons opened her second eyelid—another surprise—and the great fires within her eyes flickered.

It was then that the Great-Grandfather of All Dragons said quietly in dragon words, "Let us begin."

The wonder of it was that the young Man understood.

"My name," he replied in Man talk, in a loud, sensible voice, "is Georgi." He pointed to himself and said "Georgi" again.

The Great-Grandfather of All Dragons tried. He said "Ssgggi," which we have to admit was not even close.

The Great-Grandmother of All Dragons did not even try.

So the youngling stood and walked over, being careful not to make any sudden gestures, and pointed straight at Great-Grandfather's neck.

"Sskraken," roared Great-Grandfather, for as you know a dragon always roars out his own name.

"Sskar!" roared Sskar, shattering a nearby tree. A small, above-the-frost-line tree. The others were silent, caught up in the story's spell.

And when the echo had died away, the youngling said in a voice as soft as the down on the underwing of an owl, "Sskraken." He did not need to shout it to be heard, but every syllable was there. It made the Great-Grandfather shiver. It made the Great-Grandmother put her head on the floor and think.

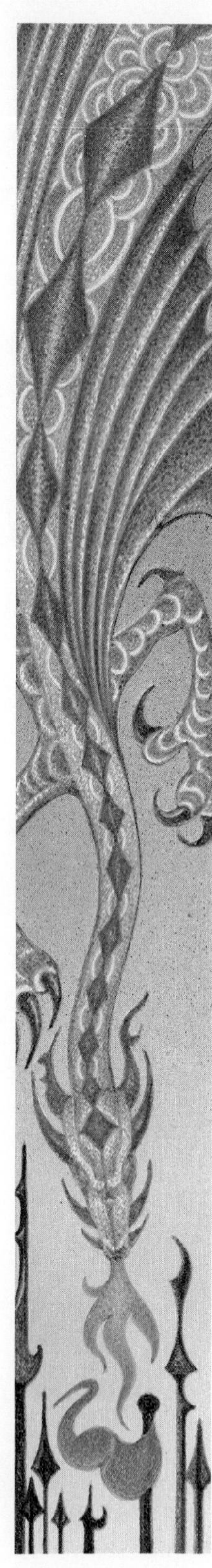

"Sskraken," the youngling said again, nodding as if telling himself to remember. Then he turned to Sskraken's mate and pointed at her. And the pointing finger never trembled.

"Sskrema," she said, as gently as a lullaby. It was the first time in her life that she had not roared out her name.

The youngling walked over to her, rubbed the spot on her nose that had lately been made sore. "Sskrema," he crooned. And to both their astonishments, she thrummed under his hand.

"She thrummed!" said Sskitter. "But you have told us . . ."

"Never to thrumm except to show the greatest happiness with your closest companions," the youngest two recited dutifully.

"So I did," said Grandfather Dragon. With the tip of his tail, he brushed away a fire-red tear that was caught in his eye. But he did it cleverly, so cleverly the little dragons did not notice. "So I did."

"Fah!" said Sskar. "It was a mistake. All a mistake. She never would have thrummed knowingly at a Man."

"That's what makes it so important," answered Sskarma. She reached up with her tail and flicked another tear from the old dragon's eye, but so cleverly the others never noticed. Then she thrummed at him. "Tell us more."

—· 5 ·—

The youngling Georgi lived with the two saurs for a year and a day. He learned many words in the old tongue: "sstek" for red meat and "sstik" for the dry, white meat of birds; "ssova," which means egg, and "ssouva," which means soul. Learning the old tongue was his pleasure, his task, and his gift.

In return, the Great-Grandfather of All Dragons and his mate learned but one word. It was the name of the Man—Georgi. Or as they said it, "Ssgggi."

At the end of the year and a day, the Great-Grandfather called the boy to him, and they walked away from the sweet-smelling nest of grasses and pine needles and attar of wild rose that Georgi had built for them. They walked to the edge of the jagged mountainside where they could look down on the rough waste below.

"Ssgggi," said the Great-Grandfather of All Dragons speaking the one word of Man's tongue he had learned, though he had never learned it right. "It is time for you to go home. For though you have learned much about us and much from us you are not a dragon but a Man. Now you must take your learning to them, the Men, and talk to them in your own Man's tongue. Give them a message from us. A message of peace. For if you fail, we who are but two will be none." And he gave a message to the Man.

Georgi nodded and then quietly walked back to the cave. At his footsteps, the Great-Grandmother of All Dragons appeared. She looked out and stared at the boy. They regarded one another solemnly, without speaking. In her dark eyes the candle flame flickered.

"I swear that I will not let that light go out," said Georgi, and he rubbed her nose. And then they all three thrummed at one another, though the Man did it badly.

Then he turned from the saurs without a further good-bye. And this was something else he had learned from the Great-Grandfather, for Men tend to prolong their good-byes, saying meaningless things instead of leaping swiftly into the air.

"It is their lack of wings," said Sskarma thoughtfully.

Georgi started down the mountain, the wind in his face and a great roar at his back. The mountains shook at his leaving, and great boulders shrugged down the cliff sides. And high above him, the two saurs circled endlessly in the sky, guarding him though he knew it not.

And so the Manling went home and the dragons waited.

"Dragons have a long patience," the two youngest saurs recited dutifully. "That is their genius." And when no one applauded their memories, they clattered their own claws together and smiled at one another, toothy smiles, and slapped their tails on the stone floor.

— 6 —

In Dragon years *continued Grandfather Dragon* it was but an eyelid's flicker, though in Man years it was a good long while.

And then one day, when the bright eye of the sun was for a moment shuttered by the moon's dark lid, a great army of Men appeared at the mouth of the canyon and rode their horses almost to the foot of the mountain.

The Great-Grandmother of All Dragons let her rough tongue lick around her jaws at the sight of so much red meat.

"Sstek," she said thoughtfully.

But the Great-Grandfather cautioned her, remembering how many dragons had died in fights with Men, remembering the message he had sent with the Manling. "We wait," he said.

"I would not have waited," hissed Sskar, lashing his tail.

His sister Sskitter buffeted him on the nose. He cried out once, and was still.

At the head of the Men was one man in white armor with a red figure emblazoned on his white shield.

It was when he saw this that Great-Grandfather sighed. "Ssgggi," he said.

"How can you tell?" asked the Great-Grandmother. "He is too big and too wide and too old for our Ssgggi. Our Ssgggi was this tall," and she drew a line into the pine tree that stood by the cave door.

"Men do not grow as dragons grow," reminded the Great-Grandfather gently. "They have no egg to protect their early days. Their skin is soft. They die young."

The Great-Grandmother put her paw on a certain spot on her nose and sighed. "It is not *our* Ssgggi," she said again. "He would not lead so many Men to our cave. He would not have to wear false scales on his body. He would come to the mountain by himself. I am going to scorch that counterfeit Ssgggi. I will roast him before his friends and crack his bones and suck out the marrow."

Then Great-Grandfather of All Dragons knew that she spoke out of sorrow and anger and fear. He flicked a red tear from his own eye with his tail and held it to her. "See, my eyes cry for our grown-up and grown-away Manling," he said. "But though he is bigger and older, he is our Ssgggi nonetheless. I told him to identify himself when he returned so that we might know him. He has done so. What do you see on his shield?"

The Great-Grandmother rose to her feet and peered closely at the Man so many slithes below them. And those dragon eyes which can see even the movement of a rabbit cowering in its burrow, saw the red dragon crouched on the white shield.

"I can see a mole in its den," said Sskar. "I can see a shrew in its tunnel. I can see . . ."

"You will see very little when I get finished with you if you do not shut up," said Sskitter and hit him once again.

"I see a red dragon," said the Great-Grandmother, her tail switching back and forth with anger.

"And what is the dragon doing?" asked the Great-Grandfather even more gently.

She looked again. Then she smiled, showing every one of her primary teeth. "It is covering a certain spot on its nose," she said.

—· 7 ·—

Just then the army stopped at a signal from the white knight. They dismounted from their horses and waited. The white knight raised his shield toward the mountain and shouted. It took a little while for his voice to reach the dragons, but when it did, they both smiled, for the white knight greeted them in the old tongue.

He said: "I send greetings. I am Ssgggi, the dragon who looks like a Man. I am taller now, but nowhere near as tall as a dragon. I am wiser now, but nowhere near as wise as a dragon. And I have brought a message from Men."

"Of course they did not trust him. Not a Man," hissed Sskar.

"They trusted this Man," said Sskitter. "Oh I know they did. I know I do."

Sşkarma closed her eyes in thought. The other two little dragons were half asleep.

Grandfather Dragon did not answer their questions, but let the story answer the questions for him.

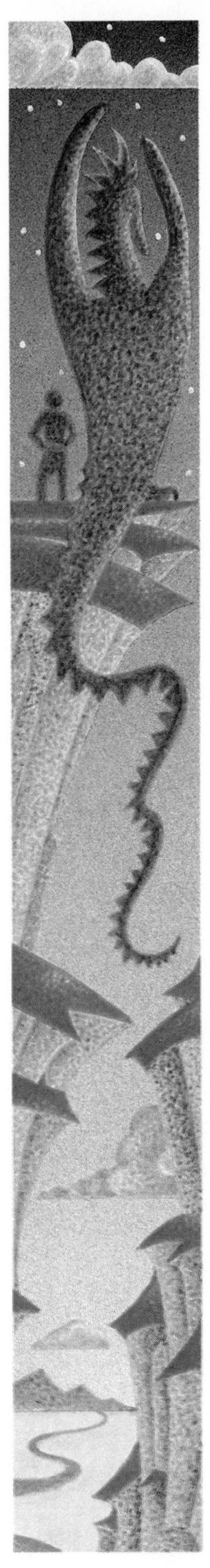

The Great-Grandfather of All Dragons stretched and rose. He unfurled his wings to their farthest point and opened his mouth and roared out gout after gout of flames. All the knights save the white knight knelt in fear then. And then Great-Grandfather pumped his wings twice and leaped into the air. Boulders buffeted by the winds rolled down the mountainside toward the Men.

The Great-Grandmother followed him, roaring as she flew. And they circled around and around in a great, widening gyre that was much too high for the puny Man arrows to reach.

Then the white knight called on all his archers to put down their bows, and the others to put aside their weapons. Reluctantly they obeyed, though a few grumbled angrily and they were all secretly very much afraid.

When the white knight saw that all his knights had disarmed themselves, the white knight held his shield up once more and called out "Come, Worm" in his own tongue. He made the Man sign again, head to heart, shoulder to shoulder. At that signal, the Great-Grandfather of All Dragons and his mate came down. They crested a current of air and rode it down to the knight's feet.

When they landed, they jarred nearly fifty slithes of earth, causing several of the Men to fall over in amazement or fear or from the small quaking of the ground. Then they lowered their heads to Ssgggi.

And the Man walked over to them, and first to the Great-Grandmother and then to the Great-Grandfather he lifted his fist and placed it ever so gently on a certain spot on the nose.

The Great-Grandmother thrummed at this. And then the Great-Grandfather thrummed as well. And the white knight joined them. The two dragons' bodies shook loud and long with their thrumming. And the army of Men stared and then laughed and finally cheered, for they thought that the Great-Grandparents were afraid.

"Afraid? Afraid of puny Men? They were shaking because they were thrumming. Only lower *animals like rabbits and lions and deer—and Men—shake when they are afraid. I'll show them afraid!" cried Sskar. He leaped into the air and roared so hard that this time real flames came out of*

his nose slits, which so surprised him that he turned a flip in the air and came back to earth on his tailbone, which hurt enormously.

Grandfather Dragon ignored him, and so did the other little dragons. Only Mother Dragon, from her corner in the cave, chuckled. It was a sound that broke boulders.

Sskar limped back proudly to his grandfather's side, eager to hear the rest of the story. "I showed them, didn't I?" he said.

—- *8* -—

"Hear this," said the white knight Georgi, first in Man talk and then in the old tongue so that the dragons could understand as well. "From now on dragons shall raid no Man lands, and Men shall leave dragons alone. We will not even recognize you should we see you. You are no longer real to us.

"In turn, dragons will remain here, in this vast mountain wilderness untouched by Men. You will not see us or prey on us. You will not even recognize us. We are no longer real to dragons."

Great-Grandfather roared out his agreement, as did Great-Grandmother. Their roaring shattered a small mountain, which, to this day, Men call Dragon Fall. Then they sprang up and were gone out of the sight of the army of Men, out of the lives of Men.

"Good," said Sskar. "I am glad they are out of our sight and out of our lives. Men are ugly and unappetizing. We are much better off without them." He stretched and curled and tried to fall asleep. Stories made him feel uncomfortable and sleepy at the same time.

But Sskitter was not happy with the ending. "What of Ssgggi?" she said. "Did they ever see him again? Of all Men, he was my favorite."

"And what of the Dragons' Thanksgiving?" said the littlest two, wide awake now.

Sskarma was silent, looking far out across the plains, across to Dragon's Fall, where the boulders lay all in a jumble.

Grandfather touched Sskarma's shoulder gently. "There is more," he said.

She turned her head to look at him, her black eyes glistening. "I know," she said. "Ssgggi came back. He would have to. He loved them so. And they loved him."

Grandfather shook his head. "No," he said. "He never came back. He could not. Dragons no longer existed for him, except in his heart. Did not exist for him—or for any Men. Of course," Grandfather added, "Men still exist for us. We do not have Man's gift of tongue or of the imagination. What is—for dragons—is. We cannot wish it away. We cannot make the real unreal, or the unreal real. I envy Man this other gift."

Sskarma closed her eyes and tried not to cry. "Never?" she said softly. "He never came back? Then how could there have been a Thanksgiving?"

Dragons keep promises *Grandfather continued,* for they do not have the imagination to lie. And so Great-Grandfather and Great-Grandmother and all their children, for they finally had many, and their children's children never bothered Men again. And, since Men did not believe Dragons existed, Men did not bother Dragons. That is what dragons give thanks for. In fact, Men believed that Saint George—as they called him in later years—had rid them forever of Dragons.

And so things have stood to this very day.

—· 9 ·—

Mother Dragon rose at the story's end. "You have a Man's imagination, old one, though you deny it. You have a gift for making up stories, which is another way of saying you lie. Sometimes I think you are more Man than dragon."

"I tell the truth," growled the old dragon. "This is dragon history." Huffily, he cleaned his front claws.

"It is true that the word history *contains the word* story*," said Mother Dragon. "But that is the only thing I will admit."*

Grandfather Dragon houghed, and the smoke straggled out of his nose slits.

"And now if we are to have a real old-fashioned Dragon Thanksgiving, to celebrate the end of stories and the beginning of food, I will have to go hunting again," said Mother Dragon. "A deer I think. I saw a fat herd by Dragon's Fall, grazing on the sweet spring grass."

"May I come?" asked Sskar.

Mother Dragon smiled and groomed his tail for him. "Now that you have real flames you may."

"The others and I will gather chestnuts," said Grandfather. "For the celebration. For Thanksgiving."

Sskarma shook her head. "I would like to stay behind and clean the cave."

The others left without an argument. No one liked to clean the cave, sweeping the bones over the side of the cliff. Mother Dragon and Sskar rose into the air, banked to the left, and winged out of sight so that they could approach the Fall from downwind. Grandfather Dragon and the three young dragons moved slowly along the deeply rutted mountain path.

Sskarma waited until they had all left; then she went out and looked at the great old pine tree that grew near the cave mouth. About five slithes up was a slash of white, the mark left by a dragon nail, a slash they all called Ssgggi's mark. *She looked at it for a long time and calculated how quickly trees grow. Then she stood up alongside the tree. The mark came up to her shoulder.*

"Ssgggi," she said. Then she said it three more times. The fourth time she said it, it came out "Georgi."

"Georgi," she said a fifth time. This time it sounded right. Smiling quietly to herself, Sskarma glanced around the wilderness and then once into the sky. Far away she could see one of the great silver birds Grandfather always warned them about. "Georgi," she said, and went back in to clean the cave.

Did you feel sympathy for the dragons in the story? Why or why not?

Do you think the dragons have a good reason to celebrate Thanksgiving? Explain your answer.

Why do you think Grandfather Dragon insists on finishing the story for the little dragons?

Why do men exist for dragons while dragons no longer exist for men?

WRITE Grandfather Dragon says that he envies man's gift of imagination. Do you think imagination is a valuable gift? Explain your answer in a paragraph.

AWARD-WINNING AUTHOR

AN INTERVIEW WITH THE AUTHOR

Jane Yolen

Jane Yolen was born in New York City and grew up in a family of writers and storytellers. Here, writer Ilene Cooper and Jane Yolen discuss the importance of storytelling and how it helped her become a successful writer.

MS. COOPER: Storytelling is a tradition in your family, isn't it?

MS. YOLEN: Yes. All my aunts and uncles are great storytellers, and I understand my great-grandfather was a storyteller in his small town in Russia. He owned an inn, so perhaps he had a captive audience—no room or meal unless you listened to his tales.

MS. COOPER: What kind of stories did you hear growing up?

MS. YOLEN: I didn't hear story stories, I heard family stories which were wild and woolly and which I'm beginning to collect now.

MS. COOPER: Would you share one?

MS. YOLEN: My favorite is about Uncle Louie, who was a scamp and a scoundrel. He was sent away to military school to be shaped up, but he gambled away the gold buttons on his uniform. Dismissed from school, he was sent home, but he never arrived. This was in Russia, during a long and cold winter, and my poor grandmother was distraught worrying about Louie. She had seven other children, but he was her firstborn. One day, when it was near spring, but not quite, she looked out the window and there was Louie coming down the street followed by twelve Chinese acrobats. He had run away and joined the circus! When things got bad, he brought the acrobats home because he knew his mother would feed them.

MS. COOPER: That's a wonderful story. If young people are interested in storytelling, I would imagine the first thing they should do is listen to the stories being told in their own homes.

MS. YOLEN: Family stories are some of the first things you can hear, but there are also the old, old stories—myths, legends, and fairy tales that we can read in books. Of course, it is even better if you hear them. There are many people today, myself included, who tell stories. Sometimes it's in traditional settings like libraries, schools, bookstores; sometimes it's outside or at storytelling festivals.

MS. COOPER: When did you start to tell stories?

MS. YOLEN: Professionally, I began as a writer, not a storyteller; but personally, I started young. I was telling stories to my brother and at summer camp to the other kids. I was always making up stories.

MS. COOPER: Did you read a lot?

MS. YOLEN: Yes, I read a lot of myths and fairy tales, and I think if you read enough of that kind of thing, it takes over. You begin thinking that way. There have been studies that show that children who hear stories when they are very young have an almost intuitive grasp of language and logic, because stories do have logic to them. You don't live happily ever after until you've followed the proper path.

MS. COOPER: What are some of the enduring themes of myth and folklore, and how do they affect us?

MS. YOLEN: There are many stories about finding true love, and the lengths people will go to to do that. There are warning tales—watch out for the stranger. Some stories carry history, like those about King Arthur. There's the tradition of loyalty unto death and being

restored when you show loyalty. A strong theme that runs through stories is the Golden Rule, or loving kindness. Interestingly, often the stories have strange messages. Take "Rumpelstiltskin." A father asks his daughter to deceive the king; she in turns tries to deceive the person she has struck a deal with. The only person who tells the truth is Rumpelstiltskin, and look what happens to him.

MS. COOPER: There has been controversy about the role of women in folklore. They always seem to be waiting around for their prince to come and rescue them.

MS. YOLEN: There are also many stories where the girl or princess takes quite an active role. In the original Cinderella story, she went out and got her prince for herself. One reason the stories seem to have weak heroines is that folklore really began to be collected during Victorian times. These early collectors would adapt the stories to reflect their society. So they deliberately chose stories where women were not portrayed as strong, or in some cases, they changed the stories to fit their own moral standards. Women in the late nineteenth century were perceived as being sweet and helpless, so that's the way they appeared in the stories.

MS. COOPER: When you go to write an original story, where do you come up with your ideas?

MS. YOLEN: I've read so many things now, I don't know where some of the ideas originate. When I wrote *The Girl Who Cried Flowers,* the impetus came from a picture by Botticelli called *Primavera* or *Spring,* in which Spring has flowers coming from her mouth. I wanted to write about that picture, but when I sat down to do it, I had just written a story in which a girl spoke in slivers of ice. From my knowledge of folklore, I knew that there was a history of stories in which women cried pearls

and diamonds, so I came up with the idea for a girl crying flowers.

MS. COOPER: What about "Great-Grandfather Dragon's Tale"?

MS. YOLEN: I love dragons, I love writing about them. The dragon story everyone knows, of course, is St. George and the dragon. It occurred to me, when I was doing some research for a speech, that dragons have a point of view, too. I wrote this and it just kept getting longer and longer.

MS. COOPER: You write so many different kinds of things. How do you decide what you are going to work on?

MS. YOLEN: I just write what feels right at the moment. Sometimes it is realistic, sometimes fantasy, sometimes poetry or science fiction. When young people ask me how I keep it all straight, I say look at the average school day. You do math for an hour, English for an hour, and you don't feel like you should be conjugating verbs when you're doing social studies.

MS. COOPER: Do you think it's strange that in this age of television, when so much of the emphasis is on visual images, storytelling would be making a comeback?

MS. YOLEN: I think storytelling is making a comeback almost in response to television. Kids are programmed to sitting in front of a set, but sitting in front of a storyteller is different. The storyteller makes an immediate adjustment during the telling to his or her audience. The storyteller can speed the story up or slow it down, which of course television can't. People, whether adults or children, respond to a personal telling. After all, storytelling has been around for thousands of years. It's what makes us human. It distinguishes us from the animals.

The Girl Who Cried Flowers
and Other Tales
Jane Yolen
illustrated by David Palladini

The Girl Who Cried Flowers

Golden Kite Award

by **Jane Yolen**

illustrated by **David Palladini**

In ancient Greece, where the spirits of beautiful women were said to dwell in trees, a girl was born who cried flowers. Tears never fell from her eyes. Instead blossoms cascaded down her cheeks: scarlet, gold, and blue in the spring, and snow-white in the fall.

No one knew her real mother and father. She had been found one day wrapped in a blanket of woven grasses in the crook of an olive tree. The shepherd who found her called her Olivia after the tree and brought her home to his childless wife. Olivia lived with them as their daughter, and grew into a beautiful girl.

At first her strangeness frightened the villagers. But after a while, Olivia charmed them all with her gentle, giving nature. It was not long before the villagers were showing her off to any traveler who passed their way. For every stranger, Olivia would squeeze a tiny tear-blossom from her eyes. And that is how her fame spread throughout the land. But soon a tiny tear-blossom was not enough. Young men wanted nosegays to give to the girls they courted. Young women wanted garlands to twine in their hair. The priests asked for bouquets to bank their altars. And old men and women begged funeral wreaths against the time of their deaths.

To all these requests, Olivia said yes. And so she had to spend her days thinking sad thoughts, listening to tragic tales, and crying mountains of flowers to make other people happy. Still, she did not complain, for above all things Olivia loved making other people happy—even though it made her sad.

Then one day, when she was out in her garden looking at the far mountains and trying to think of sad things to fill her mind, a young man came by. He was strong enough for two, but wise enough to ask for help when he needed it. He had heard of Olivia's magical tears and had come to beg a garland for his own proud sweetheart.

But when he saw Olivia, the thought of his proud sweetheart went entirely out of the young man's mind. He sat down by Olivia's feet and started to tell her tales, for though he was a farmer, he had the gift of telling that only true storytellers have. Soon Olivia was smiling, then laughing in delight, as the tales rolled off his tongue.

"Stop," she said at last. "I do not even know your name."

"I am called Panos," he said.

"Then, Panos, if you must tell me tales—and indeed I hope you never stop—tell me sad ones. I must fill myself with sorrow if I am to give you what you want."

"I want only you," he said, for his errand had been long forgotten. "And that is a joyous thing."

For a time it was true. Panos and

Olivia were married and lived happily in a small house at the end of the village. Panos worked long hours in the fields while Olivia kept their home neat and spotless. In the evenings they laughed together over Panos' stories or over the happenings of the day, for Panos had forbidden Olivia ever to cry again. He said it made him sad to see her sad. And as she wanted only to make him happy, Olivia never let even the smallest tear come to her eyes.

But one day, an old lady waited until Panos had gone off to the fields and then came to Olivia's house to borrow a cup of oil.

"How goes it?" asked Olivia innocently, for since her marriage to Panos, she had all but forsaken the villagers. And indeed, since she would not cry flowers for them, the villagers had forsaken her in return.

The old lady sighed. She was fine, she explained, but for one small thing. Her granddaughter was being married in the morning and needed a crown of blue and gold flowers. But, the crafty old lady said, since Olivia was forbidden to cry any more blossoms her granddaughter would have to go to the wedding with none.

"If only I could make her just one small crown," thought Olivia. She became so sad at the thought that she could not give the girl flowers without hurting Panos that tears came unbidden to her eyes. They welled up, and as they started down her cheeks, they turned to petals and fluttered to the floor.

The old lady quickly gathered up the blossoms and, without a word more, left for home.

Soon all the old ladies were stopping by for a cup of oil. The old men, too, found excuses to stray by Olivia's door. Even the priest paid her a call and, after telling Olivia all the troubles of the parish, left with a bouquet for the altar of his church.

All this time Panos was unaware of what was happening. But he saw that Olivia was growing thin, that her cheeks were furrowed, and her eyes rimmed with dark circles. He realized that she barely slept at night. And so he tried to question her.

"What is it, dear heart?" he asked out of love.

But Olivia did not dare answer.

"Who has been here?" he roared out of fear.

But Olivia was still. Whatever she answered would have been wrong. So she turned her head and held back the tears just as Panos wished, letting them go only during the day when they would be useful to strangers.

One day, when Olivia was weeping a basket full of Maiden's Breath for a wedding, Panos came home unexpectedly from the fields. He stood in the doorway and stared at Olivia who sat on the floor surrounded by the lacy blossoms.

Panos knew then all that had happened. What he did not know was why. He held up his hands as if in prayer, but his face was filled with anger. He could not say a word.

Olivia looked at him, blossoms streaming from her eyes. "How can I give you what you want?" she asked. "How can I give *all* of you what you want?"

Panos had no answer for her but the anger in his face. Olivia jumped up and ran past him out the door.

All that day Panos stayed in the house. His anger was so fierce he could not move. But by the time evening came, his anger had turned to sadness, and he went out to look for his wife.

Though the sun had set, he searched for her, following the trail of flowers. All that night the scent of the blossoms led him around the village and through the olive groves. Just as the sun was rising, the flowers ended at the tree where

Olivia had first been found.

Under the tree was a small house made entirely of flowers, just large enough for a single person. Its roof was of scarlet lilies and its walls of green ivy. The door was blue Glory-of-the-snow and the handle a blood-red rose.

Panos called out, "Olivia?" but there was no answer. He put his hand to the rose handle and pushed the door open. As he opened the door, the rose thorns pierced his palm, and a single drop of his blood fell to the ground.

Panos looked inside the house of flowers, but Olivia was not there. Then he felt something move at his feet, and he looked down.

Where his blood had touched the ground, a small olive tree was beginning to grow. As Panos watched, the tree grew until it pushed up the roof of the house. Its leaves became crowned with the scarlet lilies. And as Panos looked closely at the twisted trunk of the tree, he saw the figure of a woman.

"Olivia," he cried, for indeed it was she.

Panos built a small hut by the tree and lived there for the rest of his life. The olive tree was a strange one, unlike any of the others in the grove. For among its branches twined every kind of flower. Its leaves were covered with the softest petals: scarlet, gold, and blue in the spring, and snow-white in the fall. There were always enough flowers on the tree for anyone who asked, as well as olives enough for Panos to eat and to sell.

It was said by the villagers—who guessed what they did not know—that each night a beautiful woman came out of the tree and stayed with Panos in his hut until dawn.

When at last Panos grew old and died, he was buried under the tree. Though the tree grew for many years more, it never had another blossom. And all the olives that it bore from then on were as bitter and salty as tears.

Do you feel satisfied with the ending of this story, or do you wish it had ended differently? Explain.

Who do you think is to blame for Olivia's fate? Explain your response.

WRITE Do you think that a gift can be good and bad at the same time? Explain your answer in a paragraph.

Once upon a Time

What elements of fantasy do you find in the settings, the characters, and the plots of these two stories by Jane Yolen?

Writer's Workshop

Think of a place that you might use as the setting for a fantasy story. It might be a woods, your school, or even your bedroom. Does it look familiar—but with a few surprises? Write a description of the place that will make those who read your writing see it clearly in their mind's eye.

Writer's Choice *Once upon a time* makes a wonderful beginning! Write three different sentences that begin with those words. Choose the sentence that you like the best, and expand on that sentence. For example, you might want to use it to start a fantasy story or a fairy tale.

THEME

TRADITIONAL TALES

All cultures have stories that have been passed down from generation to generation, often changing as they are retold or written down. The next selections illustrate the variety of traditional stories that continue to be told today. Perhaps they will give you ideas for tales of your own.

CONTENTS

GREECE
ATHENS
SPARTA
CYCLADES
DELOS
PAROS
SAMOS
CALYMNE
TURKEY
AEGEAN SEA
N
KNOSSOS
CRETE
Kilometers 0 100 200 300 400
Miles 0 100 200 300

A Fall from the Sky

BY IAN SERRAILLIER • ILLUSTRATED BY DON DEWITT

The story of Daedalus[1] *is an ancient Greek myth. According to the story, Daedalus was a brilliant inventor who enjoyed great fame, especially in Athens, his home city in Greece. For many years his inventive skills were unequaled. Then Daedalus learned that his nephew, Talos, was also held in high esteem as an inventor. He became so jealous of Talos that he planned to get rid of him. One day, as the two were on a rooftop working, Daedalus caused Talos to fall from a ledge to his death. When the terrible crime was discovered, Daedalus was imprisoned and later exiled from Athens.*

Daedalus was sure that if he could get to the island of Crete, he would be given safe refuge. So he made his way to the harbor where the Blue Dolphin, *a ship bound for Crete, was anchored offshore. Frightened and miserable, he swam out, begged passage, and finally got on board.*

As they reached the open sea, the sail with its huge painted dolphin filled out, and he felt the ship heel over, then recover and run straight before the wind. The helmsman set his course for Crete.

No one took much notice of Daedalus. Provided he kept out of the way and did not interfere, he was left alone. The captain seemed to think that this ragged creature from the sea was in some way responsible for the fair winds. He only spoke to him once—to warn him that, if the winds changed, he would be thrown back into the sea from which he had come.

But their luck held and they reached Crete in less than a week. At the port of Heracleion Daedalus was put under guard and

---

[1] Daedalus [ded′ə•ləs]

MAP BY BERNEY KNOX

marched up the hill through five miles of olive trees to the palace of Cnossus, where King Minos held court.

At his first sight of the palace he gasped with amazement. It was built of stone, not of wood like the palace on the Acropolis.[2] As it climbed up the slope and spread itself along the crest, it looked more like a city than a palace. But as he came closer, he saw that some of the walls and pillars had tumbled down; the main hall was roofless, and the building looked more like a splendid shell than a royal palace.

When he was told that a man who claimed to be the master craftsman Daedalus had arrived, King Minos ordered his bonds to be cut and received him ceremoniously in his throne-room. Courtiers and ladies dressed in bright colors were sitting on the stone benches all round. On the walls on either side of the throne a flower garden had been painted, with two eagle-griffins lying in it. King Minos, besides being a great war-lord, was also a lover of beautiful things. Daedalus was so enchanted that he could not take his eyes away.

The king welcomed him warmly.

"I know your fame, Daedalus," he said. "There is no man in the world I would rather see than you." He pointed outside to the devastated courtyard. "We have suffered an earthquake and I need your help."

"Sir, it is I who can learn from you," said Daedalus humbly. "Your palace fills me with wonder. Even in Athens there is nothing to compare with it. Your builders can teach me much."

"There are many problems that they have failed to solve," said King Minos. "Ten years have passed since the earthquake. The main hall is still in ruins because the secret of the roof has been lost. No light reaches the inner rooms. When the rains are heavy, we are swamped. If you can solve these problems, you may live in the palace and I will reward you well." He added darkly, "I know why you left Athens. I know what happened to Talos. Serve me with devotion and I will forget your past. But if you fail me, I will destroy you."

---

[2] Acropolis [ə•krop′ə•ləs]: a hilltop in Athens where several important buildings stood

ICARUS

So Daedalus set to work for King Minos, and he was happier than he had ever been.

His first task was to rebuild the hall. To support the roof he used wooden beams and elegant columns that tapered downwards to the base. He made a statue of the Cretan snake goddess, with snakes uncoiling from her hair; he painted the walls with bright pictures of animals and sea creatures, and of bull-leaping—a favorite Cretan sport.

King Minos was so delighted that he told him to choose a wife from among the palace ladies. But Daedalus did not care for any of them. Wasp-waisted in their flounced skirts, they sat idly about the halls all day long. Too lazy to walk, they would not stir outside into the streets without a litter to ride in, and he could not bear the sound of their endless tittle-tattle. Besides, they meddled in men's affairs in a way that no Athenian lady would dare to do. Instead he chose a slave girl. Her name was Naucrate, and she had dark eyes, an olive skin, and quiet pleasing ways.

She bore him a son named Icarus, who brought him great joy. The boy grew up with none of his father's inventive skill. But he was spirited and full of gusty laughter; boldly adventurous too, for he liked to join in the dangerous bull dance and to go hunting. On the hills he was as sure-footed as a mountain goat. There was nothing in his nature to excite his father's jealousy, but everything to inspire affection and protective love. And Daedalus was drawn to him as honey-bees are drawn to fields of spring flowers.

As the years passed, Daedalus made the palace so splendid that it soon became known as one of the wonders of the world. He built a grand staircase with five broad and sweeping flights and a central well to let in the light. To brighten the inner rooms he devised a system of deep shafts. In the halls and corridors he painted frescoes—one of Minoan shields, another of double-edged axes. In the Queen's Hall the fresco of star-fish, sea-urchins, and blue dolphins sporting in the sea made it a place of beguiling charm.

To cope with the torrential rainfall of the Cretan winter, he invented a complicated network of drains. Small terra-cotta pipes, designed so that they could not fill with sediment, connected up with wide vertical shafts built into the walls. Beside the north-east staircase he made an open channel, with a series of catchpits ranged down the slope to sieve the rain and make it pure for drinking. Then stone tanks were built for storing it.

For all these achievements Daedalus was held in the highest honor. He was almost able to forget that he was only an exile, toiling for a foreign king. But as the years rolled on, he felt an increasing longing to return to his native land before he died. Surely by now the Athenians would have forgotten his crime.

Some months later his wife Naucrate died. Now a shared grief made the bond between himself and Icarus even closer than before. He went to the king and spoke of his desire to return to Greece now that his work had been completed.

But King Minos refused to let him go. "I need you here. I cannot do without your skill," he told him.

Daedalus dropped to his knees and asked again, but the king remained firm. With one of those sudden bursts of anger to which Daedalus had long been accustomed, he accused him of base ingratitude.

"You came to me a branded murderer," he stormed. "Yet I received you into my court and treated you like a nobleman. You shall not go."

But nothing could shake Daedalus from his purpose.

One night he and Icarus tried to escape in a fishing boat. But soon after dawn they were spotted and overhauled by a galley of the royal fleet, and the king had Daedalus imprisoned in the labyrinth.[3]

Deep inside the maze lurked the Minotaur. Its snorting and bellowing were like the blast of Zeus's[4] thunderbolts and the roaring of all the winds. Half deafened by the noise, Daedalus worked feverishly at the lock before the monster could scent him out. Even in darkness no lock, however intricate, could defeat him. It came apart in his fingers and he escaped.

---

[3] labyrinth [lab'ə•rinth]: a maze, built by Daedalus himself at the king's command, to hold a monster called the Minotaur

[4] Zeus [zo͞os]: the king of the gods in Greek mythology

PLAN OF ESCAPE

With Cnossus no longer safe for him, Daedalus and his son took refuge in the woods farther down the coast. Crete is a long mountainous island, at this time thinly sprinkled with settlements of farmers and shepherds, of fishermen and pirates. As King Minos had offered a large reward for their arrest, the fugitives moved from one settlement to another, never staying long in one place. Finally they hid in a cave on the western coast. Here they would sit together for hours on end, gazing across the sea toward Greece.

"King Minos rules the land and the sea. We cannot escape that way," said Daedalus, as he watched the seagulls swooping down from ledges in the cliffs, flapping their wings above the waves, then mounting again. "But he does not rule the air. The sky is open to us, and that is the way we will go."

At once he set to work on the problem of how man could change the laws of nature and fly like a bird. He watched the gulls, the blackheaded ones with their keen eyes and pointed red beaks. How effortless was their flight, as they dived or planed or hovered to rest their wings, their feet tucked close under their tails. Alive to every trick of the air, they used the wind currents to lift them; when checking speed or turning, they spread out their tails like fans.

He sent Icarus to collect the many feathers that lay scattered on the hills and in the crevices of the rocks, and started to make them into wings. He arranged the feathers in rows, threading the larger ones together and fixing the smaller ones with wax. Then he bent the finished shape into a gentle curve, so that it looked like the wing of a huge bird.

All this time Icarus had been standing beside him, watching him at work. He admired his father's skill and was always at his side. Sometimes a gust of wind caught the feathers and blew them away, and he laughed and ran to fetch them. Sometimes they flew into the water; then he dried them in the sun and handed them back. He pressed his thumb into the yellow wax to fix them, but he was clumsier than his father, and Daedalus had to fix them again. Light-hearted and full of spirit, he went on helping his father with the work. He little knew what peril he was handling.

At last two pairs of wings were ready. Daedalus had the larger pair fixed to his body and along his arms and shoulders. Standing on a rock, he spread his wings and leaped into the air and hovered above his son, then landed gracefully beside him. He flew again and swept in a great circle above the shore. And when he was higher than the cliff, he looked out to sea far over the bounding wave toward his native land, and his heart leaped within him.

When he came down he began to fix the smaller pair onto his son, and he told him how to use them. All the time he was working and talking, the old man's cheeks were wet with tears and his hands were trembling.

Then Icarus with his shining wings bounded from the rock. The feathers beat the air with a rushing sound, and he laughed aloud as he soared upwards. Soon he was twice as high as the cliff, pretending not to hear his father's voice calling him down.

"You must not be so rash," said Daedalus, as soon as the boy came down. And when he had recovered his breath and they were ready to leave, Daedalus told him again to be careful. "If you fly too low, the waves will soak your wings and weigh them down. If you fly too high, the sun will melt the wax. Fly between the two. And at night among the dazzling stars do not fly north to the Great Bear or the flashing sword of Orion—you will freeze to death. Follow me closely."

He felt the boy's wings to see that they were still sound and that the straps had not slipped, then kissed him—for the last time ever. And he sprang into the air and led the way.

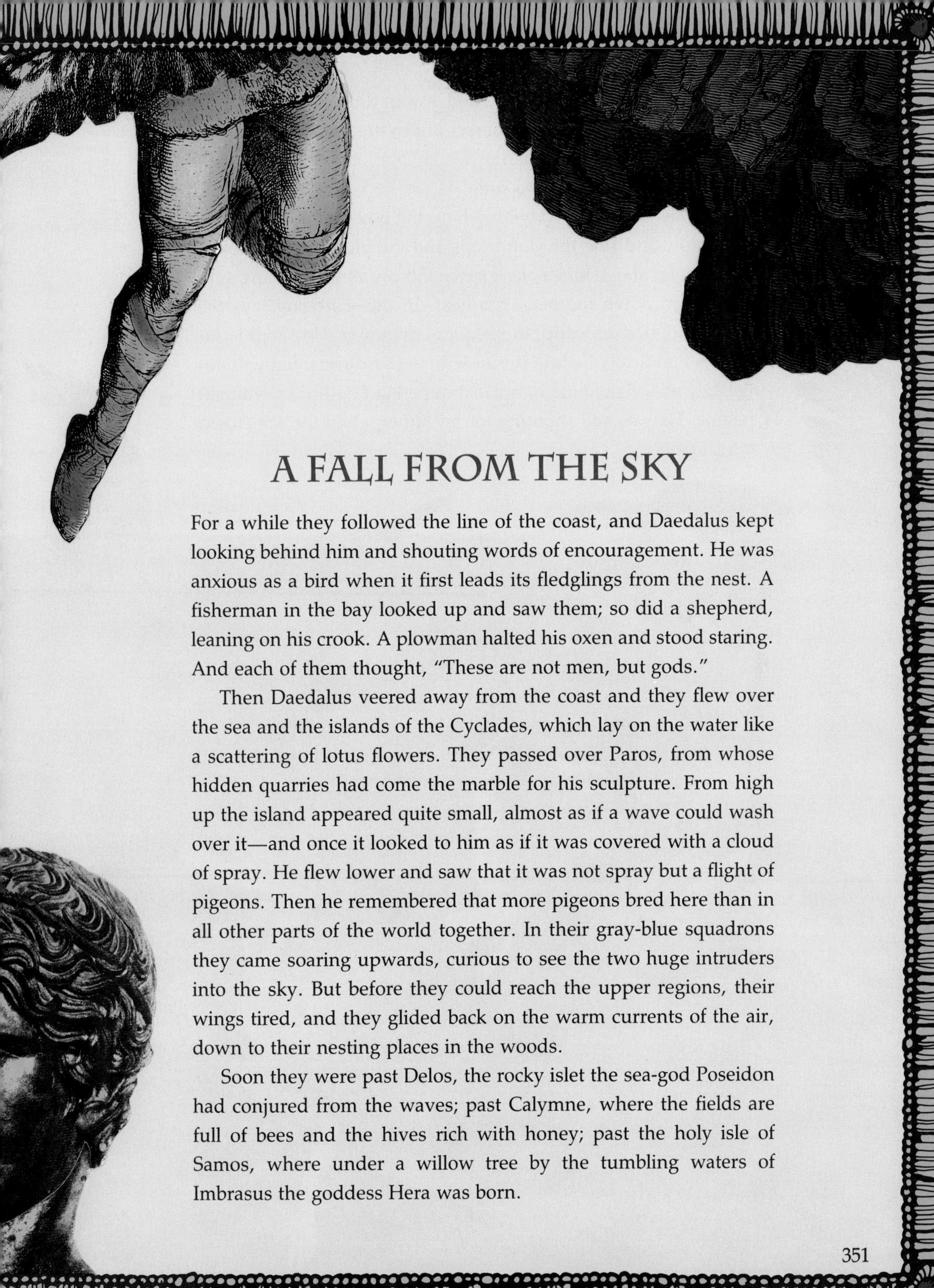

A FALL FROM THE SKY

For a while they followed the line of the coast, and Daedalus kept looking behind him and shouting words of encouragement. He was anxious as a bird when it first leads its fledglings from the nest. A fisherman in the bay looked up and saw them; so did a shepherd, leaning on his crook. A plowman halted his oxen and stood staring. And each of them thought, "These are not men, but gods."

Then Daedalus veered away from the coast and they flew over the sea and the islands of the Cyclades, which lay on the water like a scattering of lotus flowers. They passed over Paros, from whose hidden quarries had come the marble for his sculpture. From high up the island appeared quite small, almost as if a wave could wash over it—and once it looked to him as if it was covered with a cloud of spray. He flew lower and saw that it was not spray but a flight of pigeons. Then he remembered that more pigeons bred here than in all other parts of the world together. In their gray-blue squadrons they came soaring upwards, curious to see the two huge intruders into the sky. But before they could reach the upper regions, their wings tired, and they glided back on the warm currents of the air, down to their nesting places in the woods.

Soon they were past Delos, the rocky islet the sea-god Poseidon had conjured from the waves; past Calymne, where the fields are full of bees and the hives rich with honey; past the holy isle of Samos, where under a willow tree by the tumbling waters of Imbrasus the goddess Hera was born.

They flew through the night, and Icarus did not climb to the stars or stray from his father's course. But in the morning, exulting in his powers, he rose on soaring wings. He longed for the open sky; he was drawn toward the sun.

When Daedalus glanced behind him, the boy was not there. He looked below and saw the cloud tops and the blue sea. He looked up and saw far above him a black speck in front of the burning sun.

Icarus had flown too near, too near. In the scorching rays the wax began to melt and drip, the feathers slid away. He shouted for his father. Frantically he beat the air with his bare arms, but without wings they would not hold him. He dropped out of the sky, straight as a stone. He was still shouting for his father when the sea closed over his lips.

"Where are you, Icarus?" cried Daedalus. "Where are you?"

He swooped down toward the sea, toward a sprinkling of white foam on the waves. As he came nearer he saw that it was not foam but feathers, drifting on the tide towards a lonely shore. For a while he circled above, calling "Icarus!" and flapping his wide melancholy wings. Then he followed the drifting feathers and landed on the shore and took off his wings. There were feathers everywhere, some floating on the sea, some lying bedraggled in the sand. He did not touch them, but bitterly cursed his skill.

Soon the body was washed up at his feet, onto the island which was afterwards to be named Icaria after the boy. Gently he picked it up, while the gulls dipped and climbed above him. Then he followed a track between the cliffs and buried the body under an oak tree.

As he stood there, dazed and silent among the crying gulls, a partridge flew up from the ditch and perched on the bough above his head. He looked up and saw the flash of white on its feathers. It was clapping its wings and chattering gaily.

Daedalus could not bear to watch it. He turned and ran, weeping, into the lonely island.

How did you feel at the end of the story? Explain your response.

Do you think that Daedalus' desire for freedom was greater than his concern for his son's safety? Support your response with details from the story.

What do you think is the lesson, or moral, of this story?

WRITE In a paragraph, explain whether you think Daedalus' gift for creating brought him more satisfaction or misery.

The FORCE of LUCK

Retold by Rudolfo A. Anaya

Illustrated by Kim Lefeve

Once two wealthy friends got into a heated argument. One said that it was money which made a man prosperous, and the other maintained that it wasn't money, but luck, which made the man. They argued for some time and finally decided that if only they could find an honorable man then perhaps they could prove their respective points of view.

One day while they were passing through a small village they came upon a miller who was grinding corn and wheat. They paused to ask the man how he ran his business. The miller replied that he worked for a master and that he earned only four bits a day, and with that he had to support a family of five.

The friends were surprised. "Do you mean to tell us you can maintain a family of five on only fifteen dollars a month?" one asked.

"I live modestly to make ends meet," the humble miller replied.

The two friends privately agreed that if they put this man to a test perhaps they could resolve their argument.

"I am going to make you an offer," one of them said to the miller. "I will give you two hundred dollars and you may do whatever you want with the money."

"But why would you give me this money when you've just met me?" the miller asked.

"Well, my good man, my friend and I have a long-standing argument. He contends that it is luck which elevates a man to high position, and I say it is money. By giving you this money, perhaps we can settle our argument. Here, take it, and do with it what you want!"

So the poor miller took the money and spent the rest of the day thinking about the strange meeting which had presented him with more money than he had ever seen. What could he possibly do with all this money? Be that as it may, he had the money in his pocket and he could do with it whatever he wanted.

When the day's work was done, the miller decided the first thing he would do would be to buy food for his family. He took out ten dollars and wrapped the rest of the money in a cloth and put the bundle in his bag. Then he went to the market and bought supplies and a good piece of meat to take home.

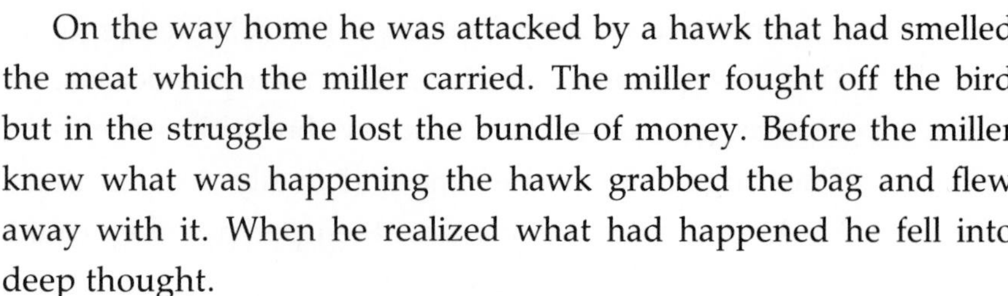

On the way home he was attacked by a hawk that had smelled the meat which the miller carried. The miller fought off the bird but in the struggle he lost the bundle of money. Before the miller knew what was happening the hawk grabbed the bag and flew away with it. When he realized what had happened he fell into deep thought.

"Ah," he moaned, "wouldn't it have been better to let that hungry bird have the meat! I could have bought a lot more meat with the money he took. Alas, now I'm in the same poverty as before! And worse, because now those two men will say I am a thief! I should have thought carefully and bought nothing. Yes, I should have gone straight home and this wouldn't have happened!"

So he gathered what was left of his provisions and continued home, and when he arrived he told his family the entire story.

When he was finished telling his story his wife said, "It has been our lot to be poor, but have faith in God and maybe someday our luck will change."

The next day the miller got up and went to work as usual. He wondered what the two men would say about his story. But since he had never been a man of money he soon forgot the entire matter.

Three months after he had lost the money to the hawk, it happened that the two wealthy men returned to the village. As soon as they saw the miller they approached him to ask if his luck had changed. When the miller saw them he felt ashamed and afraid that they would think that he had squandered the money on worthless things. But he decided to tell them the truth and as soon as they had greeted each other he told his story. The men believed him. In fact, the one who insisted that it was money and not luck which made a man prosper took out another two hundred dollars and gave it to the miller.

"Let's try again," he said, "and let's see what happens this time."

The miller didn't know what to think. "Kind sir, maybe it would be better if you put this money in the hands of another man," he said.

"No," the man insisted, "I want to give it to you because you are an honest man, and if we are going to settle our argument you have to take the money!"

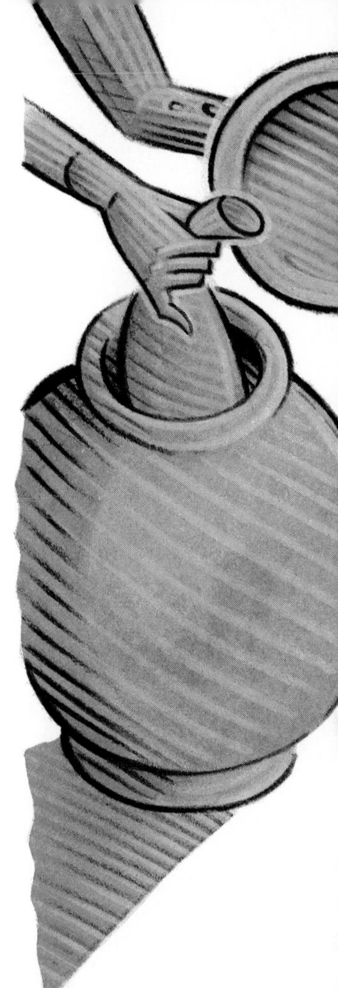

The miller thanked them and promised to do his best. Then as soon as the two men left he began to think what to do with the money so that it wouldn't disappear as it had the first time. The thing to do was to take the money straight home. He took out ten dollars, wrapped the rest in a cloth, and headed home.

When he arrived his wife wasn't at home. At first he didn't know what to do with the money. He went to the pantry where he had stored a large earthenware jar filled with bran. That was as safe a place as any to hide the money, he thought, so he emptied out the grain and put the bundle of money at the bottom of the jar, then covered it up with the grain. Satisfied that the money was safe, he returned to work.

That afternoon when he arrived home from work he was greeted by his wife.

"Look, my husband, today I bought some good clay with which to whitewash the entire house."

"And how did you buy the clay if we don't have any money?" he asked.

"Well, the man who was selling the clay was willing to trade for jewelry, money, or anything of value," she said. "The only thing we had of value was the jar full of bran, so I traded it for the clay. Isn't it wonderful, I think we have enough clay to whitewash these two rooms!"

The man groaned and pulled his hair.

"Oh, you crazy woman! What have you done? We're ruined again!"

"But why?" she asked, unable to understand his anguish.

"Today I met the same two friends who gave me the two hundred dollars three months ago," he explained. "And after I told them how I lost the money they gave me another two hundred. And I, to make sure the money was safe, came home and hid it inside the jar of bran—the same jar you have traded for dirt! Now we're as poor as we were before! And what am I going to tell the two men? They'll think I'm a liar and a thief for sure!"

"Let them think what they want," his wife said calmly. "We will only have in our lives what the good Lord wants us to have. It is our lot to be poor until God wills it otherwise."

So the miller was consoled and the next day he went to work as usual. Time came and went, and one day the two wealthy friends returned to ask the miller how he had done with the second two hundred dollars. When the poor miller saw them he was afraid they would accuse him of being a liar and a spendthrift. But he decided to be truthful and as soon as they had greeted each other he told them what had happened to the money.

"That is why poor men remain honest," the man who had given him the money said. "Because they don't have money they can't get into trouble. But I find your stories hard to believe. I think you gambled and lost the money. That's why you're telling us these wild stories."

"Either way," he continued, "I still believe that it is money and not luck which makes a man prosper."

"Well, you certainly didn't prove your point by giving the money to this poor miller," his friend reminded him. "Good evening, you luckless man," he said to the miller.

"Thank you, friends," the miller said.

"Oh, by the way, here is a worthless piece of lead I've been carrying around. Maybe you can use it for something," said the man who believed in luck. Then the two men left, still debating their points of view on life.

Since the lead was practically worthless, the miller thought nothing of it and put it in his jacket pocket. He forgot all about it until he arrived home. When he threw his jacket on a chair he heard a thump and remembered the piece of lead. He took it out of the pocket and threw it under the table. Later that night after the family had eaten and gone to bed, they heard a knock at the door.

"Who is it? What do you want?" the miller asked.

"It's me, your neighbor," a voice answered. The miller recognized the fisherman's wife. "My husband sent me to ask you if you have any lead you can spare. He is going fishing tomorrow and he needs the lead to weight down the nets."

The miller remembered the lead he had thrown under the table. He got up, found it, and gave it to the woman.

"Thank you very much, neighbor," the woman said. "I promise you the first fish my husband catches will be yours."

"Think nothing of it," the miller said and returned to bed. The next day he got up and went to work without thinking any more of the incident. But in the afternoon when he returned home he found his wife cooking a big fish for dinner.

"Since when are we so well off we can afford fish for supper?" he asked his wife.

"Don't you remember that our neighbor promised us the first fish her husband caught?" his wife reminded him. "Well this was the fish he caught the first time he threw his net. So it's ours, and it's a beauty. But you should have been here when I gutted him! I found a large piece of glass in his stomach!"

"And what did you do with it?"

"Oh, I gave it to the children to play with," she shrugged.

When the miller saw the piece of glass he noticed it shone so brightly it appeared to illuminate the room, but because he knew nothing about jewels he didn't realize its value and left it to the children. But the bright glass was such a novelty that the children were soon fighting over it and raising a terrible fuss.

Now it so happened that the miller and his wife had other neighbors who were jewelers. The following morning when the miller had gone to work the jeweler's wife visited the miller's wife to complain about all the noise her children had made.

"We couldn't get any sleep last night," she moaned.

"I know, and I'm sorry, but you know how it is with a large family," the miller's wife explained. "Yesterday we found a beautiful piece of glass and I gave it to my youngest one to play with and when the others tried to take it from him he raised a storm."

The jeweler's wife took interest. "Won't you show me that piece of glass?" she asked.

"But of course. Here it is."

"Ah, yes, it's a pretty piece of glass. Where did you find it?"

"Our neighbor gave us a fish yesterday and when I was cleaning it I found the glass in its stomach."

"Why don't you let me take it home for just a moment? You see, I have one just like it and I want to compare them."

"Yes, why not? Take it," answered the miller's wife.

So the jeweler's wife ran off with the glass to show it to her husband. When the jeweler saw the glass he instantly knew it was one of the finest diamonds he had ever seen.

"It's a diamond!" he exclaimed.

"I thought so," his wife nodded eagerly. "What shall we do?"

"Go tell the neighbor we'll give her fifty dollars for it, but don't tell her it's a diamond!"

"No, no," his wife chuckled, "of course not." She ran to her neighbor's house. "Ah yes, we have one exactly like this," she told the miller's wife. "My husband is willing to buy it for fifty dollars—only so we can have a pair, you understand."

"I can't sell it," the miller's wife answered. "You will have to wait until my husband returns from work."

That evening when the miller came home from work his wife told him about the offer the jeweler had made for the piece of glass.

"But why would they offer fifty dollars for a worthless piece of glass?" the miller wondered aloud. Before his wife could answer they were interrupted by the jeweler's wife.

"What do you say, neighbor, will you take fifty dollars for the glass?" she asked.

"No, that's not enough," the miller said cautiously. "Offer more."

"I'll give you fifty thousand!" the jeweler's wife blurted out.

"A little bit more," the miller replied.

"Impossible!" the jeweler's wife cried, "I can't offer any more without consulting my husband." She ran off to tell her husband how the bartering was going, and he told her he was prepared to pay a hundred thousand dollars to acquire the diamond.

He handed her seventy-five thousand dollars and said, "Take this and tell him that tomorrow, as soon as I open my shop, he'll have the rest."

When the miller heard the offer and saw the money he couldn't believe his eyes. He imagined the jeweler's wife was jesting with him, but it was a true offer and he received the hundred thousand dollars for the diamond. The miller had never seen so much money, but he still didn't quite trust the jeweler.

"I don't know about this money," he confided to his wife. "Maybe the jeweler plans to accuse us of robbing him and thus get it back."

"Oh, no," his wife assured him, "the money is ours. We sold the diamond fair and square—we didn't rob anyone."

"I think I'll still go to work tomorrow," the miller said. "Who knows, something might happen and the money will disappear, then we would be without money and work. Then how would we live?"

So he went to work the next day, and all day he thought about how he could use the money. When he returned home that afternoon his wife asked him what he had decided to do with their new fortune.

"I think I will start my own mill," he answered, "like the one I operate for my master. Once I set up my business we'll see how our luck changes."

The next day he set about buying everything he needed to establish his mill and to build a new home. Soon he had everything going.

Six months had passed, more or less, since he had seen the two men who had given him the four hundred dollars and the piece of lead. He was eager to see them again and to tell them how the piece of lead had changed his luck and made him wealthy.

Time passed and the miller prospered. His business grew and he even built a summer cottage where he could take his family on vacation. He had many employees who worked for him. One day while he was at his store he saw his two benefactors riding by. He rushed out into the street to greet them and asked them to come in. He was overjoyed to see them, and he was happy to see that they admired his store.

"Tell us the truth," the man who had given him the four hundred dollars said. "You used that money to set up this business."

The miller swore he hadn't, and he told them how he had given the piece of lead to his neighbor and how the fisherman had in return given him a fish with a very large diamond in its stomach. And he told them how he had sold the diamond.

"And that's how I acquired this business and many other things I want to show you," he said. "But it's time to eat. Let's eat first; then I'll show you everything I have now."

The men agreed, but one of them still doubted the miller's story. So they ate and then the miller had three horses saddled and they rode out to see his summer home. The cabin was on the other side of the river where the mountains were cool and beautiful. When

they arrived the men admired the place very much. It was such a peaceful place that they rode all afternoon through the forest. During their ride they came upon a tall pine tree.

"What is that on top of the tree?" one of them asked.

"That's the nest of a hawk," the miller replied.

"I have never seen one; I would like to take a closer look at it!"

"Of course," the miller said, and he ordered a servant to climb the tree and bring down the nest so his friend could see how it was built. When the hawk's nest was on the ground they examined it carefully. They noticed that there was a cloth bag at the bottom of the nest. When the miller saw the bag he immediately knew that it was the very same bag he had lost to the hawk which fought him for the piece of meat years ago.

"You won't believe me, friends, but this is the very same bag in which I put the first two hundred dollars you gave me," he told them.

"If it's the same bag," the man who had doubted him said, "then the money you said the hawk took should be there."

"No doubt about that," the miller said. "Let's see what we find."

The three of them examined the old, weatherbeaten bag. Although it was full of holes and crumbling, when they tore it apart they found the money intact. The two men remembered what the miller had told them and they agreed he was an honest and honorable man. Still, the man who had given him the money wasn't satisfied. He wondered what had really happened to the second two hundred he had given the miller.

They spent the rest of the day riding in the mountains and returned very late to the house.

As he unsaddled their horses, the servant in charge of grooming and feeding the horses suddenly realized that he had no grain for them. He ran to the barn and checked, but there was no grain for the hungry horses. So he ran to the neighbor's granary and there he was able to buy a large clay jar of bran. He carried the jar home and emptied the bran into a bucket to wet it before he fed it to the horses. When he got to the bottom of the jar he noticed a large lump which turned out to be a rag covered package. He examined it and felt something inside. He immediately went to give it to his master who had been eating dinner.

"Master," he said, "look at this package which I found in an earthenware jar of grain which I just bought from our neighbor!"

The three men carefully unraveled the cloth and found the other one hundred and ninety dollars which the miller had told them he had lost. That is how the miller proved to his friends that he was truly an honest man.

And they had to decide for themselves whether it had been luck or money which had made the miller a wealthy man!

Which do you think makes the miller a prosperous man—luck or money? Explain your answer.

Explain what you admire most or like least about the miller.

What do you see as the point or message of this story?

WRITE According to an old saying, "Money can't buy happiness." In a paragraph or two, explain why you agree or disagree with this statement.

THE FROG WHO WANTED TO BE A SINGER

By Linda Goss

Illustrated by Jill Karla Schwarz

Well, friends, I got a question for you. Have you ever been frustrated? That's right, I said *frustrated.* Tell the truth now. Everybody in this room should be screaming, "Yeah, I've been frustrated," because you know you have, at least once in your lives. And some of us here are frustrated every single day.

How do you tell when you are frustrated? Do you feel angry? Do you feel depressed? Are you full of anxiety? Are you tense? Are you nervous? Confused? Sometimes you can't stop eating. Sometimes you don't want to eat at all. Sometimes you can't sleep. And sometimes you don't want to wake up. *You are frustrated!*

Well, friends, let's go back. Back to the forest. Back to the motherland. Back to the days when the animals talked and walked upon the earth as folks do now.

Let's examine a little creature who is feeling mighty bad, mighty sad, mighty mad, and mighty frustrated. We call him the frog. There's nothing wrong in being a frog. But this particular frog feels that he has talent. You see, he wants to be a singer. And there's nothing wrong in wanting to be a singer except that in this particular forest where this particular frog lives, frogs don't sing. Only the birds are allowed to sing. The birds are considered the most beautiful singers in the forest.

So, for a while, the frog is cool. He's quiet. He stays to himself and practices on his lily pad, jumping up and down, singing to himself. But one day all of this frustration begins to swell inside him. He becomes so swollen that frustration bubbles start popping from his mouth, his ears, his nose, even from his eyes, and he says to himself (in a froglike voice): "You know, I'm tired of feeling this way. I'm tired of holding all this inside me. I've got talent. I want to be a singer."

The little frog decides to share his ambitions with his parents. His parents are somewhat worried about his desires, but since he is their son, they encourage him and say: "Son, we're behind you one hundred percent. If that's what you want to be, then go right ahead. You'll make us very proud."

This makes the frog feel better. It gives him some confidence, so much so that he decides to share the good news with his friends. He jumps over to the other side of the pond and says, "Fellows, I want to share something with you."

"Good!" they reply. "You got some flies we can eat?"

"No, not flies. I got talent. I want to be a singer."

"Fool, are you crazy?" says one friend. "Frogs don't sing in this place. You'd better keep your big mouth shut."

They laugh at the frog, so he jumps back over to his lily pad.

He rocks back and forth, meditating and contemplating his situation, and begins to realize that perhaps he should go and talk with the birds. They seem reasonable enough; maybe they will allow him to join their singing group.

He gathers up his confidence, jumps

over to their tree house, and knocks on their trunk. The head bird flies to the window, looks down on the frog's head, and says: "Oh, it's the frog. How may we help you?"

"Can I come up? I got something to ask you," says the frog.

"Very well, Frog. Do jump up."

Frog enters the tree house, and hundreds of birds begin fluttering around him.

"Come on in, Frog. Why don't you sit over there in the corner," says the head bird. Frog sits down but he feels a little shy. He begins to chew on his tongue.

"Frog, how may we help you?"

"Uh, well, uh, you see," says Frog, "I would like to become a part of your group."

"That's wonderful," says the head bird.

"Yes, wonderful," echo the other birds.

"Frog, you may help us carry our worms," said the head bird.

"That's not what I had in mind," says Frog.

"Well, what do you have in mind?"

Frog begins to stutter; "I-I-I-I want to-to-to sing wi-wi-with your group."

"What! You must be joking, of course. An ugly green frog who is full of warts sing with us delicate creatures. You would cause us great embarrassment."

"B-b-but . . ." Frog tries to plead his case, but the head bird becomes angry.

"Out! Out! Out of our house you go." He kicks the frog from the house. Frog rolls like a ball down the jungle path.

When he returns home, he feels very sad. The frog wants to cry but doesn't, even though he aches deep inside his gut. He wants to give up, but he doesn't. Instead he practices and practices and practices and practices.

Then he begins to think again and realizes that even though the birds sing every Friday night at the Big Time Weekly Concert, they don't control it. The fox is in charge. The frog jumps over to the fox's place and knocks on his cave.

"Brother Fox, Brother Fox, it's me, Frog. I want to talk to you."

The fox is a fast talker and a busy worker, and really doesn't want to be bothered with the frog.

"Quick, quick, quick, what do you want?" says the fox.

"I want to be in the concert this Friday night."

"Quick, quick, what do you want to do?"

"I want to sing," says the frog.

"Sing? Get out of here, quick, quick, quick!"

"Please, Brother Fox. Please give me a chance."

"Hmmm," says the fox, shifting his eyes. "Uh, you know something, Froggie? Maybe I could use you. Why don't you show up Friday, at eight o'clock sharp, okay?"

"You mean I can do it?"

"That's what I said. Now, get out of here. Quick, quick, quick!"

Oh, the frog is happy. He is going to

"do his thing." He is going to present himself to the world.

Meanwhile, the fox goes around to the animals in the forest and tells them about the frog's plans. Each animal promises to be there and give the frog a "little present" for his singing debut.

And so Monday rolls around, Tuesday rolls around, Wednesday rolls around, Thursday rolls around, and it is Friday. The frog is so excited, he bathes all day. He combs his little green hair, parts it in the middle, and slicks down the sides. He scrubs his little green fingers and his little green toes. He looks at his little reflection in the pond, smiles, and says, "Um, um, um, I am *beauuuutiful!* And I am going to 'do my thing' tonight." And soon it is seven o'clock, and then it is seven thirty, and then it is seven forty-five, and there is the frog trembling, holding on to the edge of the curtain.

He looks out at the audience and sees all the animals gathering in their seats. The frog is scared, so scared that his legs won't stop trembling and his eyes won't stop twitching. Brother Fox strolls out on stage and the show begins.

"Thank you, thank you, thank you. Ladies and gentlemen, we have a wonderful show for you tonight. Presenting, for your entertainment, the frog who thinks he's a singer. Come on, let's clap. Come on out here, Frog, come on, come on. Let's give him a big hand." The animals clap and roar with laughter. The frog jumps out and slowly goes up to the microphone.

"For-for-for-for my first number, I-I-I-I—"

Now, before that frog can put the period at the end of that sentence, the elephant stands up, pulls down a pineapple, and throws it right at the frog's head.

"Ow!" cries the frog. And the lion pulls down a banana, throws it, and hits that frog right in the mouth. "Oh," gulps the frog. Other animals join in the act of throwing things at the frog. Some of them shout and yell at him, "Boo! Boo! Get off the stage. You stink! You're ugly. We don't want to hear a frog sing. Boo, you jive turkey!"

The poor little frog has to leap off the stage and run for his life. He hides underneath the stage. Brother Fox rushes back on the stage.

"Okay, okay, okay, calm down—just trying out our comic routine. We have some real talent for your enjoyment. Presenting the birds, who really can sing. Let's hear it for the birds." The audience claps loudly. The birds fly onto the stage, their heads held up high. Their wings slowly strike a stiff, hypnotic pose as if they are statues. Their stage presence demands great respect from the audience. They chirp, tweet, and whistle, causing the audience to fall into a soft, peaceful nod.

Everyone is resting quietly except the frog, who is tired of being pushed around. The frog is tired of feeling frustrated. He leaps over the fox. He grabs him, shakes him, puts his hands around the fox's throat, and says, "You tricked me. You tried to make a fool out of me."

"Leave me alone," says the fox. "If you want to go back out there and make a fool of yourself, go right ahead."

"Hmph," says the frog. "That's just what I'm going to do."

Now that little green frog hippity-hops back onto the stage. He is shaking but determined to sing his song.

"I don't care if you are asleep. I'm gonna wake you up. I came here to sing a song tonight, and that's what I'm going to do."

In the style of what we call boogie-woogie, the frog begins to "do his thing":

DOOBA DOOBA DOOBA DOOBA
DOOBA DOOBA DOOBA DOOBA
DOOBA DOOBA DOOBA DOOBA
DOOBA DOOBA DOOBA DOOBA

The frog bops his head about as though it were a jazzy saxophone. His fingers move as though they were playing a funky bass fiddle.

DOOBA DOOBA DOOBA DOOBA
DOOBADEE DOOBADEE DOOBADEE DOOBADEE
DOOBA DOOBA DOOBA DOOBA
DOOBADEE DOOBADEE DOOBADEE DOOBADEE
DOOBA DOOBA DOOBA DOOBA
DOOBA DOOBA DOOBA DOOBA
DOOBA! DOOBA! DOOP-DEE-DOOP! . . . BLURRRRRRP!

The elephant opens one eye. He roars "Uuumphf!" He jumps from his seat. He flings his hips from side to side, doing a dance we now call the "bump." The lion is the next animal to jump up from his seat. He shouts: "I love it! I love it!" He shakes his body thisaway and thataway and every whichaway, doing a dance we now call the "twist." Soon the snakes are boogalooing and the giraffes are doing the jerk. The hyenas do the "slop" and the fox does the "mashed potato." The birds also want to join in: "We want to do Dooba Dooba, too." They chirp and sway through the trees.

Tweet Tweet Tweet Dooba
Tweet Tweet Tweet Dooba

The whole forest is rocking. The joint is jumping. The animals are snapping their fingers. They are *dancing,* doing something that they have never done before.

The fox runs back on the stage, grabs the mike, and shouts: "Wow, Frog, you are a genius. You have given us something new."

From then on, the frog is allowed to sing every Friday night at the Big Time Weekly Concert.

And, as my granddaddy used to say, that is how Rhythm and Blues was born.

DOOBA DOOBA DOOBA DOOBA
DOOBA DOOBA DOOBA DOOBA
DOOBA! DOOBA! DOOP-DEE-
DOOP! . . . BLURRRRRP!

How does Frog's eventual success illustrate the saying "If at first you don't succeed, try, try again"?

Frog only wants to "do his thing." Define the phrase *doing your own thing,* using Frog as an example.

Do you think "doing your own thing" is always a good idea, or can it lead to problems? Explain your answer.

WRITE Think about some new activity that you would like to try, and list some steps you could follow to reach your goal.

TRADITIONAL TALES

Why do you think "A Fall from the Sky," "The Force of Luck," and "The Frog Who Wanted to Be a Singer" are considered traditional stories? In your explanation, tell what makes a story traditional.

WRITER'S WORKSHOP

The myth and the folktales in this section each contain a lesson or moral. What other lesson could you share in a story? Write a folktale in your own style. Tell an interesting story, but include a lesson, too.

Writer's Choice If you were a character in one of the stories in this section, what would you want to say to the people who read about you? Choose a character you would like to speak for. What is the best way for you to reach your audience—with a letter, a comic strip, or an interview? Decide how you will share your writing with your "fans."

THEME

NEWFANGLED PRINCESSES

You have probably met many princesses in fairy tales. You know what they look like, how they behave, and even who their friends are. After you read the following selections, however, your image of a princess may never be the same again.

CONTENTS

. . . And Then the Prince Knelt Down and Tried to Put the Glass Slipper on Cinderella's Foot

by Judith Viorst

Award-Winning Author

I really didn't notice that he had a funny nose.
And he certainly looked better all dressed up in fancy clothes.
He's not nearly as attractive as he seemed the other night.
So I think I'll just pretend that this glass slipper feels too tight.

Cinderella About to Try On the Glass Slipper, 1842, oil on canvas, by Richard Redgrave (1804–1888)

In Search of Cinderella

by Shel Silverstein

From dusk to dawn,
From town to town,
Without a single clue,
I seek the tender, slender foot
To fit this crystal shoe.
From dusk to dawn,
I try it on
Each damsel that I meet.
And I still love her so, but oh,
I've started hating feet.

THE PRINCESS AND THE TIN BOX

by James Thurber
Illustrated by James Thurber

Once upon a time, in a far country, there lived a king whose daughter was the prettiest princess in the world. Her eyes were like the cornflower, her hair was sweeter than the hyacinth, and her throat made the swan look dusty.

From the time she was a year old, the princess had been showered with presents. Her nursery looked like Cartier's[1] window. Her toys were all made of gold or platinum or diamonds or emeralds. She was not permitted to have wooden blocks or china dolls or rubber dogs or linen books, because such materials were considered cheap for the daughter of a king.

When she was seven, she was allowed to attend the wedding of her brother and throw real pearls at the bride instead of rice. Only the nightingale, with his lyre of gold, was permitted to sing for the princess. The common blackbird, with his boxwood flute, was kept out of the palace grounds. She walked in silver-and-samite slippers to a sapphire-and-topaz bathroom and slept in an ivory bed inlaid with rubies.

On the day the princess was eighteen, the king sent a royal ambassador to the courts of five neighboring kingdoms to announce that he would give his daughter's hand in marriage to the prince who brought her the gift she liked the most.

The first prince to arrive at the palace rode a swift white stallion and laid at the feet of the princess an enormous apple made of solid gold which he had taken from a dragon who had guarded it for a thousand years. It was placed on a long ebony table set up to hold the gifts of the princess's suitors. The second prince, who came on a gray charger, brought her a nightingale made of a thousand diamonds, and it was placed beside the golden apple. The third prince, riding on a black horse, carried a great jewel box made of platinum and sapphires, and it was placed next to the diamond nightingale. The fourth prince, astride a fiery yellow horse, gave the princess a gigantic heart made of rubies and pierced by an emerald arrow. It was placed next to the platinum-and-sapphire jewel box.

---

[1]Cartier's [kär•tyāz′]: an expensive store

Now the fifth prince was the strongest and handsomest of all the five suitors, but he was the son of a poor king whose realm had been overrun by mice and locusts and wizards and mining engineers so that there was nothing much of value left in it. He came plodding up to the palace of the princess on a plow horse and he brought her a small tin box filled with mica and feldspar and hornblende which he had picked up on the way.

The other princes roared with disdainful laughter when they saw the tawdry gift the fifth prince had brought to the princess. But she examined it with great interest and squealed with delight, for all her life she had been glutted with precious stones and priceless metals, but she had never seen tin before or mica or feldspar or hornblende. The tin box was placed next to the ruby heart pierced with an emerald arrow.

"Now," the king said to his daughter, "you must select the gift you like best and marry the prince that brought it."

The princess smiled and walked up to the table and picked up the present she liked the most. It was the platinum-and-sapphire jewel box, the gift of the third prince.

"The way I figure it," she said, "is this. It is a very large and expensive box, and when I am married, I will meet many admirers who will give me precious gems with which to fill it to the top. Therefore, it is the most valuable of all the gifts my suitors have brought me and I like it the best."

The princess married the third prince that very day in the midst of great merriment and high revelry. More than a hundred thousand pearls were thrown at her and she loved it.

Moral: All those who thought the princess was going to select the tin box filled with worthless stones instead of one of the other gifts will kindly stay after class and write one hundred times on the blackboard "I would rather have a hunk of aluminum silicate than a diamond necklace."

Did you think the princess would choose the tin box? Explain why or why not.

Now that you have read the moral of the story, what judgment would you make about traditional fairy tale endings? Explain your response.

WRITE If you were the princess, which gift would you choose? Write an explanation for your choice.

The Hero and the Crown

by Robin McKinley ✿ Illustrated by David Wilgus

Aerin is the only child of Arlbeth, king of Damar. She has the title of first sol, the highest-ranked female in the kingdom. However, since daughters are rarely allowed to inherit, and because Aerin's mother was an unknown foreigner of suspicious origins, it is her cousin Tor, the first sola, who is heir to the throne.

At the age of fifteen, Aerin is often restless. While recovering from an illness, she makes friends with her father's old war-stallion, Talat, and finds an interesting book in the royal library.

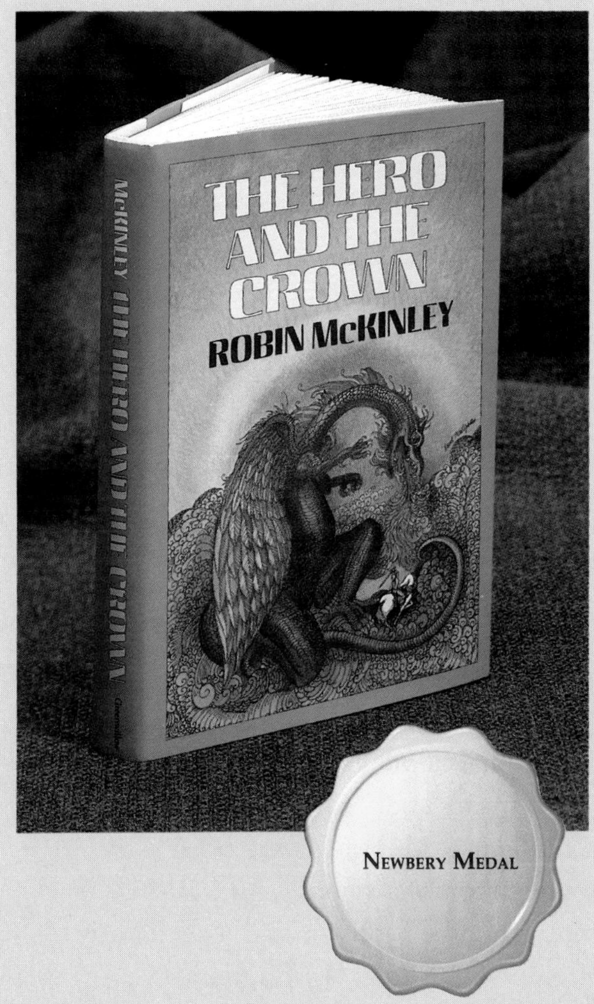

The book with the interesting binding was a history of Damar. Aerin had had to learn a certain amount of history as part of her royal education, but this stuff was something else again. The lessons she'd been forced to learn were dry spare things, the facts without the sense of them, given in the simplest of language, as if words might disguise the truth or (worse) bring it to life. Education was one of Arlbeth's pet obsessions; before him there hadn't been a king in generations who felt much desire for book learning, and there was no precedent for quality in royal tutors.

The book was faded with age, and the style of lettering was strange to her, so she had to puzzle out some of the words; and some of the words were archaic and unfamiliar, so she had to puzzle out the meanings. But it was worth it, for this book told her stories more exciting than the ones she made up for herself before she fell asleep at night. And so, as she read, she first learned of the old dragons.

Damar had dragons still; little ones, dog-sized, nasty, mean-tempered creatures who would fry a baby for supper and swallow it in two gulps if they could; but they had been beaten back into the heavy forest and the wilder Hills by Aerin's day. They still killed an occasional unwary hunter, for they had no fear, and they had teeth and claws as well as fire to subdue their prey, but they were no longer a serious threat. Arlbeth heard occasionally of one—or of a family, for they most often hunted in families—that was harassing a village or an outlying farm, and when that happened a party of men with spears and arrows—swords were of little use, for if one were close enough to use a sword, one was close enough to be badly burned—went out from the City to deal with them. Always they came back with a few more unpleasant stories of the cunning treachery of dragons; always they came back nursing a few scorched limbs; occasionally they came back a horse or a hound the less.

But there was no glamour in dragon-hunting. It was hard, tricky, grim work, and dragons were vermin. The folk of the hunt, the thotar, who ran the king's dogs and provided meat for the royal household, would have nothing to do with dragons, and dogs once used for dragons were considered worthless for anything else.

There were still the old myths of the great dragons, huge scaled beasts many times larger than horses; and it was sometimes even said that the great dragons flew, flew in the air, with wingspreads so vast as to blacken the sun. The little dragons had vestigial wings, but no one had ever seen or heard of a dragon that could lift its thick squat body off the ground with them. They beat their wings in anger and in courtship, as they raised their crests; but that was all. The old dragons were no more nor less of a tale than that of flying dragons.

But this book took the old dragons seriously. It said that while the only dragons humankind had seen in many years were little ones, there were still one or two of the great ones hiding in the Hills; and that one day the one or two would fly out of their secret places and wreak havoc on man, for man would have forgotten how to deal with them. The great dragons lived long; they could afford to wait for that forgetfulness. From the author's defensive tone, the great dragons even in his day were a legend, a tale to tell on festival days. But she was fascinated, as he had been.

"It is with the utmost care I have gathered my information; and I think I may say with truth that the ancient Great Ones and our day's small, scurrilous beasts are the same in type. Thus anyone wishing to learn the skill to defeat a

Great One can do no better than to harry as many small ones as he may find from their noisome dens, and see how they do give battle."

He went on to describe his information-gathering techniques, which seemed to consist of tirelessly footnoting the old stories for dragonish means and methods; although, thought Aerin, that could as well be from the oral tale-tellers adapting the ancient dragons to the ways of the present ones as from the truth of the author's theory. But she read on.

Dragons had short stubby legs on broad bodies; they were not swift runners over distance, but they were exceedingly nimble, and could balance easily on any one foot the better to rip with any of the other three, as well as with the barbed tail. The neck was long and whippy, so that the dragon might spray its fire at any point of the circle; and they often scraped their wings against the ground to throw up dust and further confound their enemies, or their prey.

"It is customary today to hunt the dragon with arrow and thrown spear; but if one of the Great Ones comes again, this will avail his attacker little. As their size has diminished, so has their armament; a well-thrown spear may pierce a small dragon anywhere it strikes. The Great Ones had only two vulnerable spots that might be depended upon: at the base of the jaw, where the narrow head joins the long neck; and behind the elbow, from whence the wings spring. Dragons are, as I have said, nimble; it is most unlikely that a Great One would be so foolish as to lower its head or its wings to make an easy mark. A great hero only may slay a Great One; one who by skill and courage may draw close enough to force the fatal blow.

"It is fortunate for all who walk the earth that the Great Ones bred but rarely; and that mankind has borne enough heroes to vanquish the most of them. But it is this writer's most fervid belief that at least one more hero must stand forth from his people to face the last of the Great Ones.

"Of this last—I have said one or two; perhaps there are three or four; I know not. But of one I will make specific remark: Gorthold, who slew Crendenor and Razimtheth, went also against Maur, the Black Dragon, and it he did not slay. Gorthold, who was himself wounded unto death, said with his last strength that the dragon would die of its wounds as he would die of his; but this was never known for a certainty. The only certainty is that Maur disappeared; and has been seen by no man—or none that has brought back the tale to tell—from that day to this."

In the back of the book Aerin found an even older manuscript: just a few pages, nearly illegible with age, sewn painstakingly into the binding. Those final ancient pages were a recipe, for an ointment called kenet. An ointment that was proof against dragonfire—it said.

It had a number of very peculiar ingredients; herbs, she thought, by the

sound of them. She knew just enough of the Old Tongue to recognize a few syllables; there was one that translated as "redroot." She frowned; there was a thing called redroot that showed up in boring pastoral poems, but she'd always thought it belonged to that classic category known as imaginary, like nymphs and elephants.

An ointment against dragonfire. If it worked—one person, alone, could tackle a dragon safely; not a Great One, of course, but the Black Dragon probably did die of its wounds . . . but the little ones that were such a nuisance. At present the system was that you attacked with arrows and things from a distance, with enough of you to make a ring around it, or them, so if they bolted at someone he could run like mad while the other side of the ring was filling them full of arrows. They couldn't run far, and usually a family all bolted in the same direction. It was when they didn't that horses died.

After experimenting for nearly three years, Aerin discovers how to make the dragonfire ointment. When Tor gives her a sword for her eighteenth birthday, she is excited and proud. An opportunity soon arises for Aerin to prove herself.

Aerin had begun to visit the king at his breakfast now and then, and always he looked glad to see her. Sometimes Tor ate with the king as well, and if Arlbeth noticed that Tor joined him at breakfast more often now that there was a chance he would see Aerin as well, he said nothing. Tor was home most of the time now, for Arlbeth had need of him near.

So it was the three of them lingering over third cups of malak one morning when the first petitioner of the day came to speak to the king.

The petitioner reported a dragon, destroying crops and killing chickens. It had also badly burned a child who had accidentally discovered its lair, although the child had been rescued in time to save its life.

Arlbeth sighed and rubbed his face with his hand. "Very well. We will send someone to deal with it."

The man bowed and left.

"There will be more of them now, with the trouble at the Border," said Tor. "That sort of vermin seems to breed faster when the North wind blows."

"I fear you are right," Arlbeth replied. "And we can ill spare anyone just now."

"I'll go," said Tor.

"Don't be a fool," snapped the king, and then immediately said, "I'm sorry. I can spare you least of all—as you know. Dragons don't kill people very often any more, but dragon-slayers rarely come back without a few uncomfortable burns."

"Someday," said Tor with a wry smile, "when we have nothing better to do, we must think up a more efficient way to cope with dragons. It's hard to take them seriously—but they are a serious nuisance."

Aerin sat very still.

"Yes." Arlbeth frowned into his malak. "I'll ask tomorrow for half a dozen volunteers to go take care of this. And pray it's an old slow one."

Aerin also prayed it was an old slow one as she slipped off. She had only a day's grace, so she needed to leave at once; fortunately she had visited the village in question once on a state journey with her father, so she knew more or less how to get there. It was only a few hours' ride.

Her hands shook as she saddled Talat and tied the bundles of dragon-proof suit, kenet, sword, and a spear—which she wasn't at all sure she could use, since, barring a few lessons from Tor when she was eight or nine years old, she was entirely self-taught—to the saddle. Then she had to negotiate her way past the stable, the castle, and down the king's way and out of the City without anyone trying to stop her; and the sword and spear, in spite of the long cloak she had casually laid over them, were a bit difficult to disguise.

Her luck—or something—was good. She was worrying so anxiously about what she would say if stopped that she gave herself a headache; but as she rode, everyone seemed to be looking not quite in her direction—almost as if they couldn't quite *see* her, she thought. It made her feel a little creepy. But she got out of the City unchallenged.

The eerie feeling, and the headache, lifted at once when she and Talat set off through the forest below the City. The sun was shining, and the birds seemed to be singing just for her. Talat lifted into a canter, and she let him run for a while, the wind slipping through her hair, the shank of the spear tapping discreetly at her leg, reminding her that she was on her way to accomplish something useful.

She stopped at a little distance from the dragon-infested village to put on her suit—which was no longer quite so greasy; it had reached its saturation point, perhaps, and then adapted, as well-oiled boots adapt to the feet that wear them. Her suit still quenched torches, but it had grown as soft and supple as cloth, and almost as easy to wear. She rubbed ointment on her face and her horse, and pulled on her long gloves. Shining rather in the sunlight then and reeking of pungent herbs, Aerin rode into the village.

Talat was unmistakably a war-horse, even to anyone who had never seen one before, and her red hair immediately identified her as the first sol. A little boy stood up from his doorstep and shouted: "They're here for the dragon!" and then there were a dozen, two dozen folk in the street, looking at her, and then looking in puzzlement for the five or six others that should have been riding with her.

"I am alone," said Aerin; she would have liked to explain, not that she was here without her father's knowledge but

that she was alone because she was dragon-proof (she hoped) and didn't need any help. But her courage rather failed her, and she didn't. In fact what the villagers saw as royal pride worked very well, and they fell over themselves to stop appearing to believe that a first sol couldn't handle a dragon by herself, and several spoke at once, offering to show the way to where the dragon had made its lair, all of them careful not to look again down the road behind her.

She was wondering how she could tell them delicately that she didn't want them hanging around to watch, since she wasn't at all sure how graceful (or effective) her first encounter with a real dragon was likely to be. But the villagers who accompanied her to show her the way had no intention of getting anywhere near the scene of the battle; a cornered dragon was not going to care what non-combatant bystanders it happened to catch with an ill-aimed lash of fire. They pointed the way, and then returned to their village to wait on events.

Aerin hung her sword round her waist, settled the spear into the crook of her arm. Talat walked with his ears sharply forward, and when he snorted she smelled it too: fire, and something else. It was a new smell, and it was the smell of a creature that did not care if the meat it ate was fresh or not, and was not tidy with the bones afterward. It was the smell of dragon.

Talat, after his warning snort, paced onward carefully. They came soon to a little clearing with a hummock of rock at its edge. The hummock had a hole in it, the upper edge of which was rimed with greasy smoke. The litter of past dragon meals was scattered across the once green meadow, and it occurred to Aerin that the footing would be worse for a horse's hard hoofs than a dragon's sinewy claws.

Talat halted, and they stood, Aerin gazing into the black hole in the hill. A minute or two went by and she wondered, suddenly, how one got the dragon to pay attention to one in the first place. Did she have to wake it up? Yell? Throw water into the cave at it?

Just as her spearpoint sagged with doubt, the dragon hurtled out of its den and straight at them: and it opened its mouth and blasted them with its fire—except that Talat had never doubted, and was ready to step nimbly out of its way as Aerin scrabbled with her spear and grabbed at Talat's mane to keep from falling off onto the dragon's back. It spun round—it was about the height of Talat's knees, big for a dragon, and dreadfully quick on its yellow-clawed feet—and sprayed fire at them again. This time, although Talat got them out of the worst of it, it licked over her arm. She saw the fire wash over the spear handle and glance off her elbow, but she did not feel

it; and the knowledge that her ointment did accomplish what it was meant to do gave her strength and cleared her mind. She steadied the spear-butt and nudged Talat with one ankle; as he sidestepped and as the dragon whirled round at them again, she threw her spear.

It wouldn't have been a very good

cast for a member of the thotor, or for a seasoned dragon-hunter, but it served her purpose. It stuck in the dragon's neck, in the soft place between neck and shoulder where the scales were thin, and it slowed the dragon down. It twitched and lashed its tail and roared at her, but she knew she hadn't given it a mortal wound; if she let it skulk off to its lair, it would eventually heal and re-emerge, nastier than ever.

It bent itself around the wounded shoulder and tried to grip the spear in its teeth, which were long and thin and sharp and not well suited for catching hold of anything so smooth and hard and narrow as a spearshaft. Aerin dismounted and pulled out her sword, and approached it warily. It ignored her, or appeared to, till she was quite close; and then it snapped its long narrow head around at her again and spat fire.

It caught her squarely; and dragonfire had none of the friendliness of a woodfire burning by the side of a river. The dragonfire pulled at her, seeking her life; it clawed at her pale shining skin, and at the supple leather she wore; and while the heat of it did not distress her, the heat of its malice did; and as the fire passed over her and disappeared she stood in shock, and stared straight ahead of her, and did not move.

The dragon knew it had killed her. It was an old dragon, and had killed one or two human beings, and knew that it had caught this one well and thoroughly. It had been a bit puzzled that she did not scream when it burned her arm, and that she did not scream now and fall down writhing on the earth; but this did not matter. She would not trouble it further, and it could attend to its sore shoulder.

Aerin took half a dozen stiff steps forward, grasped the end of the spear and forced the dragon to the ground, swung her sword up and down, and cut off the dragon's head.

Then there was an angry scream from Talat, and she whirled, the heat of the dead dragon's fresh-spilled blood rising as steam and clouding her vision: but she saw dragonfire, and she saw Talat rear and strike with his forefeet.

She ran toward them and thought, Gods, help me, it had a mate; I forgot, often there are two of them; and she chopped at the second dragon's tail, and missed. It swung around, breathing fire, and she felt the heat of it across her throat, and then Talat struck at it again. It lashed her with its tail when it whirled to face the horse again, and Aerin tripped and fell, and the dragon was on top of her at once, the claws scrabbling at her leather tunic and the long teeth fumbling for her throat. The smoke from its nostrils hurt her eyes. She yelled, frantically, and squirmed under the dragon's weight; and she heard something tear, and she knew if she was caught in dragonfire again she would be burned.

Then Talat thumped into the dragon's side with both hind feet, and the force of the blow lifted them both—for the dragon's claws were tangled in leather

laces—and dropped them heavily. The dragon coughed, but there was no fire; and Aerin had fallen half on top of the thing. It raked her with its spiked tail, and something else tore; and its teeth snapped together inches from her face. Her sword was too long; she could not get it close enough for stabbing, and her shoulder was tiring. She dropped the sword and struggled to reach her right boottop, where she had a short dagger, but the dragon rolled, and she could not reach it.

Then Talat was there again, and he bit the dragon above its small red eye, where the ear hole was; and the dragon twisted its neck to spout fire at him, but it was still dazed by its fall, and only a little fire came out of its mouth. Talat plunged his own face into the trickle of smoke and seized the dragon by the nostrils and dragged its head back; and still farther back. Its forefeet and breast came clear of the ground, and as the dragon thrashed, Aerin's leg came free, and she pulled the dagger from her boot and thrust it into the dragon's scaleless breast. The dragon shrieked, the noise muffled by Talat's grip on its nose, and Aerin stumbled away to pick up her sword.

Talat swung the dying dragon back and forth, and slashed at its body with one forefoot, and the muscles of his heavy stallion's neck ran with sweat and smudges of ash. Aerin lifted up the sword and sliced the dragon's belly open, and it convulsed once, shuddered, and died. Talat dropped the body and stood with his head down, shivering, and Aerin realized what she had done, and how little she had known about what it would involve, and how near she had come to failure; and her stomach rebelled, and she lost what remained of her breakfast over the smoking mutilated corpse of the second dragon.

She walked a few steps away till she came to a tree, and with her hands on its bole she felt her way to the ground, and sat with her knees drawn up and her head between them for a few minutes. Her head began to clear, and her breathing slowed, and as she looked up and blinked vaguely at the leaves overhead, she heard Talat's hoofbeats behind her. She put out a hand, and he put his bloody nose into it, and so they remained for several heartbeats more, and then Aerin sighed and stood up. "Even dragons need water. Let's look for a stream."

Again they were lucky, for there was one close at hand. Aerin carefully washed Talat's face, and discovered that most of the blood was dragon's, although his forelock was singed half away. "And to think I almost didn't bother to put any kenet on your head," she murmured. "I thought it was going to be so easy." She pulled Talat's saddle off to give him a proper bath, after which he climbed the bank and found a nice scratchy bit of dirt and rolled vigorously, and stood up again mud-colored. "Oh dear," said Aerin. She splashed water on her face and hands and then abruptly pulled off all her dragon-tainted clothing and submerged. She came up again when she needed to breathe, chased Talat back into the water to wash the mud off, and then brushed and rubbed him hard till she was warm and dry with the work and he was at least no more than damp.

She dressed slowly and with reluctance, and they returned to the battlefield. She tried to remember what else she ought to have thought of about dragons. Eggs? Well, if there were eggs, they'd die, for new-hatched dragons depended on their parents for several months. And if there were young dragons, surely we'd have seen them—?

With much greater reluctance she tied together some dry brush and set fire to it from her tinder box, and approached the dark foul-smelling hole in the rock. She had to stoop to get inside the cave at all, and her torch guttered and tried to go out. She had an impression of a shallow cave with irregular walls of rock and dirt, and a pebbly floor; but she could not bear the smell, or the knowledge that the grisly creatures she had just killed had lived here, and she jerked back outside into the sunlight again, and dropped her torch, and stamped out the fire. She didn't think there were any eggs, or dragon kits. She'd have to hope there weren't.

She thought: I have to take the heads with me. The hunters always bring the heads—and it does prove it without a lot of talking about it. I don't think I can talk about it. So she picked up her sword again and whacked off the second dragon's head, and then washed her sword and dagger in the stream, resheathed them, and tied her spear behind the saddle. The dragons looked small now, motionless and headless, little bigger and no more dangerous than rabbits; and the ugly heads, with the long noses and sharp teeth, looked false, like masks in a monster-play for the children during one of the City holidays, where part of the fun is to be frightened—but not very much. Who could be frightened of a dragon?

I could, she thought.

She tied the heads in the heavy cloth she'd carried her leather suit in, and mounted Talat, and they went slowly back to the village.

The villagers were all waiting, over a hundred of them, gathered at the edge of town; the fields beyond the village were empty, and men and women in their working clothes, looking odd in their idleness, all stood watching the path Aerin and Talat had disappeared down only an hour ago. A murmur arose as the front rank caught sight of them, and Talat raised his head and arched his neck, for he remembered how it should be, coming home from battle and bearing news of victory. The people pressed forward, and as Talat came out of the trees they surrounded him, looking up at Aerin: Just the one girl and her fine horse, surely they have not faced the dragon, for they are uninjured; and they were embarrassed to hope for a sol's burns, but they wished so sorely for the end of the dragon.

"Lady?" one man said hesitantly. "Did you meet the dragon?"

Aerin realized that their silence was uncertainty, and she smiled in relief, and the villagers smiled back at her, wonderingly. "Yes, I met your dragon; and its mate." She reached behind her and pulled at the cloth that held the heads, and the heads fell to the ground; one rolled, and the villagers scattered before it as if it still had some power to do them harm. Then they laughed a little sheepishly at themselves; and then everyone turned as the boy who had announced Aerin's arrival said, "Look!"

Seven horsemen were riding into the village as Aerin had ridden in. "You weren't supposed to get here till tomorrow," she murmured, for she recognized Gebeth and Mik and Orin, who were cousins of hers a few times removed and members of her father's court, and four of their men. Gebeth and Orin had been on many dragon hunts before; they were loyal and reliable, and did not consider dragon-hunting beneath them, for it was a thing that needed to be done, and a service they could do for their king.

"Aerin-sol," said Gebeth; his voice was surprised, respectful—for her father's sake, not hers—and disapproving. He would not scold her in front of the villagers, but he would certainly give Arlbeth a highly colored tale later on.

"Gebeth," she said. She watched with a certain ironic pleasure as he tried to think of a way to ask her what she was doing here; and then Orin, behind him, said something, and pointed to the ground where the small dragons' heads lay in the dust. Gebeth dropped his gaze from the unwelcome sight of his sovereign's young daughter rigged out like a soldier boy who has seen better days, realized what he was looking at, and yanked his eyes up again to stare disbelievingly at red-haired Aerin in her torn leather suit.

"I—er—I've gotten rid of the dragons already, if that's what you mean," said Aerin.

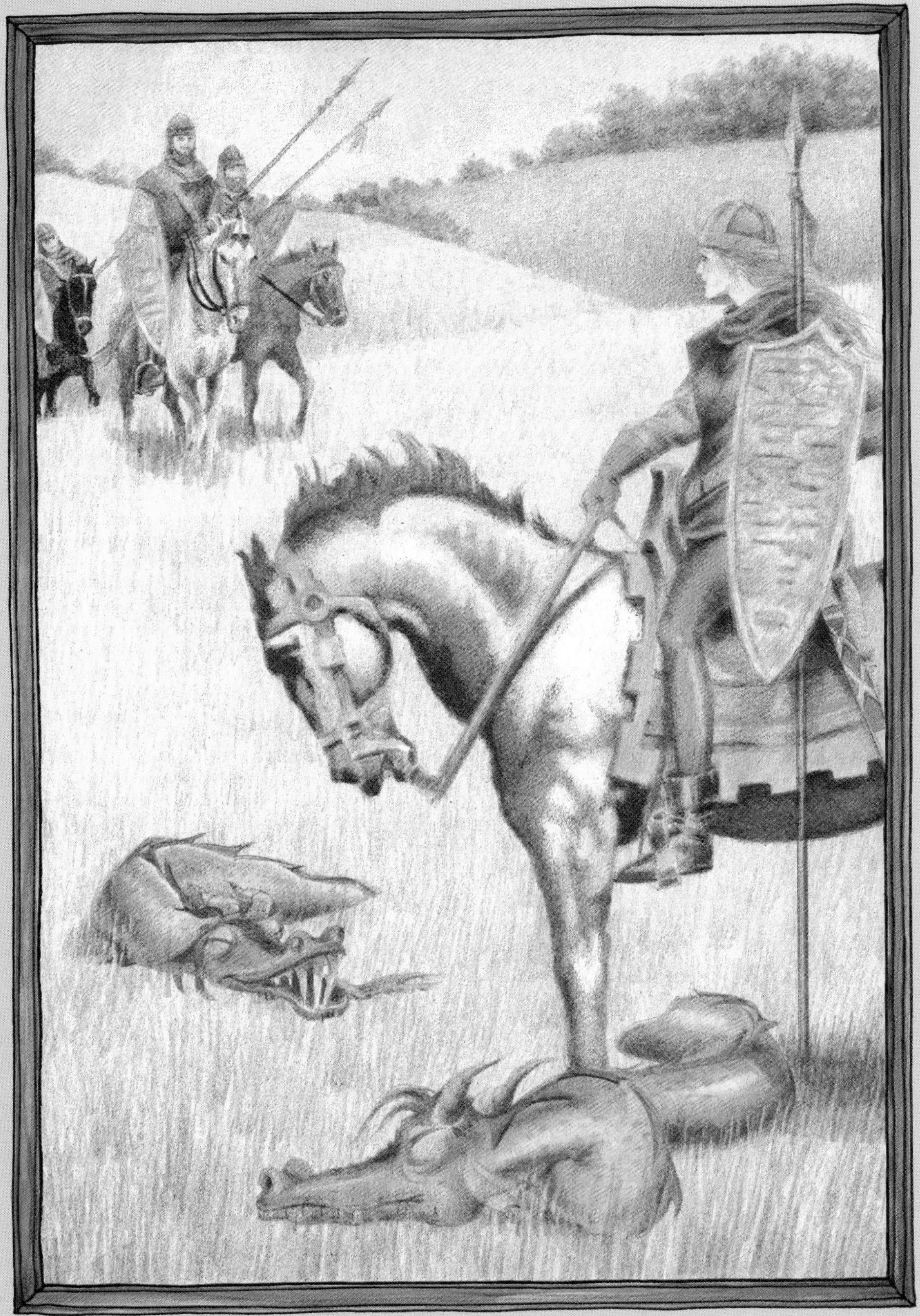

Gebeth dismounted, slowly, and slowly stooped down to stare at her trophies. The jaws of one were open, and the sharp teeth showed. Gebeth was not a rapid nor an original thinker, and he remained squatting on his heels and staring at the grisly heads long after he needed only to verify the dragonness of them. As slowly as he had stooped he straightened up again and bowed, stiffly, to Aerin, saying, "Lady, I salute you." His fingers flicked out in some ritual recognition or other, but Aerin couldn't tell which salute he was offering her, and rather doubted he knew which one he wanted to give. "Thank you," she said gravely.

Gebeth turned and caught the eye of one of his men, who dismounted and wrapped the heads up again; and then, as Gebeth gave no further hint, hesitated, and finally approached Talat to tie the bundle behind Aerin's saddle.

"May we escort you home, lady?" Gebeth said, raising his eyes to stare at Talat's pricked and bridleless ears, but carefully avoiding Aerin's face.

"Thank you," she said again, and Gebeth mounted his horse, and turned it back toward the City, and waited, that Aerin might lead; and Talat, who knew about the heads of columns, strode out without any hint from his rider.

The villagers, not entirely sure what they had witnessed, tried a faint cheer as Talat stepped off; and the boy who announced arrivals suddenly ran forward to pat Talat's shoulder, and Talat dropped his nose in acknowledgment and permitted the familiarity. A girl only a few years older than the boy stepped up to catch Aerin's eye, and said clearly, "We thank you." Aerin smiled and said, "The honor is mine." The girl grew to adulthood remembering the first sol's smile, and her seat on her proud white horse.

Do you think that Aerin's decision to hunt for the dragons is wise or foolish? Explain your response.

What kind of person is Aerin?

How is the battle with the dragons more difficult than Aerin anticipated?

What makes Aerin's battle with the dragons different from previous battles of other dragon slayers?

WRITE Write a diary entry in which Aerin tells what she thinks she accomplished by slaying the dragons.

WORDS ABOUT THE AUTHOR

Robin McKinley

Jennifer Carolyn Robin McKinley was born November 16, 1952, in Warren, Ohio. Robin's love of stories and books began when she was very young. Being read to by her mother, a teacher, is one of her earliest childhood memories. Her father, an officer in the United States Navy and the Merchant Marine, traveled extensively and brought home books from abroad for Robin.

AWARD-WINNING AUTHOR

Books became both home and friends for Robin because she was an only child and her parents relocated frequently. She actually remembers the events of her life by recalling the books she was reading at the time.

Along with Robin McKinley's love of reading came a preoccupation with creating stories. She told herself stories about young girls who were misfits or who were misunderstood but became unlikely heroes during their adventuresome and exciting lives. These stories were the seeds from which several of her published works grew.

At an early age she developed a love of horses, which she has maintained throughout her life. At age eight, she moved to Japan, where she was able to take horseback riding lessons for several years. Later McKinley took dressage lessons while working part-time on a horse farm outside of Boston. Although neither she nor the horse was a natural at this disciplined riding, she realized that through hard work and determination they could both succeed. This realization is illustrated in the character of Aerin, whose hard-won success is a matter of hard work and determination, not luck.

Although McKinley describes writing as hard work, she finds it exhilarating, which enables her to press on. Sometimes as she writes, the stories seem to happen automatically, ending altogether differently from what she had expected, or not ending at all. When that happens, the result is more adventures or books.

When asked by young writers for advice, Robin McKinley tells them to read and write as much as possible. She reminds them that good writing takes practice, as does anything else done well.

NEWFANGLED PRINCESSES

Which character in these selections seems the least like one that you would find in a traditional fairy tale? Explain your answer.

WRITER'S WORKSHOP

How would you add a new and interesting twist to a familiar fairy tale? Might you tell about another kind of newfangled princess? Might you set the story in modern times? Write a play or a skit in which you present your own version of a scene from a fairy tale.

Writer's Choice Think about your favorite TV actor or character. Does he or she remind you of any fairy-tale character? What part in a fairy tale can you imagine the actor playing? Respond in any kind of writing you like, and share the results.

CONNECTIONS

MULTICULTURAL CONNECTION

TELLING TALES

In Indonesia, two classic tales are told in unique and fascinating ways: through dance and puppet plays. The two tales are Indian epic poems, the *Ramayana* and the *Mahabharata*, which tell stories about Hindu heroes and gods. They were brought to Indonesia more than a thousand years ago and have become a vital part of Indonesian culture.

In classical Indonesian dance, these tales are told through intricate and symbolic gestures and movements. The graceful motion of a dancer's hands can convey a powerful emotion or message to the audience. The dance is enhanced by elaborate costumes and the music of a gamelan [gam'ə•län] orchestra, which includes up to thirty gongs, drums, and xylophones.

Another storytelling tradition of Indonesia is the shadow puppet play, in which the audience views the shadows of flat, detailed puppets held behind a white screen. A puppet master tells the story, moves the intricately made puppets, and provides their voices, while directing a gamelan orchestra. Sometimes the puppet master adds scenes or dialogue that comments on current events. Puppet plays are very popular and can last all night.

In class, brainstorm some ideas for a puppet play. You might think of a traditional tale that would make a good puppet play, or you can invent your own story with interesting characters and an action-filled plot.

LANGUAGE ARTS/ART CONNECTION

SHADOW PUPPET PLAY

With a partner or small group, write a script based on one of your puppet play ideas. Also design the puppet characters for your play, and sketch scenes showing their actions at important moments in the play. Share your story and designs with classmates. You might even enjoy making your puppets out of stiff paper, mounting them on sticks, and performing your play in class.

SOCIAL STUDIES/MATH CONNECTION

INDONESIAN DATA

Indonesia is an island nation with the fifth-largest population in the world. Find out the area of Indonesia in square miles and the total population of the country. Then calculate the population density per square mile. Next, find out the area and population of Java, the island on which most Indonesians live, and calculate the population density of Java. What conclusions can you draw about the country from your calculations?

Clockwise from top: An Indonesian puppet master working behind a screen; Legong dancers, Bali, Indonesia; Audience view of an Indonesian puppet play; a close-up of a Wayang Kulit puppet, showing the intricate details

UNIT FIVE

HOME PLANET

It is only a little planet
But how beautiful it is.
Robinson Jeffers

The first pictures of the earth from space gave us a new perspective on our planet. From space, the boundaries between countries do not exist; the earth belongs to everyone, and all people must work together to protect this "little planet" and preserve its beauty. In this unit you will see how Native Americans of today continue their tradition of respect for the earth and how scientific exploration can enhance our appreciation of our home planet. As you read, think about what you might do to make our planet a better place.

THEMES

BOOKSHELF

THE SIERRA CLUB BOOK OF OUR NATIONAL PARKS

BY DONALD YOUNG WITH CYNTHIA OVERBECK BIX

The national parks of the United States contain many natural wonders. Here is the story of how these wonders came to belong to all Americans.

HARCOURT BRACE LIBRARY BOOK

THE BIG WAVE

BY PEARL S. BUCK

In this story about the big wave that destroys families and an entire village, a young Japanese boy learns to be brave in the face of adversity and to appreciate life.

Child Study Association's Children's Book Award

SURTSEY: THE NEWEST PLACE ON EARTH

BY KATHRYN LASKY

Illustrated with spectacular photographs, this book describes the recent emergence of the island of Surtsey off the coast of Iceland.

ALA Notable Book, Outstanding Science Trade Book for Children

BLUE PLANET

BY BARBARA EMBURY HEHNER

Based on the IMAX® film *Blue Planet*, this book offers a panoramic view of our home planet as it explores the forces that shape Earth and the natural cycles that make life possible.

EARTHQUAKE

BY BRIAN KNAPP

This fascinating book describes the causes of earthquakes, landslides, and tsunamis. It also examines ways that people can be prepared for such disasters.

THEME

APPRECIATING THE EARTH

Many people today are concerned with the need to protect our natural environment. One threatened environment is the Everglades in Florida. The following selections will take you to the Everglades and explain why this area, as well as the earth itself, should be respected.

CONTENTS

EVERGLADES COUNTRY

*by **Patricia Lauber***

Tucked in the southern tip of Florida, Everglades is the third largest national park. It is nearly twice the size of Rhode Island, containing some one and a half million acres of land and water. Everglades is, like the other parks, a piece of wilderness set aside to be preserved in its natural state. But in one way it stands alone. Other parks were established to preserve geological or scenic features of the North American continent. Everglades was established to protect and preserve the many forms of life within its boundaries. Here are no soaring snow-capped mountains, no geysers, no giant canyons, no glaciers. This is a park of life: of birds and mammals, of fish, reptiles, and amphibians, and of plants.

The Everglades was once a free-running river. Like any other river, it had a channel through which water flowed from higher to lower ground as it moved toward the sea. It had a place where it began: Okeechobee, the large lake in the center of Florida. It had a place where it

ended, where its waters met the sea: the tidal estuaries of the Gulf of Mexico and of Florida Bay. Here the resemblance to other rivers ended. The Everglades was not the kind of river that appears on maps as a thin blue line.

Sweeping in an arc through south Florida, the Everglades was only about one hundred twenty miles long, but it was, on the average, forty miles wide. Its waters were seldom more than two feet deep, and they flowed so slowly that they seemed to lie unmoving, like a lens upon the land.

Draining toward the sea, the water wove its way through vast tracts of saw grass, broken only by occasional islands of trees. Saw grass is the plant most characteristic of the Everglades, and that is why the region has been called a "river of grass" and why the Indians named it *Pa-hay-okee,*[1] meaning Grassy Water. Saw grass, however, is really a sedge, not a grass. A true grass has a round hollow stem, whereas a sedge has a triangular solid one, usually with sharp edges. The blades of saw grass are edged with tiny sawlike teeth, as sharp as points of glass.

In the northern Everglades the saw grass grew thick and tall, as tall as fifteen feet. Farther south its stands were less dense, and it grew to heights of four to six feet. Wherever it grew, saw grass was the plant that created the Everglades,

[1] Pa-hay-okee [pä · hī′ō · gē]

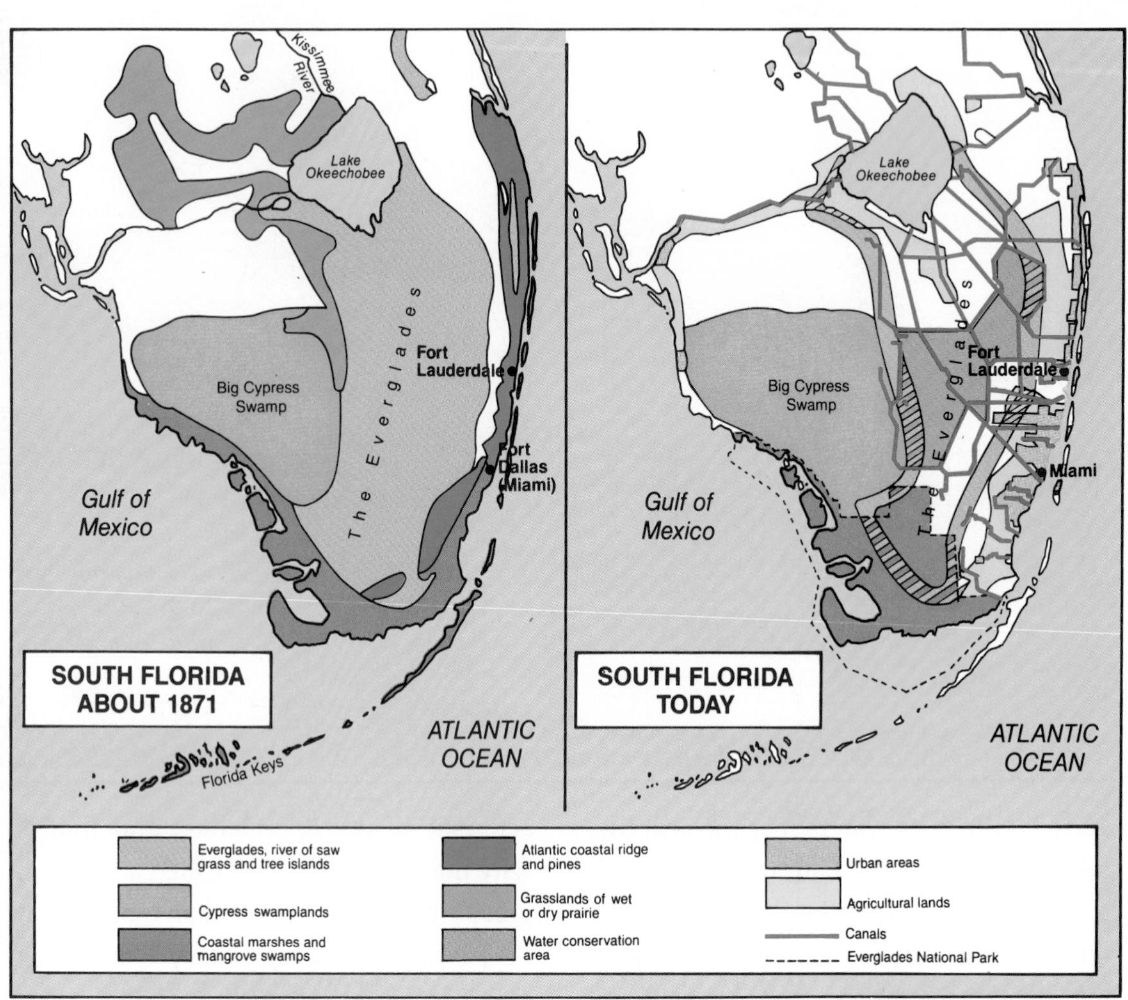

that laid a covering of soil over the bare limestone that had risen from the sea. For hundreds and hundreds of years, saw grass sprang up out of the shallow river, lived, and died. The dead saw grass decayed and, in rotting, began to lay down a thick layer of peat.

The peat covered the limestone. Like a sponge, it absorbed water, stored it, and then released it to go its way. In time, the vast river of grass took shape, curving south from Okeechobee and covering twenty-eight hundred square miles of central Florida.

The river was seasonal, depending on the rains for water. Then, as now, the rains fell only at certain times of year.

All life in the Everglades is tuned to the rains and to water that lies upon the land for months at a time. This has been true for the thousands of years that there has been an Everglades. But in time gone by there was more water and it lay longer upon the land. In those days, before man changed it with canals and levees, the Everglades was a broad, slow-moving river for nine or ten months of the year, and sometimes even longer. Its water came not only from the rains that fell on it but also from the north, from Okeechobee and the Kissimmee Valley.[2]

Okeechobee's lake bed was shaped like a giant shallow saucer. When rains fell in torrents, the lake filled, then spilled over its southern rim. The water flowed slowly into the Everglades. Sometimes hurricane winds scooped water out of the lake and sent it southward too.

The dry season brought an end to the rains and hurricanes. But by then still more water was reaching Okeechobee. It came from a chain of shallow lakes in the Kissimmee Valley to the north. Filled to overflowing by heavy rains, the lakes spilled over into the Kissimmee River. The river wound slowly south, draining the rain-soaked land, spilling into marshes, and emptying eventually into Okeechobee. Again, that big lake filled to the brim and overflowed. The water flowed slowly down the Everglades.

The flow was slow because the land was flat. The southern edge of Okeechobee was only seventeen feet above sea level, and the sea lay one hundred twenty miles distant. The land fell away by about two inches to the mile. Over this flat course the water spread and crept at a rate measured in inches per day rather than the feet per second of other rivers.

Under natural conditions, at least a part of the Everglades was always covered by water. In the dry season, water covered perhaps 10 percent of the land. Then the rains came, drenching the land, healing the cracked mud, filling the hollows, raising the water table, and starting the slow movement of water toward the sea. Later, Okeechobee overflowed and, as water from the Kissimmee reached it, went on overflowing. Water levels in the Everglades rose steadily until by late autumn some 90 percent of the land was under water. Throughout the winter and early spring, water levels dropped and then, with the coming of the rains, began to rise again.

This annual cycle was sometimes broken by natural catastrophes. There were years when hurricanes brought bad floods, and there were also years of drought and fires. But the many kinds of plants and animals survived. They survived flood, drought, and fire, as they survived the changing water levels of a normal year. Each kind was adapted in one or more ways to the land that was the Everglades.

The same thing is true today. That is the reason for the park, which is meant to preserve these many kinds of life. And that is also the problem, for the park does not control its own watery destiny. It lies

[2] Kissimmee [kis · sim′ē]

Everglades National Park is home to many animals such as (left) the alligator and (right) the purple gallinule.

at the southern tip of the Everglades, and it cannot control the flow of water from the north.

The true Everglades, the great river of grass, no longer exists. South of Okeechobee, land has been cleared and drained to open it up for farms, ranches, and towns. Other parts of the Everglades are now surrounded by levees to form huge swampy reservoirs. Water no longer flows freely and seasonally through what was once the Everglades. It moves instead through canals and through gates controlled by man.

Such control has put the park's life under stress and its future in danger. To be the Everglades, even a small piece of it, the park needs the right amounts of water at the right times of year, for its plants, like its animals, are adapted to the conditions that made the Everglades unique.

What do you think is the biggest problem facing Everglades National Park? Explain your answer.

How does Patricia Lauber give this subject a sense of urgency? Use details from the text to support your response.

WRITE Do you think people were right to build canals and clear the land? Or do you think they should have left the Everglades in its natural state? Write a brief statement of your opinion.

Song of the Sky Loom

Tewa Indian song
translated by Herbert Spinden

Oh our Mother the Earth oh our Father the Sky
Your children are we
    with tired backs we bring you the gifts you love

So weave for us a garment of brightness

May the warp be the white light of morning
May the weft be the red light of evening
May the fringes be the falling rain
May the border be the standing rainbow

Weave for us this bright garment
that we may walk where birds sing
    where grass is green

Oh our Mother the Earth oh our Father the Sky

Saddle blanket with tassels
Navajo, New Mexico
Museum of the
American Indian

AWARD-WINNING AUTHOR

Billie Wind, a modern-day thirteen-year-old Seminole Indian, doubts the legends of her ancestors. Having been to school at the Kennedy Space Center, she has little respect for the stories about talking animals and the great serpent who lives in the Everglades. Her uncle Charlie Wind, the tribal medicine man, is concerned about her doubts. With the approval of her parents, Iron Wind and Mamau Whispering Wind, he sends her out into the Everglades to learn that "there is more to the Earth than only the things you can see with your eyes." She is to stay only overnight, but a fire in the Everglades traps her for many days in a cave at the bottom of a sinkhole.

After the earth has cooled, Billie Wind makes a boat from a cypress tree and begins her journey home. She rescues a panther kitten she calls Coootchobee (the Seminole word for panther*), who travels with her until his father appears and carries him away. Then she takes in a gopher turtle, which she names Burden because of an Indian legend that says the quiet turtle carries all the troubles of Earth on its back. Lost in the Everglades, Billie Wind travels for several weeks, following the river's flow toward the sea. Near the coast she sees signs that a hurricane is coming, and she starts looking for a safe place to survive the storm.*

The Talking Earth

by Jean Craighead George
illustrated by Wayne McLaughlin

Burden at her feet, her leggings tucked in her boots, Billie Wind paddled toward the mouth of the river on the incoming tide. She followed the route the spoonbills had taken. Occasionally she glanced back. The clouds were drab sponges, heavy with water, pocked and gray. Her ears ached as the atmospheric pressure dropped lower and lower.

"That's what the animals heard," she said, shaking her head. "The voice of the low."

Three white herons flew overhead, their wings bowing deeply in a strenuous effort to keep aloft in the humid air.

"Mamau Whispering Wind," Billie Wind murmured as the birds of good fortune flew over. "You gave me a strong back. It is better than a charm. But you also gave me a practical mind and I am going to follow the path of the white herons. They are flying to safety."

The birds soared over an island and dropped out of sight. Billie Wind paddled harder, skimming along the edge of the island and into a corridor overhung with mangroves. A violet-blue bay gleamed at the end. She could see the white herons. They were resting on a stump beyond the corridor.

Protected by the trees from the gusting winds, she rode the speeding water down the tunnel. A wrecked sailboat was jammed among some tree trunks. She wished she had time to stop and search it for useful articles. A sail caught her eye. She backwatered and came alongside the boat.

Lifting up a broken mast, she tugged loose a small nylon sail and stuffed it under the mats. Quickly she climbed back into the bow and paddled hard to make up for lost time.

The tide had almost stopped running out. She had about an hour before it turned and started galloping in with such force that she would not be able to withstand it.

"Thirteen feet," she said. "I must get thirteen feet above sea level to be safe from the tidal wave." She recalled the warnings posted in the Florida schools and public places.

The white herons unfolded their wings, flapped them and glided out over the bay. She dug in her paddle and followed. Sliding out of the corridor she saw that the bay was really the wide mouth of a river. The herons crossed the ruffled surface and dropped onto a beach. After a moment they took to their wings again and flew up the river. She stood up. Far ahead of them the land bulged distinctly.

"High land." She sat down. "Could that be the village?"

If so she would have to cross the choppy bay to get to it. If the tide turned when she was in the middle she might be swept away. She thought she had better cling to the shore. But it was miles and miles around. Should she chance it and follow the birds across the bay?

She decided to follow the birds. The bay was growing quieter. The gusts had stopped and the tide had not turned. Lifting her paddle, getting down on her knees, she plunged the dugout onto the steely water. Swiftly she slipped across the surface.

Out of the corner of her eyes she watched the twigs and leaves on the water. Gratefully, she saw they were not moving, going neither inland nor out to sea. They were standing still waiting ominously for the change. She lowered her head and stroked harder. Burden looked up, then pulled her head inside her shell.

The leaves started out to sea. At first they barely moved, but as the storm drew the bay water into its center of low pressure, they began to move faster and faster. Faster and faster. Billie Wind shouted as she fought the tide. The dugout moved slower and slower. Then it stopped. She paddled forward furiously. It slipped and moved backward.

She was only one hundred feet from the beach where the herons had been. She glanced behind her in terror. A straight path led to the sea.

Her eyes fell on the upturned stump of a tree. She steered toward it with one hand while pulling out the sail with the other. As she came alongside she threw the sail over the roots. The snags caught it and she held on. The dugout slowed down and came to a stop.

The tide ran on seaward.

Now what to do?

In five hours the tide would turn again and start back. Could she hang on that long? And if she could, would the storm and the tidal wave come with it? She wrapped the sail around her wrists and held on tighter. She counted. She sang. She listed the herbs in the black drink. She thought of Mamau Whispering Wind and of Charlie Wind. What would they do? Never mind what Charlie Wind would do, what would Whispering Wind do? She took off her headband and tied her wrists to the sail. She tensed her thigh muscles to hold the boat beneath her.

Then the sail went slack. She was no longer straining. She looked over the gunnel. The dugout was grounded on the bottom of the bay. She was high, dry and safe.

Slowly she got to her feet, untied her wrists and studied her situation. She was far from the trickle of water that was the river, but close to the beach. She must abandon her boat and walk. Slinging her deerskin pouch on her back, she picked up the fish spear and tucked the sail into her belt. She took a long drink of fresh water and picked up Burden.

Billie Wind eased out of the dugout, testing the depth of the mire. It was only a few inches deep. Beneath the black residue from the swamp was firm sand. She walked swiftly, not even turning around to bid her dugout good-bye.

Safely on the beach she dropped her possessions, promptly climbed a tree and searched the landscape for the white herons. There was no sign of them; but north along the river was a mound covered with fig and palm trees.

"Calusa mound!" She slid to the ground. "Let's go, Burden." She picked up the turtle, who was digging into the ground again.

Billie Wind recounted the little she knew about the mysterious Calusa. "They understood hurricanes," she said to herself. "They built their villages on stilts above the tidal waves. They constructed forty-foot-high shell mounds on which, some people said, their chiefs lived. That makes sense. From such heights they could see enemies, ships; plan strategies; and, above all, avoid the deadly hurricanes."

Lining up three trees with the mound she walked from one to the next, keeping herself on a beeline course with her destination. Once she climbed a tree and looked back. The bay was empty. The bottom gleamed like quicksilver in the eerie light.

"In five hours it will all come raging back." Shifting Burden to her other arm, she lined up three more trees and plunged into a red mangrove swamp, the worst walking in the world.

The looping roots and interlocking limbs slowed her down to a turtle's pace, for she was forced to climb over some and wedge herself under others. Occasionally she took out her machete and slashed through the binding meshes. She slipped in the mire, fell, got up and walked on.

Two hours later the mosquitoes stopped buzzing and clung to the undersides of the leaves. The wind ceased blowing and an awesome stillness was upon the land. She looked around and plugged on.

After a long struggle that seemed to be getting her nowhere, she decided to climb a tree again and take stock of her position. She should have been at the mound.

The bay was still empty. The storm clouds were rolling over the ground, but the mound was not to be seen. She climbed higher. In the opposite direction from which she had been walking stood the tree-covered rise.

A bird screamed almost in her ear. She shook her head, leaped to the ground and plugged back along her trail. The mire at her feet released stinky bubbles of methane gas.

Learning from her mistake, she climbed trees frequently now to make sure she was on the correct course. Presently there were smaller roots, smaller trees and, at last, she came out of the mangrove forest and stood on the edge of an empty canal. On the other side was the Indian mound. She ran full speed for it.

At its base grew more mangroves, but she barely noticed them in her excitement and relief. Whacking a path up the slope with her machete, she noticed, after a

short climb, that the trees had changed. Mangroves gave way to figs, hardwoods and pines, trees of higher ground. That was encouraging, for she was above the flood mark. Burden thrust her head out of her shell and began digging the air.

At last on the summit, Billie Wind put her down and shinnied up another tree. An innocent landscape awash in a soft veil of clouds stretched out in beauty before her. She clung to the trunk for a long while, enchanted by the drowsy peacefulness of the scene.

A leaf stirred, then another and another.

"Here it comes," she said and slid down the tree to search for a hiding place behind a log or tree where she could pitch her sail and make a tent. Then a powerful gust struck her and almost knocked her over, and she knew a fragile tent would not do. Hurricanes, she remembered, could rip up trees and hurl them through the air like toothpicks.

She must dig into the ground. Make a burrow. And she must dig on the lee side of the mound out of the direct blast of the wind. She took out the adz, found a treeless spot about ten feet below the summit and dug. The first drops of rain struck. They were like cold needles.

"What are you doing here?"

Billie Wind rolled her eyes and looked at Burden.

"What are you doing here?" The turtle's voice was croaky like a frog's.

"Forgive me, Charlie Wind, forgive me. The animals *really* do talk." A pair of running shoes stepped into her peripheral vision. She got slowly to her feet, her eyes following the shoes to the pants, the pants to the shirt, the shirt to the black eyes of an Indian boy. The eyes were wide and frightened, but he held his chin high and his shoulders did not tremble.

"Digging," she finally answered and dropped to her knees. Then she stood up again, reached out and touched him. He was real. He had real cheeks, eyelashes, teeth, fingernails and his breath came and went softly.

"What are *you* doing here?" she asked.

"I'm on my name-seeking quest." His face grew solemn, and he pressed his full lips tightly against his teeth. "I am out adventuring to get a new name."

"You're alone?"

"Yes."

A limb cracked overhead and he glanced into the trees. Leaves twisted and spun on their stems. "Looks like a bad storm."

"It is. The bay is empty of water. That means hurricane." She pulled her machete out of her belt and handed it to the boy.

"Dig," she said. "We've got to make a shelter."

He dropped to his knees and brought the implement down with a smart blow. Billie Wind raked out the shells he had loosened with her adz. Glancing at each other, they set a rhythm and went to work. He striking, she hoeing. When they were three feet into the mound, the shells moved, slid, and the cave collapsed.

"Now what do we do?" the boy asked,

rocking back on his heels. He wore his hair shoulder length and tied with a red thong around his head. His clothes were blue jeans and a T-shirt. A windbreaker was tucked in his belt at his hip.

"Dig," she said and went back to work. He swung the machete without further comment. Billie Wind glanced over her shoulder at him. If he was scared he did not show it.

They dug more carefully now, packing the roof as they tunneled.

"We'll cover the entrance with my sail," she said. "By the way, what day is it?"

"It's the third week in September."

She counted in her head while she hoed out the shells, then whistled a low note. "Twelve weeks. I've been paddling around in this wilderness for twelve weeks."

"What for?"

A section of the ceiling started crumbling and she could not answer.

"What's your name?" she asked when she had stopped the rain of shells.

"Oats," he answered. "Oats Tiger."

She was about to laugh when she thought better of it. After all, her name was pretty funny, too.

"My name's Billie Wind." He did not laugh or comment, just nodded and dug. Presently he sat back on his heels.

"Billie Wind? Did you say Billie Wind?" She shook her head "yes."

"Then you must be the girl the Panther Paw tribe is looking for. Word went out through the medicine men to watch the rivers for a girl in a dugout. Some bulldozer operators said they saw her heading toward the Fahkahatchee. Is that you?"

She did not answer immediately. The wind-gusted rain stung her face and thoughts of Charlie Wind and Mamau Whispering Wind swept over her.

She shook her head to forget. There was no time for self-pity now. She must dig and dig furiously. Billie Wind concentrated her thoughts on her new friend.

"Oats," she said. "Well, that's an easy name to remember."

"It's a dumb name," he snapped. "That's why I'm here. I'm only twelve; not really old enough for an adventure to find a new name. But I don't want to be called Oats anymore, so I persuaded my mother to let me go.

"I've been gone for three days." He paused. "The forecast was sun, with stormy weather next week."

"What name would you like?"

"I don't know. But the council will know when I come home and tell them I found the nest of a rare Everglades kite, tracked a wild cat and . . . dug a shelter from a hurricane." He cast the machete deep.

"They named my brother Cattle Jumper after he stopped a stampede up north of Lake Okeechobee. Maybe they'll call me Machete Joe." He drove the long blade into the ground.

"Watch out!" he shouted. "It's collapsing." They threw their backs against the ceiling, but gravity was relentless. The shells cascaded like water and filled the shelter.

"Now what?" Billie Wind asked. "We've got to crawl under tree roots or do something. The wind will blow us away."

"I'll lash us to a tree with my belt."

"We'll sail off with the tree."

She squatted on the ground, wondering if they would have time to cut off the limbs of a fig tree and lash them together. Fig trees sent down hundreds of roots from their limbs deep into the ground. They would hold even under the worst blows. They could wedge themselves between the roots and limbs and wrap up in the sail. But was there time?

The rain was falling steadily now and turning into spray as stout winds gusted it. Billie Wind's hand touched a chunk of limestone shells fused by water and time. She rolled to her knees and hands.

"A huge hunk of rock," she said. "We can dig under it. It won't collapse." She picked up her adz and crawled to its downhill side.

"Oats! Oats! There's already a cave here." Lying flat on her belly she wiggled her head and shoulders under the rock and looked into a dark room. From far in the back came a hiss.

"Snakes," she called.

"I'm not afraid of snakes," he answered. "Go on in. I'm following." He threw himself down on his belly and caterpillared forward.

"Snake Tiger," he said. "I like that. A snake pit is a good place to hide. It will be dry even in a storm. Snakes don't like to get wet when they sleep."

Billie Wind backed out to get Burden and her deerskin pouch. Coming down the slope, she stepped in a hole beside the limestone rock. It avalanched and carried her into the cave. She was looking at a flat ledge just above her shoulder.

Hissst. Taking her penknife in hand she raised her arm. When her eyes adjusted to the dim light she could make out a low room tilted upward. She was pleased to see that. Water would not collect on the slope. She felt the ground. It was dry.

Hissst. She studied the ledge near the ceiling.

"Are you all right?" Oats called, wiggling his way in.

Two eyes gleamed from the ledge and she dared not answer. She had not heard snakes. She had heard a panther.

A soft purr of recognition vibrated the shelter and the smudge-faced Florida panther came out of the shadows and crouched in a squat.

"Coootchobee!" She reached for him. "I'd know you anywhere with that snub face." She patted his big paw and rubbed

his forehead. "Hello, hello." He rubbed her with his head in greeting.

"Either I have paddled in a circle and am back in the Fahkahatchee Strand, or you have taken your long trek away from your home to settle down on your own territory." She studied him. "I think you're on your own."

The panther licked his paw and washed his face.

"Oats," she whispered. "Come here. Meet my old friend Coootchobee, the panther."

She could hear the shells clatter as he wedged his way toward her.

"A panther?" His voice was tense. She grabbed his hand and pulled him up the incline until he could dig in his shoes and sit up. His jaw was clenched bravely. He did not whimper. Outside the wind whistled as it drove the rain horizontally through the air.

"Listen," said Billie Wind. A low rumble sounded from far away. It slowly grew louder, as if some comet were approaching the earth.

"Tidal wave. It's coming."

Oats moved closer to Billie Wind and the panther. Taking a deep breath, he turned his head until he was looking at Coootchobee.

"He's beautiful," he said, licking his fear-dried lips.

Billie Wind was no longer thinking of Coootchobee. The sound of the sea returning held her spellbound. It moaned like a being. Oats heard and shivered. The air was icy cold. Billie Wind snuggled closer to warm Coootchobee and gave Oats the sail to wrap himself in.

They watched the entranceway. Nothing could be seen but a wall of solid rain. Hours passed. The sun set, and they were in darkness.

Presently Oats lifted his head from his knees.

"The waves are smashing the bottom of the mound. What a tide!"

"We're okay," she said reassuringly. "Coootchobee is not worried; and he knows a lot. Charlie Wind once told me we must keep the animals on Earth, for they know everything: how to keep warm, predict the storms, live in darkness or blazing sun, how to navigate the skies, to organize societies, how to make chemicals and fireproof skins. The animals know the Earth as we do not."

All through the night and the small hours of the morning, Billie Wind and Oats sat still and listened. The cave grew warm with their body heat, and Coootchobee panted in his sleep.

At last the cave brightened. The sun had come over the horizon and was sending its light through the storm clouds into the cave.

"We made it so far," whispered Oats and stretched out his cramped legs. The panther lifted his head.

"Hello," Oats said hoarsely to the sleek beast.

Coootchobee raised his lips and wrinkled his nose. He held the warning expression.

"Oats is all right," Billie Wind said to

the irritated panther and stroked his flat head.

The lips remained lifted.

"He likes you," Billie Wind said.

"He doesn't look like it."

"He hasn't showed his canine teeth. Just lifting his lips and wrinkling his nose means you get a passing grade."

"I want an A," Oats said. "How do I get that?" He sat perfectly still.

Presently Coootchobee lowered his lip, closed his mouth and put his head on his paw, and as he did so, Billie Wind heard a soft expulsion of air.

"Pheww." It was Oats letting out his breath.

The waves continued to boom at the bottom of the mound most of the morning. Then they climbed higher, sending salt spray into the air. The wind sounds increased. The rain deluged the mound.

"We are nearing the height of the storm," Oats said in a low voice. The waves crashed constantly.

"I'm hungry," said Billie Wind. "Want a piece of fish?"

"I can't eat. I must fast like my forefathers did."

"But you need your strength."

"I have strength." He wrapped his arms around his knees as Billie Wind unwrapped the fish and ate.

"I would cheat if I were you."

"I want a new name."

The rain sounded like bullets hitting the earth; the wind shrieked and whistled.

Billie Wind glanced down at Burden. She was halfway into the floor of the den, digging slowly and skillfully as if nothing were happening.

"That turtle is fearless," she said. "She has to be. She carries the Earth on her back."

"You believe that?"

She did not answer. The storm had reached its height, and they were both afraid.

* * *

Sometime before noon the voice of the wind lowered and the waves boomed far away. Half asleep, half awake, Billie Wind heard the change and glanced at Oats. He was still hugging his knees, his eyes wide open.

"Hear that?" she whispered.

"Yes," he answered. "The worst is over."

Coootchobee heard the change, too. He lifted his tawny head, and twisted his ears and listened. Then he yawned, curling his red tongue to the roof of his mouth. His pointed teeth were very white. Billie Wind thought about his presence here on the mound.

"Are we near the Fahkahatchee Strand?" she asked Oats.

"Ten or fifteen miles."

"Very close for an animal that travels twice that far every night."

"Why?"

"I must have paddled backward farther than I thought," she answered. "I last saw Coootchobee on the Fahkahatchee Strand. Where are we?"

"My village is not far from this mound on the Chobee River." He paused. "I hope everyone got to high land. We get hurricane warnings. I am sure my clan went to Naples or the Highway village, where the land is higher.

"I hope my brother went. He was always saying how he would stay home if a hurricane hit so that he could see what it was like. My village is low. Right on the water. But everyone knows what to do."

Oats talked on and on. His fears gone, his life intact, he was thinking about other people.

"Billie Wind," he finally said. "I was afraid. Is that terrible?"

"So was I," she answered. "But it's smart to be afraid sometimes. We are alive because our ancestors were afraid of the hurricanes and built mounds and villages above the storm tides."

"But—Coootchobee. How did you dare go into a panther's den not knowing who he was? That scared me worse than the wind and rain."

"I had no choice. I was avalanched in, but when I saw his face I knew all was going to turn out all right. I saved Coootchobee's life. Now he has saved mine." She rubbed her chin. "That sounds like an old Indian legend, doesn't it?"

Oats nodded and crept down the incline to the den entrance. He thrust his head out.

"Sun!" he called. "The sun is out. Wow, it's wonderful." Billie Wind slid to the entrance and wiggled into the sunlight right behind Oats. She stood up and lifted her arms.

"It's a beautiful summer day. The sky is clear, the sea is blue, the air is warm."

"We must be in the eye of the storm," Oats said. "This must be the hole in the center of the whirling clouds that the weathermen talk about. It's really beautiful; but it's a tease. There's more to come."

Billie Wind ran to the top of the mound. Uprooted trees lay like giant clubs down its side.

"Everything has been destroyed," she whispered uncomfortably.

"Scary," added Oats. "Not even my leather belt would have held us. We would have been blown to our deaths for sure."

After a short time, the clouds covered the sun and circled counterclockwise.

"Here comes the other side of the storm," Oats said. "We're not out of it yet."

The first shower of rain hit the ground as they wiggled back into the den. Coootchobee lifted his head as they came sprawling in.

"Why didn't you get up to see the sun?" Billie Wind asked him. "Did you

know the storm was not over? I think you did. I think the pressure of the air tells you."

Oats crawled up on the ledge away from Coootchobee and stretched out. Presently Billie Wind heard the boy's quiet breathing that told her he was, at last, at ease. The den grew dark. The rain washed down again.

"Oats?"

"What?"

"Do you think the animal gods talk?"

"No."

"I do."

"That's silly. That's just old legends."

"Coootchobee spoke to you."

"Coootchobee spoke to me?"

"He said as plain as he could: 'The storm is not over.'"

Oats thought about that. "That's true. He didn't go out. And that sort of said, 'Why get up when there's more to come?'"

The wind shrieked again and the rain pelted the leaves on the ground; but there was no tidal wave. The fury had gone out of the storm. The sea was back in its bed and could barely be heard as it beat on the shores of the bay. The constant sound put them all to sleep.

Billie Wind awoke in the late afternoon and lay on her back listening to a gentle swish of the rain. She could not hear the wind. Slowly she rolled to her knees and sat up. Burden was in her burrow. Coootchobee was stretched on his side, his eyes open. Oats was still sleeping.

She put her ear to the ground. The turtle was scratching and digging deeper and deeper into the earth.

"I hear what you are saying, Burden. At last, I hear your message. It's the Earth that matters. Not the stars or the comets, but the plain old Earth. And you are right. It's all we've got. Dig it lovingly."

She dozed off again, dreaming not of the galaxies and her distant star, but of grass blades and otters and pure clear water.

The next thing she knew Oats was shouting from the top of the mound.

"The sun! Here it comes again." She slid out the den entrance and ran up the hill to his side, laughing excitedly. Then she became quiet as she looked down on the bay, the islands, the Gulf of Mexico. Not a leaf remained on the once-green mangroves. They had been ripped off by the hundred-mile-an-hour wind and the pounding salt tide. Cast among the trees were boards, splintered boats, seaweed, dead fish, house tops and birds. Billie Wind put her hands to her mouth. The destruction before her was awesome.

"Looks like a nuclear bomb hit it," said Oats. "Nothing is left." He shuddered.

"I heard the turtle speak today," Billie Wind said.

"The turtle speak?" Oats scratched his head. "What did she say?"

"That we must love the Earth or it will look like this."

"What else did she say?"

"That life can be destroyed unless we work at saving it."

"That's true. But, hey, look we survived." He turned his hands palms up, closed them, opened them and held them close to his face.

"I lived through a hurricane."

"I know your new name," Billie Wind said.

"What is it?"

"Hurricane Tiger."

He turned his head quickly and smiled at her.

"I like it. I like it." Throwing his arms above his head he shouted to the clearing sky.

"Hurricane Tiger is my name."

Billie Wind went back for her pouch, took out the fish and coconut and placed it on top of the mound. She sat down.

"Hurricane Tiger," she said, passing the food to him. "Eat up."

He laughed proudly and sat down beside her.

What is your favorite part of this selection? Explain why you like that part.

How does Billie Wind's understanding of the Earth and the animals help her survive the hurricane? Give three examples from the story.

Billie Wind's uncle, Charlie Wind, wants her to learn that "there is more to the Earth than only the things you can see with your eyes." What does she learn?

Do you think Oats has earned the name Hurricane Tiger? Explain your response.

Write In a paragraph or two, comment on Billie Wind's statement that "life can be destroyed unless we work at saving it." How might life on Earth be destroyed? How can we work to save it?

Words About the Author:

Jean Craighead George

Jean Craighead George does a lot of research to get ready for her writing, but not all of her work is done in libraries or museums. Ms. George likes to get out into the world and see things for herself. Much of her preparation for writing involves patiently observing wildlife. When she wrote the *Thirteen Moons* books, she traveled all over the United States to observe animals in their natural settings. She spent six weeks off the coast of Alaska learning about bowhead whales for her book *Water Sky.* Temperatures of thirty-five degrees below zero didn't stop Ms. George from camping on the sea ice during part of this time. In 1979 Ms. George took a raft trip down the Colorado River to get the experience she needed to write *River Rats, Inc.* While researching wolves in Alaska for a *Reader's Digest* article, she was chased by an unfriendly grizzly bear.

AWARD-WINNING AUTHOR

Her experiences with the wolves in Alaska inspired one of her most successful books. "When I returned home from Alaska, I was unable to publish my article on the wolf for the *Reader's Digest,*" she remembers. "I was frustrated. I had notebooks of material from generous scientists, and I had lived with and talked to wolves." She was unable to ignore her experiences and what they had taught her. She worked her ideas into a book for young people that she titled *Julie of the Wolves*. Ms. George says it took her a year and a half to write the book, and she had to rewrite it three times to get it right.

All her time and effort paid off. In 1973 *Julie of the Wolves* earned Jean George one of the highest honors a book for young people can earn, the Newbery Medal. That same year, *Julie of the Wolves* was named one of the ten best children's books of the last 200 years.

The Time We Climbed Snake Mountain

AWARD-WINNING AUTHOR

by Leslie Marmon Silko

Seeing good places
  for my hands
I grab the warm parts of the cliff
    and I feel the mountain as I climb.
Somewhere around here
   yellow spotted snake is sleeping on his rock
     in the sun.

So
 please, I tell them
   watch out,
don't step on the spotted yellow snake
     he lives here.
The mountain is his.

The Three Tetons by Thomas Moran, The White House Collection

The Delight Song of Tsoai-talee

by N. Scott Momaday

View of Rocky Mountain
by Albert Bierstadt (1830–1902)
White House, Washington, D.C.

I am a feather in the bright sky.
I am the blue horse that runs in the plain.
I am the fish that rolls, shining, in the water.
I am the shadow that follows a child.
I am the evening light, the lustre of meadows.
I am an eagle playing with the wind.
I am a cluster of bright beads.
I am the farthest star.
I am the cold of the dawn.
I am the roaring of the rain.
I am the glitter on the crust of the snow.
I am the long track of the moon in a lake.
I am a flame of four colors.
I am a deer standing away in the dusk.
I am a field of sumac and the pomme blanche.
I am an angle of geese upon the winter sky.
I am the hunger of a young wolf.
I am the whole dream of these things.

You see, I am alive, I am alive.
I stand in good relation to the earth.
I stand in good relation to the gods.
I stand in good relation to all that is beautiful.
I stand in good relation to the daughter of Tsen-tainte.
You see, I am alive, I am alive.

APPRECIATING THE EARTH

What attitudes toward the earth do the selections in this section express? Give examples to explain your answer.

WRITER'S WORKSHOP

In "The Talking Earth," Billie Wind hears the turtle say that "life can be destroyed unless we work at saving it." Choose an issue to which that comment could apply. It might be an environmental issue or an issue about the ways that people treat each other. Then write a persuasive essay. Give evidence to get your readers to agree with your opinion or to take an action that you recommend.

Writer's Choice Water—rivers, rain, tidal waves—is mentioned in most of these selections. Choose and carry out a writing idea that relates to water. A poem or a research report, for example, may help you and your readers appreciate the importance of water.

THEME

OUR DYNAMIC PLANET

What is the most outstanding display of nature's power that you have ever witnessed? Earthquakes, volcanoes, and storms remind us that our earth is a dynamic, ever-changing planet. The next selections explore some of these forces of change, showing how they affect both the earth and people's lives.

CONTENTS

by Neill Bell

from *The Book of Where, or How to Be Naturally Geographic*

What would you see if you could look at the world as an astronaut does—from the edge of space? Mostly you would see water.

Earth is a water planet, with more than 70 percent of its surface covered by oceans and seas. It seems almost a mistake to call our world "Earth," since so little of it is actually solid ground.

Some of the land areas are tiny islands, specks that you could hardly see from way up there, hundreds of miles above the earth. Others are huge chunks of land that stretch for thousands of miles: the super-islands that we call continents.

Fits and Pieces

"I think I've found something over here," shouts Judy to the others in the crew. She carefully brushes the dirt away from the smooth, shiny surface of a piece of pottery she has found buried in the Arizona desert. The others continue the search, and by the end of the day, more than 20 pieces have been found nearby.

These bits and pieces of clay are brought back to the laboratory, where they are painstakingly fitted together. Even though a few small chunks are missing, the archaeologists—scientists who specialize in digging up the past—can see that they have found a beautiful bowl made by the Anasazi Indian peoples more than 800 years ago.

The young German scientist studied his maps thoroughly. He felt that the fit between the two continents seemed too good to be a mere accident. If he cut South America from the left side of the map and turned it just a little, it fit almost perfectly into the coast of Africa.

To Alfred Wegener it looked as if the continents had once been joined together and had somehow drifted apart across the Atlantic Ocean to the places where they are now. Maybe, just maybe, he thought, they were once joined like a bowl that has since been broken apart. In his mind he put the bits and pieces back together, and it seemed to him that they fit very well.

Scientists have long agreed that it is all right to reconstruct pottery from fragments found in the same vicinity. But until recently they have rejected the idea that the continents might have once fit together. Most scientists felt certain that Wegener had been working too many jigsaw puzzles. Surely continents of solid rock could not have broken apart and wandered thousands of miles from where they had formerly been joined together. Preposterous!

Today, however, most earth scientists agree that Wegener's farfetched idea that the continents were once joined together is essentially correct. Many clues besides the good fit between the pieces led them to believe that the giant superislands have moved around over the face of our planet.

Look at a world map or a map of the Atlantic Ocean. Can you see possible fits between the lands? Which pieces seem to

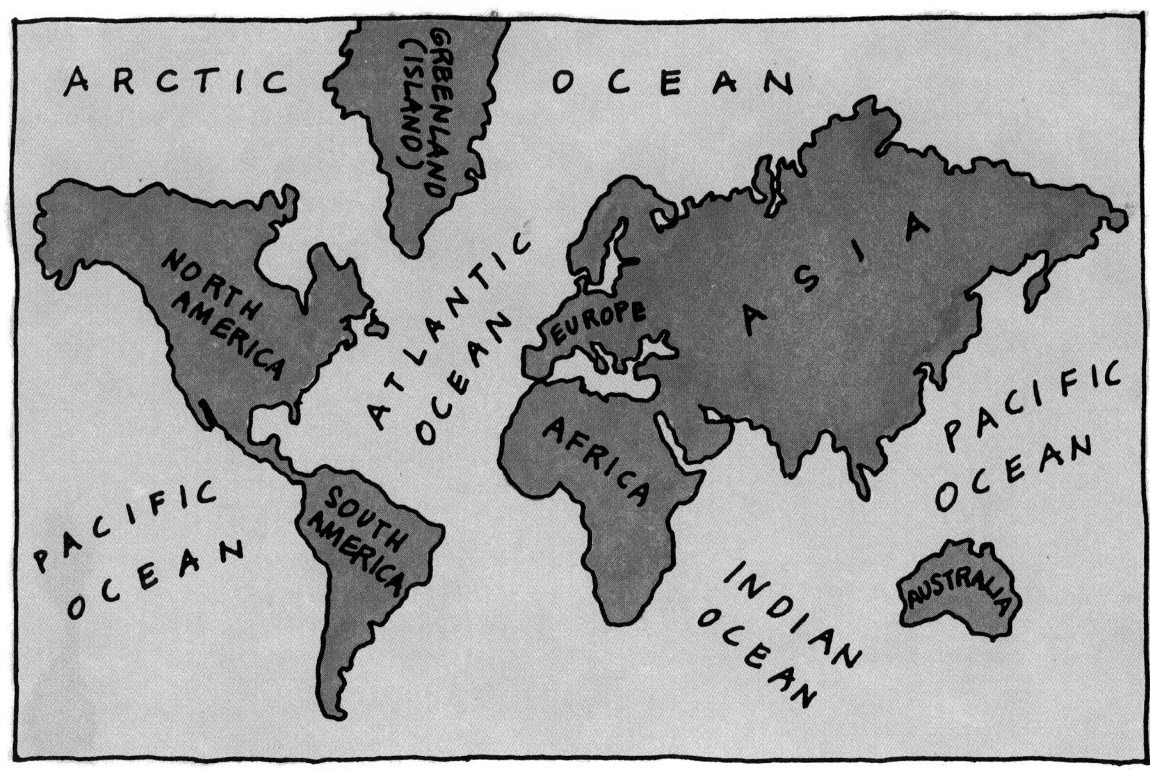

fit together neatly? Where are there gaps? You can probably see where Wegener first got his ideas, but it was many years before proof to support his ideas was collected from all over the world.

Plates That Go Bump in the Night

The idea of drifting continents began to make much more sense when scientists developed the theory that the earth's crust is made up of plates.

An easy way to visualize the plates is to think of a hard-boiled egg. You know how an egg will sometimes crack when it is being boiled in water? The pressure inside causes it to expand, but the shell is too brittle to stretch. Crack! The eggshell breaks into a number of pieces—looking like the plates of the earth's crust.

The difference is that the crustal plates don't stay where they are. It might be the heat inside the earth, or perhaps the force of the earth's spinning that causes the plates to move. No one is certain exactly why they move about, but they do. Most of the time the movement is too slight for us to notice—the plates move only a few inches per year—but sometimes, we may feel the movement as earthquakes or volcanic eruptions.

The real action takes place at the edges of the plates. In some places—such as in the middle of the Atlantic Ocean—the plates are spreading apart. Plates in other areas are being squeezed together.

In fact, some plates are pushed or pulled so hard that they are forced underneath other ones and are finally melted deep inside the earth.

Some of the big chunks of crust carry only ocean on their backs, while some of them carry the huge blocks of light rock that we call continents. Most plates carry some of each.

Where the plates carrying continents bump into each other, tall mountain ranges are often formed—the crust is squeezed together, and mountains are shoved up in towering ranges. In other places, plates carrying continents collide with oceanic plates. The result is that the oceanic plate is forced under the continent, creating deep trenches and arcs of islands.

If all this sounds too difficult to imagine, you can see how it works for yourself by making your own plates. You'll need some stiff paper—index cards, or even paper plates, should work—and a blob of clay (play dough or dry, stiff mud) to serve as your continents.

First try the plates (paper) without continents (clay) on them. If you are using

paper plates, turn them upside down. As you slide the plates together, they should either slip past each other—one going under the other—or collide. What if they collide? If you push them together slowly, you can feel tension increasing as they buckle upward or downward.

What happens if you keep pushing one against the other? The same thing that takes place when two oceanic plates meet head on—one eventually is forced under the other.

Let's see what happens when a plate carrying a continent meets another without one. Put a good-size hunk of clay (or whatever you are using for your continents) on one plate and bring them together again.

If they don't collide, and the continental plate overrides the oceanic one, they slide on without much trouble. (In reality the continental plate also has a blob of rock just as deep on the bottom as on the top. The plate diving underneath scrapes this rock, with earthquakes and volcanic activity resulting.)

What if the continental plate starts to go under the oceanic plate? Try it and see.

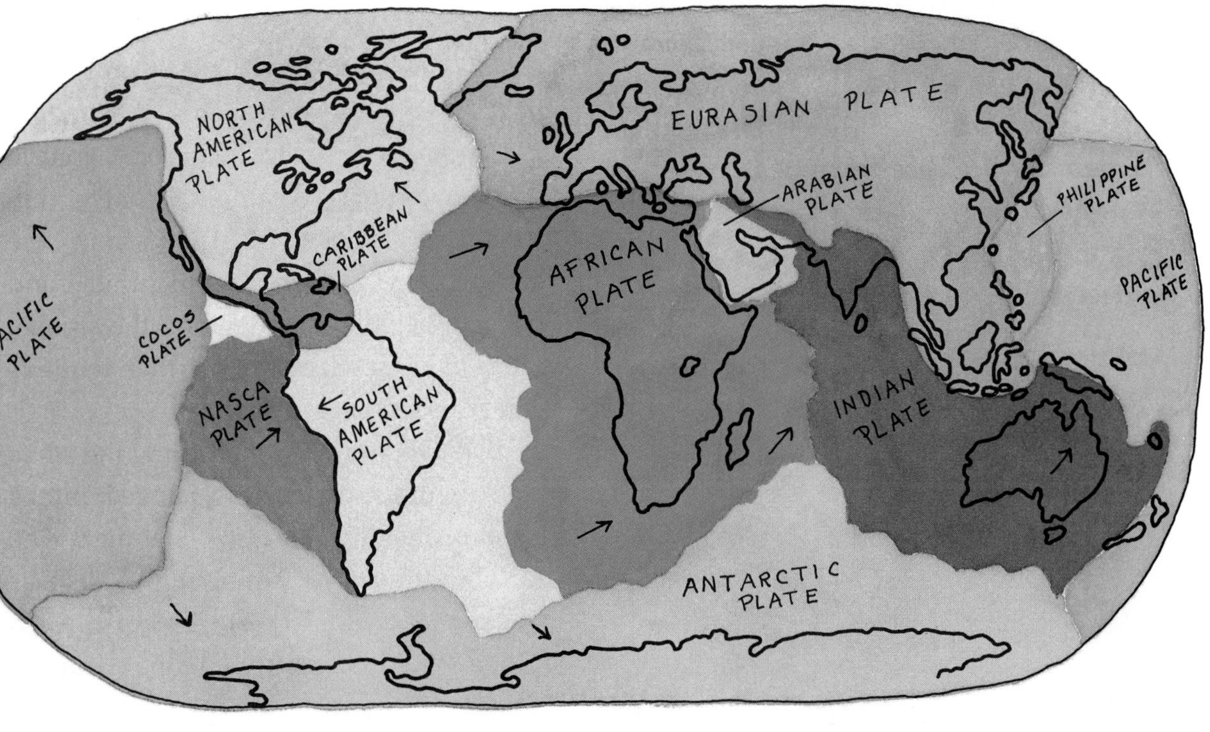

You may be able to push your plates hard enough to move your continental blob, or you may find that your plates act the same way the earth's crust does. The continental rock forces the oceanic plate to flip-flop and turn under the plate carrying it.

See what happens when two plates carrying continental material come together. The plates carrying them are bent and squeezed together until one is forced down. Then the blobs run into each other, and there occurs a dramatic folding of the crust—something your soft clay probably won't do. The earth's highest mountains are believed to be the result of crashes between continental blocks carried on the backs of plates that have crunched together.

Where are the edges of the plates that go bump in the night—and the daytime too? If you trace the centers of the earthquakes and active volcanoes around the world, you will find the outlines of the dozen or more plates that make up the crust of our ever-changing planet.

Middle America, Where the Earth Shakes

Imagine yourself in a Mexican cornfield on a sunny afternoon in February 1943. As you watch farmer Dionisio Pulido working, you notice that a thin stream of smoke is rising from the ground. The earth begins to rumble and fine ash begins to accompany the smoke. There is a smell in the air that reminds you of rotten eggs.

By daylight the next morning the small hole in the ground has changed into a cone of smoking cinders 30 feet high. The earth continues to rumble and shake as smoke, ash, and large rocks are thrown into the air. This noisy outpouring continues all day long, building an even larger cone of cinders that reaches 150 feet above the surrounding fields.

The events of the next day are even more startling. Thick chunks of molten rock come pouring out of cracks near the base of the growing cone, covering the cornfield to a depth of more than ten feet. The hissing of steam and the roar of the explosions from inside the cone are deafening to anyone standing within a mile, and smoke billows upward thousands of feet into the darkening sky.

Within a few weeks the molten rock flows and ash have buried not only the cornfield, but Dionisio's home village of Paricutin (pa-ree-ku-TEEN).

That little puff of smoke you saw was the birth of a volcano 1,500 feet high, whose lava flows buried more than 15 square miles of farmland.

The area between the continents of North and South America has seen many sights similar to this one. That long, narrow strip of land known as Central America is the place where several of the earth's crustal plates are pushing together. It was there in the centuries before the arrival of Columbus that the Aztec, Maya, and Toltec peoples built their great cities of stone.

The records these native civilizations left tell us that their lands have been shaking for thousands of years. A line of volcanoes runs the length of Central America, from just north of Paricutin, south through Panama, including the towering twin peaks of Popocatepetl

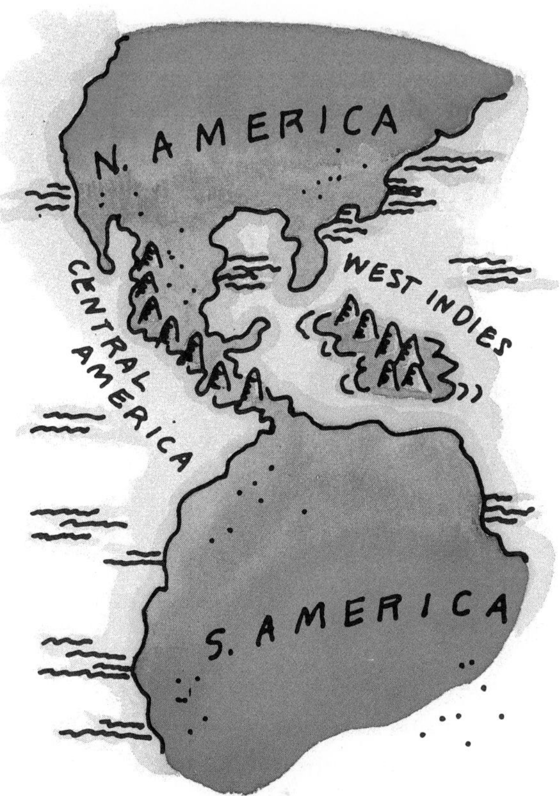

(po-po-cah-tay-PET-il), which is 17,887 feet high, Citlaltepetl (seat-lol-tay-PET-il), which is 18,701 feet high, and fiery Izalco (ee-ZAHL-co) in El Salvador.

Volcanoes are no strangers to the islands of the West Indies either. A few of the islands in the group called the Lesser Antilles have active volcanoes that have proven destructive in this century, the most famous of which is Mt. Pelee (PAY-lay) on the island of Martinique (mar-ti-NEEK).

Pelee had been sending rumbling signals for several months before the big eruption took place, and worried islanders from all over Martinique had come to the town of St. Pierre to seek refuge. But on the morning of May 8, 1902, the side of the volcano blew open, and a cloud of superheated steam and ash roared down toward the town. Within minutes the fiery cloud engulfed St. Pierre, killing the entire population of 30,000 people, except one scorched prisoner who was in a cell below ground.

A RETIRED VOLCANO

The same crustal plate movements that produce volcanic activity have also produced many devastating earthquakes in Central America. During the 1970s alone, two earthquakes destroyed the capital cities of Managua, Nicaragua, and Guatemala City, Guatemala. These earthquakes left more than a million and a half people homeless.

The "land bridge" connecting the two Americas is thus a shaky one. Yet some of the land's restlessness has been helpful to people because the soils produced by volcanic activity are unusually fertile. Many of the bananas and coffee beans enjoyed by people around the world would not grow so well had it not been for the scary events that gave the region its rich soil.

What about the area where you live—has there been a history of volcanic activity or earthquakes? We ordinarily think of volcanoes and earthquakes occurring only on the western edge of North America, where the earth is very restless. The Cascade Range in California, Oregon, Washington, and British Columbia has shown that it is far from extinct—a term best reserved for retired volcanoes. Mt. St. Helens in the Cascade Range erupted explosively in 1980.

Most people who have studied the geologic, or earth science, history of the West expect strong earthquakes there again at any time.

Even if you don't live in the West, you may be able to find some shaky earth in

your area's background. Surprisingly, powerful earthquakes have been known to shake such places as Boston, Massachusetts; Charleston, South Carolina; and the Mississippi Valley. See if you can find out if there has ever been a quake in your area, and if so, when it happened.

There may even have been volcanoes in your area's past. The granite rock that is found in many parts of the eastern United States was formed by volcanic action within the earth's crust many years ago, and there are other places where ancient lava once poured out of the earth to form features that can be identified even today. Do you have any remnants of a fiery eruption in your own backyard? What is that smell? Whew, it's only some eggs boiling.

AN EARTHQUAKE-RESISTANT HOME

Did any of the information in this selection change your ideas about the earth? Explain.

Explain the theory of crustal plates.

How can learning about earthquakes and volcanic eruptions in past history help us understand what to expect from those in the future?

Write Do you live or would you live where earthquakes or volcanic eruptions have occurred? In one or two paragraphs, share your thoughts about living in such an area.

CHARLES RICHTER

EARTHQUAKE MAN

BY CATHERINE PLUDE

Just before six o'clock in the morning on February 9, 1971, many residents of the northern Los Angeles area were jolted awake by the shaking and rumbling of an earthquake. One of those residents was Charles Francis Richter, who, according to his wife, "jumped up screaming and scared the cat." This was certainly not a very scientific reaction, especially coming from one of the world's leading seismologists. Those who knew Dr. Richter well, however, probably figured his screams were more of delight than terror, for earthquakes were his life's work, and this was a firsthand experience!

Richter was born on April 26, 1900, on a farm near Hamilton, Ohio. He moved with his family to the Los Angeles area when he was nine years old. At the age of twenty, he received a bachelor's degree in physics from Stanford University, then enrolled at the California Institute of Technology (Caltech) in Pasadena for graduate study in theoretical physics.

In 1927, a year before he received his doctoral degree, Richter began a "temporary" job as a physicist at Caltech's new Seismological Laboratory. That job turned out to be the beginning of a lifelong career at Caltech. He not only continued his research at the laboratory, but he also joined the institute's teaching staff. He achieved the rank of full professor of seismology in 1952, and when he retired in 1970, he was given the honorary title of "professor emeritus."

When Richter was still a young research assistant at Caltech, he was given the task of collecting data on Southern California's earthquakes so that an annual catalog could be published comparing those quakes. While working on this assignment, Richter became very frustrated with the scale then being used to measure earthquake intensity. That scale, the Mercalli scale, depended mainly on human observation of damage done to structures and on the impressions of the people who experienced a quake. Richter believed that too much misinterpretation would result if he used the Mercalli scale for his data, so he set about developing a scale that would be more scientific and objective.

Richter devised such a scale in 1935. It provided a much more accurate method of comparing earthquakes than the Mercalli scale because it relied on seismic data and mathematics to determine the ground motion of a quake. It also allowed seismologists a means to estimate the energy released at the epicenter.

Because Richter was assisted in the development of his scale by Beno Gutenberg, who was then the director of the Caltech laboratory, some seismologists believe the scale should be called the "Richter-Gutenberg scale." Richter himself referred to it as "the scale," "the magnitude scale," or, sometimes, "that confounded scale." Nevertheless, "Richter scale" caught on with the general public, and today this term is used by seismologists all over the world to describe the magnitude of an earthquake.

In addition to his research and teaching duties at Caltech, Richter wrote two books about seismology, one of them coauthored with Gutenberg. Also, he spent one year as a Fulbright research scholar at Tokyo University in Japan. He devoted long hours to his work, and although he enjoyed literature as well as long hikes in the mountains, he spent much of his leisure time analyzing data on the seismograph he had installed in his living room.

One of his colleagues called Richter "a walking encyclopedia of seismic data," and supposedly he never forgot anything about earthquakes. This was not true about the more ordinary things in life, however. One time he showed up at a formal dinner party wearing a shoestring for a tie because he

had forgotten the black tie he was supposed to wear. While he was skeptical about earthquake prediction as a science, Richter was very concerned about earthquake *preparedness.* "Most loss of life and property has been due to the collapse of antiquated and unsafe structures," he once said. After his retirement from Caltech, Richter helped establish a consulting firm that offered seismic evaluations of structures, and it was his hope that this situation would someday be remedied.

The "earthquake man" died on September 30, 1985, after suffering from heart disease for several years. Just a few days before his death, Mexico City was rocked by two giant earthquakes in which thousands of people were killed by toppled buildings. Many of those buildings were structurally unsafe and built on unstable soils. It is certain that Charles Richter, watching scenes of the earthquake damage on the television set in his hospital room, felt that many of those lives had been needlessly lost.

What have you learned about the study of earthquakes that you did not know before?

How might Richter's life's work have been both frustrating and rewarding? Explain your response.

WRITE List some things you think a seismologist must study in order to predict earthquakes and help communities prepare for them

The Richter Scale

The scale that Charles Richter and Beno Gutenberg devised is "open-ended," meaning that it has no upper or lower limits. Although no earthquake has yet been measured above a magnitude-9,* there is no highest number on the scale, and a very small tremor might be assigned a number below zero.

Each number on the Richter scale represents a tenfold increase in seismic wave activity, or ground motion, and approximately a thirtyfold increase in energy released by a quake. This means that a quake that has a magnitude-8 on the Richter scale has ten times more ground motion than a 7, one hundred times (10 x 10) more than a 6, and one thousand times (10 x 10 x 10) more than a 5. In the measurement of energy, or force, a magnitude-8 quake is about thirty times more powerful than a 7, nine hundred times (30 x 30) more powerful than a 6, and twenty-seven thousand times (30 x 30 x 30) more powerful than a 5.

* Two earthquakes—one in Alaska (1964) and one in Chile (1960)—were recalculated at a magnitude over 9.

The Cloud-Mobile

AWARD-WINNING AUTHOR

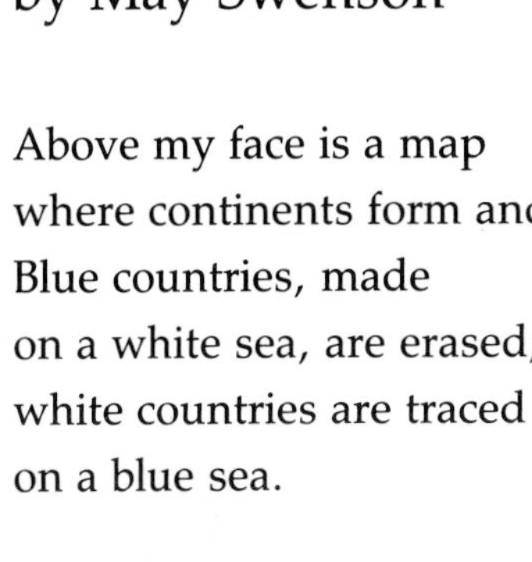

by May Swenson

Moonlight Seascape 2,
Artist Unknown

Above my face is a map
where continents form and fade.
Blue countries, made
on a white sea, are erased;
white countries are traced
on a blue sea.

It is a map that moves
faster than real
but so slow;
only my watching proves
that island has being,
or that bay.

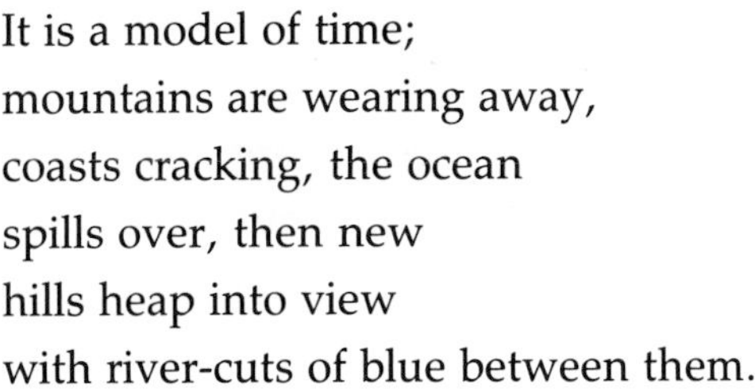

It is a model of time;
mountains are wearing away,
coasts cracking, the ocean
spills over, then new
hills heap into view
with river-cuts of blue between them.

It is a map of change:
this is the way things are
with a stone or a star.
This is the way things go,
hard or soft,
swift or slow.

TORNADO POWER

By Dennis Brindell Fradin

FROM DISASTER! TORNADOES

After the 1979 tornado in Vernon, Texas, Suzy Thomas's family was missing some important papers. They figured they'd never see those papers again. But the papers were sent back to them. They had been blown by the tornado to Woodward, Oklahoma—more than 150 miles away.

The tornado also uprooted 100-foot-tall trees in the horse pasture outside Suzy Thomas's house. Two years later, the gigantic trees were still scattered throughout the pasture.

Such occurrences happen often during tornadoes. Their powerful winds can do many astounding things.

Cars are often sent flying long distances by tornadoes. So are other heavy objects. In 1975, a Mississippi twister lifted a home freezer and blew it more than a mile through the air before dropping it. In 1931, a Minnesota tornado lifted a train car weighing 160,000 pounds and carried it 80 feet through the air before throwing it in a ditch. Of the 117 people in the train car, only one man died.

Buildings, too, have been moved by tornadoes. A 1966 tornado in Topeka, Kansas, moved a ten-story building right off its foundations. Do you remember how Dorothy in *The Wizard of Oz* had her house lifted by a twister? In Ponca City, Oklahoma, a man and his wife were eating supper when their house was suddenly lifted by a tornado. Except for the floor, the

house was blown to pieces. The floor—with the man and woman on it—was set back down on the ground. The unhurt couple weren't in the land of Oz, though. They were still in Ponca City, Oklahoma.

Many strange things have happened to animals during tornadoes. Chickens have had all their feathers plucked out by the strong winds. Sheep have had their wool sheared off.

Animals have found themselves going on unexpected trips inside tornadoes. Once in Kansas, a herd of steers was sent flying through the sky. One person who saw them said that they looked "like a flight of gigantic birds."

You've heard the expression "It's raining cats and dogs." Once, frogs actually rained down from the sky. This happened after a tornado sucked up a pond that contained hundreds of frogs. When the pond water was set down, so were the frogs.

During a 1970 tornado in Radcliffe, Iowa, Louise Hyland's horse was picked up and blown a mile through the air. "Cheyenne Lady came down on a fence post that poked a hole in her back," Mrs. Hyland remembers. "But she recovered." During the 1979 tornado in Vernon, Texas, a horse was picked up and blown through the air for about two hundred yards. The horse landed near what had been the kitchen of Juan and Isabel Martinez.

People, too, have been carried through the air by tornadoes. A 1913 Nebraska twister carried a young woman through the air for a quarter of a mile. She landed unharmed. Back in 1899, a young boy was lifted by a tornado with his mother and another woman in Kirksville, Missouri. The twister also picked up a horse. According to witnesses, the horse went over a church steeple. After a flight of several blocks, the three people and the horse were set down on the ground. The boy later said that he had seen the horse while in the air. "At one time it was directly over me," he said, "and I was very much afraid I would come in contact with its flying heels."

After tornadoes have passed, people often find objects driven like spears into other objects. It is common to find straw and grass driven into trees and buildings. After a tornado struck St. Louis in 1896, weather bureau chief Willis Moore found a garden spade driven six inches into a tree limb. Before the tornado struck Vernon, Texas, in 1979, the Nava family had a deck of cards on a shelf. "The ace card was driven right into the wall—where it stuck," remembered twelve-year-old Billy Joe Nava.

The power of tornadoes also has made deep impressions on the minds of people. An 1861 tornado that struck Camanche, Iowa, was witnessed by a farmer named Benjamin F. Gue. Gue, later lieutenant governor of Iowa, wrote this description:

Suddenly the funnel rose into the air and I could see falling to the earth tree tops, rails, boards, posts, and every conceivable broken fragment of wrecked buildings. . . . It was an awe-inspiring sight. . . . The cloud of inky blackness settled down to the earth again in the distance, sweeping on with a mighty power, glowing with a thousand forked tongues of lightning as the very earth seemed to tremble beneath the incessant roar of thunder. No pen or tongue can convey to the mind a true picture of the frightful sights and sounds . . . of that irresistible tornado.

One hundred and twenty years later, newspaperman Dennis Spruill sat in his office and remembered how he felt when the Wichita Falls tornado almost sucked him out of his house: "I've never felt anything like the power of that tornado," he said. "I felt it could overcome any obstacle I could think of. I could feel and sense its power all around me. I can't even put into words the feeling of its great power. I've never had to describe something like that before. It was that ultimate phenomenon of nature we've named a tornado."

Journalist Dennis Spruill said that a tornado is the "ultimate phenomenon of nature." Do you agree or disagree? Explain your response.

Compare the tornado stories in this selection. Then tell which story you found the most astonishing and why.

WRITE Reread Benjamin F. Gue's description of a tornado. Then write your own description of a display of nature's power that you have seen.

How to Tell a TORNADO

By Howard Mohr

Listen for noises.
If you do not live
near railroad tracks,
the freight train you hear
is not the Northern Pacific
lost in the storm:
that is a tornado
doing imitations of itself.
One of its favorite sounds
is no sound.
After the high wind, and
before the freight train,
there is a pocket of nothing:
this is when you think
everything has stopped:
do not be fooled.
Leave it all behind
except for a candle
and take to the cellar.

Afterwards
if straws are imbedded
in trees without leaves,
and your house—except
for the unbroken bathroom mirror—
has vanished
without a trace,
and you are naked
except for the right leg
of your pants,
you can safely assume
that a tornado
has gone through your life
without touching it.

What the Twister DID

by **Bill Franzen**

This morning while Daryl Eckner was equalizing my sideburns with his electric clippers, I thought I saw the ring pull from a window shade hanging down from his glasses. At first, it was just dangling down in front of his face, but it started dancing around when Daryl said to me, about the big tornado that hit us a while back, "It could have been worse." Then, just like all the other weird things I'd seen since that tornado, the ring pull was gone.

Daryl was right: it could have been a whole lot worse. Because what the big Palm Sunday twister *didn't* do, fortunately, was harm any man, woman, or

child here. But that was probably only because our heroic ham-radio operators got such speedy advance warnings out around town. And the fact that we all have good, strong storm cellars didn't hurt, either. After that, we were just plain lucky, I guess, because when the big twister lifted (Dad always used to say they can take off as quickly as they land), and people came out of hiding and started looking over the damage to their homes, property, and livestock, the old-timers in town agreed that the twister had been pretty nasty.

It seemed nasty to me, too, even though it was my first experience with one. But there was something else about it. I mean, I didn't have to survey what was left of Mom's and my home and belongings or of my bicycle-repair shop in the barn for very long to understand why people always call tornadoes mischievous. Because you know what the big twister did? It yanked the little man off the top of my horseshoes trophy (seven years ago, in high school, I pitched a pretty accurate shoe) and blew him right into a small soft-drink bottle. Didn't even disturb the right arm he's got cocked back. And you know where we finally found the bottle? Inside one of Mom's empty hatboxes. (Ever since Dad passed on, it seems Mom can't collect enough empty cardboard boxes.) And that turned up in the front seat of my truck, which was discovered about two-thirds of a mile down the road from our place, sitting on top of the Metcalfs' silo, where the dome had been.

Now, if that had been the tornado's only weird trick on us, it wouldn't have seemed so remarkable. But there was a lot more. Take the big Swiss army knife I kept in my top bureau drawer. I found it inside the grass-seed spreader, which had its T-shaped handle stuck through one of the holes of the big birdhouse, which was still sitting undisturbed on its pole in our front yard. And all the blades and tools on the knife were flipped out—same as in the poster they used to have taped up in the window at the hardware store—minus the fish scaler/hook disgorger, which was gone completely. The next week, when the insurance agent was going around the place with me, *that* showed up, with the starter rope from the lawn mower wrapped around it, inside the banjo Dad made for me, from a locally grown gourd, when I was born.

The twister didn't pick on just me and Mom, though. It was to blame for similar "jokes" all over town. Frank Nisswa, the half-Sioux whose farm is on the opposite side of town from us, said the tornado sucked all the water out of his well and carried his china cabinet eight hundred yards before setting it down again in his cornfield, without breaking a single cup or dish. And Frank told me that inside, sitting on top of a stack of dinner plates, he found the vise that had been clamped to his workbench. Yvette Kenner, one of those courageous ham-radio operators I mentioned before, said that she and her boyfriend and her twins came out of their storm cellar expecting the very worst, but all they found was their electronic fun organ's bossa-nova beat playing and their parakeet plucked clean of feathers but otherwise okay. And Daryl Eckner himself, barber and captain of our State Champion tug-of-war team, has told everyone over and over how he climbed out of his cellar to find that the traveling van, with the team's name painted in fancy circus lettering on both sides, which was normally parked in his backyard, had vanished. It hasn't shown up yet. According to Daryl, a spiderweb between the legs of his barbecue—only twenty feet from where the van had been sitting—hadn't been touched. All there was, he said, was the purple foil wrapping from an Easter candy stuck in the middle.

Word of what the big twister did must have gotten out fast, because a man in a red beret—some sort of carnival big shot—showed up during our cleanup. In no time, with the help of our eager ham-radio operators, he had the news out that he'd be setting up a tent where the self-service car wash used to be, and was ready to pay cash for our "tornado curiosities." Even before he got all the tent stakes in the ground he bought Chet Rittie's shotgun-with-seven-blades-of-straw-and-a-mascara-applicator-driven-into-the-stock, and Herman Joplin's phone-receiver-embedded-in-the-leaf-from-a-dinner-table, and Gladys Wells's sneaker-lodged-inside-a-twenty-foot-length-of-hose.

I wonder if it was really that great an idea to be pitching easy money around a town in such disrepair, where everyone's state aid and insurance money was still two weeks away. It was tempting to me, I know, since it came right when I needed cash to get the crane to come in and take my truck down off the Metcalfs' silo. I didn't want to sell my horse-shoe-pitcher-in-the-soft-drink-bottle, though. How many times is a guy—even a guy living in twister country—going to get ahold of a keepsake like that? So, several nights running, once Mom was asleep (it seems she can't sleep enough since Dad passed on), I did something I'm not proud of: I fashioned my *own* twister jokes. I figured the carnival guy wouldn't know the difference, and maybe I'd get my truck down.

It wasn't easy, what with half my bicycle-repair tools scattered who knows where, but after a few sleepless nights in the barn I'd assembled quite a group of "authentic" twister curiosities. There was the half-a-bowling-ball-with-the-bicycle-tire-pump-lodged-in-the-thumb-hole. And the tricky ball-of-piano-wire-and-salad-forks-and-umbrella-skeleton-and-bicycle-spokes-jammed-inside-a-big-goldfish-bowl. And my favorite, which I really wished I could keep—the ice-cream-scoop-coming-out-of-bongos-with-gardening-shears-going-in. Well, the carnival man really went for them—he even whistled when he first picked up the bowling-ball thing. And so I hired the crane for a hundred and seventy-five dollars *and* kept my man-in-the-bottle.

But about two months after the big twister, I put him in one of Mom's empty shoe boxes that still had the white tissue in it and buried it. I didn't need it anymore to know how weird things could be after a tornado, because even though our town was pretty much back together, I couldn't walk down Center Street without, for a moment, seeing some kind of twister curiosity mirage, like a lamp-shade on a fire hydrant, or the float ball from a toilet tank drifting across a big puddle. And once I even thought I saw

Mom's rocker, which we never did find, hooked upside down on the town-hall clock. I even planned how I would wait for the hand to lower to twenty after the hour and catch the thing when it slid off. But it disappeared at ten past. The worst time had to be when I was driving home in my rescued truck, with the annoying new whine it makes over thirty, to share some homemade soup with Mom and finish replacing the shingles. I glanced up at the top of the Metcalfs' silo, where the new dome was under way, and for just a moment I saw myself up there in my truck on twister-lookout, with a portable ham radio on my knees and my half-a-pair-of-binoculars around my neck.

This condition let up all last week, but this morning, in the barber chair, there was that ring pull swinging from Daryl Eckner's glasses. It didn't last long, though, and next thing I knew Daryl was going on and on about the upcoming dance that's supposed to raise money for our tug-of-war team's new van. "We're all bouncing back now, huh?" Daryl said, spinning me around to look at myself in the mirror. And I saw a largemouth bass on my head—until Daryl spun me back a hundred and eighty degrees from the mirror, and I realized it was just the old prizewinner that had always been mounted on Daryl's wall. And tonight, while reorganizing the hall closet, I came across the fancy Sunday bonnet Mom used to wear to church before she started sleeping through the bells. I almost yanked the long peacock feather from under the hatband, but then I realized that that was exactly where it belonged. So while I'm hoping that the ring pull was the last of my mirages, I'm beginning to wonder now if I'll ever again see anything the way I used to.

Why might someone who has experienced a tornado like or dislike this story?

Which, if any, of the tornado curiosities in the story do you think could occur as the result of a real tornado? Explain.

At first the narrator does not want to part with his man-in-the-bottle. Why do you think his feelings about keeping it change?

WRITE In a paragraph, explain whether you think it is a good idea for writers to create humor from serious subjects, as Bill Franzen did in this story.

OUR DYNAMIC PLANET

Which do you think is easiest to predict: a tornado, an earthquake, or a volcanic eruption? Explain your answer.

WRITER'S WORKSHOP

What would you do if an earthquake occurred or a tornado struck? Find out how to prepare for a natural disaster that could happen in your area. Make plans for both your home and your school. Then write a how-to essay for other students in your school to read.

Writer's Choice The word *dynamic* comes from the Greek word *dynamis*, meaning "power" or "strength." Choose a person or an event in your life that could be described as dynamic. Use any form of writing you like to express your thoughts about the power or strength of your topic.

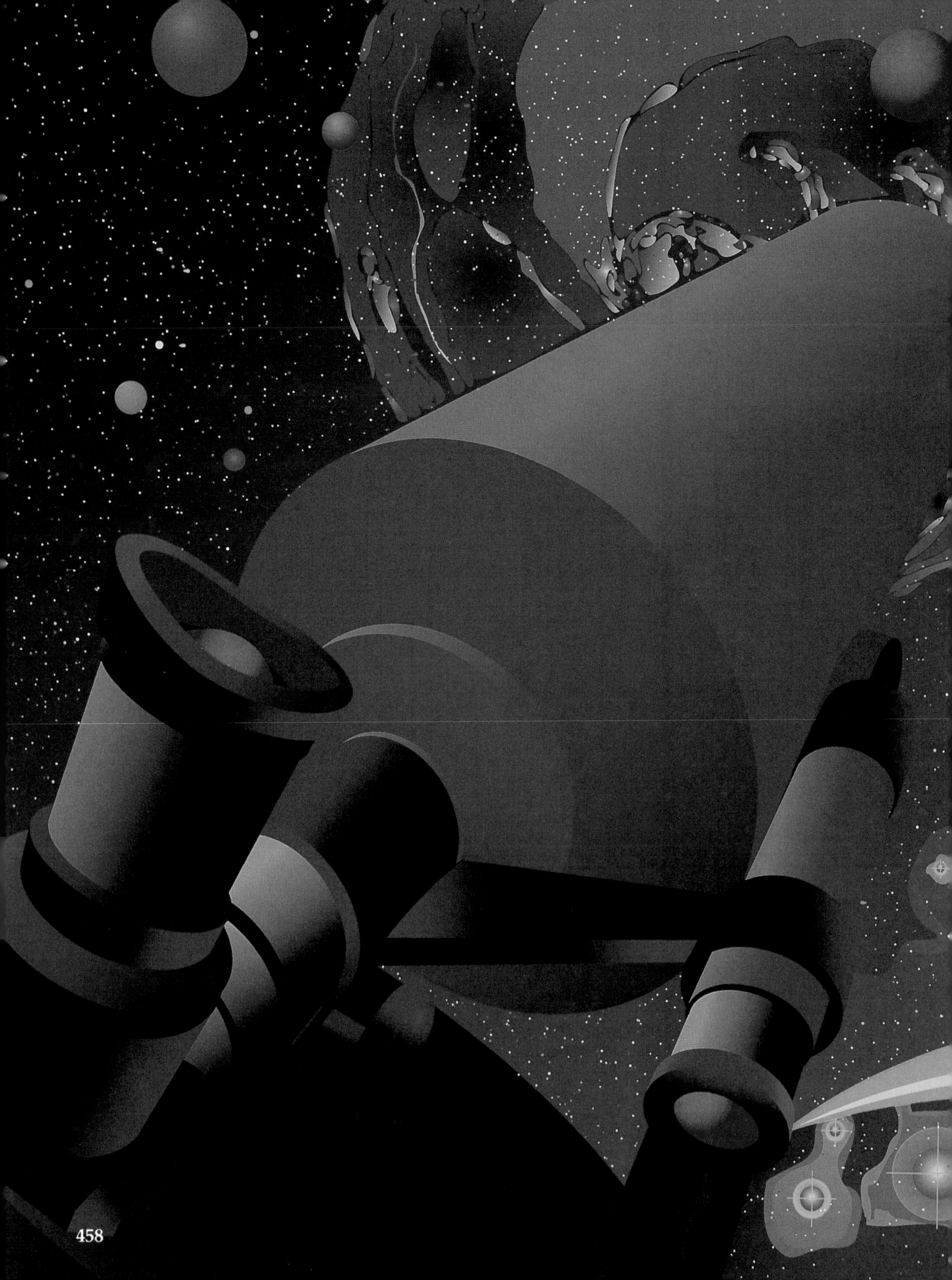

THEME

BEYOND THE EARTH

What would it be like to leave the earth and then return? The astronauts' accounts that follow may help you to think about our world and beyond in a new way.

CONTENTS

MEN FROM EARTH

by
Buzz Aldrin
and
Malcolm
McConnell

Kennedy Space Center,
Cape Kennedy,
July 16, 1969

Campfires twinkled on the beaches and along the causeways near the Cape. Over a million people had come to watch the launch of* Apollo 11*. Even at 3:00* AM *on this muggy Wednesday morning, the headlights of over 200,000 cars cut through the darkness, intensifying the excitement. There were tents and

campers along the roads, and thousands of boats were anchored on the Indian and Banana rivers. For most of the night before, people had sweated in bumper-to-bumper traffic on the highways from Cocoa Beach and Titusville. This was an event no one was about to miss.

At 4:15 AM Deke Slayton woke us. "It's a beautiful morning," he said. "You're go."

Joe Schmitt and his crew had our equipment laid out in the suiting room. The place looked like an anatomy lab for robots. I was hooked up to my portable ventilator and Joe snugged down the brown and white "Snoopy cap" with my earphones and microphone. When Joe snapped my clear bubble helmet in place, I couldn't hear anything anymore.

It was almost dawn when the van stopped at the base of the gray mobile launching platform. The pad was deserted because Rocco Petrone's launch team had already loaded the Saturn[1] with more than 2,000 tons of supercold LOX[2] and liquid hydrogen propellant. The booster had the explosive power of an atomic bomb.

We were to enter the command module according to our seat assignments for liftoff. Neil would be in the left couch because the abort handle was there. Mike would take the right until after translunar injection (TLI), our actual departure toward the moon. That left the center couch for me, which meant I was responsible for sealing the hatch. I'd be the last man to enter. Gunter led Neil and Mike out the swing-arm bridge to the white room, leaving me standing on the platform, holding my portable suit ventilator like a commuter carrying a briefcase.

The only sound I could hear was the whirring ventilator fan. When I walked I could feel my soft pressure boots twang on the grating. The sun was just rising. Surf rolled soundlessly onto the beach, half a mile away. Across the Banana River thousands of cars were parked around the VAB.[3] Millions of people lined the roads and beaches around the Cape, all gazing at this launch pad. Across America and Europe, millions more were watching on television. But here I was completely alone, breathing cool oxygen inside the sterile cocoon of my suit. A feeling of calm confidence rose inside me.

The marathon training was over. We were actually going. Two nights before, NASA administrator Tom Paine had joined us for dinner in the crew quarters. He'd ordered us not to take any chances on this mission. "If you have to abort,"

[1] *Saturn: the rocket that launched Apollo*

[2] *LOX: liquid oxygen*

[3] *VAB: vehicle assembly building, where spacecraft are assembled and prepared for flight*

he'd said, "I'll see that you fly the next moon landing flight. Just don't get killed."

Sheets of frost drifted off the booster beside me. The Apollo spacecraft, all 50 tons of the command, service, and lunar modules—over a million separate parts—was hidden beneath the launch shroud. When we reached the moon, the command module would be called *Columbia* and LM[4] Number 5 would become *Eagle.* They were American names that showed the pride we took in our country's greatest adventure.

I looked south down the coast and saw the older launch pads of the Cape. First were the rusty Redstone and Atlas gantries[5] and then the taller girders and assembly buildings of the Titan[6] complex. I stared for a moment at Launch Pad 34, where Gus, Ed, and Roger[7] had died 30 months before. In a special pocket of my spacesuit I had an *Apollo 1* mission patch and Soviet medals honoring cosmonauts Vladimir Komarov—killed on *Soyuz 1*—and Yuri Gagarin, the first man in space, who had died in a plane crash the year before. I was taking them to leave on the moon.

Joe Schmitt appeared on the platform. They were ready for me in the white room.

"T minus ten, nine . . ." The voice from the firing room sounded calm. I looked to my left at Neil and then turned right to grin at Mike. ". . . four, three, two, one, zero, all engines running." Amber lights blinked on the instrument panel. There was a rumble, like a freight train, far away on a summer night. "Liftoff! We have a liftoff."

It was 9:32 AM.

Instead of the sudden G forces[8] I remembered from the Titan that launched *Gemini XII*,[9] there was an unexpected wobbly sway. The blue sky outside the hatch window seemed to move slightly as the huge booster began its preprogrammed turn after clearing the tower. The rumbling grew louder, but was still distant.

All five F-1 engines[10] were at full thrust, devouring tons of propellant each second. Twelve seconds into the flight, the Houston capcom,[11] astronaut Bruce McCandless, announced that Mission

[4] *LM: lunar module*

[5] *gantries: structures used to hold rockets*

[6] *Redstone, Atlas, Titan: names of America's early rockets*

[7] *Gus Grissom, Ed White, and Roger Chaffee: astronauts for* Apollo 1, *who died in a fire on the launch pad during a test*

[8] *G forces: the forces of gravity*

[9] *Gemini: The Gemini flights, which used a two-man crew, prepared the way for Apollo.*

[10] *F-1 engines: huge engines that powered the first stage of the Saturn rocket*

[11] *capcom: capsule communicator*

Control had taken over from the firing room at the Cape. We were approaching Max Q,[12] one minute and 20 seconds after liftoff. It felt like we were at the top of a long swaying pole and the Saturn was searching the sky to find the right trajectory into orbit.

"You are go for staging," Bruce called.

Neil nodded, gazing at the booster instruments on his panel. He had a tuft of hair sticking out from the front of his Snoopy cap that made him look like a little kid on a toboggan ride. "Staging and ignition," he called. The gigantic S-IC[13] burnt out and dropped away toward the ocean, 45 miles below us.

Oddly enough the S-II's[14] five cryogenic engines[15] made very little noise, and the Gs built gently. Three minutes into the flight, the escape tower automatically blasted free, dragging the boost protection cover with it.

Now that the cover was gone, we could look out and see the curved Atlantic horizon recede. Six minutes later, we could clearly make out the division between the arched blue band of Earth's atmosphere and the black sky of space. The S-II dropped away and the single J-2 engine of our S-IVB third stage

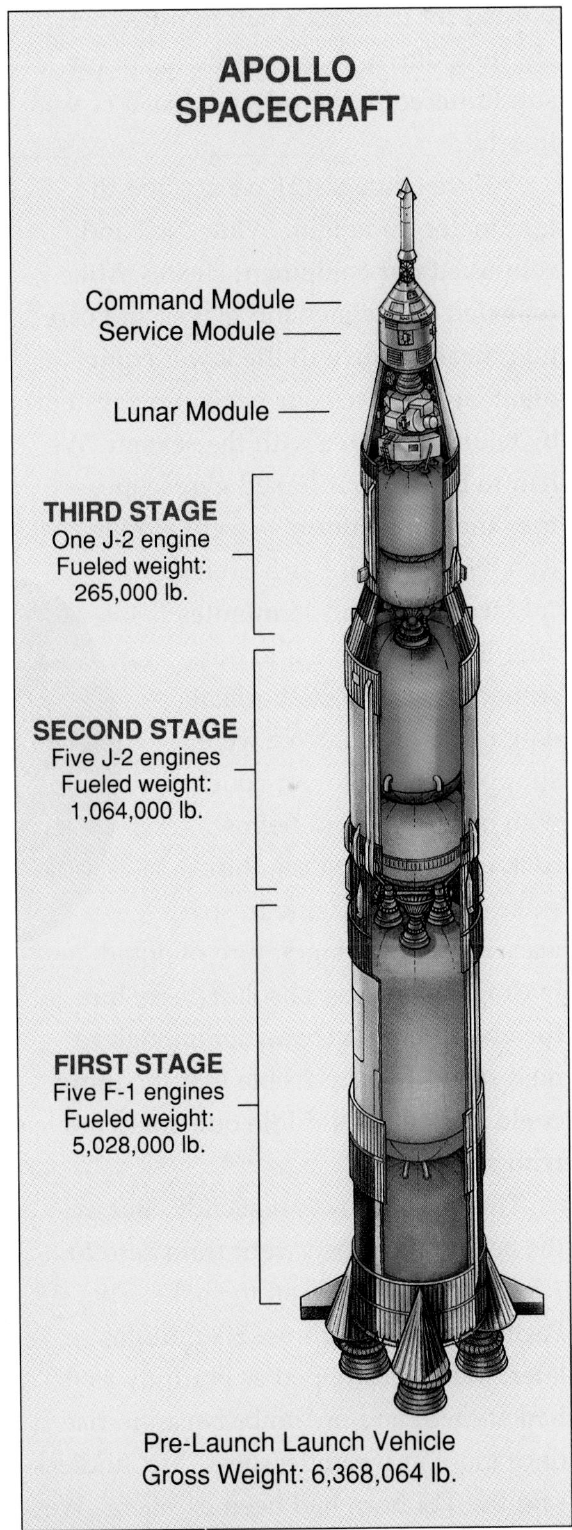

[12] *Max Q: maximum aerodynamic pressure, the point where the drag due to atmosphere is greatest on the rocket*
[13] *S-IC: first stage of the Saturn*
[14] *S-II: second stage of the Saturn*
[15] *cryogenic engines: engines that use supercold fuels*

burned for two and a half minutes before shutting down. A tab on the leg of my suit fluttered in the zero G. *Apollo 11* was in orbit.

Above Madagascar we crossed the terminator into night. While Neil and I continued our equipment checks, Mike removed his helmet and gloves and carefully floated down to the lower equipment bay to check our navigation system by taking star fixes with the sextant. We had to be sure our linked gyroscopes—the "inertial platform"—were working well *before* we left Earth orbit.

Two hours and 45 minutes after liftoff we were into our second orbit, just past orbital dawn near Hawaii. We were strapped tightly to our couches, with our gloves and helmets back on. Restarting the third-stage cryogenic engine in space was risky. The temperature of liquid hydrogen was near absolute zero, but the engine's plume was hot enough to melt steel. It was possible that the thing could explode and riddle our spacecraft with shrapnel.

. . . the engine's plume was hot enough to melt steel.

The TLI burn began silently. But as the acceleration load went from zero to 1.5 Gs, our cabin began to shake. The Pacific tilted beneath us. Six minutes later, the burn stopped as abruptly as it had started, and my limbs began to rise once more in weightlessness. McCandless said the TLI burn had been excellent. We were traveling at a speed of 35,570 feet per second and were passing through 177 nautical miles above Earth. "It looks like you are well on your way now," he added.

I looked out my window and could make out the cloud-covered mouth of the Amazon. Even at this speed, there was no way to actually sense Earth receding, but if I glanced away from the window, then looked back, more of the planet was revealed. The next time I stared out, I was startled to see a complete bright disk. We were 19,000 miles above Earth, our speed slowly dropping as Earth's gravity tugged at us and the distance grew.

Flying steadily this way may have given us a nice view of Earth, but it also meant that one side of the spacecraft was constantly in sunshine, while the other was in darkness. You can't do this for very long because in space the sun's heat will literally broil delicate equipment and burst propellant tanks on the hot side, while on the shaded side the gear will freeze in the deep cold. We had to begin the "barbecue roll," turning slowly on our long axis so that we would distribute the sun's heat evenly. Most people probably thought *Apollo 11* was shooting toward the moon like a bullet, with its pointed end toward the target. But actually we were moving more like

The Earth as viewed during the Apollo 11 *moon mission*

a child's top, spinning on the nozzle of our SPS engine.[16]

This movement meant that every two minutes Earth disappeared, then reappeared from left to right, moving from one window to another, followed by the hot searchlight of the sun. We could see the crescent moon out a couple of our windows, though the view was obscured by the LM's many bulges. By this point we had entered the limbo of so-called cislunar space, the void between Earth and the moon. We didn't have any sense of moving up or down, but in fact we were climbing out of the deep gravity well of Earth. And as we coasted upward, our speed dropped. In 20-some hours, we would be over halfway to the moon, but moving at only a fraction of our original 25,000-mile-per-hour escape velocity. A little later, when we would reach the crest of the hill and come under the moon's gravitational influence, we'd speed up again.

After five hours in space, we removed our bulky suits, and the cabin seemed more spacious. We could curl up in any corner we chose, and each of us soon picked a favorite spot. I settled in the lower equipment bay, and Neil seemed to like the couches. Mike moved back and forth between the two areas, spending as much time at the navigation station down below as with the hundreds of spacecraft system instruments grouped around the couches.

Our first Apollo meal went better than we expected. None of us was spacesick—we'd been careful with head movements—so we were actually quite hungry for the gritty chicken salad and sweet applesauce. The freeze-dried shrimp cocktail tasted almost as good as the kind you get on Earth. We rehydrated food with a hot-water gun, and it was nice to eat something with a spoon, instead of squirting it through tubes the way we'd done on Gemini.

The deep-space tracking station at Goldstone in southern California (there were two others, one outside Madrid and another near Canberra, Australia) wanted us to test our television system. Neil was the narrator, and he gave the weather report for Central and South America. I got some good shots of Mike floating from one window to another, and then he held the camera while I took the TV audience on a little tour of the navigation station below.

When this impromptu TV show was over, I realized I was very tired. It had been a full day, and we needed sleep. When I curled up in my lightweight

[16] *SPS engine: service propulsion system engine, designed to insert the spacecraft into lunar orbit and then thrust it out of lunar orbit back toward Earth*

sleeping bag, I couldn't help thinking how adaptable humans are. There we were, three air-breathing creatures bedding down for the night in this tiny bubble of oxygen. Our spacecraft was like a miniature planet, built by humans like us. We were able to live inside it comfortably, though only an inch or two of alloy and plastic separated my face from the vacuum outside.

Somehow I still felt secure. Ventilators whirred softly and thrusters thumped at odd times. The radio was turned low; Houston would call us only in an emergency. We shaded our windows and dimmed the cabin. I hooked up my sleeping bag beneath the couch and stretched, floating in the luxury of weightlessness. It was time to rest.

A Shadowy Sphere

On our second day outbound, *Apollo 11* flew into the shadow of the moon, which was now less than 40,000 miles away. From where we were the moon eclipsed the sun, but was lit from the back by a brilliant halo of refracted sunlight. There was also a milky glow of Earthshine highlighting the biggest ridges and craters. This bizarre lighting transformed the moon into a shadowy sphere that was three-dimensional but without definition.

"The view of the moon that we've been having recently is really spectacular," Neil reported. "It's a view worth the price of the trip."

We strapped ourselves to the couches again the next day to get ready to swing around the left-hand edge of the moon. Hidden around the far side, we would experience loss of signal and would be out of touch with Houston for 48 minutes; that would be when Mike would punch the PROCEED button that would fire the SPS engine for lunar orbit insertion. I gazed to my right out the small window. All I saw was the corrugated, grayish-tan moonscape. The back side of the moon was much more rugged than the face we saw from Earth. This side had been bombarded by meteors since the beginning of the solar system millions of centuries ago. Mike read off the digits from his DSKY screen.[17] The burn began exactly on time. My hand settled on my chest, and the calves of my legs flexed. This had to go right. For six minutes the SPS engine burned silently, slowing the spacecraft to just over 3,600 miles per hour, the speed necessary for us to be "captured" by lunar gravity. When the engine finally stopped, we rose again, weightless against our couch straps.

[17] *DSKY: display-keyboard of a computer*

Earth rising above the moon's horizon as viewed from Apollo 11

Mike was beaming. We had slipped over the rim of the moon's gravity well. Tomorrow, Neil and I would board the LM and slide all the way down to the surface.

The next day Neil and Buzz moved into the lunar module, while Mike stayed in the command module. Then the two spacecraft separated. The LM was now called the Eagle, *and the command module was* Columbia. Columbia *would orbit the moon while* Eagle *descended to the moon's surface.*

Lunar Module Eagle, *July 20, 1969*

We were just 700 feet above the surface when Charlie Duke, the capcom on duty, gave us the final "Go," just as another 12 02 alarm flashed. Neil and I confirmed with each other that the landing radar was giving us good data, and he punched PROCEED into the keyboard. All these alarms had kept us from studying our landing zone. If this had been a simulation back at the Cape, we probably would have aborted. Neil finally looked away from the DSKY screen and out his triangular window. He was definitely not satisfied with the ground beneath us. We were too low to identify the landmark craters we'd studied from the *Apollo 10* photographs. We just had to find a smooth place to land. The computer, however, was taking us to a boulder field surrounding a 40-foot-wide crater.

Neil rocked his hand controller in his fist, changing over to manual command. He slowed our descent from 20 feet per second to only nine. Then, at 300 feet, we were descending at only three and a half feet per second. As *Eagle* slowly dropped, we continued skimming forward.

Neil still wasn't satisfied with the terrain. All I could do was give him the altimeter[18] callouts and our horizontal speed. He stroked the hand controller and descent-rate switch like a motorist fine-tuning his cruise control. We scooted across the boulders. At two hundred feet our hover slid toward a faster descent rate.

"Eleven forward, coming down nicely," I called, my eyes scanning the instruments. "Two hundred feet, four and a half down. Five and a half down. One sixty. . . ." The low-fuel light blinked on the caution-and-warning panel, ". . . quantity light."

Neil slowed the descent again. The horizon of the moon was at eye level. We were almost out of fuel.

"Sixty seconds," Charlie warned.

The ascent engine fuel tanks were full, but completely separate from the descent engine. We had 60 seconds of fuel remaining in the descent stage before we had to land or abort. Neil searched the ground below.

"Down two and a half," I called. The LM moved forward like a helicopter flaring out for landing. We were in the so-called dead man's zone, and we couldn't remain there long. If we ran out of fuel at this altitude, we would crash into the surface before the ascent engine could lift us back toward orbit. "Forward. Forward. Good. Forty feet. Down two and a half. Picking up some dust. Thirty feet. . . ."

Thirty feet below the LM's gangly legs, dust that had lain undisturbed for a billion years blasted sideways in the plume of our engine.

"Thirty seconds," Charlie announced solemnly, but still Neil slowed our rate.

The descent engine roared silently, sucking up the last of its fuel supply. I turned my eye to the ABORT STAGE button. "Drifting right," I called, watching the shadow of a footpad probe lightly touching the surface. "Contact light." The horizon seemed to rock gently and then steadied. Our altimeter stopped blinking. We were on the moon. We had about 20 seconds of fuel remaining in the

[18] *altimeter: instrument for measuring altitude*

descent stage. Immediately I prepared for a sudden abort, in case the landing had damaged the *Eagle* or the surface was not strong enough to support our weight.

"Okay, engine stop," I told Neil, reciting from the checklist. "ACA out of detent."

"Got it," Neil answered, disengaging the hand control system. Both of us were still tingling with the excitement of the final moments before touchdown.

"Mode controls, both auto," I continued, aware that I was chanting the readouts. "Descent engine command override, off. Engine arm, off. . . ."

"We copy you down, *Eagle,*" Charlie Duke interrupted from Houston.

I stared out at the rocks and shadows of the moon. It was as stark as I'd ever imagined it. A mile away, the horizon curved into blackness.

"Houston," Neil called, "Tranquillity Base here. The *Eagle* has landed."

It was strange to be suddenly stationary. Spaceflight had always meant movement to me, but here we were rock-solid still, as if the LM had been standing here since the beginning of time. We'd been told to expect the remaining fuel in the descent stage to slosh back and forth after we touched down, but there simply wasn't enough reserve fuel remaining to do this. Neil had flown the landing to the very edge.

"Tranquillity Base here. The *Eagle* has landed."

"Roger, Tranquillity," Charlie said, "we copy you on the ground. You've got a bunch of guys about to turn blue. We're breathing again. Thanks a lot."

I reached across and shook Neil's hand, hard. We had pulled it off. Five months and 10 days before the end of the decade, two Americans had landed on the moon.

"It looks like a collection of just every variety of shapes, angularities, granularities, every variety of rock you could find . . .," I told Houston. Everyone wanted to know what the moon looked like. The glaring sunrise was directly behind us like a huge searchlight. It bleached out the color, but the grays swam in from the sides of my window.

Charlie said there were "lots of smiling faces in this room, and all over the world."

Neil grinned at me, the strain leaving his tired eyes. I smiled back. "There are two of them up here," I told Charlie.

Mike's voice cut in much louder and clearer than Mission Control. "And don't forget the one in the command module."

Charlie told Mike to speak directly to us. "Roger, Tranquillity Base," Mike said. "It sounded great from up here. You guys did a fantastic job."

That was a real compliment coming from a pilot as skilled as Mike Collins.

"Thank you," Neil said. "Just keep that orbiting base ready for us up there now."

We were supposed to do a little housekeeping in the LM, eat a meal, and then try to sleep for seven hours before getting ready to explore the surface. But whoever signed off on that plan didn't know much psychology—or physiology, for that matter. We'd just landed on the moon and there was a lot of adrenaline still zinging through our bodies. Telling us to try to sleep *before* the EVA[19] was like telling kids on Christmas morning they had to stay in bed until noon.

I decided to begin a ceremony I'd planned with Dean Woodruff, my pastor at Webster Presbyterian Church. He'd given me a tiny Communion kit that had a silver chalice and wine vial about the size of the tip of my little finger. I asked "every person listening in, whoever and wherever they may be, to pause for a moment and contemplate the events of the past few hours, and to give thanks in his or her own way." The plastic note-taking shelf in front of our DSKY became the altar. I read silently from Dean's Communion service—*I am the vine and you are the branches . . .*—as I poured the wine into the chalice. The wine looked like syrup as it swirled around the sides of the cup in the light gravity before it finally settled at the bottom.

Eagle's metal body creaked. I ate the tiny Host and swallowed the wine. I gave thanks for the intelligence and spirit that had brought two young pilots to the Sea of Tranquillity.

Magnificent Desolation

Suiting up for the moon walk took us several hours. Our PLSS[20] backpacks looked simple, but they were hard to put on and tricky to operate. They were truly our life-support systems, with enough oxygen, cooling water, electrical power, and radio equipment to keep us alive on the moon and in constant contact with Houston (via a relay in the LM) for four hours. On Earth, the PLSS and spacesuit combination weighed 190 pounds, but here it was only 30. Combined with my own body weight, that brought me to a total lunar-gravity weight of around 60 pounds.

Seven hours after we touched down on the moon, we depressurized the LM, and Neil opened the hatch. My job was to guide him as he backed out on his hands and knees onto the small porch. He worked slowly, trying not to jam his backpack on the hatch frame. When he reached the ladder attached to the

[19] *EVA: Extra-Vehicular Activity (*extra *means "out of"), space walks or moon walks*
[20] *PLSS: portable life support system*

would be no way we would be able to keep from breathing some of that dust. If strange microbes *were* in this soil, Neil and I would be the first guinea pigs to test their effects.

Bruce told us that President Richard Nixon wanted to speak to us. More stage fright. The president said, "For one priceless moment, in the whole history of man, all the people on this Earth are truly one."

I looked high above the dome of the LM. Earth hung in the black sky, a disk cut in half by the day-night terminator. It was mostly blue, with swirling white clouds, and I could make out a brown landmass, North Africa and the Middle East. Glancing down at my boots, I realized that the soil Neil and I had stomped through had been here longer than any of those brown continents. Earth was a dynamic planet of tectonic plates, churning oceans, and a changing atmosphere. The moon was dead, a relic of the early solar system.

Time was moving in spasms. We still had many tasks to accomplish. Some seemed quite easy and others dragged on. It took me a long time to erect the passive seismometer (the "moonquake" detector). We were supposed to level it by using a BB-type device centered in a little cup. But the BB just swirled around and around in the light gravity. I spent a long time with that, but it still wouldn't go level. Then I looked back, and the ball was right where it should be.

"You have approximately three minutes until you must commence your EVA termination activities," Bruce told us. Our time walking on the moon was almost over.

". . . all the people on this Earth are truly one."

I was already on the ladder when Neil reminded me about the mementos we had planned to leave on the moon. From a shoulder pocket I removed a small packet that held the two Soviet medals and the *Apollo 1* patch, as well as a small gold olive branch, one of four we'd bought. We'd given the other three to our wives as a way of joining them to our mission. The packet also contained the tiny silicone disk marked "From Planet Earth" and etched with goodwill messages from the leaders of 73 nations, including the Soviet Union. I tossed the pouch onto the soil among our jumbled footprints.

Inside the LM, we still had to stow 40 pounds of moon rocks in two aluminum boxes. Houston needed endless exchanges of data so we could align our navigation computer. Then we had to discard our PLSS backpacks, our overshoes, and all the other refuse of our brief stay to cut down on our weight for the ascent. Mission Control told us that our moonquake

Buzz Aldrin (right) walking on the surface of the moon. One member of the Apollo crew (below) conducts scientific experiments while on the surface of the moon.

seismometer had recorded the impact of our gear being tossed out the hatch.

Finally it was time to eat and sleep. After we snacked on cocktail sausages and fruit punch, I stretched out on the deck beneath the instrument panel, and Neil propped himself across the ascent engine cover, with his boots wedged into a sling under the DSKY. With the windows shaded, the LM grew cold. Neil was having trouble getting to sleep because of the glare of Earth reflected through our telescope on his face. We had moon dust smeared on our suit legs and on the deck. It was like gritty charcoal and smelled like gunpowder from the fireworks I'd launched so many years before on the New Jersey shore.

Homeward Bound

Seven hours later we prepared for ascent. There was an almost constantly active three-way loop of radio traffic connecting *Columbia, Eagle,* and Mission Control. We discovered during a long checklist recitation that the ascent engine's arming circuit breaker was broken off on the panel. The little plastic pin simply wasn't there. This circuit would send electrical power to the engine that would lift us off the moon. Finally I realized my backpack must have struck it when I'd been getting ready for my EVA.

Neil and I looked at each other. Our fatigue had reached the point where our thoughts had become plodding. But this got our attention. We looked around for something to punch in this circuit breaker. Luckily, a felt-tipped pen fit into the slot.

At 123 hours and 58 minutes GET,[21] Houston told us, "You're cleared for takeoff."

"Roger," I answered. "Understand we're number one on the runway."

I watched the DSKY numbers and chanted the countdown: "Four, three, two, one . . . *proceed.*"

Our liftoff was powerful. Nothing we'd done in the simulators had prepared us for this amazing swoop upward in the weak lunar gravity. Within seconds we had pitched forward a sharp 45 degrees and were soaring above the crater fields.

"Very smooth," I called, "very quiet ride." It wasn't at all like flying through Earth's atmosphere. Climbing fast, we finally spotted the landmark craters we'd missed during the descent. Two minutes into the ascent, we were batting along at half a mile per second.

Columbia was above and behind us. Our radar and the computers on the

[21] *GET: ground elapsed time, the amount of time that had passed on Earth since the launch*

The Apollo 11 lunar module ascending from the surface of the moon as viewed from the command and service module

two spacecraft searched for each other and then locked on and communicated in a soundless digital exchange.

• • •

Four hours after Neil and I lifted off from the Sea of Tranquillity, we heard the capture latches clang shut above our heads. Mike had successfully docked with *Eagle*. I loosened the elastic cords and reached around to throw more switches. Soon Mike would unseal the tunnel so that Neil and I could pass the moon rocks through and then join Mike in *Columbia* for the long ride back.

I hadn't slept in almost 40 hours and there was a thickness to my voice and movements. Still I could feel a calmness rising inside me. A thruster fired on *Columbia*, sending a shiver through the two spacecraft.

Seven hours later, we were in our last lunar orbit, above the far side, just past the terminator into dawn. We had cast

Eagle's ascent stage loose into an orbit around the moon, where it would remain for hundreds of years. Maybe, I thought, astronauts will visit our flyweight locomotive sometime in the future. Mike rode the left couch for the trans-Earth injection burn. Our SPS engine simply had to work, or we'd be stranded. The burn would consume five tons of propellant in two and a half minutes, increasing our speed by 2,000 miles per hour, enough to break the bonds of the moon's gravity.

We waited, all three of us watching the DSKY. "Three, two, one," Mike said, almost whispering.

Ignition was right on the mark. I sank slowly into my couch. NASA's bold gamble with Lunar Orbit Rendezvous had paid off. Twenty minutes after the burn we rounded the moon's right-hand limb for the final time.

"Hello. *Apollo 11*, Houston," Charlie Duke called from Earth. "How did it go?"

Neil was smiling. "Tell them to open up the LRL doors, Charlie," he said, referring to our quarantine in the Lunar Receiving Laboratory.

"Roger," Charlie answered. "We got you coming home."

The moon's horizon tilted past my window. Earth hung in the dark universe, warm and welcoming.

Buzz Aldrin saw the mission to the moon as "our country's greatest adventure." Would you agree or disagree with him? Explain your response.

Do you think Tranquillity Base is a good name for the place on the moon where the *Eagle* landed? Why or why not?

Near the end of this selection, Aldrin makes the comment that "NASA's bold gamble with Lunar Orbit Rendezvous had paid off." Explain how the mission was a bold gamble.

Many astronauts who have flown on space missions have said that looking at Earth from space has given them a better understanding of the word *home*. What do you think they mean?

Write List three questions you would like to ask Buzz Aldrin about his mission to the moon.

WORDS ABOUT THE AUTHOR

EDWIN E. ALDRIN, JR. ("BUZZ")

Most people think Buzz Aldrin got his nickname as a fighter pilot, but it was given to him, almost as soon as he was born, by his slightly older sister Fay Ann, who referred to him as her "baby buzzer." The Aldrin children grew up in Montclair, New Jersey, with their father, who was an aviator, and their mother, whose family name had been Moon. Young Buzz loved sports and outdoor life more than his studies, but his father encouraged him to put school first.

At sixteen Edwin E. Aldrin, Jr., "Buzz," left home for West Point, where he became the leading freshman in both academics and athletics. Following graduation, he served as a fighter pilot during the Korean War, flying sixty-six combat missions and earning the Distinguished Flying Medal.

Aldrin became an astronaut after doing advanced studies at the Massachusetts Institute of Technology (M.I.T.). As a crew member on *Gemini XII,* before the *Apollo 11* mission that is described in "Tranquillity Base," he took a space walk that lasted over two hours. He has handled all his assignments with the cool thinking, the outspoken enthusiasm, and the sense of humor that have become his trademarks.

Now in his sixties, Aldrin campaigns for a more creative and sustained space program. In a 1990 interview with Leonard David of *Ad Astra* magazine, Buzz Aldrin summarized his philosophy: "I came up with a phrase several years ago of trying to 'go through life cutting a wide swath.' Reach your arms out and then just kind of waltz through it. It's surprising what you can encounter and collect. Don't focus too narrow. Open up. Change direction. Add to somebody's idea or bring two people together who are working on the same problem, but from different points of view. Polish your ideas as much as possible, then try them out on others. You may have to give away a little bit in order to become a cooperative person. To say you need an open mind is obvious."

Perspective

by Alfred M. Worden, Apollo astronaut

Floating effortlessly, freely,
Magnet-drawn to a target in the blackness
We venture
Moving easily in the confines of our small world,
Sustaining life.

Stars in slow ballet pirouette;
Passive thermal control
We barbecue to the moon.

We believe we can illuminate our history
By visiting this ancient lovely sphere.
What value is this flight
In a hostile ocean to an alien shore?
What can the living learn from the dead?

Slowly the lunar disc slides by the window
Familiar, but much larger,
And then earth drifts into sight.
Of all the stars, moons, and planets,
Of all I can see or imagine,
This is the most beautiful;
All the colors of the universe
Focused on one small globe;
And it is our home, our refuge.

Now I know why I'm here:
Not for a closer look at the moon,
But to look back
At our home
The earth.

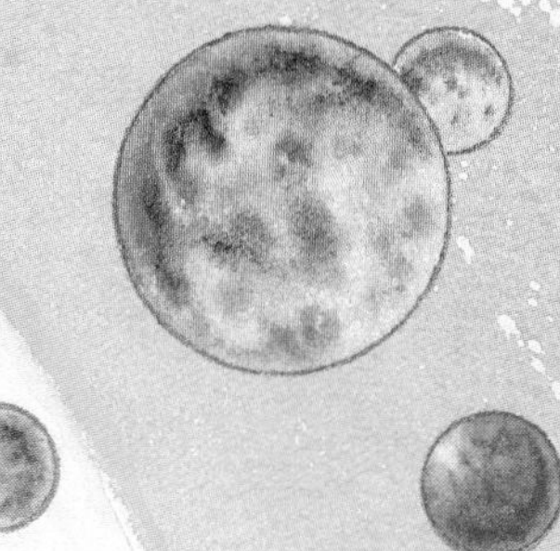

BEYOND THE EARTH

What did Buzz Aldrin and Alfred M. Worden find amazing when they looked back at Earth from space?

WRITER'S WORKSHOP

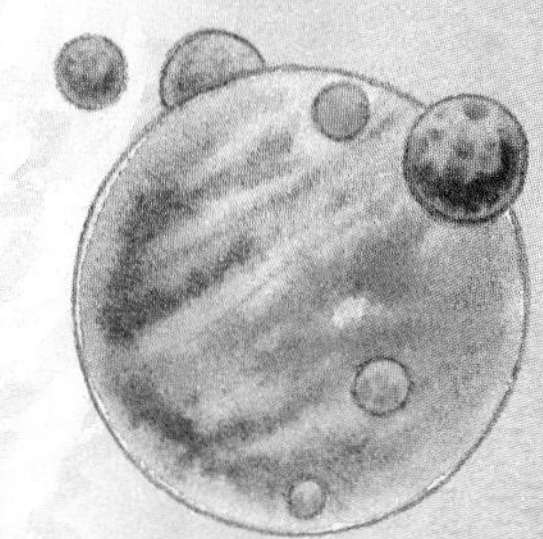

To request information about preparing for a journey beyond Earth, write a business letter to one of the organizations below.

- To join the Young Astronauts Club—or to form a chapter at your school—write to this address:
Young Astronauts Council, 1308 19th Street NW, Washington, DC 20336
- To attend a camp for future astronauts, write to this address:
U.S. Space Camp, U.S. Space and Rocket Center, P.O. Box 070015, Huntsville, AL 35807

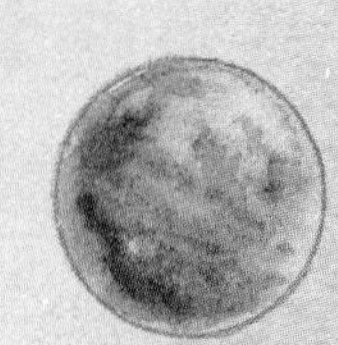

Writer's Choice If you lived in space, how would your life be different? Write about and share an idea that is "out of this world"!

CONNECTIONS

MULTICULTURAL CONNECTION

A MAN OF TWO WORLDS

Like many Native Americans, Jim Shore lives in two worlds. As the son of a Seminole leader, he shares many of his people's traditions, including their love for the land. As a lawyer, he is trying to help his people succeed in the modern world.

During his boyhood on the Seminole reservation at Brighton, Florida, Shore loved to hunt and fish and always assumed that he would become a rancher. School held little interest for him. Then he had a car accident, which left him blind. When he finally sorted out his life, he decided to go to college—for himself and for his people. By studying with the help of cassette tapes, he earned a law degree in 1980.

Today, Shore is the General Counsel for the Seminole Tribe. He handles legal affairs for the Seminoles in crucial areas such as land rights and economic development. Through law, he is working to strengthen the Seminole nation and ensure a better life for his people.

In class, discuss how a more modern way of life might clash with the Seminoles' traditional respect for the land. Can modernization take place without damage to the environment? Explain.

SOCIAL STUDIES CONNECTION

HISTORICAL INVESTIGATION

The Seminole Indians were originally part of the Creek confederation of tribes and lived in the areas that are now Alabama and Georgia. In the early 1700s, some of the Creeks moved into Florida, where they became known as Seminoles. In the 1800s, the United States government forced most of the Seminoles to leave Florida. Find out what happened to the Seminoles, how they got the name *Seminole*, and where most of the Seminoles live today.

SCIENCE CONNECTION

THREATENED ENVIRONMENTS

The Seminoles who live in the Everglades have traditionally depended on its resources for their survival. Now the environment of the Everglades is threatened. Find out about another threatened environment in the United States, perhaps one close to where you live. It may be a large area such as the Everglades or a small area such as a lake or woods. List the dangers the area faces, and predict what you think will happen to the area.

Top right: Jim Shore; members of a Seminole family in traditional clothing

UNIT SIX

INSPIRATIONS

By putting these special happenings into words and writing them down, I was trying to hold onto and somehow preserve the magic of those moments. And I guess that's really what books and writing are all about.

Yoshiko Uchida

Where does inspiration come from? The great painters of Mexico often found inspiration in the history of their country. Yoshiko Uchida implies that writers are often inspired by events in their own lives. This unit will enable you to compare several writers' autobiographies and other personal comments with their fiction or poetry and see how their experiences have influenced their work. As you read, think of experiences that you could record and share with others—in paint or in words.

THEMES

BOOKSHELF

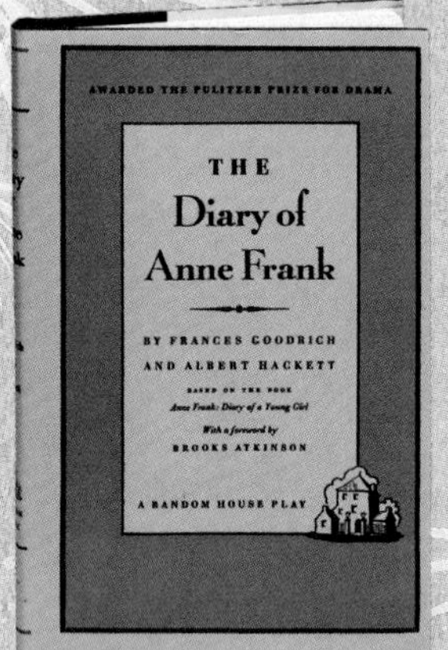

THE DIARY OF ANNE FRANK

BY FRANCES GOODRICH AND ALBERT HACKETT

This dramatization based on the book tells the story of a young Jewish girl and seven other people who hide in an attic for more than two years to avoid being captured by the Nazis.

Antoinette Perry Award, Critics' Circle Award, Pulitzer Prize

HARCOURT BRACE LIBRARY BOOK

JULIA MORGAN: ARCHITECT OF DREAMS

BY GINGER WADSWORTH

This biography tells the story of Julia Morgan, the architect of the Hearst Castle in San Simeon, California. Designer of more than 700 buildings, Julia Morgan paved the way for women in the field of architecture. Illustrations that show some of her buildings will amaze you!

What's Your Story? A Young Person's Guide to Writing Fiction

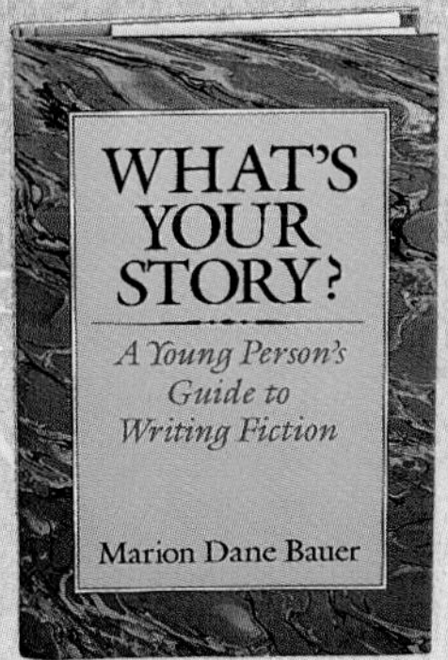

BY MARION DANE BAUER

An award-winning novelist offers useful suggestions for beginning writers on such matters as how to find a topic, develop characters, and structure a story.

ALA Notable Book

Rising Voices: Writings of Young Native Americans

SELECTED BY ARLENE B. HIRSCHFELDER AND BEVERLY R. SINGER

The poems and essays in this collection present a variety of viewpoints on topics such as the search for identity, the importance of family and tradition, and the struggle for survival.

Children's Choice, IRA Teachers' Choice, Notable Children's Trade Book in the Field of Social Studies

In the Forest

BY JIM ARNOSKY

Find out what inspires an artist to paint a particular scene. Jim Arnosky reveals what he was thinking as he painted various views of a forest.

Outstanding Science Trade Book for Children

THEME

SHARING EXPERIENCES

If you were going to write a story about a child learning to ride a bicycle, you might use your own experience of learning to ride to help you write your story. In the following selections, you'll find out how authors Jean Little and Yoshiko Uchida drew from their experiences to write works of fiction.

CONTENTS

LISTEN FOR THE *Singing*

AWARD-WINNING AUTHOR

by Jean Little

Listen for the Singing *begins in 1939, when German soldiers invade Poland, and Britain declares war on Germany. It has been five years since the Solden family came from Germany to Toronto, Canada. Anna Solden, the youngest member of the family, has very poor vision. For several years she attended a special Sight Saving class taught by Mrs. Schumacher, who was the wife of the family doctor. Anna and Mrs. Schumacher became good friends. Now Anna is entering regular high school.*

At first Anna is anxious about school, but she soon makes two good friends, Maggie and Suzy; and through her brother Rudi's tutoring, she comes to understand math for the first time. Rudi also teaches her to dance so that she can go to the school's Christmas dance. He is no longer the brother who teased and mocked her when they were younger.

Anna has just finished ninth grade when Rudi enlists in the navy to fight against Hitler. Soon after Rudi's ship leaves Toronto, the Soldens receive a telegram saying that he has been blinded in an accident.

Illustrated by S.M. Saelig

apa did not go to get Rudi until September was half over. Dr. Schumacher made many telephone calls the night the telegram came. Finally, he got in touch with the doctor in charge of Rudi's case. Afterwards he and Papa came immediately home.

"Dr. Bricker says Rudi is doing well and seems quite cheerful," he said, "but he is not ready to travel yet and he has said that he does not want any of the family to come. He also told me that Rudi is suffering from profound shock but is being very courageous. He sounded very impressed by him."

"How did it happen?" Mama asked. "Did he say how long it would be before he is better? He will get better, won't he?"

"He said it was some freak accident. Cleaning fluid got splashed into his face. Both eyes were badly burned. When the burns heal, there will be scars. He holds out no hope that Rudi will be able to see again. I'm so sorry, Klara."

"Cleaning fluid," Mama repeated. "But how . . .?"

"It was no one's fault, Dr. Bricker said. He didn't give me the details. How it happened doesn't lessen the tragedy."

Anna heard the words but could not make herself feel they were true. Not about Rudi with his eyes that were bluer than anyone's. She waited dully for Mama to begin to cry. Mama sat very straight and did not shed a tear.

She doesn't believe it either, Anna thought.

Later, lying in bed unable to sleep, she suddenly remembered thinking one day that it would be simpler for her if she were blind. Then she had seen something. What? The sunlight turning Maggie's hair to gold. And she had known what a miracle vision was. Then she thought of Rudi and wept.

But the days that followed were busy ones and she had little time to brood. She set out for school on the first morning of the new term with scarcely a qualm. She would have to explain about her poor eyesight to any new teachers but she was getting used to explaining. She had come to understand and deal with her own limitations in a new way, during the previous year. She had even discovered hitherto hidden abilities. She could serve a volleyball perfectly!

It had been arranged ahead of time that she and Maggie would not be separated. The two of them had gone to see Mr. Appleby about it before school ended.

As it turned out, the whole gang was put into the same class with Miss Sutcliff as their homeroom teacher. This fall, Anna, instead of going on home as she had the year before because she could not see, went with the others to the school football games. She loved wearing the school colors, long white and green ribbons streaming down from a small rosette pinned to her coat. She knew all the cheers. Any friend of Suzy's could not help learning them. Suzy chanted them whenever there was a moment's silence. Anna found herself having a wonderful time, even though she had no clear idea of what was happening in the game. She groaned, screamed, and jumped up and down with everyone else. Maggie tried to remember to tell her afterwards what they had been excited about.

She felt guilty having fun when she thought of Rudi. Yet she knew that sitting alone and sorrowing over his tragedy would help neither him nor her. Mama, this time, did nothing dramatic like refusing to eat. She too realized that the only way to hold onto her sanity and help her family through this dark time was to behave as normally as possible. Anna understood her mother better than ever before.

A letter arrived before Rudi came home. He had dictated it to someone. It sent everyone individual greetings. The others looked relieved because his words sounded so normal. But Anna heard the words meant for her without any response except uneasiness. "Hi, Anna. Keep smiling." He had never told her to keep smiling before. Why hadn't he said something with meaning?

He asked only one thing, that they somehow manage to give him a room to himself.

"I know this will make a problem," he said, "but if Anna could move in with the other girls, I'd be glad to have her corner."

They moved Fritz down to the couch in the living room instead. He didn't care. Anna sighed with relief and she was sure her two sisters did too. There just was not room for the three of them, each so different, in that one bedroom. Gretchen and Frieda had over the years worked out an arrangement by which they managed to keep the peace, but with Anna added it would never have worked.

Then Papa went to get Rudi. The house seemed extra quiet, waiting. Mama baked Rudi's favorite cookies. Nobody talked about it much. Nobody knew what to say. But everyone was nervous.

Before they felt ready, the two were home. Papa, looking older than Anna had ever seen him, and Rudi with dark glasses on and a cane in his hand, smiling, saying the right things.

"He's so normal," Gretchen half-whispered when Papa had taken him up the stairs, away from them, "but . . ."

But he isn't normal at all, Anna thought, not saying the words aloud. And it's not just that he's blind. He's gone away from us inside. His feelings are blind too.

In the following week, a routine was set up. Rudi ate alone in his room. He came downstairs in the evenings, when the whole family was home, and sat in the living room with them. He listened to the news with Papa. He told Mama how good her torte was. He insisted that she not stay at home with him, that he just wanted to rest by himself. He never mentioned his blindness. When he needed help, he asked for it directly, in as few words as possible. It was only then that the studied cheer went out of his voice and they could hear the hurt.

"But what can we *do*?" Frieda said desperately, one evening, when Rudi had already gone up to his room.

"Give him time," Papa said tiredly. "That's what Dr. Bricker told me. He said

he is wounded in spirit as well as in his eyes. Just leave him to get over it, he said."

"He won't let us do anything else," Mama said. Now tears did come. "Yet he does seem cheerful. He eats well. I think . . . I'm sure he is getting better."

Anna knew he was not. She could hear him in the night when he thought everyone was sleeping. Often he paced back and forth, back and forth in his room, with no light on. Anna knew he did not need light but still it made it all the more terrible somehow. Then she heard him crying. She knew how he must look. She had seen him the day the news came about Aunt Tania. She had reached out to him then. Maybe now she could do it again.

She lay still, listening.

What could she say?

He did not know anyone heard him. He never let them see him cry.

She stayed where she was.

The next afternoon, she went up to him and asked him about a problem she was having with geometry.

"I can't help you, Anna," he said, quite calmly. "Ask Mr. McNair."

"But, Rudi," she started, forcing herself to go on in spite of his indifference, "if you could just explain . . ."

"I'm sorry. I can't," he said. "You're too clever for me now, Anna."

She retreated and sat by herself, thinking hard.

The girls at school were fascinated by Rudi. To them, he seemed a wounded war hero. In a way he was, Anna knew. But she did not want to talk about him.

Finally a night came when she could no longer lie still and listen. She got up and went to his door.

"Rudi," she said softly, to the pacing in the darkness. "Rudi, can I do anything for you?"

There was a silence in the room, a silence so complete it was frightening. She waited.

Then a rasping voice said, "Leave me alone, Anna. I'm sorry I wakened you."

She stood still, not sure what to do.

"Please," he said, his voice a whisper now, "just leave me alone."

She turned and was halfway out the door when he asked abruptly, "Have I ever wakened you before?"

Anna swallowed. She must make him believe her.

"No," she said steadily, "I just happened to wake up."

"Good night," he said.

"Good night," she returned, yawning what she hoped sounded like a normal, sleepy yawn.

She had not talked with Rudi; she had talked to a stranger. When she reached her bed, she had to bury her face in the pillow or he would have heard her cry.

The next afternoon, after school, she went to Mrs. Schumacher. She phoned first from the office at school. She let the secretary assume she was phoning her parents. Although nobody seemed to be listening, she kept her voice low.

Mrs. Schumacher did not ask her to speak more clearly. She simply said, "Of course, you may come. As soon as you can get here is fine."

As Anna neared the Schumachers' house, she felt apprehensive. What if she could not make Mrs. Schumacher understand? Yet she was the most understanding person, except for Papa, that Anna knew. She had, after all, understood Anna herself when nobody else could get past the sullen, stubborn, uncaring face she had turned toward the world, the wall of pride she had built around herself. Now, she was sure Rudi was behind a wall, too. And Anna longed to find a way to get him out.

Mrs. Schumacher opened the door before Anna had time to ring the bell.

"Elizabeth's sleeping," she said. "She's a very considerate child really. She won't wake up for a couple of hours."

Anna smiled. She had spent a lot of time with Elizabeth that summer. Mrs. Schumacher had taught her how to give the baby a bath, had let her feed her and take her out in the carriage. Anna had loved pushing that buggy along, pretending the baby inside it was hers, sometimes. She was proud to be trusted with Elizabeth. But right now she was glad the baby was out of the way.

Mrs. Schumacher led the way into the living room. She seemed to know, from the beginning, that this was not one of Anna's customary visits, that she had come about something serious. She knew, of course, about Rudi. But not about his nights. Only Anna knew that.

Anna told Eileen Schumacher everything, all the small things and the big ones that were worrying her.

A man from the Canadian National Institute for the Blind had come to see Rudi, soon after Papa brought him home. Anna had just come in from school so she stayed to listen.

"Rudi was perfectly polite," she told Mrs. Schumacher. "But, at the end, he said, 'I don't think I'm quite ready yet for the things you're suggesting, sir. I just want to rest at the moment. I'll have my father telephone your office when I think you can help me.' "

"That sounds good," Mrs. Schumacher said. "It sounds as though he realizes he has to give himself a while to adjust, and then he'll ask for help."

"It does sound like that," agreed Anna, struggling to put her anxiety into words. "His words always sound all right. But there's nothing underneath what he says. It's as though he's not really there. Just politeness and words but not Rudi himself. I'm sure he only listens enough so he can make the right answers. Otherwise he doesn't care. And nothing he says really means anything."

She paused and took a deep breath. Mrs. Schumacher waited for her to go on.

"And, oh, in the night . . ." Anna's story came spilling out.

"Once I heard him praying to die," Anna said, the horror of that moment still dark in her eyes. "He begged! But that's not the most frightening thing. It's hard for me to know how to say it. To me, the worst part is that he is going further and further away from us. He's disappearing, escaping maybe, into some safe secret place where nobody can reach him or hurt him anymore."

She stopped, trying to get her thoughts in order. Although she didn't want to repeat herself, she had to make it clear. Her friend still said nothing, seeing Anna had not finished.

"What's wrong is you can't live in that place. I've been somewhere like it. A little like it, anyway. It's like being shut up inside a shell with no way out. I remember. I still dream about it sometimes."

"Oh, Anna," Eileen Schumacher said.

Anna paid no attention. She was not sorry for that little girl now; she was worried about Rudi.

"When I was small and everything seemed so hard and Rudi was mean, I went there, but I couldn't love anybody from inside that place. You and Bernard and Ben and Isobel and Papa all rescued me. You just broke the shell, a little at a time, until you could come in and I couldn't stop you. You could come in and I could come out."

Mrs. Schumacher smiled at that. She even laughed softly.

"You were extremely prickly at first, I must admit," she said. "I thought of you, I remember, as a little porcupine with all its quills sticking out. And I can see why you are concerned now. But what do you want to do?"

"I want to rescue Rudi," Anna said simply. "I think—I don't know why—that we could wait too long. He might go so far in we'd never be able to bring him back."

Mrs. Schumacher sat still, on a low hassock, her arms clasped around her knees. She looked at the child—no, the young woman—facing her.

"I think you have a plan, don't you, Anna?" she said. "I can see it in your face. Tell me. That's what you really came for, isn't it?"

Anna nodded, not surprised that Mrs. Schumacher had guessed. She had always been good at reading the minds of the children she taught. But she wanted this plan to be a secret. It had to be or it wouldn't work. This was going to be the tricky part. She had no choice but to trust her old teacher.

"It's like this," she said, and explained. She did not confide her whole idea, not the last part she would play in it by herself, if she had to. She would only do it if the first part wasn't enough and, whatever happened, it would be between Rudi and her, no one else.

"Can you help?" Anna asked. "Will you?"

"That's a tall order, Anna, but I think perhaps I can. I can try anyway," Mrs. Schumacher said slowly, thinking ahead as she spoke. "I'll have to do some persuading but Franz can help. You don't mind him knowing, Anna?"

Anna shook her head. She felt giddy with relief. There had been the chance that Mrs. Schumacher would not go along with the idea.

"Maybe, very likely in fact, we're going about this all wrong and we should leave it to the professionals," Mrs. Schumacher said, hesitating for one moment.

"I know Rudi better than anyone," Anna said, surprised to realize this was true. "I know how he can put people off. I think . . . you see, he was so mean to me once, not just one time but often, back a few years before I knew you even. We don't speak of it now but he feels sorry when he thinks of it. Or he did, before he went away. Then last year we got to be a sort of team. Maybe, because of those things, I can get through to him. I do want to try. If I fail and it doesn't help, then someone else, some grown-up, can still do the professional things."

Getting ready to put Anna's plan into operation took nearly a month. She had to go over to the Schumachers' almost every day after school.

"What's gotten into you? I've hardly seen you for days," Maggie protested.

"It's something I'm trying to do for Rudi," Anna said, knowing that would silence all objections.

"Can we help?" Suzy wanted to know.

Anna shook her head.

"I can't talk about it so don't ask," she said.

Can *I* help? she wondered.

It was too late to back down. The night came when she had to try it, good or bad, right or wrong. She went up to Rudi's room and got things ready in an out-of-the-way corner where he would be sure not to trip over anything. She went back down, waited the long, long hours till bedtime, and tried not to grow so afraid, while she was waiting, that she would be unable, in the end, to carry her plan through. She also had to keep all of this inner turmoil hidden from her family. She had never in her life been more grateful than she was that night when Mama said, as usual:

"Off to bed, Anna. Sleep well."

The time had almost come.

* * *

Anna had worried about falling asleep but she was far too tied up in knots even to doze. She heard all the noises of the household settling down: water running in the bathroom, Papa and Mama talking downstairs, light switches being clicked off, the last news broadcast signing off with "God Save the King," beds creaking. Papa began to snore. After an endless stretch of time, she heard Rudi start to walk, back and forth, as though he were locked in a cage.

She took a small flashlight, borrowed from Dr. Schumacher, eased out of bed without making a sound, inched her way cautiously to his bedroom, opened the door soundlessly and slid her body around it, beamed the thin line of light down at the talking book machine and reached for the knob that turned it on. She waited till Rudi was on the far side of the room. He was talking to himself. She couldn't hear the words, only muttering, but they made him miss the one little click. She had worried about that click ahead of time and never dreamed it would be so simple.

Breathing shallowly, doing her level best to keep her hand steady, she moved the phonograph needle into place.

"*A Tale of Two Cities,*" a man's voice read out, startling even Anna who had known what was coming, "by Charles Dickens. Read by Stanley Wellman."

Having practiced at the Schumachers' over and over, Anna then moved the needle a little further on in order to miss all the part about it being a talking book to be used exclusively by blind people, and to reach the story itself. It caught the tail end of the last word of what she wanted to skip and then went on, the deep voice speaking the words with love, with respect, exactly the way they should be read.

> "It was the best of times, it was the worst of times, it was the age of wisdom, it was the age of foolishness, it was the epoch of belief. . . ."

"What is it? Turn it off. Stop it! Who's there?" Rudi cried out.

She had been amazed he had let the record play that long. She switched it off.

"It's only me, Anna," she said. "That was the first record of a talking book. I picked it because I knew you liked it, even though you had read it before. I thought . . ."

"Anna please, I told you, leave me alone," Rudi said.

"I will in a minute," she answered, keeping on even though she could hear her voice starting to shake. "But first I have to do one more thing. Listen, just this once. I want to read you something."

Rudi said nothing but she could feel his mind set against her. If anything, the wall was stronger.

Slowly, painstakingly slowly, she began to read. She had marked off the breaks in the first paragraph with bits of paper glued to the page. Since she had been following, she knew how to pick up exactly where the reader on the record had been cut off.

"It . . . was . . . the . . . epoch . . . of . . . in . . . cre . . . du . . . li . . . ty . . . it . . . was the . . . sea . . . son . . . of . . . light. . . ."

"Anna," he stopped her.

"Yes?" she said.

"Why are you reading like that, so slowly?"

"It's very fast for me. I only know the basic alphabet, none of the abbreviations. If I didn't have it practically memorized, I'd have been slower still," she said, not giving him a direct answer, trying to make him go on talking.

"Anna," he said again.

"Yes?" Anna said, her heart lifting a fraction for his voice sounded alive. Not warm or understanding or welcoming. But curious and really Rudi's.

"How are you reading?"

"In Braille," Anna said.

"Were you looking at it?"

"No. How could I be? I didn't turn on the light."

There was a long silence. Then she began to talk to him in a quiet, level, almost angry voice.

"Rudi, stop being the way you are. You're not you at all. If I can read Braille after only a few lessons from Mrs. Schumacher, you can too. You can listen to this book all night here in the darkness instead of pacing up and down, up and down."

"So you did hear me other nights," he said softly, bitterly.

"Yes. I've always heard you. But I'm talking about something else. You're going away inside. Mama says you're getting better. You have even Papa nearly fooled. . . ."

"But not smart little Anna," he mocked.

"No, not me," she said. "Because I know how it is."

"You know!" he jeered again.

But once more she was glad, for he sounded ready to fight. She had not heard him ready to fight for weeks. Now she would have to use her last weapon, the one she had withheld till now.

"I couldn't see much till I was nine," she said, "and you, you called me Awkward Anna and made fun of me and kept saying I was stupid. Do you remember that? I was more afraid of you than of anyone."

"But I didn't know," he said, taken off guard by her sudden attack.

"Oh, it's all over long ago, that hurting. And I wasn't like you because I didn't know either that I couldn't see properly. I believed you were right, that I was stupid and clumsy and no good. I believed you so much that I went away inside myself where you couldn't reach me to keep hurting. Like you, now."

"Where's the phonograph?" he asked suddenly.

Anna knew when to stop.

"Let me turn on the light for myself," she said, "and I can get you to it. I used a tiny flashlight to help me find it before, so you wouldn't hear me and I could surprise you."

"You're just lucky I didn't have a heart attack," her brother said, as she pulled his hand into the crook of her elbow and led him to the talking book machine. Showing him how to operate it was simple. "The records go around much more slowly than on our own phonograph," she explained, "and here are all the other records that make up the rest of the book."

He picked them up and carefully put them back down.

"I can teach you the Braille alphabet, which is how everybody begins, after school—if you help me with my math, that is."

She held her breath while she waited. Had she gone too far?

Then he laughed, a cracked little laugh which sounded something like a sob. But Anna knew it was laughter.

"Go back to bed, Little Stupid, little Awkward Anna," he said. "We'll see what tomorrow brings when we get there. Turn out the light when you go."

She got up and left him, without another word, because she couldn't speak with such a lump in her throat. She ran to her alcove, fell onto her bed and lay there, listening.

Would the pacing begin again?

What had she done?

He hadn't promised anything.

"It was the best of times, it was the worst of times . . .," the voice began again.

Then it said, *". . . it was the season of light, it was the season of darkness, it was the spring of hope. . . ."*

Anna hugged her pillow to her and let the tears of joy come any old way they wanted to.

What did you learn from this selection about how to help someone in trouble?

Anna's "last weapon" is to remind Rudi of how he once treated her. What is its effect on Rudi?

Given Rudi's response to Anna's offer to help, what changes do you predict might happen in his life?

At the end of the selection, the record plays ". . . it was the season of light, it was the season of darkness, it was the spring of hope. . . ." How do these lines express a theme of the story?

WRITE Write a short description of a time when you tried to help someone, as Anna does. Compare your experience to Anna's.

ALA Notable Book

Boston Globe–Horn Book Award

Little by Little

A Writer's Education

by Jean Little

Jean Little drew on many of her own experiences in writing Listen for the Singing. *Like Anna Solden, for example, Jean Little had very poor eyesight, attended a Sight Saving class, and lived in the Toronto area as a teenager. However, it was her father, not her brother, who enlisted in the navy during World War II. In this excerpt from her autobiography, Little tells about her first publication—two Christmas poems written when she was seventeen—and the events that followed.*

The publication of the poems made a sensation among my teachers and even impressed my classmates. Early in January, when I came home for lunch, I found a letter for me on the hall table. I carried it into the living room where the light was better. From there I could glimpse Dad still standing in the hall, reading his mail.

The envelope was from *Saturday Night*. I tore it open and stared at the slip of paper that fell into my hand. I had never had anything like it before. It said $30.00. I could make that out.

"Dad," I said uncertainly, "I think *Saturday Night* has sent me a bill for thirty dollars."

He came and looked over my shoulder. Then he grinned.

"It's not a bill. It's a cheque. They are paying you for the poems."

I stared from him to the cheque and back again. I would gladly have paid *Saturday Night* for the delight they had given me. It had not crossed my mind that they would pay me.

"You mean, it's mine? Thirty dollars?" I said, sounding dazed.

"You wrote the poems, didn't you?" my father said, laughing at my look of stupefaction. "You are a writer, Jean. Writers get paid for their work."

Work! It hadn't been work. It had been something I did for the love of doing it.

Thirty dollars! I wrote in my diary:

I got the shock of my life in a cheque for $30.00 (thirty dollars) from Saturday Night. I really feel professional at last. I sent them another poem immediately, mercenary creature that I am.

The poem was turned down with a kind letter from B. K. Sandwell himself. I was disappointed, but not surprised. I knew in my heart of hearts that I had a lot to learn yet.

When I arrived at school one January morning, Miss Sinclair, my Latin teacher, met me in the hall.

"Jean, did you know there's a letter asking about you in the Letters to the Editor column in *Saturday Night*?"

"No!" I said, thrilled to the core to hear from my admiring public.

We went to the library and there was the letter.

On Christmas Day the year I turned 16.

January 23, 1951

> Thank you for those two finely sensitive poems, Mary and Joseph, published in the Dec. 25 issue. I hope the author is a Canadian.
>
> J. A. Alexander
> Toronto, Ont.

Beneath the letter, the Editors had replied: "Yes, she is a Canadian, living in Guelph, Ont."

I beamed at Miss Sinclair. She smiled mistily back at me.

"That's quite a compliment, Jean. You've done well," she said. Then she cleared her throat.

All morning, teachers stopped me in the hall to congratulate me. Even Mr. Hamilton, the principal, sought me out.

"This will be a proud day for your father," he said.

I felt like a celebrity. Much as I enjoyed the attention, however, I yearned to race home to show my family the letter. Instead I had to wait until noon. When at last I was free, I positively flew the mile and a half to our house. I burst into the dining room where the family was assembling for lunch. When I came to a halt, I gasped out, "Mum, somebody wrote to *Saturday Night* asking about me. Some man named J. A. Alexander. He liked my poems."

Mother did not say a word to me. Instead she sent a searching look down the table to where my father sat.

"Llew, you didn't!" she exclaimed. I did not understand. What had Dad to do with some strange man from Toronto? My puzzled gaze followed her accusing one. Dad was grinning. And blushing!

"Well, I just . . . " he began to defend himself.

At last the meaning of my mother's question registered. J. A. Alexander was my father.

I wanted to kill him. He had made me a laughingstock. If anybody found out that my own father had written that letter, I'd never live it down. Humiliated and speechless with rage, I sank into a chair.

He was proud of himself. He had signed the letter with an alias, and he had driven to Toronto to mail it so it would not have a Guelph postmark.

"If you keep still," Mother told me, "nobody need ever know. Jean, calm down. It isn't the end of the world."

I did not calm down. I did not fully forgive him until after his death. I did not begin to see how endearing it was of him until I was thirty. I did not tell the story in public until I was forty-five. My fond father was the kind of parent every aspiring writer should be lucky enough to have.

I still had my thirty dollars. I kept

looking for exactly the right way to spend it. I saw an advertisement in the *Globe and Mail* for a Great Dane puppy worth thirty dollars. My parents were unmoved by my pleas.

"No Great Dane puppy!" they said in unison.

Buying lots of books tempted me. But I wanted to spend the whole, huge amount on one grand purchase. After all, no eighteen-year-old I knew had thirty dollars to spend in any way he or she saw fit.

Dad tried to get me to start a bank account.

"If you are going to be a writer, you'd better start learning to use money wisely. You won't have a lot of it."

I had no interest whatever in being practical. I wanted to celebrate.

"No," I said stubbornly. "I don't want to invest it. I want to spend it."

"Do you know what I think you should do with your money?" Mother said suddenly.

"What?" I asked warily, braced to withstand another sensible idea.

"I think you should buy some material, have a dress made, and get Jamie to take you to the At Home," she said.

Was she serious? Why would I want to go to a formal dance with my big brother?

I cringed at the thought of the two or three "tea dances" and class parties I had gone to in grade nine. I had never been asked to dance by a boy. I had only danced with other wallflowers. At the last party I had attended, the well-meaning chaperone had pushed me into a sort of Sadie Hawkins dance. When the music stopped, the person who stood opposite you had to be your partner. The boy opposite me took one look, grimaced and said clearly, "Oh, no!" He had then walked off the floor, leaving me deserted. All around me couples had started to dance. Keeping an iron grip on my self-control, I had gone to stand behind the record player. I had stayed there until it was time to go home. I had not been to a dance since.

Standing are Aunt Gretta, Dad and Mother. Grandma is holding Pat, and Hugh, Jamie and I are sitting on the steps.

"I hate dances," I told my mother now.

"But I think this would be different," she said. "You are going to graduate from high school without ever attending a real dance. I don't think your friends would look down on you if Jamie took you. After all, he's a college man. Hugh would be there, too. You could practise dancing with him ahead of time. Think about it."

I thought about it. Betty Hall, Hugh's girlfriend, had become my friend, too. I told her in a joking way what my mother had suggested. She did not laugh. She said I should do it. Both my brothers sounded enthusiastic. Mum and Dad never told me what they had said to make Jamie so courtly. He actually wrote me a letter inviting me to go with him.

When I nervously agreed, Mother and I went shopping for material for my dress. The shop had just gotten in a roll of lustrous, soft green velvet from Paris, France. When they moved it, light shimmered along its folds. I held it up and watched it ripple and gleam. I had never seen anything look so rich. I spent all my Mary and Joseph money on eight yards of it, hoping I was not making a colossal mistake.

The dressmaker made me a lovely dress. There was enough material left to make gloves that stretched from my elbows to two points on the backs of my hands. We also bought a pair of silver sandals.

The night of the dance began to loom ahead like an iceberg. My stomach lurched every time I thought about it.

We pushed the pingpong table out of the way and Hugh and I began to practise dancing. "You're doing fine . . . ouch!" he kept saying. He taught me to waltz and, at the finish, to spin in circles the full length of the pingpong room.

"When the waltz contest is announced, save it for me," he said. "Betty's so short that she falls over my foot when we pivot. You and I pivot perfectly."

On the day of the dance, I had my hair curled. I wore lipstick and pink nail polish. The dress helped me to feel braver as it slid over my head and settled around me in gleaming folds. When I came down the long staircase, dressed up but inwardly shaking, my brother Jamie stepped forward and handed me a florist's box.

Hugh and Betty were watching. Mum and Dad stood waiting. Mother, as chairman of the board of education, was to be in the reception line with Dad beside her. Pat and Rose were planning to come and look on for awhile from the upstairs gallery that ran around the gymnasium. Grandma was the only one staying home.

I opened the box. Before I saw the gardenia, its heady fragrance reached my nose. I lifted it out with unsteady hands. I had never received a corsage before and had not expected such a thoughtful gesture from my big brother. Feeling shy, I turned to look at him. Had it been his idea or Dad's?

He looked elegant. Debonair, even.

"Thank you," I said uncertainly.

"I had nothing to do with it," my father said, smiling warmly at Jamie.

"Well, I like that!" Jamie pretended to be affronted. "Do you think I don't know how to treat my date?"

I apologized. This was not the brother who, many years before, had dropped me into a creek when he was supposed to be carrying me across it. This was a prince among brothers.

The gym was decorated to look like a huge Valentine. As we waited to go through the heart-shaped gates that let onto the dance floor, I felt a finger run along the rolled collar of my dress.

"It's so soft," a girl whispered. "Feel it."

"I can't," her escort muttered.

"Go on," the girl urged. "She'll never know."

A much heavier finger ran the length of my collar. I felt like giggling. I pretended to have noticed nothing.

When Jamie and I began to dance, I found that Hugh's coaching had worked. I knew what to do with my feet. What's more, I loved doing it. When Jamie asked if I'd like to sit out a dance, I shook my head. Hugh cut in on us and Betty and I changed places. Mother, Dad, Rose and Pat all went home before the waltz contest was announced. Hugh came to get me.

"1 . . . 2 . . . 3, 1 . . . 2 . . . 3," he was counting in a mutter as we waltzed around the gym.

Couples began to leave the floor as the judges tapped them on the shoulder. We kept dancing. Both of us were counting now. We did not miss a beat. There were only five couples left. Four . . .

"You two are the winners," one of the judges told us, smiling at our astonished laughter. "You were the only couple on the floor doing proper ballroom waltzing."

With Jamie at the dance (I felt like Cinderella at the ball).

Up to that moment, the winners of each contest had gone up on stage and been given their prize. They had then done a few steps across the width of the platform. Hugh and I, however, had the entire floor to ourselves.

"Okay, Jean," he murmured, "we'll waltz to the far end. Then, when I give you the signal, we'll pivot."

My heart was pounding. What if I missed the signal? What if I found myself falling over his foot?

We waltzed up to the end. Then, as scattered applause began, Hugh said, "Now, *pivot*!" We were off, spinning around and around, down the entire length of the gym. The applause was real now. As we finished, flushed and laughing, I knew how Cinderella felt dancing with the prince. No wonder she stayed past midnight. I never wanted to go home, either.

When we got home, we woke my parents up so they could see Hugh and me pivot and admire our prize. As we waltzed around their bedroom, careening into the furniture and laughing like idiots, I remembered that my father had wanted me to put my thirty dollars in the bank. If it had lain somewhere collecting interest for forty years, it could never have bought me another such enchanted evening.

And J. A. Alexander knew it.

In a later chapter, Jean Little describes some experiences that led her to become a writer.

I wanted to be a writer. But I had been told over and over again that you could not make a living as a writer. You had to get a real job and write in your spare time.

But what real job could a legally blind girl with a B.A. in English do?

Then I learned that the Rotary Crippled Children's Centre planned to start a small class for handicapped children and would need a teacher for it. I had no teaching qualifications, but I had worked with children with motor handicaps for three summers at Woodeden Camp.

The Rotarians agreed to hire me if I would first go to Montreal for two weeks to take a course on educating children with motor handicaps. The course was taught by Ellen Thiel from the Institute for Special Education at the University of Utah in Salt Lake City. I was intimidated by the other students, most of whom were experienced teachers and, although I enjoyed the course itself, I decided I would have to give up the idea of being a teacher. They kept talking a language I did not understand. Phonics, for instance. It was clearly of paramount importance, and I did not know what it meant. When I went in for my final interview, I explained all this to Ellen.

She laughed. "Phonics notwithstanding, I think you just may be a born teacher. I'm about to give a six-week course in Salt Lake on teaching children with motor handicaps. How would you like to come home to Utah with me and we could find out if I'm right?"

I stared at her, not knowing for a second whether or not she was kidding. Then I saw her grin. It was very friendly and had in it the same challenge that Dad's had had so often.

"All right," I said dazedly. "Where's Utah?"

I called home half an hour later to tell Mother that I was coming home to pack tomorrow and, the day after, was meeting this strange woman, Ellen Thiel, in Urbana and setting out for the American West.

"Wonderful," Mother said after only the shortest of hesitations. "I'll be there to meet you. You can tell me all about it while we pack."

At the end of that summer, I made a list in my diary of all the "new experiences" I had had since I left home. There are forty-nine items listed. I stopped only because I had filled the last page in that diary.

I did discover what Phonics meant, but I learned far more than that. The children in the demonstration class taught me a lot. So did Ellen's three children, Paula, Mary and Joe.

One evening I was reading *The Secret Garden* to the Thiel kids. Paula and Mary were enthralled by the story, but Joe kept fiddling with odds and ends on his bed and behaving as though he were extremely bored. When I closed the book, however, and started to shepherd the girls out of his room, he demanded that I give him the phone.

"Why?" I asked. "It's time you went to sleep. I read two extra chapters because the girls were so interested."

"I have to tell Mama something," Joe said.

Ellen was working late at the university. But I knew she was alone and besides, who was I to come between a boy and his mother?

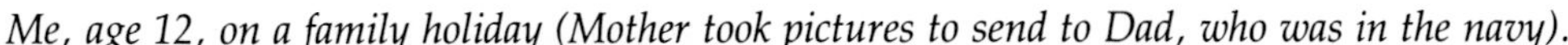

Me, age 12, on a family holiday (Mother took pictures to send to Dad, who was in the navy).

I handed him the telephone on its long cord. Returning after tucking in the girls, I heard him say in a voice filled with wonder and delight, "Mum, they got into the garden!!!"

Never again did I make the mistake of thinking that a child who appeared inattentive was getting nothing out of a book. His tone held exactly the joy Mary Lennox herself felt when she stepped through the ivy-covered green door.

At the end of the summer, Ellen wrote me a glowing letter of recommendation, and I went back to Guelph to start preparing for my teaching job at the Crippled Children's Centre.

I was not an ideal teacher. When your students continually correct your arithmetic, it keeps you humble. But I did one important thing well. I read to them.

I found that these were deprived children, not because they were not loved, but because they had largely been kept indoors due to their handicaps. Not one of them had ever seen a rainbow or been to a circus. They could not swim. They had not been taken to a zoo. Most of them had not ridden on a city bus. None had been on a train journey. Most had never eaten in a restaurant.

We did all these things, and Phonics, too.

Remembering how I had never found a cross-eyed heroine in a book, I decided to search for books about children with motor handicaps. I did not for one moment intend to limit my students to reading about crippled kids. I knew that they completely identified with Anne Shirley and Homer Price, that they actually became Bambi, Piglet and Wilbur. I did not think they needed a book to help them adjust. I did believe, however, that crippled children had a right to find themselves represented in fiction.

I began to search.

I found a book about a girl with polio. None of my students had polio. The Salk vaccine had already been discovered. I found several books that contained invalid children who completely recovered before the book ended. None of my students was ever going to recover completely.

I was looking for a book in which the child's handicap was present only in the background. The kids I taught were not conscious of their disabilities most of the time. They minded when people stared at them, or when their brothers and sisters got bicycles, of course. But usually they were too busy living to brood. Physio and occupational therapy were like arithmetic and reading, an accepted part of their days.

When we read *The Secret Garden,* Alec said, "What's the matter with Colin? Why doesn't he have therapy?"

"I guess it was written too long ago for them to know about therapy," I said weakly.

"What I can't figure out," Clifford complained, "is how he stood up for the first time in June and was well enough to beat Mary in a race by August. That's crazy."

The others loved the ending so much that they defended Colin's rapid recovery. But even they sounded a bit dubious.

We went through the same questions when we read *Heidi.* Clara got well even faster than Colin.

"Miss Little, what was wrong with Clara?"

It didn't say. I began to feel angry on their behalf. Why couldn't there be a happy ending without a miracle cure? Why wasn't there a story with a child in it who resembled the kids I taught?

Somebody should write one, I thought.

It did not yet cross my mind that that somebody might be me.

Do you agree with Jean Little that children with physical disabilities have "a right to find themselves represented in fiction"? Why do you think this is or is not important?

Explain how Jean's feelings toward her father for writing the letter about her poems changed over the years.

Do you think Jean used her thirty dollars wisely, or should she have put the money in the bank? Explain your answer.

What qualities of a good teacher do you think Jean Little has?

WRITE Suppose you are planning to interview Jean Little for a magazine article. List several questions you would like to ask her.

THE INVISIBLE THREAD

by Yoshiko Uchida

ALA Best Book for Young Adults

Yoshiko Uchida was born in Alameda, California, the daughter of Japanese immigrants. Her family experiences made her aware of an "invisible thread" that connected her parents to the country they had left behind and that also extended into her own life. Uchida became the first full-time professional Japanese American writer of books for young people.

In this excerpt from her autobiography, she explains how she began writing and tells about one of the experiences that most strongly influenced her writing—the internment of Japanese Americans during World War II.

"Mama, can't we get a puppy? Please?"

"Please, Mama, can't we?"

Keiko and I begged shamelessly and finally wore Mama down. When a five-month-old collie puppy finally came into our lives, we named him Brownie. I was so excited, I simply had to do something to hold on to the magical happiness so it would never fade away.

That was when I remembered the booklet with blank pages I'd made at school. It was covered with silver and gold Christmas wrapping paper and was so special I hadn't known what to do with it. All I had written in it so far was my name and address and the word *private*.

Now at last I'd discovered a perfect use for it. I kept in it an account of everything Brownie did, from the day he was scratched by a cat, to the time he ate the rind of half a cantaloupe and his poor belly expanded to the size of a full melon. I recorded the day he learned to raise his leg at a tree and also the tragic day he came down with distemper.

Our neighbor, who was a Christian Scientist and believed in spiritual healing, came to pray for Brownie. "Mrs. Harpainter is taking care of him and is doing Christian Science," I wrote in my booklet. I truly believed she could heal him, but he was too sick to be saved and had to be put to sleep.

Nothing I truly loved had died before. Keiko and I cried so much, refusing even to go outside to play, that Papa finally bought a hammock to console us. He hung it in the backyard between the peach and the apricot trees and told us to try it out.

I lay on the striped canvas hammock, gently swaying to and fro. I looked up between the mass of green leaves at the cloudless blue sky, but all I could see were Brownie's sad eyes as we left him at the vet's. I was too desolate and devastated to enjoy the hammock. I decided then that I would do something for Brownie in my special booklet.

My sister, Keiko (right), and myself, when she was about seven and I was about three.

I used a whole page to draw a tombstone for him bearing the words *Died*

March 16, 1932. Ten months old. Then, using my crayons, I surrounded the tombstone with four magnificent floral wreaths and bouquets of flowers, similar to those I had seen at the cemetery. I also drew him a tree. I thought he would like that.

When I finished, I felt better. I had found a way to give Brownie a proper ending to his brief life. I had also discovered that writing in the booklet was a means, not only of holding on to the special magic of joyous moments, but of finding comfort and solace from pain as well. It was a means of creating a better ending than was sometimes possible in real life. I had discovered what writing was all about.

Fortunately, I was able to write about other happier moments as well. There was the glorious day we got another dog—a beautiful Scotch collie we named Laddie. And the day we got our first refrigerator, enabling us to enjoy the luxury of making our own ice and even ice cream.

The refrigerator was a special boon for me because I no longer had the odious chore of emptying the pan under the ice box where water from the melting ice collected. I was also relieved of the task of hanging the sign in our window to tell the ice man how many pounds of ice we needed each day.

When my booklet was filled, I began a black leather three-ring binder notebook that I called "My Diary of Important Events." My first entry was about our sixth-grade graduation party at school. I was so impressed by the vanilla ice cream with a green Christmas tree center that I illustrated the page with a colored drawing of it.

One day when I was in the sixth grade, my favorite teacher, Miss Wolfard, put up several intriguing pictures taken from magazine covers. One was of an aproned woman watering geraniums in her window box. Another showed a boy delivering newspapers with his golden retriever. There was also a man wearing a green eyeshade and black sleeve protectors bent over a desk. There were several other pictures as well.

"Who do you think these people are?" she asked. "What's happening in their lives? See if you can write a story about one of them."

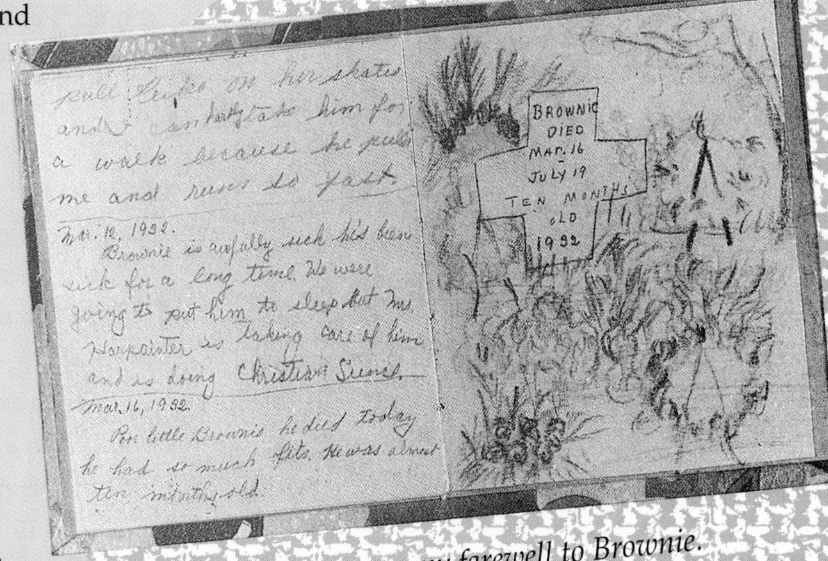

pull [illegible] on her skates
and I [illegible] take him for
a walk because he pulls
me and runs so fast.

Mar. 12, 1932.
Brownie is awfully sick he's been
sick for a long time. We were
going to put him to sleep but Mrs.
Harpainter is taking care of him
and is doing Christian Sience.

Mar. 16, 1932.
Poor little Brownie he died today
he had so much fits. He was almost
ten months old.

BROWNIE
DIED
MAR. 16
JULY 19
TEN MONTHS
OLD
1932

A page from my first diary—my farewell to Brownie.

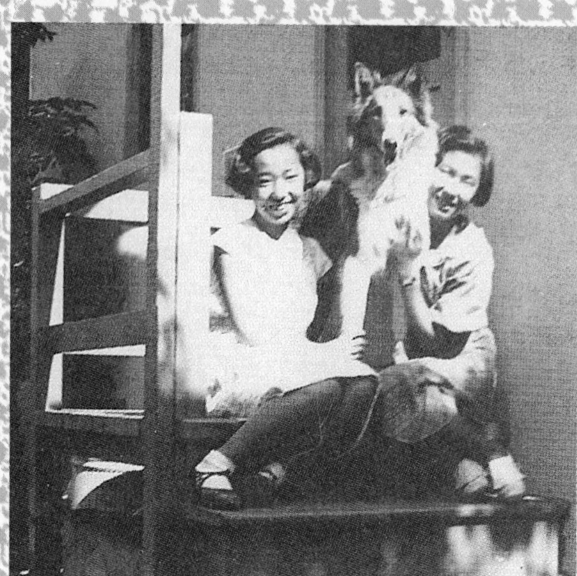

My sister and I with Laddie on our back porch.

My head began to buzz with ideas, and I could hardly wait to get started. That might well have been the day I discovered how much fun it was to write stories of my own. Soon I was writing short stories in little booklets, and because like my parents, I was also frugal, I made them out of brown wrapping paper.

My first attempt was called "Jimmy Chipmunk and His Friends—a Short Story for Small Children." The back cover read "by Yoshi Uchida, Age Ten, Low Sixth Grade." My next story was called "Willie, the Squirrel."

Two years later I allowed myself to advance to white typing paper, and using my father's typewriter, I wrote and illustrated a seven-chapter book called "Sally Jane Waters."

It never in my wildest dreams occurred to me to write about a Japanese American child, which may seem strange today. But the books I was reading at the time were only about white children and were written by white authors. The best world, it seemed to me then, was the white American world. So that was what I wrote about.

The written word was always important in our family, and I was surrounded by books. Papa bought us a complete set of *The Book of Knowledge*, a sort of junior encyclopedia, and Mama also bought many books for us, as well as for herself.

One corner of her bureau was usually piled high with magazines and books that she hoped someday to read. But unfortunately, she never found the time, and the unwieldy pile continued to grow, spilling over onto any nearby table or shelf.

Mama also kept a diary. She filled up dozens of small brown-leather five-year diaries with golden clasps to record our daily doings. But I never liked those cramped pages that forced you to squeeze a whole day into a tiny one-inch space. Instead of a daily entry, I liked to wait for a special event and fill up a whole page or more with the full glory of it.

When Mama had a few free moments, she often sat at the table in the breakfast nook, pushed aside the books, magazines, and papers spread out on it, and scribbled her poems on bits of scrap paper or the backs of old envelopes. It was as though she felt her poems were not worthy of a nice clean page in a notebook and that she could only indulge in writing them after completing her tasks as a mother and wife.

The poems she wrote were the thirty-one-syllable Japanese *tanka* and were published every other week in a small publication put out by our good friend, Mrs. Wasa.

My first brown wrapping paper book.

I had a great interest in Mrs. Wasa as well, but for entirely different reasons. She seemed more of a grandmother to me than my real grandmother, and because she lived only two blocks from us, I visited her often.

I usually found her in the sunny kitchen, wearing an apron that seemed to swallow up her tiny person, daintily licking her fingers as she baked custard or a vanilla sponge cake.

"Ah, Yo Chan, you are just in time for a little taste," she would say, making me a cup of hot cocoa to go with it.

I always thought I was incredibly lucky to arrive each day at exactly the right moment, but she no doubt thoughtfully timed her baking to gladden my heart on those after-school visits.

Poetry and diary entries certainly were not the primary items of writing in our house. Both my parents were avid letter writers, communicating not only with friends and relatives in Japan, but with many friends scattered across the United States.

Of course all these people wrote back, so our mailbox was always bulging, and the mailman was a good friend. He made two deliveries each day and always had something for us in his big leather pouch.

Besides writing letters, my father kept all our financial records. His fingers could make the beads of the abacus dance in lively rhythm as he checked bills and maintained our household accounts. He wrote all the checks in the neat flowing script he had learned at night school and never left an unpaid bill on his desk for more than two days.

A page from "My Diary of Important Events."

He liked to read, too, but his taste was quite different from Mama's. He liked reading such magazines as *The Literary Digest, The Christian Century*, and *National Geographic*, and he never left for the office without a copy of the *San Francisco Chronicle* to read on the ferry.

Because there were no baby-sitters in the world of my childhood, our parents took us everywhere they went—to church, to the movies, to visit friends, to San Francisco's art museums (because Mama loved art), and to concerts (because Papa loved music).

My diary was filled with such entries as "Tonight we went to hear the Cossacks Chorus. They were keen!" Or "to hear Roland Hayes sing." Or "to hear Ignace Jan Paderewski play the piano." Or "to see 'The Merry Widow'" or "A Midsummer Night's Dream" or "Mme Butterfly." All of which I could only describe as "perfect!" or "swell" or "just keen!"

When I was writing about a concert or a play, one page of my diary was quite sufficient, even including an illustration. But when we went on summer trips to Los Angeles to visit my grandmother, or to Livingston to visit friends on a farm, I needed at least three pages. And my limited vocabulary of "keen" and "swell" suddenly began to seem woefully inadequate.

At the age of sixteen, Yoshiko Uchida entered the University of California in Berkeley, where she studied English, philosophy, and history. During her senior year, in December 1941, Japan bombed Pearl Harbor.

"No company for lunch?" I asked, surprised.

It was Sunday, but there were only the four of us going home from church. It seemed strange, but I was glad for the peace and quiet. Finals were starting soon at the university, and I was anxious to have a quick lunch and go to the library to study.

As we were having lunch, an urgent voice suddenly broke into the program on the radio. Japan, the announcer said, had attacked Pearl Harbor.

"Oh, no!" Mama gasped. "It must be a mistake."

"Of course it is," Papa agreed.

He turned up the volume. It didn't sound like a mistake.

"It's probably the work of some fanatic," Papa insisted.

Not one of us believed it was war. Kay went with my parents to visit friends, and I went to the campus library to study. I didn't return until almost five o'clock.

The minute I got home, I knew something was wrong. A strange man sat in our living room, and my father was gone.

Mama and Kay explained that two FBI men had taken my father for questioning. A third remained to guard us, intercepting all phone calls and preventing friends from coming to see us.

"We're prisoners in our own home," Kay said ominously. "The police even broke in and searched our house while we were out."

As upset as she was, in her usual thoughtful way, Mama was making tea for the FBI man in the kitchen. She always served tea to anyone who called, even the "Real Silk Lady," who came with her satchel of silken samples to sell Mama stockings and undergarments.

"You're making tea for the FBI man?" I asked, indignant.

But Mama respected everybody regardless of the work they did. The man who delivered our dry cleaning, the People's Bread man who sold doughnuts and bread from his truck, the boy who delivered rice and tofu from the Japanese grocery store, or the Watkins door-to-door salesman. She treated them all with equal respect and courtesy.

"He's only doing his job," Mama said now of the FBI man. "He's trying to be pleasant." And she carried a tray of tea things into the living room.

But I wasn't about to have tea with someone guarding us as though we were prisoners. I went to my bedroom and stayed there until the FBI man got instructions to leave.

When at last the three of us were alone, we made supper, but none of us felt like eating. Papa was gone, and we had no idea what happened to him or when he would be back. We finally went to bed, leaving the porch light on for him.

As I lay in bed in my cold, dark room, I heard the mournful wail of the foghorns on the bay. I felt a clammy fear come over me, as though I was at the bottom of a deep well and couldn't climb out.

My father didn't return that night or for the next three days. We had no idea where he was or what had happened to him. But Mama persuaded me to continue going to classes, and somehow I managed to get through my finals.

Five days after he was taken, we finally learned that my father was being held at the Immigration Detention Quarters in San Francisco with about one hundred other Japanese men.

The FBI had apprehended all the leaders of the Japanese American community—businessmen, teachers, bankers, farmers, fishermen—and held them incommunicado.

The following day we got a postcard from Papa asking us to send his shaving kit and some clean clothing. We arranged for permission to visit him, and Kay drove us to San Francisco.

My heart sank when I saw the drab gray building that looked like a jail. And as though to confirm my impression, a guard brought Papa to the visiting room like a prisoner.

"Papa! Are you all right?"

He looked tired and haggard, but assured us that he was fine. The news he gave us, however, was terrible. All the men in his group were being sent in a few days to a prisoner-of-war camp in Missoula, Montana.

"Montana! Then we won't be able to visit you anymore."

"I know," Papa answered, "but we can write to each other. Now, girls, be strong, and take good care of Mama for me, will you?"

Kay and I began to cry as we said our good-byes and watched Papa go back down the bleak hallway. It was Mama who was the strong one.

From the moment we were at war with Japan, my parents (and all the Issei[1]) had suddenly become "enemy aliens." They were not citizens because by law the United States prevented Asians from becoming naturalized citizens. Now Kay, as the oldest U.S. citizen, became head of our household.

She had graduated from Mills College in 1940 with a degree in early childhood education, but the only job she could find was as a nursemaid to a three-year-old white child. Her employers asked her to stay on in spite of the war, but I wondered why they felt compelled to say that. After all, Kay was still the same person, and she was an American, just as they were.

However, strange ideas seemed to be erupting in the minds of many Americans. I was astonished when a white friend of many years asked, "Didn't you have any idea it was going to happen?"

I was hurt that she had asked. Her question implied that we somehow knew of Japan's war plans simply because we were Americans of Japanese ancestry. It was a ridiculous assumption.

Eventually Kay left her job to devote all her time to managing our household affairs. Papa's bank account had been blocked immediately, and for a while we could withdraw only $100 a month for living expenses. She needed important papers from his safe-deposit box, but found that the FBI had confiscated all his keys.

She needed to pay the premiums on his car and life insurance policies, file his income tax returns, and at his request, purchase U.S. Defense Bonds. It was a difficult job for Kay, trying to manage all the tasks that Papa had handled until then.

Papa wrote often, trying to help us manage without him, but his letters often arrived looking like lace doilies. The censors had cut out whatever they didn't want us to read.

"Don't forget to lubricate the car," Papa wrote. Or, "Be sure to have the roses pruned, brush Laddie every day, send

---

[1]Issei [ē' sā]: Japanese immigrants in the U.S.; first generation

Grandma her monthly check, and take our Christmas offering to church."

We could tell he was trying to anticipate all our problems from his snowbound camp in Montana. He also tried to cheer us up, and asked us to tell our church friends not to be too discouraged.

Having a good time with our neighbors. Left to right, Solveig, Yoshiko, Marian, Keiko.

Still, it was hard not to worry. Japan was now the despised enemy, and every Japanese American became a target of the same hatred directed at Japan. It was not because we had done anything wrong, but simply because we *looked* like the enemy.

One evening I went out with some friends for a late evening snack to a restaurant where we'd often gone before. We hadn't been there long when an angry Filipino man came to our table. His fists were clenched, and his eyes flashed with anger.

"You know what your Jap soldiers are doing to my homeland?" he shouted. "They're killing my people!"

"But we're not from Japan," we said, trying to reason with him. "We're Americans!"

He continued to harass us, not listening to anything we said. Then having had his say, he left, still scowling. But he had ruined our evening, for we knew there were many others who hated us as much as he did. We left the restaurant quickly and went home in silence.

I was frightened as I saw newspaper accounts accusing Japanese Americans of spying and sabotage in Hawaii. These rumors were later completely refuted, but at the time most Americans accepted them as the truth.

Soon racist groups began calling for a forced eviction of all Americans of Japanese ancestry along the West Coast. They called it an "evacuation"—a word implying removal for the protection of the person being removed—but actually it was an uprooting.

Hatred against Asians, however, was not new to California. It had existed for a hundred years. Laws that restricted immigration and land ownership already existed, and now groups who would benefit economically from our removal joined in the calls for a mass uprooting.

As new rumors spread, we grew more and more uneasy. Several of my classmates from out of town left the university to rejoin their families. And in Montana my father worried helplessly about what would happen to us.

We thought we should start packing some of our belongings, in case we were actually uprooted. One evening, as we were packing books into wooden crates, a friend stopped by to see us.

"What on earth are you doing?" he asked. "There will never be a mass evacuation. Don't you realize we're American citizens? The U.S. government would never intern its own citizens. It would be unconstitutional."

Of course his facts were right. Still, we knew that the attorney general of California claimed, incorrectly, that Japanese Americans had "infiltrated . . . every strategic spot" in the state.

On the floor of the House of Representatives, Congressman John Rankin had shouted, "I say it is of vital importance that we get rid of every Japanese . . . Damn them! Let us get rid of them now!"

Our government did nothing to stop these hysterical outcries or to refute the false rumors. We learned many years later that although President Franklin D. Roosevelt had seen a state department report testifying to the "extraordinary degree of loyalty" among the West Coast Japanese Americans, he chose instead to listen to the voices of the hatemongers.

On February 19, 1942, the President signed Executive Order 9066, which resulted in the forcible eviction of all Japanese, "aliens and nonaliens,"

The Uchida family lived in a single horse stall in an old stable at the Tanforan Racetrack.

from the West Coast of the United States. He stated that this was a military necessity, and because we did not know otherwise at the time, we believed him. The Supreme Court of the land sanctioned his decision.

It was a sad day for all Americans of Japanese ancestry. Our government no longer considered us its citizens, simply referring to us as "nonaliens." It also chose to ignore the Fifth and Fourteenth Amendments to the Constitution that guaranteed "due process of law" and "equal protection under the law" for all citizens. We were to be imprisoned in concentration camps without a trial or hearing of any kind.

"But we're at war with Germany and Italy, too," I objected. "Why are only the Japanese Americans being imprisoned?"

No one, including our government, had an answer for that.

Under the direction of Lieutenant General John L. DeWitt of the Western Defense Command, 120,000 men, women, and children of Japanese ancestry (two-thirds of whom were American citizens) were to be uprooted from their homes on the West Coast of the United States.

We were told we could "evacuate voluntarily" outside the military zone, but most of us had no place to go. How could we suddenly pick up everything and move to a new and unknown location? Some of our friends moved to inland towns, but when the exclusion zone was later extended, they were uprooted once again and eventually interned in a camp anyway.

We felt like prisoners even before our actual eviction. We had to observe an 8:00 P.M. curfew and were not permitted to travel more than five miles beyond our home. We had to turn in all shortwave radios, cameras, binoculars, and firearms. We also had to register. Each family was given a number, and ours was 13453.

I shuddered when I read the headlines of our local paper on April 21. It read, "JAPS GIVEN EVACUATION ORDERS HERE." On May 1, we were to be sent to the Tanforan Racetrack, which had been hurriedly converted into an "Assembly Center."

"But how can we clear out our house in only ten days?" Mama asked desperately. "We've lived here for fifteen years!"

"I guess we just have to do it, Mama," Kay answered. "We can't argue with the U.S. Army."

Friends came to help us clear out our belongings. But no one could help us decide what to keep and what to discard. We had to do that for ourselves. We grew frantic as the days went by. We sold furniture we should have kept and stored things we should have thrown out.

Mama was such a saver. She had drawers and closets and cartons overflowing with memory-laden belongings. She saved everything from old string and wrapping paper to valentines, Christmas cards, clay paperweights, and drawings that Kay and I had made for her. She had dozens of photograph albums and guest books and packets of old letters from friends and family.

We put off until the last minute a decision none of us wanted to make. What were we going to do with our beloved Laddie? We knew no friends who could take him. Finally, it occurred to me to put an ad in the *Daily Californian* at the university.

"I am one of the Japanese American students soon to be evacuated," I wrote, "and have a male Scotch collie that can't come with me. Can anyone give him a home? If interested, please call me immediately at Berkeley 7646W."

Our family in happier days after WW II.

The day my ad appeared, I was deluged with sympathetic calls, but we gave him to the first boy who called because he seemed kind and caring. We gave him Laddie's doghouse, leash, brushes, favorite toy, and everything else he would need.

The boy promised he would write us at Tanforan to let us know how Laddie was doing. We each gave Laddie a hug and watched him climb reluctantly into the strange car.

"Be a good boy now, Laddie," I said. "We'll come back for you someday."

"How can I throw all this away?" she asked bleakly.

In the end she just put everything in trunks that we stored at the Bekins Storage Company. We also stored there the furniture that was too large to be left with friends offering us space in their basements.

Mama, Kay, and I couldn't bear to go inside. We stood at the curb watching as the boy drove off. And we could still hear Laddie's plaintive barking even after the car turned the corner and we could no longer see it.

Yoshiko Uchida

Yoshiko Uchida tells about the kinds of writing she and her family members did. What kinds of writing are important for you and for other members of your family? Explain.

How did Yoshiko and her mother differ in their attitudes toward the FBI man who watched the Uchida family in their home? How would you feel in Yoshiko's situation?

How was the government's treatment of the Japanese Americans during World War II unconstitutional? You may want to look up the Fifth and Fourteenth Amendments to the Constitution.

Do you think the Japanese Americans should have refused to leave their homes? What might have happened if they had refused?

WRITE In a paragraph, explain one or more of the causes of prejudice. Include at least one reference to events in the selection.

THE BRACELET

BY YOSHIKO UCHIDA

"Mama, is it time to go?"

I hadn't planned to cry, but the tears came suddenly, and I wiped them away with the back of my hand. I didn't want my older sister to see me crying.

"It's almost time, Ruri," my mother said gently. Her face was filled with a kind of sadness I had never seen before.

I looked around at my empty room. The clothes that Mama always told me to hang up in the closet, the junk piled on my dresser, the old rag doll I could never bear to part with; they were all gone. There was nothing left in my room, and there was nothing left in the rest of the house. The rugs and furniture were gone, the pictures and drapes were down, and the closets and cupboards were empty. The house was like a gift box after the nice thing inside was gone; just a lot of nothingness.

It was almost time to leave our home, but we weren't moving to a nicer house or to a new town. It was April 21, 1942. The United States and Japan were at war, and every Japanese person on the West Coast was being evacuated by the government to a concentration camp. Mama, my sister Keiko and I were being sent from our home, and out of Berkeley, and eventually, out of California.

The doorbell rang, and I ran to answer it before my sister could. I thought maybe by some miracle, a messenger from the

ILLUSTRATIONS BY FLOYD COOPER

government might be standing there, tall and proper and buttoned into a uniform, come to tell us it was all a terrible mistake; that we wouldn't have to leave after all. Or maybe the messenger would have a telegram from Papa, who was interned in a prisoner-of-war camp in Montana because he had worked for a Japanese business firm.

The FBI had come to pick up Papa and hundreds of other Japanese community leaders on the very day that Japanese planes had bombed Pearl Harbor. The government thought they were dangerous enemy aliens. If it weren't so sad, it would have been funny. Papa could no more be dangerous than the mayor of our city, and he was every bit as loyal to the United States. He had lived here since 1917.

When I opened the door, it wasn't a messenger from anywhere. It was my best friend, Laurie Madison, from next door. She was holding a package wrapped up like a birthday present, but she wasn't wearing her party dress, and her face drooped like a wilted tulip.

"Hi," she said. "I came to say good-bye."

She thrust the present at me and told me it was something to take to camp. "It's a bracelet," she said before I could open the package. "Put it on so you won't have to pack it." She knew I didn't have one inch of space left in my suitcase. We had been instructed to take only what we could carry into camp, and Mama had told us that we could each take only two suitcases.

"Then how are we ever going to pack the dishes and blankets and sheets they've told us to bring with us?" Keiko worried.

"I don't really know," Mama said, and she simply began packing those big impossible things into an enormous duffel bag—along with umbrellas, boots, a kettle, hot plate, and flashlight.

"Who's going to carry that huge sack?" I asked.

But Mama didn't worry about things like that. "Someone will help us," she said. "Don't worry." So I didn't.

Laurie wanted me to open her package and put on the bracelet before she left. It was a thin gold chain with a heart dangling on it. She helped me put it on, and I told her I'd never take it off, ever.

"Well, good-bye then," Laurie said awkwardly. "Come home soon."

"I will," I said, although I didn't know if I would ever get back to Berkeley again.

I watched Laurie go down the block, her long blond pigtails bouncing as she walked. I wondered who would be sitting in my desk at Lincoln Junior High now that I was gone. Laurie kept turning and waving, even walking backwards for a while, until she got to the corner. I didn't want to watch anymore, and I slammed the door shut.

The next time the doorbell rang, it was Mrs. Simpson, our other neighbor. She was going to drive us to the Congregational church, which was the Civil Control Station where all the Japanese of Berkeley were supposed to report.

It was time to go. "Come on, Ruri. Get your things," my sister called to me.

It was a warm day, but I put on a sweater and my coat so I wouldn't have to carry them, and I picked up my two suitcases. Each one had a tag with my name and our family number on it. Every Japanese family had to register and get a number. We were Family Number 13453.

Mama was taking one last look around our house. She was going from room to room, as though she were trying to take a mental picture of the house she had lived in for fifteen years, so she would never forget it.

I saw her take a long last look at the garden that Papa loved. The irises beside the fish pond were just beginning to bloom. If Papa had been home, he would have cut the first iris blossom and brought it inside to Mama. "This one is for you," he would have said. And Mama would have smiled and said, "Thank you, Papa San," and put it in her favorite cut-glass vase.

But the garden looked shabby and forsaken now that Papa was gone and Mama was too busy to take care of it. It looked the way I felt, sort of empty and lonely and abandoned.

When Mrs. Simpson took us to the Civil Control Station, I felt even worse. I was scared, and for a minute I thought I was going to lose my breakfast right in front of everybody. There must have been over a thousand Japanese people gathered at the church. Some were old and some were young. Some were talking and laughing, and some were crying. I guess everybody else was scared too. No one knew exactly what was going to happen to us. We just knew we were being taken to the Tanforan Racetrack, which the army had turned into a camp for the Japanese. There were fourteen other camps like ours along the West Coast.

What scared me most were the soldiers standing at the doorway of the church hall. They were carrying guns with mounted bayonets. I wondered if they thought we would try to run away, and whether they'd shoot us or come after us with their bayonets if we did.

A long line of buses waited to take us to camp. There were trucks, too, for our baggage. And Mama was right; some men were there to help us load our duffel bag. When it was time to board the buses, I sat with Keiko and Mama sat behind us. The bus went down Grove Street and passed the small Japanese food store where Mama used to order her bean-curd cakes and pickled radish. The windows were all boarded up, but there was a sign still hanging on the door that read, "We are loyal Americans."

The crazy thing about the whole evacuation was that we were all loyal Americans. Most of us were citizens because we had been born here. But our parents, who had come from Japan, couldn't become citizens because there was a law that prevented any Asian from becoming a citizen. Now everybody with a Japanese face was being shipped off to concentration camps.

"It's stupid," Keiko muttered as we saw the racetrack looming up beside the highway. "If there were any Japanese spies around, they'd have gone back to Japan long ago."

"I'll say," I agreed. My sister was in high school and she ought to know, I thought.

When the bus turned into Tanforan, there were more armed guards at the gate, and I saw barbed wire strung around the entire grounds. I felt as though I were going into a prison, but I hadn't done anything wrong.

We streamed off the buses and poured into a huge room, where doctors looked down our throats and peeled back our eyelids to see if we had any diseases. Then we were given our housing assignments. The man in charge gave Mama a slip of paper. We were in Barrack 16, Apartment 40.

"Mama!" I said. "We're going to live in an apartment!" The only apartment I had ever seen was the one my piano teacher lived in. It was in an enormous building in San Francisco with an elevator and thick carpeted hallways. I thought how wonderful it would be to have our own elevator. A house was all right, but an apartment seemed elegant and special.

We walked down the racetrack looking for Barrack 16. Mr. Noma, a friend of Papa's, helped us carry our bags. I was so busy looking around, I slipped and almost fell on the muddy track. Army barracks had been built everywhere, all around the racetrack and even in the infield.

Mr. Noma pointed beyond the track toward the horse stables. "I think your barrack is out there."

He was right. We came to a long stable that had once housed the horses of Tanforan, and we climbed up the wide ramp. Each stall had a number painted on it, and when we got to 40, Mr. Noma pushed open the door.

"Well, here it is," he said, "Apartment 40."

The stall was narrow and empty and dark. There were two small windows on each side of the door. Three folded army cots were on the dust-covered floor and one light bulb dangled from the ceiling. That was all. This was our apartment, and it still smelled of horses.

Mama looked at my sister and then at me. "It won't be so bad when we fix it up," she began. "I'll ask Mrs. Simpson to send me some material for curtains. I could make some cushions too, and . . . well . . ." She stopped. She couldn't think of anything more to say.

Mr. Noma said he'd go get some mattresses for us. "I'd better hurry before they're all gone." He rushed off. I think he wanted to leave so that he wouldn't have to see Mama cry. But he needn't have run off, because Mama didn't cry. She just went out to borrow a broom and began sweeping out the dust and dirt. "Will you girls set up the cots?" she asked.

It was only after we'd put up the last cot that I noticed my bracelet was gone. "I've lost Laurie's bracelet!" I screamed. "My bracelet's gone!"

40

We looked all over the stall and even down the ramp. I wanted to run back down the track and go over every inch of ground we'd walked on, but it was getting dark and Mama wouldn't let me.

I thought of what I'd promised Laurie. I wasn't ever going to take the bracelet off, not even when I went to take a shower. And now I had lost it on my very first day in camp. I wanted to cry.

I kept looking for it all the time we were in Tanforan. I didn't stop looking until the day we were sent to another camp, called Topaz, in the middle of a desert in Utah. And then I gave up.

But Mama told me never mind. She said I didn't need a bracelet to remember Laurie, just as I didn't need anything to remember Papa or our home in Berkeley or all the people and things we loved and had left behind.

"Those are things we can carry in our hearts and take with us no matter where we are sent," she said.

And I guess she was right. I've never forgotten Laurie, even now.

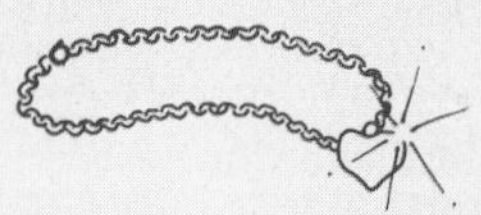

Do you find the story's ending hopeful or sad? Explain your response.

How does the appearance of the flower garden reflect the way Ruri feels?

What kind of person would you say Ruri's mother is? Use examples from the story to support your answer.

WRITE In a paragraph, explain the significance of the bracelet in the story.

SHARING EXPERIENCES

Yoshiko Uchida called writing a way of "trying to hold onto and somehow preserve the magic of [special] moments." Do you think that Jean Little would agree? Explain.

WRITER'S WORKSHOP

The authors in this section used World War II (1939–1945) as a setting for their stories. Find out and share more information about this era by writing a social studies research report. Choose a topic that interests you. Use several resources, including interviews, to learn more about the topic. Then plan a memorable way to present the information.

Writer's Choice Both the authors of these selections and their characters faced changes in their lives. When is change good, and when is it bad? Speaking for yourself or through a character that you create, respond to that question, perhaps in a letter, a diary entry, or a persuasive essay.

THEME

INVITATIONS TO POETRY

Have you ever had to write a poem and felt as if you would never find a subject? The poets whose works you are about to read would assure you that your own life is full of possibilities. You may be surprised at how these poets have turned some simple, everyday experiences into poetry.

CONTENTS

Voices and Stories

Mel Glenn and His Poetry

Mel Glenn is the author of several books of poems about high-school experiences, including Class Dismissed, Class Dismissed II, *and* Back to Class. *The students and teachers he writes about are fictional, but they are drawn from Glenn's own experiences and observations as a student and a teacher. Glenn is one of the first poets to write for and about teenagers. Here he discusses the inspiration for his poetry.*

I started writing when I was in college. I was a premed major, and I had my moment of truth in comparative anatomy when I had to look an alley cat in the eye. He looked back at me, and I knew I couldn't do what I had to do to be a doctor. So I turned to writing. I worked on the school newspaper at New York University, where I did a lot of writing —feature writing was what I liked best. As an English major, I didn't know what I was going to do after school, so I joined the Peace Corps. That got me into teaching.

Once I had taught for several years, I noticed patterns developing. I kept seeing the same kinds of kids and hearing about the same kinds of problems. The poems that I write are amalgams of all the voices I have listened to and all the stories that I've heard. Some of the poems are about real people I've known, but others come from my own experience.

Teaching is what I do. I'm at home in front of a class; it's what I do best. I wouldn't stay home and just write because my inspiration comes from teaching. I write because I'm involved with kids. Presently I'm a dean in the New York school system, which means I'm in charge of discipline and counseling. Kids come in, and I hear their problems. A writer needs material, and my material is what I do every day.

I teach at the same high school I attended, so that is very strange at times. The major difference from when I was a high schooler is that often kids don't have the same sense of security that comes from having a two-parent family, a stable income, and a stable environment. Maybe I'm romanticizing the past, but there seems to be more pressure on kids today. Some things are the same, though. Kids still want to succeed, and they still want the approval of their parents and their friends. There are still the kids whose faces will light up when they learn something or read a book.

If my audience could learn one thing from my writing, I would hope it's the feeling of not being alone. When something happens, they think, "I'm the only one going through this. I'm the only one who feels depressed, who worries about being fat." Turn to any poem in the book, and you can see you're not alone. There are other voices out there saying, "You'll get through, just keep trying."

Ms. Phyllis Shaw (SPEECH)

Period 7, Room 202

Come in, seventh-period class.
Welcome to the festivities.
It is nearly the end of the day
As well as the end of my patience.
You have made your position quite clear
Issuing your White Paper on Indifference.
But, my darlings, I don't give up that easily.
You say, "Why should we make speeches?
We already know how to talk."
I say, " 'Yo, man' does not constitute
Effective communication between
    civilized beings."
You say, "I gotta go to the nurse."
I say, "Not unless you're bleeding internally."
You say, "Can't we just ad lib?"
I say, "Babbling is for babies."
I demand thought, preparation, and intelligence.
Talk may be cheap to some.
Not in my classroom, my darlings,
Not in my classroom.

Tammy Yarbrough

Period 7, Room 202

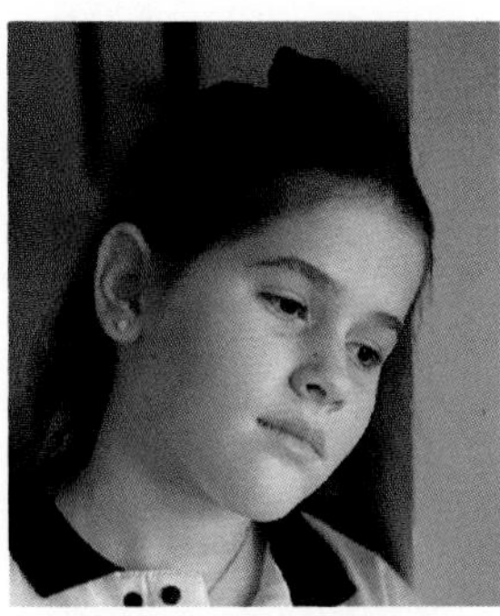

Last month when I gave my speech
My friend, Eileen, organized my notes,
Corrected my timing, applauded my delivery.
She even gave me a standing ovation.
Eileen sorta died last week.
I look at her empty chair,
Next to me in class,
And I feel like crying again.
Her parents took her away.
I couldn't bring myself to see her off
And now I feel horribly alone.
My friend, Eileen, didn't *really* die.
Her family just moved to a new city.
It's the same thing.
Please, Ms. Shaw,
I can't give my speech today.
There's nobody here to give me a hand.

Kwang Chin Ho

Period 2, Room 141

My family came from China five years ago.
My father holds a doctorate from the university.
He works in a restaurant.
My mother holds an advanced degree from
 the institute.
She works with my father.
The language is easier for me than for them,
Especially Mr. Cantor's language of
Light, magnetism, and motion.
I wish to be an engineer
And build beautiful things.
Every day I go home and
Tell my parents what I have learned.
They nod their heads in approval.
It is then we speak the same language.

Belinda Enriquez

Period 3, Room 122

When I first came to history class
I sat in the last row, last seat
So I could read my romance novels
And not be bothered.
Some teachers notice what I'm reading;
    most don't,
But Miss Parsons did.
She didn't scream,
Or rip the book out of my hands,
Or toss it in the wastebasket.
She just whispered, "Quick, read these,
I've got a million of them—
Real life is better!"
And handed me a list of biographies of
Famous women in history.
I've read many of them—
Harriet Tubman, Joan of Arc, Susan B. Anthony.
I will always remember Miss Parsons's
Gentle smile and right words at the right time.
Maybe I should become a teacher.

From Life to Poetry

ALA Best Book for Young Adults

Children's Choice

Five Poets Talk About Their Work

from *The Place My Words Are Looking For*

WILLIAM STAFFORD

JOHN UPDIKE

PHYLLIS JANOWITZ

KARLA KUSKIN

PAUL FLEISCHMAN

One Time

by William Stafford

When evening had flowed between houses
and paused on the schoolground, I met
Hilary's blind little sister following
the gray smooth railing still warm from the sun
with her hand; and she stood by the edge
holding her face upward waiting
while the last light found her cheek
and her hair, and then on over the trees.

You could hear the great sprinkler arm
of water find and then leave the pavement,
and pigeons telling each other their dreams
or the dreams they would have. We were
deep in the well of shadow by then, and I
held out my hand, saying, "Tina, it's me—

Hilary says I should tell you it's dark,
and, oh, Tina, it is. Together now—"

And I reached, our hands touched,
and we found our way home.

Talk with a little luck in it, that's what poetry is—just let the words take you where *they* want to go. You'll be invited; things will happen; your life will have more in it than other people's lives have.

Of course this kind of luck happens to everybody, when they get going in their talk or in their writing, but only those who pay attention and try in a sustained way get richer and richer in their lives.

Once someone said to me, "Think of something that happened, but don't tell what happened—tell what you wish had happened. And try to remember more of your feelings than just the look of things; tell how they felt, how they sounded, whatever. . . ." That's how my poem "One Time" came to me. I began to feel how the sun warmed the railing by the school. I could hear the pigeons "telling their dreams." And with a great rush I felt how it would be to be blind, to have the world out there signaling to you all the time.

W. S.

Icebox

by John Updike

In Daddy's day there were such things:
Wood cabinets of cool
In which a cake of ice was placed
While he was off at school.

Blue-veined, partitioned in itself,
The cake seemed cut of air
Which had exploded; one cracked star
Appeared imprisoned there.

It melted slowly through the day;
The metal slats beneath
Seeped upwards, so the slippery base
Developed downward teeth.

Eventually an egg so small
It could be tossed away,
The ice cake vanished quite, as has
That rather distant day.

These stanzas were a part of *A Cheerful Alphabet of Pleasant Objects,* from Apple to Zeppelin, written in 1957 and dedicated to my son, who was then less than one year old. That is why I speak of "Daddy's day" in the first line. Iceboxes were very common when I was a little boy, in the 1930s; they preceded refrigerators in the American kitchen. Instead of an electric engine to produce coldness, though, the icebox simply had a large cake of ice in it, perhaps a foot square, which was brought every other day or so by an "iceman" in his "ice truck." The ice was manufactured, by electrical cooling, in an "ice plant." As a child I lived near an ice plant and used to watch the men handle the big slabs of ice with big tongs and break them into smaller pieces with "ice picks." Every kitchen used to have in one of its drawers an ice pick, to break smaller pieces off of the ice in the icebox. The ice plant supplied each home with a card you could put in the window, saying if you wanted ice that day, and how big a piece.

What I explain here in prose my poem tries to suggest with poetry. More, the poem tries to convey the look of the cake, or block, of ice—how it had a kind of star in it, and how as it melted the slats it sat on would rise up inside it like teeth. Poetry tries to give the look and the feel of a thing or experience, in language that makes us stop and think, and that often tries to impress itself on our minds with rhyme and meter. The rhyme scheme here is *abcb,* and the lines are alternately iambic tetrameter and iambic trimeter: that is, they alternately have foủr beats and three, so that it's as if two seven-beat lines rhyme. When you write poetry, you hear this music in your head, like singing a song to yourself. It's not too hard, and it's fun.

J. U.

There Was a Man

by Phyllis Janowitz

My neighbor has a wooden leg
(thump, thump)
he drags on the ground.
He tells children to bang on it.

They're afraid they'll hurt him
and bang very gently
(tap, tap)
He takes out his teeth

To show them
what a fake he is.
They are amazed!

He takes off his glasses
like the man who
scratched his eyes
out and in again.

Then he hides pennies
for them to find and keep.
Finally he takes off his wooden leg
(thump, thump)
and leans it against the wall.

When I was five years old, my Uncle Leo (who died many years ago) told me that he was a very special person for a number of reasons: He could take off his eyes (eyeglasses) and put them back on, he could take out his teeth and put them back in, and he could take off his leg (a wooden one). Then, at other times, he'd say, "I'm so strong if you hit my leg it won't even hurt. Go on, hit me, hit me!" I wouldn't want to hit him, even if it didn't hurt; I loved him very much. He was a magician. He could turn a handkerchief into a mouse and make it jump out of his hand. And he would hide pennies in the living room for my sister and me to find. He had a huge crop of white hair, carried a cane, and looked fierce. Men don't look like this anymore—elegant and strong. I, for one, don't ever see any quite as handsome.

P. J.

Untitled Poems

by Karla Kuskin

Write about a radish
Too many people write about the moon.

The night is black
The stars are small and high
The clock unwinds its ever-ticking tune
Hills gleam dimly
Distant nighthawks cry.
A radish rises in the waiting sky.

I have a friend who keeps on standing on her hands.
That's fine,
Except I find it very difficult to talk to her
Unless I stand on mine.

When I used to carry a camera with me and take a lot of photographs, I paid very close attention to everything I saw. And I noticed that when I had color film in my camera my eye would be especially aware of colorful scenery, or people dressed in interesting color combinations.

But when my camera was loaded with black-and-white film I paid much more attention to light and dark, overall pattern and design, the kind of things that would show up well in black-and-white photographs. There is also a difference in my point of view when I am writing prose and when I am writing poetry. Writing prose makes me listen for stories. But if I am writing poetry I concentrate more on the rhythms and sounds of words, and on details. The smallest observation can be the start of a poem. I thought of "I have a friend . . ." as I tried to talk to my daughter Julia (then about seven years old) while she endlessly practiced standing on her hands. And "Write about a radish" began as advice to myself on a day when I was determined to write a poem about something nobody else had ever written a poem about.

So that I will not forget a particular combination of words or a funny idea I make notes. If a notebook is not handy I will use any scrap of paper lying around: my grocery list, the edge of the newspaper. You can not only write a poem *about* anything, you can also write it *on* almost anything. Poems also make nice gifts and they never need to be walked or fed.

K. K.

Water Striders

by Paul Fleischman

Detail of *Les nymphéas, le matin* by Claude Monet (1840–1926), Paris, Orangerie

Whenever we're asked
if we walk upon water
we answer

To be sure.

Whenever we're asked
if we walk on it often
we answer
Quite often.

All day through.
Should we be questioned
on whether it's easy
we answer

A snap.

Whenever we're asked
if we walk upon water
we answer
Of course.

It's quite true.
Whenever we're asked
if we walk on it often
we answer

Each day.

Should we be questioned
on whether it's easy
we answer
Quite easy.

It's a cinch.

Should we be told	Should we be told
that it's surely a miracle	that it's surely a miracle
we reply	we reply
Balderdash!	
	Rubbish!
Nonsense!	
Whenever we're asked	Whenever we're asked
for instructions	for instructions
we always say	we always say
	Come to the pond's edge
and do as we do.	
	Put down one foot
and then put down another,	
	resting upon the thin film
	on the surface.
Believe me, there's no call	
at all to be nervous	
	as long as you're reasonably
	mindful that you—
But by that time our student	But by that time our student
no matter how prudent	
has usually	has usually
	don't ask me why
sunk from view.	sunk from view.

"Water Striders" comes from Paul Fleischman's book *Joyful Noise: Poems for Two Voices*.

"Poetry begins in the mouth," the poet Donald Hall has written. For me, it began as well with the shortwave radio, the alto recorder, and the Swiss Army knife.

I received the radio when I was ten. After my parents and sisters had gone to bed, I would plug in the headphones and cruise the airwaves, no light in the room but the radio's dials. I heard broadcasts in Japanese, Swedish, Arabic, Hindi, and dozens of other languages I didn't speak. Not knowing the sense of the words, I heard only their sound—their music.

I learned to play the recorder in high school. A few years later I became friends with a flute player. For hours on end we played duets, never wanting to stop. I discovered that two voices were much better than one. And that performing a piece was infinitely more fun than merely listening to it.

The knife was a twenty-first birthday present. Since childhood I'd made impromptu sculptures out of driftwood, pine needles—whatever was at hand. But that knife had an awl, perfect for making holes. A technological leap that spurred a burst of building that still hasn't subsided.

In consequence of all of which, I was struck one day by the desire to write some poems for two voices. Verbal music, making use of the sounds of words as much as their meaning. Duets for two readers, to be performed aloud. Sculptures built not of sticks, but words. I've never enjoyed writing anything else as much.

P. F.

INVITATIONS TO POETRY

Karla Kuskin says, "The smallest observation can be the start of a poem." How do the poems by the other poets support this statement? Give several examples.

WRITER'S WORKSHOP

Try out Paul Fleischman's theory that "two voices [are] much better than one." Write a poem in two voices. As you write, read the lines aloud so you can hear how they sound. When you are finished, read the poem aloud with a partner.

Writer's Choice Review the experiences that have been shared in these poems. Does one experience remind you of something that happened to you? Share your experience in writing. Decide on a form of writing that will best convey your thoughts to your audience.

THEME

IN SEARCH OF ADVENTURE

Gary Paulsen writes about something he knows and loves: dogsledding. By first reading an excerpt from one of Paulsen's novels and then part of his autobiography, you will learn how this author's work reflects his own experiences, as well as how he uses his imagination to create a fictional world.

CONTENTS

NEWBERY HONOR
SCHOOL LIBRARY JOURNAL AWARD

B Y . G A R Y   P A U L S E N

Russel Susskit lives with his father in a government house in an Eskimo village. Now fourteen years old, Russel is beginning to feel unhappy with his life. At his father's suggestion, he goes to talk to Oogruk, an old, wise man of the village. Oogruk, who is blind, explains how the people of the village once had "songs for all of everything" but lost them when they abandoned traditional Eskimo ways. Encouraged by Oogruk to find his own song, Russel decides to learn more about the old ways by taking Oogruk's dog team out to run.

I L L U S T R A T E D   B Y   J A C K   U N R U H

North and east of the village the land rose away from the sea in rolling hills that led to mountains. Even in the middle of the winter the land fought to hold the snow. The short tundra grass gave no foothold and so often the surface was blown free of snow and the grass was out all winter.

Arctic hares fed in the bare areas, as did ptarmigan, the small white grouselike birds sometimes flocking two and three hundred birds in a single place. Now and then, even in the dark-cold of winter, it was possible to see a frozen blue or purple flower—winter flowers.

Russel sat on the edge of the sled and looked down at one such flower by his foot. It had four petals, and he did not understand how it could have gotten through the fall and into the middle of winter. But it had. And it had grown in beauty for it, the color rich against the cold brown of the grass.

Much had changed.

Oogruk had talked until he was done and when he was done he had fallen silent. It might have taken days and nights, it felt like years, and when he was finished Russel had fallen asleep, a real sleep this time. He slept without moving, leaning against the wall and when he awakened the room was cool—still not cold—and he got up stiffly and stretched.

Oogruk was silent, with his eyes closed, the lamp burned out. For a moment Russel thought he was dead, but he was still breathing and Russel took a deerskin and wrapped it around the old man's shoulders.

He knew what to do. From the walls he took the lances and bow and arrows. He also took a pair of bearskin pants and the squirrel underparka and the deerskin outerparka with the hair on the inside. Some of the hair was brittle on the deerskin but it was still thick and warm.

He did not think of the objects as belonging to him, just thought of them as being what he needed. Oogruk had told him to use what he needed, including the dogs and sled and Russel followed those thoughts as if they had been his own, as in some way they were.

He was wearing store pants and a coat and he took them off and hung them on the pegs. For a moment he stood naked in the cooling room, felt his skin tighten. Then he pulled on the bearskin pants, with the hair out, the skin soft and supple. Oogruk had worked oil into the leather to maintain them as he had taken care of everything. At the top there was a drawcord and he pulled it tight. The pants were just slightly large, but the right length.

On the wall were sealskin mukluks. He took them down and felt inside. The grass bottoms were still good and he pulled them on, tied them up around his calves over the bearskin.

Then came the squirrelskin innerparka with the hair out, soft and fine, like leather silk. Last he pulled over the outerparka, thick deerhide, with the hair in, and when that was on and shrugged in place he took down a pair of deerhide mittens with a shoulder thong and pulled them on.

As soon as he was dressed he went outside before he could heat up. He had to get the sled out of the lean-to on the side of the house and see how much work it needed. The harnesses were also there and the gangline.

It was cold, standing cold. So cold you could spit and it would bounce. When the wind hit him he pulled up the hood and tightened the drawstring through the wolverine ruff. The long fur came in around his face and stopped the wind. Then he pulled up the mitten cuffs and felt the air movement through the parka stop. His body brought the temperature up almost immediately.

Around the sea side of the house Oogruk or somebody had made a lean-to. The door had leather hinges and a wooden pin through the latch. Russel pulled the pin and worked the door open against the snow.

Inside stood a dogsled and there were harnesses on a peg on the wall. He reached in and pulled the sled out to examine it more closely. The sky was light now, a gray all-around haze off the sea and out of the clouds at the same time, and he thought he'd never seen anything so beautiful as the sled in the gray light.

It was the old kind of sled, the kind they called basket sleds. When the modern, white mushers ran the races, they used toboggans made with plastic and bolted together. Ugly little tough sleds. But in the old days the people used sleds of delicate hardwood lashed with rawhide, all flexible and curved gracefully. Oogruk's was like a carving of a sled, with birch rails down the side and elegant curved stanchions. Around the front was a warped-wood brushbow—something he'd never need unless he ran where there were trees—and it had one-eighth-inch brass runner shoes that looked almost new.

There was a steel snowhook tied to the bridle and a rope gangline with tugs and neck-lines already in place.

He spread it out on the snow and studied everything carefully. The lashing on the sled looked old, but had been oiled and was in good shape. The rope on the gangline was a corded nylon and looked also to be in top condition.

He pulled the harnesses down and spread them out and went over them carefully as well. They were clean, had been patched a few times but were good for all of that.

All he needed was a dog team.

The harnesses all seemed the same size so he put them on the tugs, using the small ivory toggles to tie them in. Then he set the snowhook and pulled the gangline out in front of the sled and stopped to see what he had.

He had never run a team himself. But he'd seen mushers go by in races—one long-distance race went by the village—and he knew how things should look.

He took the lead dog off the chain. It growled at him and raised its hair but he tightened his grip and paid no attention to the snarl. The dog held back and Russel had to drag him to the gangline. The dogs had run for Oogruk but that was more than two years earlier. They had not run since for anybody. And this stranger had to earn their respect, earn the run. The leader turned his shoulder in the curve that meant threat, the curve that meant attack, and lifted his lip to Russel. It was an open challenge and Russel cuffed him across the head with a stiff hand. Still the dog growled and now took a cut at Russel's leg and Russel hit the dog harder.

Then a thing happened, a thing from the trance with Oogruk, and he leaned down so his head was over the top of the leader's head and he growled down at the dog. He did not know why he did this, did not know for certain what the growl meant but when it was finished he curved his head over the dog's head and, still without knowing for sure why, he bit down, hard, across the bridge of the dog's nose.

The leader growled and flashed teeth but quickly backed down and that was the end of it. He stood to in harness, pulling the gangline out tight while Russel turned to bring the rest of the team.

The other four dogs came nicely and settled into harness as if they'd been working all along. Russel smiled. It almost looked like a dog team.

He had in mind this first time to just take the dogs out on the ice and see what happened. He took no weapons or other gear because he wasn't sure if he could control the team and didn't want to lose anything if the sled flipped.

The first run was rough. The dogs ran as a gaggle, wide open, in a tangled bunch and not lined out as they should have been. Russel ran into them with the sled more than once when they stopped —before he could get the brake on—and when they hit the so-called pressure ridges a mile offshore, where the ice from the sea ground against the shore ice and piled up, he almost lost the sled.

They tipped him and dragged him on his face for a quarter of a mile before he could get the snowhook set in a crack.

When he had stopped them he put the sled upright and sat on it for a moment to think. It was close to dark, the quick three-hour day all but gone, and he would have to head back to the village, yet he did not want to leave the run.

The wind cut at his cheeks and he turned his hood away from the force, took the cold.

"You will have to know me," he said quietly to the dogs after a time. "Just as I will have to know you."

Two of them looked back at him. It was perhaps not an invitation. It was perhaps not a look that meant anything at all except that they looked back and their eyes caught his eyes and he knew they would run. He *knew* they would run. He knew when he put his feet to the sled and took the handlebar in his hands that they would run and he did not know how he knew this but only that it was so.

When he was on the runners he reached down and disengaged the snowhook and used the small lip-squeak sound that Oogruk had told him to use to get the dogs running.

They were off so fast he was almost jerked backward off the sled.

It wasn't a gaggle now, but a pulling force with all the dogs coordinating to line the sled out across the ice, a silent curve of power out ahead of him.

The feeling, he thought, the feeling is that the sled is alive; that I am alive and the sled is alive and the snow is alive and the ice is alive and we are all part of the same life.

He did not try to steer them that first time and they ran up the coast on the ice for three or four miles before their fat caught up with them and they slowed. When they were down to a trot, tongues slavering off the heat from their run, Russel stopped them again.

Oogruk said the leader had been gee-haw trained the same as the white freighters did—to go right on gee, left on haw.

"Gee!" Russel made it a loud command but he needn't have. The lead dog turned off to the right and started out again, back in toward shore. When they got along the beach edge, where the ice was mixed with sand, Russel turned right again and headed back for the village.

The dogs automatically headed for Oogruk's house and their chains, and Russel let them go. When they pulled in he took them out of harness and put them back on the chains and went into the house.

Oogruk was awake and sitting by the lamp. He had moved, Russel could tell by his position, but he was back and he smiled when Russel came in.

"Did they run for you?" the old man asked. "Did they run for you?"

Russel shrugged out of the parkas, down to bare skin. He laughed. "They ran, Grandfather. They ran for me like the wind."

"Ahh. That is fine, that is fine."

"It was a feeling, a feeling like being alive. The sled flew across the ice and I was alive with the sled."

"Yes. Yes. That is so—this is how it should be. You are correct."

"Is there meat left? We should eat meat."

The old man laughed. "You are a true person. Eat when you are happy. No. We ate it all last time. Get more from the cache. But first feed the dogs. Give them meat three times bigger than your fist. Always take care of the dogs first."

On his next trip with the dogs, Russel practices the old way of hunting he has learned from Oogruk. He even manages to kill a deer with a bow and arrow so that they will have meat. Soon he is ready for a greater challenge.

Sea ice is not the same as fresh-water ice. The salt-water ice is stronger, more elastic, isn't as slippery. Also the sea ice moves all the time, even when it is thick. Sometimes whole cakes of the ice will go out to sea, miles across, sliding out to sea and taking anybody on the cake with it.

On the fourth day after taking the deer with the arrow Russel took the team out on the ice to find seals. Oogruk wanted oil for the lamp and he wanted some seal meat and fat to eat and he said these things in such a way that Russel felt it would be good to find a seal to take with the harpoon. It wasn't that he actually asked, or told Russel to go for seal, but he talked about how it was to hunt in the old days.

"Out on the edge of the ice, where it meets the sea but well back from the edge, sometimes there are seal holes. The seals come up through them and sit on the ice and if you are there when they come you can get the small harpoon point in them. That is the way it was done. Men would leave their dogs well back and pile a mound of snow in front of them and wait for the seal. Wait and wait." Oogruk had scratched with his nails on the wall of the house. "When the seal starts to come there is a scratching sound and the hunter must be ready to put the point in then."

"How long must one wait?" Russel asked.

"There is not a time. Waiting for seals is not something you measure. You get a seal, that is all. Some men go a whole winter and get none, some will get one right away. Hunting seals with the small point and the killing lance is part of the way to live."

So Russel went out on the ice. He took the team away in the daylight and was twenty miles out, working heavily through pressure ridges, when the storm came off the sea.

He had seen many storms. In his years with the village, every winter brought violent storms off the sea, white walls of wind and driven snow. Twice he had been caught out on a snowmachine and had to run for the village ahead of the wall coming across the ice.

But with a dog team you did not run ahead of the wall. As he was crossing a pressure ridge, pushing the dogs up and over the broken, jagged edges, he heaved up on the sled and looked out across the ice, out to sea, and a great boiling wall of white was rising to the sky. In seconds it was impossible to tell where the sky ended and the sea ice began and Russel knew he would have to hide before it hit. He fought the sled down the pressure ridge and brought the dogs around into a small hole under an overlapping ice ledge. There was barely room to pull his legs in.

He tipped the sled over to make a rough door across the opening to block the wind and pulled the dogs in on top of him. Working as fast as he could he tried to pack snow into the slats of the sled bottom but before he could make any headway the wind roared into the pressure ridge.

Russel drew the hood tight on his parka and huddled into the dogs, closing the small opening in the front of his hood by burying his face in dog fur.

The dogs whined for a few moments, then squirmed into better positions, with their noses under their tails, and settled in to ride the storm out the same way dogs and wolves have ridden storms out forever—by sleeping and waiting.

Russel felt a couple of small wind-leaks around the edge of his parka and he stopped them by pulling the drawstrings tighter at the parka's bottom hem. When he had all air movement stopped he could feel the temperature coming up in his clothing and he listened to the wind as it tore at his shelter.

In what seemed like moments but might have been an hour, the wind had piled a drift over his hole and he used a free arm to pack the snow away and clear the space around his body. The dogs remained still and quiet, their heat tight around Russel.

After a time he dozed, and when he awakened it seemed that the wind had diminished to some degree. He used a mittened hand to clear away a hole and he saw that it was getting darker—the short day almost gone again—and that indeed the wind was dying.

He stood, broke through the drift and shrugged the snow off. It was still cloudy but everything seemed to be lifting. The dogs were curled in small balls covered with snow, each of them completely covered except for a small blowhole where a breath had kept the snow melted. Each hole had a tiny bit of steam puffing up as the

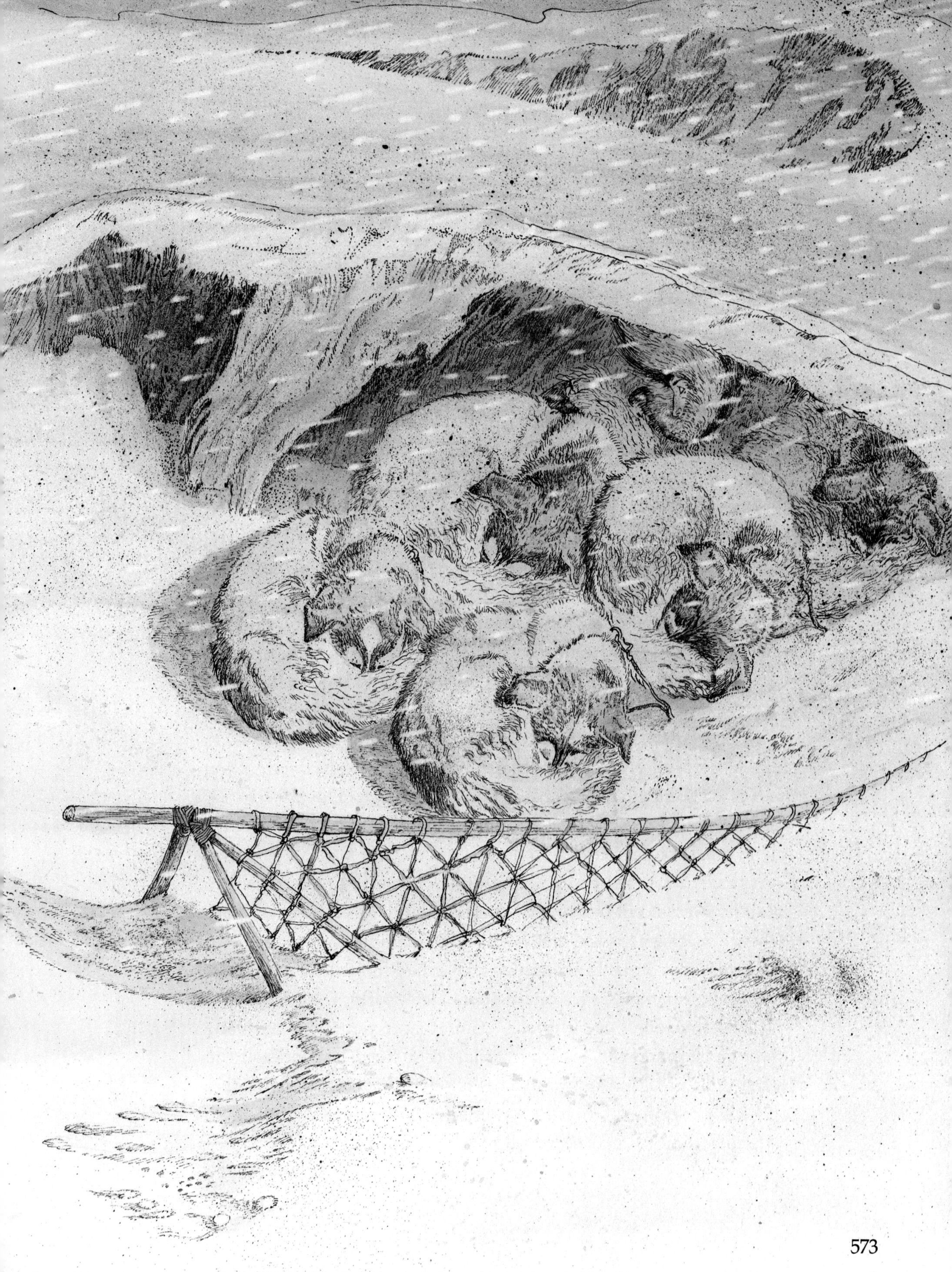

dogs exhaled and Russel was reluctant to make them stir. They looked so comfortable in their small houses.

Still he had to get home.

"Ha! Hay! Everybody up!" He grabbed the gangline and shook it. The leader stood up and shook his fur clean of snow and that brought the rest of them up.

In a minute he had them lined out, aimed for home—or where he thought the village was—and when he called them to run they went about thirty yards and stopped. It wasn't abrupt. They were running and they slowed to a trot and then a walk and finally they just stopped.

"What is it?" Russel snorted. "Are we still asleep in our houses? Hai! Get it up and go."

Again they started and went forty or so yards and stopped.

Russel swore. "Get up! Run now or I will find a whip."

And after a time, hesitating still, they finally got moving. Slowly. At a trot first, then a fast walk, then back up to a trot, they headed across the ice fields.

Russel nodded in satisfaction. He had not run dogs enough to know for certain what it meant when they didn't want to run, but he supposed that it was because they had anticipated staying down for a longer time.

But the man had to run the dogs. That's what Oogruk had said to him. "You must be part of the dogs, but you must run them. If you do not tell them what to do and where to go they will go where they want. And where a dog wants to go is not always the same as where the man wants to go."

The wind had stopped almost as suddenly as it came, in the way of arctic storms, but before it died it seemed to have changed a bit. When it first came it was out of the west, straight in from the sea, but before it stopped Russel noted that it had moved around to the north, was coming down from the blue-black north, the cold places.

Twice more the dogs tried to come to the right, but he made them go back and run his way. At last they lined out and went to work and Russel looked for the lights of the village. He had come out a way, but as the wind died he knew they should show, especially the light up on the hill near the fuel tanks.

He saw nothing. The clouds were still thick and low so he

couldn't see the stars. He had nothing to help him tell his true direction.

He ran for several hours, letting the dogs seek their own speed, and once he was sure he should have run into the village he called them down and set the snowhook.

He was going the wrong way.

What has happened, he thought, is that during the storm the ice has caked and turned. A whole, huge plate of ice with Russel and the dogs had rotated and changed all his directions. That's why the dogs had hesitated, held back. They knew the way home and had wanted to head back to the house.

He could have let them run and they would have taken him home. But now—now what would they do?

More now, he thought. More is coming now. It was getting cold, colder than he'd ever seen it. He could feel the cold working into his clothing, see the white steam of the dogs' breath coming back over their backs. His feet were starting to hurt. He was lost and the cold was working in and he did not know where to go.

There were just the dogs—the dogs and the sled and him. And the ice, and the snow and the northern night. Nobody would come to look for him because they expected him to be out late—or didn't expect anything at all. He had told nobody other than Oogruk that he was going out for seals and since he was staying at Oogruk's house nobody else could know that he was gone. And Oogruk would not expect him back because Russel was hunting the old way.

He was alone.

And a part of him grew afraid. He had seen bad weather many times. But he'd always had the chance to get out of it. On a snowmachine, unless it broke down, you could ride to safety. But he would have to face the cold now.

He debated what to do for three or four minutes. If he went down without a fire the cold would get bad later—maybe too bad. He had nothing to burn and there was no wood or fuel on the ice.

And what had Oogruk said about that? He fought to remember the trance but nothing came. He knew about problems growing in the cold, or during a storm, from other people. But Oogruk had said nothing about being lost on the ice.

Lost on the ice.

People died when they were lost on the ice. He had heard stories of people dying, of whole families lost. The ice moved out and away from land and the people had starved to death or drowned when the ice broke up beneath them, stories that came down in the long nights, sad stories.

And now Russel. Now Russel lost on the ice with a dog team and sled.

In the sled bag he had a small piece of meat left over from when he and Oogruk had cooked the deer. He could eat. That would help him stay warm. And then what?

He could wait until the clouds cleared off and he could see stars and they would guide him home. But it might be many days. Sometimes the clouds stayed for weeks.

"So." He talked aloud to the dogs, saw a couple of tails wag in the darkness with his voice. "So there is some trouble. What should we do?"

The leader looked around at him, although it was too dark for Russel to see his face. Still, there was something there, a desire to understand or to help. Russel smiled, a quick sign back in the fur of his hood.

The dogs.

They were the answer. He could not trust himself, couldn't see anything to help him, but he could trust the dogs. Or he thought he could. He would let them run and decide where to go.

"Hai! Enough rest. It is time to take me home. Take me back to the village."

He squeaked with his lips and they got up and started off. At first they traveled in the direction Russel had forced them to go. But as they settled into their trot the leader moved them gently to the right, more and more to the right until he had them going where he had first started them off before Russel had corrected him.

Russel nodded, let them run. They had a purpose in their backs, a pulling sense that he could believe in. He was learning about dogs, just in the few runs he'd taken. He was learning.

And one thing he had to know was that in some ways they were smarter than men. Oogruk had said that to him.

"Men and dogs are not alike, although some men try to make

them so. White men." Oogruk had laughed. "Because they try to make people out of dogs and in this way they make the dogs dumb. But to say that a dog is not smart because it is not as smart as a man is to say that snow is not smart. Dogs are not men. And as dogs, if they are allowed to be dogs, they are often smarter than men."

The problem, Russel knew, was learning when to recognize that dogs were smart. The dogs knew how to run in the dark and see with their heads, with their feet, with their hair and noses. They saw with everything.

At last Russel *knew* that they were heading back for the village in the cold and dark, knew it because he felt it inside.

But they were not home yet.

Running in the dark, even in the tight dark of the north when there is no moon, it is possible to see out ahead a great distance. The snow-ice is white-blue in the dark and if there is no wind to blow the snow around, everything shows up against the white.

Now, suddenly, there was a dark line ahead of the lead dog. A dark line followed by a black space on the snow, an opening of the ice. A lead of open water, so wide Russel could not see across.

Open water. Steam rising into the cold. The ice was moving and he was moving with it.

The team stopped. The lead dog whined and moved back and forth across the edge of the ice. The dogs hated open water, hated to get wet, but they knew that the way home was across the lead.

For a few moments the leader continued to whine and pull back and forth. "Haw! We go left along the ice and see."

The leader slammed to the left gratefully, happy to be relieved of the responsibility.

But the open lead was long. They ran mile after mile along the broken edge of the ice, in and out of the steam wraiths that came from the sea water. New ice was forming rapidly in the deep cold but it was not safe and would not be safe for several days, if then. Besides, it kept breaking away with the shifting of the cake that Russel was running on.

Yet the fear was gone. The fear had come from the unknown, from not acting, and now that he had made a decision to act the fear had gone. He might not make it, he might die on the ice, but he would not die with fear. He would die working to not die.

That was something he could tell Oogruk when he got back. If he got back. The thing with dying was to try to not die and make death take you with surprise.

And with the end of the fear came a feeling of strength. The cold was less strong along the lead because the warmth from the sea water came up as steam. The steam froze on everything, on the gangline and the sled and the dogs. Soon everything glistened with ice, even the dogs looked like jewels running ahead of him in the dark with the ice frozen on their backs.

It was a beauty he could not measure. As so much of running the dogs proved to be—so much of it had a beauty he saw and took into himself but could not explain.

And while he was looking at the beauty he saw that the lead had narrowed. There was still open water, but there were large chunks floating in it and the idea came to him of bridging the open water with one of the chunks.

He stopped the team.

The leader whined. It is perhaps possible that Oogruk has done this, Russel thought, and the dog is scared because he's done it before.

Or it was possible that the dog was reading Russel's mind and knew what they were going to do. Or it might be that the dog had figured out what had to be done on his own.

Whatever the reason, the dog knew and he didn't like it. Russel set the hook and took the harpoon with the line on it

out of the sled. He walked to the edge of the lead, holding back to make sure he wouldn't break off the edge and fall in. Death would come instantly with the water. With the weight of the parka and pants wet, he would go down like a stone.

There were several chunks floating in the lead, which had now narrowed to thirty or so feet. Most of them were smaller than he could use, but one was about twenty feet long and four feet wide. It lay sideways, halfway across the opening.

He laid the harpoon line on the ice, in a small loop, and held one end with his left hand. With his right he hefted the harpoon and with an easy toss threw it across the large chunk of ice.

Then he tried to ease it back so that the butt end of the harpoon would hang up on an edge. It was harder than it looked and took him ten or twelve tries before the harpoon shaft caught in a small hole. When it drew tight the point jammed and he took up the strain until he had the weight of the chunk moving. Slowly he pulled the ice through the dark water, slowly and gently heaving on the great weight.

He gradually brought the chunk across the lead until the end butted against the edge he stood on, then, using the harpoon as a prod he jammed and pushed until the ice lay the long way across the lead.

When it was in position he went back to the sled and pulled out the hook. "Up! Up and across the ice."

The leader knew what he wanted, but he held back, whining louder now. The ice didn't look that steady, didn't look safe. He didn't move to the side, but he wouldn't go, either.

Twice more Russel urged him from the sled but the dog wouldn't go and Russel threw the sled over on its side and walked to the front. The leader shook and crouched down but didn't move away. Russel took his mittens off and hung them by their cords behind his back. Then he grabbed a handful of hair on the dog's neck and another at the root of his tail and heaved the dog out onto the chunk.

The leader fought for balance, found it on the teetering ice, then drove with all his might for the other side of the lead, clawing and scrabbling.

So powerful was his tearing struggle that he pulled the next two dogs after him, and those three then pulled the rest of the team and the sled in a great leap onto the floating ice bridge.

Russel grabbed the handle as it went by and barely got his feet on the runners. A kick left, another to the right and the sled flew across the gap of water at the far end, splashed once as Russel threw his feet up to stay out of the water—and he was across.

Across onto the land ice. Off the floating pack ice. Safe.

Safe with the dogs. Safe and heading for the village. Safe and moving to where he could now see the light of the fuel tank on the hill. Safe out of the steam of the water and back on the solid ice.

Pick out a description in the story that you especially like, and explain your choice.

Oogruk tells Russel that in some ways dogs are smarter than men. How do the dogs in the story prove to be smarter than Russel?

Compare a new plastic sled with Oogruk's older wooden one. How do the two sleds reflect the changing times of the Eskimo people?

How does Russel overcome his fear of dying on the ice?

WRITE For Russel, the sight of the dogs running in the dark with the ice frozen on their backs has "a beauty he could not measure." In a paragraph, describe something you have seen or experienced that you think is beautiful.

An Interview with the Author

GARY PAULSEN

Gary Paulsen has written many books for young people. In this interview, Paulsen discusses with writer Ilene Cooper how he began writing and where he got the idea for *Dogsong*. He also tells about the relationship between *Dogsong* and his autobiography, *Woodsong*.

MS. COOPER: Which did you write first, Woodsong *or* Dogsong*?*
MR. PAULSEN: I wrote *Dogsong* first. I got the idea while I was running the Iditarod, which I later wrote about in *Woodsong*. I pulled into an Eskimo village very late at night, and a kid came running up and grabbed at my team. That's very dangerous. If the dogs turn in, they can start fighting among themselves, and whatever—or whoever—is in the middle when that happens is going to get mauled. Pulling at my lead dog, he tried to get it to go toward his house, a small log hut. I grabbed the kid—he was kind of small—and put him up over my head. I said, "What are you doing out here in the middle of the night?" and he said, "I want you to teach me about dogs."
MS. COOPER: An Eskimo boy didn't know about sled dogs?
MR. PAULSEN: I couldn't believe it. He had almost no knowledge of dogs. He didn't even know enough not to grab them. You see, a lot of the Eskimo villages now have snowmobiles. They've gotten rid of their dogs. So I started thinking, what if an Eskimo boy used a team of dogs to find his heritage? The two books intermingle, but that incident is what set me off.
MS. COOPER: You've become a very popular writer, especially for young adults, but your life hasn't always gone smoothly, has it?

MR. PAULSEN: No. But I must say the army squared me away. I shaped up and became a field engineer and went on to work in the aerospace industry. I was involved in the Gemini space program with all the "right stuff" guys. One night at a deep-tracking station in California, when I was twenty-seven years old, I sort of freaked out. I didn't like what I was doing and saw that I had built my own prison. What had I done? I realized right then that what I wanted to do was write. I drove to Hollywood, got a job as a proofreader at a magazine, and started to learn how to write. I worked hard at it, but, then, I still work hard at it.

MS. COOPER: What was the first thing you wrote for publication?

MR. PAULSEN: The first book was a humorous exposé about the space industry. It sold about eight and a half copies. The second book was a young-adult novel called *Mr. Tucker*, a historical western. Throughout my career, I've moved back and forth between adult and young-adult books.

MS. COOPER: You've had some rough spots with your career, too, haven't you?

MR. PAULSEN: I've had some bad luck. One time I had borrowed money against my book advances, and when I didn't get paid what I thought I was due, I went bankrupt. I decided to quit writing. My family and I had been living in Colorado, and we drove to Minnesota. We moved into a lean-to in the woods. No plumbing, no electricity. Then they repossessed the car.

MS. COOPER: How did you pull yourself out of it?

MR. PAULSEN: At first, we lived off the land, hunting and

gardening. That's how I got into dogs. Someone gave us four dogs and a broken sled, so I learned about training dogs. When I heard about the Iditarod, I knew I wanted to do it, but a race like that requires money. So I started writing again because I needed money for the race.

MS. COOPER: How did you feel when you finally knew you'd be able to run it?

MR. PAULSEN: I didn't honestly think I was going to run it. It was one of those things you say, like "I'm going to climb Mt. Everest someday," but you don't believe it will happen. I had seven dogs when I said I was going to do the Iditarod. You need to train at least two teams. I didn't have a car to get up to Alaska. But then people started giving me dogs, somebody gave me an old Chevy pickup, and Bemidji, Minnesota, sponsored me. The next thing I knew, I was driving to Anchorage, and I still didn't think I was going to run it. I got to Anchorage in December and trained all winter. But it was only when I was in the shoots, ready to go, that I believed it. And then I thought, what have I done?

MS. COOPER: Looking back, how well prepared were you?

MR. PAULSEN: Poorly prepared. At that point, only three people in the "lower forty-eight" had run the race. I called one, and he said, "Wear mukluks" (Eskimo snowboots). That was all the advice I got until I was in Alaska. There the other mushers helped me a lot. At that time you didn't have to really qualify for the race. You just went out with three Iditarod mushers and ran with them on overnighters. Then they signed a form saying you could live through it—that was just an opinion, of course. But when you got the signatures, you could turn in your entry form. Nobody thought I was going to finish, but I finished in seventeen days and fourteen hours. I came in forty-second out of the sixty-eight that went the distance.

MS. COOPER: When you were running the race, did you know you'd write about it?

MR. PAULSEN: I write all the time. I have notebooks with me, and I'm constantly making entries. I kept a journal during the race. I meditated, too. I knew I'd write about it, and as I've said before, there's no substitute for personal introspection at zero latitude.

MS. COOPER: In Woodsong, *you write about the dogs' lying down and refusing to run for you. How did you feel about that?*

MR. PAULSEN: It was insulting. There were also feelings involving my self-worth. Maybe I'm not worthy as a human to do this thing. The bond between people and dogs—even if they're house dogs—is very fragile. For them to become so upset, you have to feel there is something wrong with you and your capacity for compassion. You think, "I have done something wrong—and not just here with the dogs. Maybe I'm not a very good person."

MS. COOPER: What about Dogsong? *How did you research that?*

MR. PAULSEN: Well, again, I jumped right in the middle of it. I went to Eskimo villages, and I talked to the people. I also did a lot of reading.

MS. COOPER: You mentioned meditation earlier. Is there a mythic quality to your experiences?

MR. PAULSEN: I think *spiritual* is a better word. I don't mean religious. But each person does have a spirit, and I use meditation to become serene. I don't try to overtly write about this sort of thing, but I think it comes through because it's a part of me.

MS. COOPER: It's really balance you're speaking of, isn't it?

MR. PAULSEN: Yes, and I think it's critical that young people find that kind of balance in their own lives. There's so much coming at them. Kids today need to learn survival—physical, emotional, and spiritual. I really believe we are at a critical point.

Wood-SONG

ALA Best Book for Young Adults
School Library Journal Award

BY GARY PAULSEN

In *Woodsong* Gary Paulsen describes his own adventures with dogsledding. Living with his family in the wilderness of northern Minnesota, he became involved with sled dogs at the age of forty, when some friends gave him four dogs and a broken sled. At first he used the dogs for trapping animals, but he soon grew to feel it was wrong for him to kill. He began to train for the Iditarod, a dogsled race across Alaska. In this excerpt from his autobiography, Paulsen tells about some of the lessons he learned from his dogs.

Illustrated by DOUGLAS SMITH

Different dogs of course have different tempers. Some are more short-tempered than others, but on one occasion I had a whole team mad at me.

It made for a wild ride.

The thing is, it started gently enough. My leader was a sweet dog named Cookie and I had six dogs, all cheerful. It was on the trapline. I had checked several sets and the weather had turned sour. By late afternoon there was a full storm blowing snow so hard it was impossible to see where we were going.

The dogs always know direction but this was before I learned to trust them—learned to understand that lead dogs know more than the person on the sled. Afraid I would get lost in the storm, I challenged every decision. If Cookie wanted to go left, I wanted to go right, if she wanted to go right, I wanted to go left or straight ahead.

Each time she persisted, overriding my commands, I scolded her for fighting me, and each time I would find later that she was right.

Still I did not learn and I continued to challenge them, often causing the team to get tangled. In time they grew sick of my idiocy. When I went up to pull them over, floundering in the deep snow, they ignored me, tried to shrug away my hand.

Finally I went too far.

We were running along the top edge of a long ridge, higher and higher. The wind was tearing at us. I had my head buried in my parka hood and couldn't even see the front end of the team.

But I was sure I knew the ridge, knew where we were, felt that I had been there before.

I was absolutely, dead wrong.

The team went slower and slower until they were walking, lugging up the middle of the ridge and—perhaps after a quarter of a mile—they stopped. I yelled at them to turn right ("Gee" is the command for right, "Haw" for left). I knew where we were now—was sure of it—but Cookie tried to turn them left, down a long, shallow incline.

I became furious at their mutiny, swore, yelled at the team, then stomped forward, grabbed Cookie by the back of her harness and half-pulled, half-threw her off to the right.

She vanished in the driving snow and wind, moving angrily in the direction I had thrown her. The team followed her, and I jumped on the sled as it went by.

For one or two seconds it was all right. I stood on the brake and held the sled back and we slithered down the hill.

Then it all blew apart. With a great lurch I felt the sled fly out into empty space and drop beneath me. I barely had time to fall backward and go into a tuck before I hit the side of a nearly vertical incline and began to tumble.

I flapped and rolled for what seemed like hours, end over end. I heard the dogs falling beneath me, the sled rolling over and over, and all the gear and food being tossed out, crashing around me.

With a resounding thump the whole pile—sled, dogs, gear, and me, upside down—plummeted into a heap in the bottom of what seemed to be a deep gully.

It was impossible for a moment to understand what had happened. There was not a place where I ended and the dogs and junk began. One dog—named Lad—had his nose jammed squarely in my mouth, another was in my armpit. The sled was on top of me, and if you'd asked me my name I couldn't have told you.

Cookie had knowingly taken the team over the edge of a sharp drop. It was something she never would have done on her own, but I had pushed and griped and hollered too much and she thought it time to give me a lesson.

If I wanted to be stupid, if I persisted in being stupid, if I just couldn't resist being

stupid, then she figured I had it coming and she wouldn't hold me back.

It was a good lesson.

But it wasn't over yet. I stood and shook the snow out of my clothes—it was actually packed in my ears—and tipped the sled upright. It took me fifteen minutes to find all the gear and repack the sled and the dogs watched me quietly the whole time.

When the sled was loaded I set to work on the dogs. They were an unholy mess, tangled so badly the gangline was in knots.

The dogs were . . . strange. While I worked to untangle them, it was almost as if I weren't there, as if a robot were working on them. They were pleasant enough, but they did not make eye contact with me. They looked straight ahead while I untangled them. They almost, but not quite, ignored me. Even the dogs that would normally be jumping all over me held back.

It was eerie, quiet even with the wind blowing over the top of the gully. But after a moment I dismissed it as all in my head and went back to the sled.

I pulled the snowhook and stood on the runners.

And the whole team lay down.

They did not drop instantly. But each and every dog, as if by a silent command from Cookie, dug a bit and made a bed and lay down in the snow and went to sleep. I tried every way I knew to get them to run. Fed them, begged them, bit their ears, but they completely ignored me. I wasn't even there.

They didn't get up for eighteen hours.

I had gone over the line.

In the storm, in the pushing and yelling and driving, I had passed the point where they would accept me, run for me, pull for me, and they told me there in that gully. In that wild place they told me so that I would understand that they were the team, they were all of it, and if I ignored them or treated them wrong I would know it.

Finally I pulled out my sleeping bag and made a camp of sorts and heated some tea and dozed and drank tea and thought of how it is to be stupid.

And later, when they felt I'd had enough—late the next day while I was still in the sleeping bag—Cookie stood and shook the snow off. The rest of the dogs did the same, shook and marked the snow. I got out of the bag and fed them and packed and stood on the sled and they pulled up and out of the gully like a runaway train. They pulled up and into the sun and loped all the way home in great joy and glee; joy they were happy to share with me.

Unless I grew stupid again.

It is always possible to learn from dogs and in fact the longer I'm with them the more I understand how little I know. But there was one dog who taught me the most. Just one dog.

Storm.

First dog.

Joy, loyalty, toughness, peacefulness—all of these were part of Storm. Lessons about life and, finally, lessons about death came from him.

He had a bear's ears. He was brindle colored and built like a truck, and his ears were rounded when we got him so that they looked like bear cub ears. They gave him a comical look when he was young that somehow hung onto him even when he grew old. He had a sense of humor to match his ears, and when he grew truly old he somehow resembled George Burns.

At peak, he was a mighty dog. He pulled like a machine. Until we retired him and used him only for training puppies, until we let him loose to enjoy his age, he pulled, his back over in the power curve so that nothing could stop the sled.

In his fourth or fifth year as a puller he started doing tricks. First he would play jokes on the dog pulling next to him. On long runs he would become bored and when we least expected it he would reach across the gangline and snort wind into the ear of the dog next to him. I ran him with many different dogs and he did it to all of them—chuckling when the dog jumped and shook his or her head—but I never saw a single dog get mad at him for it. Oh, there was once a dog named Fonzie who nearly took his head off, but Fonzie wasn't really mad at him so much as surprised. Fonzie once nailed me through the wrist for waking him up too suddenly when he was sleeping. I'd reached down and touched him before whispering his name.

Small jokes. Gentle jokes, Storm played. He took to hiding

things from me. At first I couldn't understand where things were going. I would put a bootie down while working on a dog and it would disappear. I lost a small ladle I used for watering each dog, a cloth glove liner I took off while working on a dog's feet, a roll of tape, and finally, a hat.

He was so clever.

When I lost the hat it was a hot day and I had taken the hat off while I worked on a dog's harness. The dog was just ahead of Storm and when I kneeled to work on the harness—he'd chewed almost through the side of it while running—I put the hat down on the snow near Storm.

Or thought I had. When I had changed the dog's harness I turned and the hat was gone. I looked around, moved the dogs, looked under them, then shrugged. At first I was sure I'd put the hat down, then, when I couldn't find it, I became less sure and at last I thought perhaps I had left it at home or dropped it somewhere on the run.

Storm sat quietly, looking ahead down the trail, not showing anything at all.

I went back to the sled, reached down to disengage the hook and when I did, the dogs exploded forward. I was not quite on the sled when they took off so I was knocked slightly off balance. I leaned over to the right to regain myself, and when I did I accidentally dragged the hook through the snow.

And pulled up my hat.

It had been buried off to the side of the trail in the snow, buried neatly with the snow smoothed over the top so that it was completely hidden. Had the snowhook not scraped down four or five inches I never would have found it.

I stopped the sled and set the hook once more. While knocking the snow out of the hat and putting it back on my head I studied where it had happened.

Right next to Storm.

He had taken the hat, quickly dug a hole, buried the hat and smoothed the snow over it, then gone back to sitting, staring ahead, looking completely innocent.

When I stopped the sled and picked up the hat he looked back, saw me put the hat on my head, and—I swear—smiled. Then he shook his head once and went back to work, pulling.

Along with the jokes, Storm had scale eyes. He watched as the sled was loaded, carefully calculated the weight of each item, and let his disapproval be known if it went too far.

One winter a friend gave us a parlor stove with nickel trim. It was not an enormous stove, but it had some weight to it and some bulk. This friend lived twelve miles away—twelve miles over two fair hills followed by about eight miles on an old, abandoned railroad grade. We needed the stove badly (our old barrel stove had started to burn through) so I took off with the team to pick it up. I left early in the morning because I wanted to get back that same day. It had snowed four or five inches, so the dogs would have to break trail. By the time we had done the hills and the railroad grade, pushing in new snow all the time, they were ready for a rest. I ran them the last two miles to where the stove was and unhooked their tugs so they could rest while I had coffee.

We stopped for an hour at least, the dogs sleeping quietly. When it was time to go my friend and I carried the stove outside and put it in the sled. The dogs didn't move.

Except for Storm.

He raised his head, opened one eye, did a perfect double take—both eyes opening wide—and sat up. He had been facing the front. Now he turned around to face the sled—so he was facing away from the direction we had to travel when we left—and watched us load the sled.

It took some time as the stove barely fit on the sled and had to be jiggled and shuffled around to get it down between the side rails.

Through it all Storm sat and watched us, his face a study in interest. He did not get up, but sat on his back end and when I was done and ready to go I hooked all the dogs back in harness—which involved hooking the tugs to the rear ties on their harnesses. The dogs knew this meant we were going to head home so they got up and started slamming against the tugs, trying to get the sled to move.

All of them, that is, but Storm.

Storm sat backward, the tug hooked up but hanging down. The other dogs were screaming to run, but Storm sat and stared at the stove.

Not at me, not at the sled, but at the stove itself. Then he raised his lips, bared his teeth, and growled at the stove.

When he was finished growling he snorted twice, stood, turned away from the stove, and started to pull. But each time we stopped at the tops of the hills to let the dogs catch their breath after pulling the sled and stove up the steep incline, Storm turned and growled at the stove.

The enemy.

The weight on the sled.

I do not know how many miles Storm and I ran together. Eight, ten, perhaps twelve thousand miles. He was one of the first dogs and taught me the most and as we worked together he came to know me better than perhaps even my own family. He could look once at my shoulders and tell how I was feeling, tell how far we were to run, how fast we had to run—knew it all.

When I started to run long, moved from running a work team, a trapline team, to training for the Iditarod, Storm took it in stride, changed the pace down to the long trot, matched what was needed, and settled in for the long haul.

He did get bored, however, and one day while we were running a long run he started doing a thing that would stay with him—with us—until the end. We had gone forty or fifty miles on a calm, even day with no bad wind. The temperature was a perfect ten below zero. The sun was bright, everything was moving well, and the dogs had settled into the rhythm that could take them a hundred or a thousand miles.

And Storm got bored.

At a curve in the trail a small branch came out over the path we were running and as Storm passed beneath the limb he jumped up and grabbed it, broke a short piece off—about a foot long—and kept it in his mouth.

All day.

And into the night. He ran, carrying the stick like a toy, and when we stopped to feed or rest he would put the stick down, eat, then pick it up again. He would put the stick down carefully in front of him, or across his paws, and sleep, and when he awakened he would pick up the stick and it soon became a thing between us, the stick.

He would show it to me, making a contact, a connection between us, each time we stopped. I would pet him on top of the head and take the stick from him—he would emit a low, gentle growl when I took the stick. I'd "examine" it closely, nod and seem to approve of it, and hand it back to him.

Each day we ran he would pick a different stick. And each time I would have to approve of it, and after a time, after weeks and months, I realized that he was using the sticks as a way to communicate with me, to tell me that everything was all right, that I was doing the right thing.

Once when I pushed them too hard during a pre-Iditarod race—when I thought it was important to compete and win (a feeling that didn't last long)—I walked up to Storm and as I came close to him he pointedly dropped the stick. I picked it up and held it out but he wouldn't take it. He turned his face away. I put the stick against his lips and tried to make him take it, but he let it fall to the ground. When I realized what he was doing, I stopped and fed and rested the team, sat on the sled and thought about what I was doing wrong. After four hours or so of sitting—watching other teams pass me—I fed them another snack, got ready to go, and was gratified to see Storm pick up the stick. From that time forward I looked for the stick always, knew when I saw it out to the sides of his head that I was doing the right thing. And it was always there.

Through storms and cold weather, on the long runs, the long, long runs where there isn't an end to it, where only the sled and the winter around the sled and the wind are there, Storm had the stick to tell me it was right, all things were right.

And it came to Storm to grow old. Eight, nine, then ten years and he slowed. He trained many pups and, finally, he retired and stopped pulling. We tried to make him a pet and move him into the house, as we often do when dogs retire, but he didn't want that, didn't want to leave the kennel. He rattled around in the house and kept trying to walk out through the windows and glass doors, so we let him outside and kept his food dish full and left him untied.

For a year Storm was the old man in the kennel. He sat in the sun and played with the pups and watched the team leave and come back and always he had a stick. He would hold the stick when I came out to the kennel to harness and when I returned from a run.

And another year passed and he grew blind and his thinking changed so that he was not always aware but still he was happy. He sat by his house and when he heard my steps coming, he would hold his stick out for me. Sometimes I would go to his house and sit next to it in the sun and he would lay his head in my lap with the stick in his mouth and I would think of things I had forgotten about; young things and old things, long runs and short runs, puppies and cold and wind, northern lights and firelight against snow, the creaking sound of an old-fashioned lashed sled moving beneath me, and the joy, the raw-cold joy of going again and again inside the diamond that is northern winter, and all with Storm.

And there came a time when it was supposed to end. Storm failed and began to wander aimlessly through the kennel, bouncing off other dogs' houses, and I knew it would not be long until he faced east as so many of them did when they died. I wanted to leave him loose for that, so he could find the right place.

But we had some new dogs and some of them were aggressive and insecure and wanted to fight all the time. They would even almost fight old Storm when he came too close to their circles, though it was very rare for young dogs to attack older, more respected ones. I did not want Storm to end that way, in violence, so when I went on a trip one fall day I left Storm tied to his chain.

It was a temporary thing, just until I got back, but while I was gone it came on Storm to end and in the final time of his life he somehow got the chain wrapped around his doghouse so he could not face east, could not do it properly.

I saw where he had struggled and torn at the ground with his old claws to get around, to face east as so many animals do if there is time in the end but he could not. He could not tear the chain out of the ground, could not wear it around, could not move the house, could not face the east and end it right.

And it was my fault. I should have known that this was the day he would end, should have felt that he was going to die. I should have known to let him loose, even if there was a risk of a fight. After all, it would be natural for him to fight—they love to fight.

But I did not.

It was my fault and when death came and Storm could not face east he knew that I would be upset. Storm knew I would feel bad, and he did the only thing he could do.

When I came back the next day I went to the kennel and there was silence until I came close and then the dogs went into the death song, which sounds much like the rain song, and I knew then Storm was gone. Knew before I saw him, knew before I even arrived at the kennel. It is a low song, that stays low and does not go into the keening whine that means excitement and I felt all the sadness that comes with the end of a life and went to take his body from the kennel and bury him.

I found him next to his house. He had jammed into the side, trying to get around to the east. The earth was torn beneath him, the chain held his head north.

But he didn't blame me.

I will always blame myself, but Storm did not blame me.

His last act, his last thought, was for me. Storm lay dead and in his mouth was a stick, the stick.

Our stick.

Would you be interested in going to see a movie based on Gary Paulsen's autobiography? Why or why not?

What lessons would you say Gary Paulsen learned from his dogs?

How is Gary Paulsen's autobiography like a novel? How is it different?

WRITE Think of someone you know who would enjoy reading *Dogsong* and *Woodsong,* and write to that person, recommending the books.

IN SEARCH OF ADVENTURE

In his interview, Gary Paulsen talks about why young people today need to learn survival. What do the selections by Paulsen show about how people learn to survive?

WRITER'S WORKSHOP

Write an essay comparing the dogs in "Dogsong" with the dogs in "Woodsong." What similarities and differences do you see? What can you conclude about the way Paulsen's real-life experiences affected his fiction?

Writer's Choice Picture yourself in an adventurous role. What kind of adventure do you think you would enjoy? What value does adventure have for you? Develop your own writing idea about searching for or finding adventure. Think of a way to share your writing.

CONNECTIONS

MULTICULTURAL CONNECTION

MEXICAN MURALS

The Mexican Revolution of 1910–1920 inspired a revolution in Mexican art as well. Mexican artists began to explore new themes and styles rooted in Mexican culture.

This artistic innovation is best seen in the work of three muralists, Diego Rivera, David Alfaro Siqueiros, and José Clemente Orozco, who painted scenes from Mexican history, politics, and daily life on the walls and ceilings of public buildings. Although each had his own style, their work was distinctly Mexican and focused world attention on Mexican art.

There have been other important artists. Frida Kahlo, Diego Rivera's wife, painted dreamlike scenes with a flavor of Mexican folk art. Rufino Tamayo, one of Mexico's most famous artists, was also inspired by folk art and the tones and textures of the Mexican landscape. The colors of his paintings, says one writer, are like the juices of tropical fruits.

Work with classmates to think of ideas for a mural to represent your school or community. Brainstorm people, scenes, or events that you would like to include.

ART CONNECTION

CREATE A MURAL

Use your ideas from the previous activity to paint or draw a mural with your classmates. Work in small groups, with a section of the mural assigned to each group. When all the sections are finished, tape them together on a wall and give your mural a title.

SOCIAL STUDIES/ART/ LANGUAGE CONNECTION

MEXICAN ARTS AND CULTURE

Mexico has a wealth of artistic traditions. Choose one of the Mexican arts—painting, sculpture, literature, music, dance, architecture, crafts—to research. Then prepare an oral report on your findings. Present your report in class and have a class discussion about the various art traditions.

Clockwise from top: Detail from a mosaic mural by Diego Rivera at the Theater of the Insurgents in Mexico; Self-Portrait with Monkey *by Frida Kahlo;* Woman Carrying Tub *by Rufino Tamayo; Diego Rivera and Frida Kahlo in New York City, 1933; Diego Rivera laying out a sketch of a fresco for Rockefeller Center in New York City*

GLOSSARY

The **pronunciation** of each word in this glossary is shown by a phonetic respelling in brackets; for example, [in′tō·nā′shən]. An accent mark (′) follows the syllable with the most stress: [tak′tiks]. A secondary, or lighter, accent mark (′) follows a syllable with less stress: [kôr′ə·gā′tid]. The key to other pronunciation symbols is below. You will find a shortened version of this key on alternate pages of the glossary.

Pronunciation Key*

a	add, map	m	move, seem	u	up, done
ā	ace, rate	n	nice, tin	û(r)	burn, term
â(r)	care, air	ng	ring, song	yōō	fuse, few
ä	palm, father	o	odd, hot	v	vain, eve
b	bat, rub	ō	open, so	w	win, away
ch	check, catch	ô	order, jaw	y	yet, yearn
d	dog, rod	oi	oil, boy	z	zest, muse
e	end, pet	ou	pout, now	zh	vision, pleasure
ē	equal, tree	o͝o	took, full	ə	the schwa, an unstressed vowel representing the sound spelled a in *above* e in *sicken* i in *possible* o in *melon* u in *circus*
f	fit, half	ōō	pool, food		
g	go, log	p	pit, stop		
h	hope, hate	r	run, poor		
i	it, give	s	see, pass		
ī	ice, write	sh	sure, rush		
j	joy, ledge	t	talk, sit		
k	cool, take	th	thin, both		
l	look, rule	t͟h	this, bathe		

adz

antics Strange to say, *antics* comes from a word meaning "old." What do a person's odd actions have to do with age? Not much. The public baths of the Roman Empire were decorated with carvings of a wild mixture of floral, animal, and human shapes. The later Italians called them *antico,* meaning "old." The figures were so weird that *antico* came to mean "strange" or "bizarre," too.

antiquated

A

ab·a·lo·ne [ab′ə·lō′nē *or* ab′ə·lō′nē] *n.* A shellfish with a flattened, slightly spiraled shell lined with mother-of-pearl: ***Abalone* live in the ocean, and their shells are occasionally found along the shore.**

ab·so·lu·tion [ab′sə·lo͞o′shən] *n.* A release from either guilt or punishment for sins; forgiveness: **My mother thinks I should pray for *absolution* for watching so much TV.**

ab·solve [ab·zolv′] *v.* **ab·solved, ab·solv·ing** To set free from responsibility; to pardon: **The accused man was found innocent and *absolved* of the crime.**

adz [adz] *n.* A tool with a curved blade on a handle used for cutting or digging: **Miyax used an *adz* to chop ice blocks.**

af·fix [ə·fiks′] *v.* **af·fixed, af·fix·ing** To add or attach.

af·front [ə·frunt′] *v.* **af·front·ed, af·front·ing** To insult directly: **Lilly was *affronted* when Mr. Lapinsky would not let her sing.** *syn.* offend

a·gape [ə·gāp′] *adj.* Wide open: **The door to the deserted house was *agape,* and weird sounds were coming out of it.**

ag·i·ta·tion [aj′ə·tā′shən] *n.* The act of moving or shaking due to excitement or nervousness. *syn.* disquiet

al·cove [al′kōv] *n.* A nook or partly enclosed section of a room: **In each of the *alcoves* there was enough room for a small table.**

a·li·as [ā′lē·əs] *n.* A false name: **Charles Dodgson wrote some of his books under the *alias* Lewis Carroll.**

al·i·bi [al′ə·bī] *n.* A legal defense by which a person suspected of a crime tries to prove that he was somewhere else when the crime was committed: **No witnesses were found to support the defendant's *alibi* that he was bowling on the night of the robbery.**

al·ien [āl′yən *or* ā′lē·ən] *n.* A person who is living in a country where he or she is not a citizen: **Many *aliens* enter this country to find jobs.** *syn.* foreigner

al·loy [al′oi *or* ə·loi′] *n.* A substance that is a combination of two or more metals or of a metal and some other substance: **Steel is an *alloy* of iron and carbon.**

al·lu·sion [ə·lo͞o′zhən] *n.* A slight reference to or suggestion of something: **He made an *allusion* to the beach as we talked about vacations.** *syn.* hint

am·or·tize [am′ər·tīz′ *or* ə·môr′tīz′] *v.* **am·or·tized, am·or·tiz·ing** To pay off a debt gradually: **The cost of this car can be *amortized* over three years.**

an·guished [ang′gwisht] *adj.* Agonized; extremely painful: **The athlete let out an *anguished* cry as his ankle twisted.**

a·nom·a·lous [ə·nom′ə·ləs] *adj.* Unusual; not consistent with what is ordinary: **The pig adopted the kitten in a truly *anomalous* relationship.** *syn.* uncommon

an·tics [an′tiks] *n.* Clownish or playful behavior.

an·ti·quat·ed [an′ti·kwā′tid] *adj.* Out-of-date or old-fashioned: **My grandmother still uses her *antiquated* washboard to do the laundry.** *syns.* old, ancient, obsolete

ap·pre·hend [ap′rə·hend′] *v.* **ap·pre·hend·ed, ap·pre·hend·ing** To seize and take into custody; to arrest: **Police *apprehended* the burglar as he was climbing through a window.**

ar·bi·trar·y [är′bə·trer′ē] *adj.* Without limits; based on convenience rather than logic or fairness: **I'll never know what to expect if you always make *arbitrary* decisions.**

ar·cha·ic [är·kā′ik] *adj.* Of or relating to words or phrases that are no longer in use.

ar·ti·fact [är′tə·fakt′] *n.* The handmade product, such as a tool or ornament, of a particular culture.

as·pir·ing [ə·spīr′ing] *adj.* Wanting to achieve a certain goal: **Marvelle is an *aspiring* astronaut, so she eagerly watches every rocket launch.**

as·sent [ə·sent′] *n.* Agreement: **By common *assent,* the group changed the meeting date.**

as·sid·u·ous·ly [ə·sij′o͞o·əs·lē] *adv.* With steady, constant care and attention: **By studying *assiduously* all year, Sam improved his math grade from a C to an A.**

at·ten·u·at·ed [ə·ten′yo͞o·āt′əd] *adj.* Having become thin or slender: **The old woman's rings hung loosely on her *attenuated* fingers.**

at·tune [ə·t(y)o͞on′] *v.* **at·tuned, at·tun·ing** To bring into harmony or awareness.

au·then·tic [ô·then′tik] *adj.* Genuine or real.

a·verse [ə·vûrs′] *adj.* Having distaste for something; feeling opposed: **Ursula was *averse* to the plan, though the others liked it.**

av·id [av′id] *adj.* Eager; enthusiastic: **John, an *avid* baseball fan, listens to all of his team's home games on the radio.**

B

baize [bāz] *n.* A heavy wool or cotton cloth: **The chairs are upholstered in dark green *baize.***

bar·rack [bar′ək] *n.* A structure used for temporary housing; a building to house soldiers: **The *barrack* the young soldiers had to sleep in was cramped, cold, and drafty.**

barrack

be·guil·ing [bi·gīl′ing] *adj.* Pleasing. *syn.* charming

be·lat·ed [bi·lā′tid] *adj.* Delayed; past a given time.

bel·fry [bel′frē] *n.* A tower containing a bell: **A huge bell once hung in the *belfry* of this church.**

belfry

ben·e·fac·tor [ben′ə·fak′tər] *n.* A person who has given help, money, or a gift.

be·queath [bi·kwēth′ *or* bi·kwēth′] *v.* **be·queathed, be·queath·ing** To give or hand down something to another.

be·rate [bi·rāt′] *v.* **be·rat·ed, be·rat·ing** To scold angrily and abusively.

be·ret [bə·rā′ *or* ber′ā] *n.* A soft, round cap without a visor.

beret

be·seech·ing·ly [bi·sēch′ing·lē] *adv.* In a way that begs or asks very seriously.

be·stow [bi·stō′] *v.* **be·stowed, be·stow·ing** To give as a gift. *syn.* confer

biff [bif] *v.* **biffed, biff·ing** To punch at, as in boxing: **The fight in the schoolyard erupted into punching and *biffing.***

bi·zarre [bi·zär′] *adj.* Out of the ordinary; very different: **Those students wear *bizarre* clothing and outrageous hairstyles.** *syns.* eccentric, odd

blanched [blancht] *adj.* Without color; bleached: **The *blanched* patio furniture was moved to the shade so it would not fade any more.** *syn.* whitened

bole [bōl] *n.* The trunk of a tree: **They carved their initials in the *bole* of the oak tree.**

a	add	**o͝o**	took
ā	ace	**o͞o**	pool
â	care	**u**	up
ä	palm	**û**	burn
e	end	**yo͞o**	fuse
ē	equal	**oi**	oil
i	it	**ou**	pout
ī	ice	**ng**	ring
o	odd	**th**	thin
ō	open	**th**	this
ô	order	**zh**	vision

ə = a in *above*, e in *sicken*, i in *possible*, o in *melon*, u in *circus*

brindle

brindle *Brindle* developed from the word *brand* in Old English, which meant "a partly burned piece of wood." A hot *brand* will leave a permanent mark on whatever it touches. A *brand name* is a name that seems permanently attached to a product. Oh, yes, a *brindled* dog has a coat marked with dark streaks that look like burns.

caldron

brin·dle [brin′dəl] *adj.* Having dark streaks or flecks on a tawny or grayish color: **We bought a *brindle* puppy, whose coat had brown and gray streaks.**

bun·co [bung′kō] *adj.* Swindling or cheating: **Some people think lotteries are *bunco* games.**

C

cache [kash] *n.* A hiding place for concealing or storing something.

cal·dron [kôl′drən] *n.* A large pot or kettle: **A pioneer woman cooked meals in a huge black *caldron* hanging in the fireplace.**

can·ter [kan′tər] *v.* **can·tered, can·ter·ing** To move at a gait slower than a gallop but faster than a trot: **The wild horses were *cantering* gracefully across the plain.**

ca·reen [kə·rēn′] *v.* **ca·reened, ca·reen·ing** To sway wildly from side to side while moving: **The sled was *careening* down the slope because my brother could not control it.**

cas·cade [kas·kād′] *v.* **cas·cad·ed, cas·cad·ing** To fall as water falls: **The soup *cascaded* out of the tipped pot and into the campfire.** *syns.* tumble, flow

case·ment [kās′mənt] *n.* A type of window that has hinges at the side and opens as a door does: **Because of all the snow that had collected on the windowsill, the *casement* was difficult to open.**

cen·sure [sen′shər] *n.* Criticism. *syns.* blame, reproach

clem·en·cy [klem′ən·sē] *n.* Mildness in judging; mercy: **The district attorney asked for a harsher sentence, insisting that the judge had shown too much *clemency* in his original decision.**

co·her·ent·ly [kō·hir′ənt·lē] *adv.* In an orderly and logical way: **Paco calmed down and told the details of the story *coherently*.**

com·pli·ance [kəm·plī′əns] *n.* The act of giving in or agreeing with.

com·pul·so·ry [kəm·pul′sər·ē] *adj.* Required; enforced: **Because good health is so important for a soldier, a physical exam is *compulsory* for all applicants for military service.**

con·ces·sion [kən·sesh′ən] *n.* A privilege granted by an authority: **Gloria's parents made a few *concessions* to her smaller size, such as riding their bikes slowly enough for her to keep up.**

con·coct [kən·kokt′ *or* kon·kokt′] *v.* **con·coct·ed, con·coct·ing** To make by combining ingredients: **Beverly and Kim *concocted* a stew from the leftovers.** *syn.* devise

con·fis·cate [kon′fis·kāt′] *v.* **con·fis·cat·ed, con·fis·cat·ing** To seize by authority: **The getaway car was *confiscated* as evidence.**

con·jure [kon′jər *or* kun′jər] *v.* **con·jured, con·jur·ing** To appear to summon by use of spells or magic: **The psychic claims to have *conjured* spirits from the air.**

con·sign·ee [kən·sī′nē′] *n.* One who receives a shipment of goods or materials and who may be designated to act as an agent for the sender: **The export company had to find new *consignees* for its goods when the import company closed.**

con·sis·ten·cy [kən·sis′tən·sē] *n.* The degree of firmness or thickness of a substance: **Gail mixed the water and flour to the *consistency* of buttermilk.**

con·tend [kən·tend′] *v.* To argue or maintain.

con·vulse [kən·vuls′] *v.* **con·vulsed, con·vuls·ing** To move violently: **Miriam *convulsed* with laughter when she realized her mistake.** *syn.* shake

cor·ru·gat·ed [kôr′ə·gā′tid] *adj.* Having a ridged or uneven surface.

cos·mo·naut [koz′mə·nôt] *n.* A Russian astronaut: **The *cosmonauts* talked with the American astronauts about the latest Russian launch.**

cou·ri·er [kŏŏr′ē·ər *or* kûr′ē·ər] *n.* Messenger: **The *courier* arrived with the letter a bit too late.**

cringe [krinj] *v.* **cringed, cring·ing** To shrink or wince out of fear or humility.

croon [krōōn] *v.* **crooned, croon·ing** To sing in a low, gentle, and soothing way.

cur·ren·cy [kûr′ən·sē] *n.* Money in general circulation: **Because of inflation, our *currency* isn't worth as much as it was a few years ago.**

D

deb·o·nair [deb′ə·nâr′] *adj.* Having the qualities of gentleness, good manners, and courtesy. *syn.* suave

de·but [dā′byōō *or* dā·byōō′] *n.* A first appearance: **Alanya's relatives came from all over the country to see her acting *debut.***

de·duce [di·d(y)ōōs′] *v.* **de·duced, de·duc·ing** To determine by reason; to figure out: **After I saw the keys on the table, I *deduced* that when she left, she wasn't driving her car.** *syn.* infer

de·fray [di·frā′] *v.* To pay the cost or expense of something.

del·uge [del′yōōj] *v.* **del·uged, del·ug·ing** To flood with water. *syns.* pour, inundate

de·mure·ly [di·myŏŏr′lē] *adv.* Modestly, or seemingly so: **Bianca lowered her eyes *demurely* as she thanked the soldier for his compliment.**

de·ploy [di·ploi′] *v.* To set up or put in position for use.

de·prav·i·ty [di·prav′ə·tē] *n.* An evil or corrupt condition: **At the peace talks, the officials discussed the *depravity* of the rulers who had been overthrown.**

de·rive [di·rīv′] *v.* **de·rived, de·riv·ing** To receive or to come from a particular source: **Mrs. Matsumoto teaches kindergarten, *deriving* pleasure from working with the children every year.**

des·pot·ism [des′pə·tiz′əm] *n.* A system in which the ruler has unlimited power; tyranny: **Many historians have written about the *despotism* in France when kings did whatever they wanted and the people were powerless.** *syn.* oppression

de·ter [di·tûr′] *v.* To discourage or prevent action. *syns.* dissuade, hinder

de·te·ri·o·rate [di·tir′ē·ə·rāt′] *v.* **de·te·ri·o·rat·ed, de·te·ri·o·rat·ing** To lessen or make worse. *syn.* disintegrate

dev·as·tat·ing [dev′ə·stāt′ing] *adj.* Causing destruction or leaving in ruins. *syns.* destructive, overwhelming

dex·ter·i·ty [dek·ster′ə·tē] *n.* Skill in using the hands: **The carpenter's *dexterity* was evident from the high quality of his work.**

dex·ter·ous [dek′strəs *or* dek′stər·əs] *adj.* Skillful in using the hands: **Joseph's *dexterous* fingering technique was the envy of other violinists.**

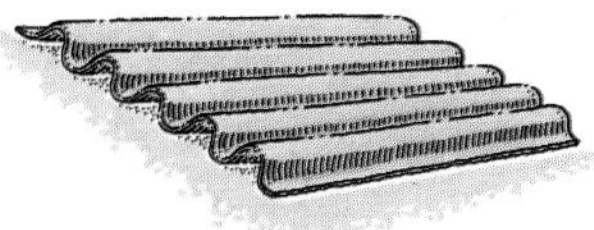

corrugated

debonair This word, borrowed from the French, was originally a three-word phrase, *de bon aire,* which meant "from a good family." The pleasant, gracious manners of a *debonair* person were once thought to be the result of good breeding.

a	add	**ŏŏ**	took
ā	ace	**ōō**	pool
â	care	**u**	up
ä	palm	**û**	burn
e	end	**yōō**	fuse
ē	equal	**oi**	oil
i	it	**ou**	pout
ī	ice	**ng**	ring
o	odd	**th**	thin
ō	open	**th̶**	this
ô	order	**zh**	vision

ə = { a in *above*, e in *sicken*, i in *possible*, o in *melon*, u in *circus* }

dilapidated

embedded

di·lap·i·dat·ed [di·lap′ə·dā′tid] *adj.* Fallen to pieces or ruined due to neglect.

dil·i·gent·ly [dil′ə·jənt·lē] *adv.* In a determined, careful way: **The teacher praised her for working *diligently* on the project.** *syn.* earnestly

di·min·ish [di·min′ish] *v.* **di·min·ished, di·min·ish·ing** To become gradually less; to make smaller: **The food supply in the pantry *diminished* after their relatives arrived and began eating their meals there.** *syns.* decrease, dwindle

dis·creet·ly [dis·krēt′lē] *adv.* In a cautious and quiet way. *syns.* prudently, tactfully

dis·em·bod·ied [dis′im·bod′ēd] *adj.* Existing free or apart from a body: **The superstitious neighbors claimed the house was haunted by *disembodied* spirits.**

dis·en·gage [dis′in·gāj′] *v.* **dis·en·gaged, dis·en·gag·ing** To release, free, or detach from something. *syns.* loosen, withdraw

dis·gorg·er [dis·gôrj′ər] *n.* A tool used to pull out fish hooks: **She used the *disgorger* to remove the hook from the trout's mouth.**

dis·or·i·ent·ed [dis·ôr′ē·en·təd] *adj.* Displaced from a sense of time, location, or identity. *syn.* confused

dis·pel [dis·pel′] *v.* **dis·pelled, dis·pel·ling** To drive away or remove. *syn.* scatter

dis·re·pair [dis′ri·pâr′] *n.* A rundown condition due to neglect.

dis·sen·sion [di·sen′shən] *n.* Discontented quarreling; conflict. *syns.* discord, disagreement

di·ver·sion [di·vûr′zhən] *n.* A change in the course of events: **Sumi's telephone call was a welcome *diversion* from cleaning out closets.** *syn.* digression

di·vi·sive·ness [di·vī′siv·nes] *n.* A state of disunity or disagreement: **The *divisiveness* in the student council began with the argument over the recycling drive.**

dog·ged·ly [dôg′id·lē] *adv.* In a persistent or stubborn way: **The firefighters worked *doggedly* for days to put out the forest fire.** *syn.* obstinately

doi·ly [doi′lē] *n.* A small, decorative mat, usually made of lace or linen, that is often placed under a vase or a dish: **Mother always put *doilies* under the flower vases when company came.**

drudg·er·y [druj′ər·ē] *n.* Dull, tiring, hard work.

du·bi·ous [d(y)ōō′bē·əs] *adj.* Doubtful. *syns.* wary, unsure

E

ec·sta·sy [ek′stə·sē] *n.* A state of overwhelming happiness or delight: **Mr. Lee was in *ecstasy* when he heard that his son was safe.** *syn.* rapture

ec·stat·i·cal·ly [ek·stat′ik·lē] *adv.* In a happy or delighted manner; with great emotion. *syn.* exuberantly

ed·i·ble [ed′ə·bəl] *adj.* Suitable for eating: **Those mushrooms are not *edible,* because they are poisonous.** *syn.* eatable

e·lat·ed [i·lā′tid] *adj.* Filled with joy. *syn.* exultant

e·lu·sive [i·lōō′siv] *adj.* Able to avoid capture: **For hours the lion patiently stalked her *elusive* prey.**

em·bed·ded [im·bed′əd] *adj.* Enclosed or stuck in a surrounding substance.

em·bla·zon [im·blā′zən] *v.* **em·bla·zoned, em·bla·zon·ing** To decorate brilliantly or adorn with a design or color.

em·i·nent [em′ə·nənt] *adj.* Important or respected because of high rank or quality; outstanding: **During his visit to America, the *eminent* physicist gave a lecture that was attended by most of the country's leading atomic researchers.** *syn.* famous

e·mit [i·mit′] *v.* To send or give off. *syn.* transmit

en·crust [in·krust′] *v.* **en·crust·ed, en·crust·ing** To cover with decorations such as jewels.

en·gulf [in·gulf′] *v.* **en·gulfed, en·gulf·ing** To surround and swallow up. *syn.* consume

en·thrall [in·thrôl′] *v.* **en·thralled, en·thrall·ing** To hold spellbound; to captivate: **We were *enthralled* by my uncle's stories of his adventures in Africa.**

ep·i·cen·ter [ep′ə·sen′tər] *n.* The point on the earth's surface directly above the focus of an earthquake: **A crack the size of a house opened up at the earthquake's *epicenter*.**

ep·och [ep′ək] *n.* An extended period of time that is important for its series of events or developments.

es·tu·ar·y [es′cho͞o·er′ē] *n.* The broad place where a river joins with a sea: **From the airplane, Marcus could easily see the rivers and *estuaries*.**

e·vac·u·ate [i·vak′yo͞o·āt′] *v.* **e·vac·u·at·ed, e·vac·u·at·ing** To move out; to vacate.

e·vince [i·vins′] *v.* To show evidence of; to reveal: **An old Navajo rug *evinces* some Spanish influence in its design.** *syns.* prove, indicate

ex·clu·sive·ly [iks·klo͞o′siv·lē] *adv.* Strictly limited to; only: **The video is to be used *exclusively* by schools and not by the general public.** *syn.* solely

ex·ot·ic [ig·zot′ik] *adj.* Strangely different and fascinating. *syns.* foreign, unfamiliar

ex·pul·sion [ik·spul′shən] *n.* The act of something being forced out. *syn.* ejection

ex·ult [ig·zult′] *v.* **ex·ult·ed, ex·ult·ing** To express great joy. *syn.* rejoice

fa·kir [fə·kir′ *or* fā′kər] *n.* A Moslem or Hindu holy person who may perform feats of endurance: **The *fakir* demonstrated his ability to walk across hot coals.**

fast·ness [fast′nis] *n.* A remote, secluded place: **Hidden deep in the woods, the hut served as a *fastness* for the knights.**

fer·vid [fûr′vid] *adj.* Eager; intense. *syns.* impassioned, fervent

flam·boy·ant [flam·boi′ənt] *adj.* Colorful or elaborate; showy: **Guido's *flamboyant* costume made him the center of attention.**

floun·der [floun′dər] *v.* **floun·dered, floun·der·ing** To struggle or act clumsily; to move awkwardly.

flus·tered [flus′tərd] *adj.* Confused; upset and nervous: **When the cat leaped at the cage, the *flustered* canary chirped and hopped wildly about.**

fo·li·age [fō′lē·ij *or* fō′lij] *n.* Leaves of a tree or any other plant.

fo·ment [fō·ment′] *v.* To stir up or arouse: **News of food shortages would *foment* a rebellion in the city.**

estuary

floundering When enough people make the same error with words, the mistake may become part of the language. This seems to be true of the verb *flounder*. People somehow combined *founder*, "to fall" or "to stumble," with *blunder*, "to move in a clumsy way." The origins of the verb *flounder* have no connection with the fish.

a	add	**o͝o**	took
ā	ace	**o͞o**	pool
â	care	**u**	up
ä	palm	**û**	burn
e	end	**yo͞o**	fuse
ē	equal	**oi**	oil
i	it	**ou**	pout
ī	ice	**ng**	ring
o	odd	**th**	thin
ō	open	**th̶**	this
ô	order	**zh**	vision

ə = a in *above*, e in *sicken*, i in *possible*, o in *melon*, u in *circus*

gaggle

grisly Hearing a *grisly* story may make you shiver with fear. Indeed, the word *grisly* comes from an Old English word meaning "to shudder." The *grizzly* bear inspires the same terror and takes its name from the same root.

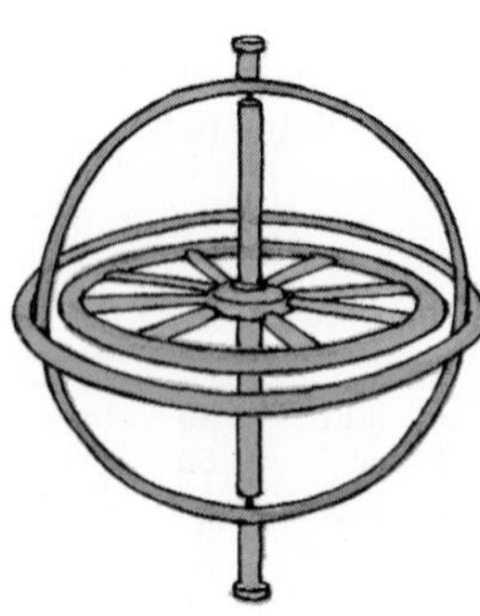

gyroscope

for·ay [fôr′ā] *n.* A raid or an expedition: **The soldiers went on a *foray* into the enemy camp to seize weapons.**

fore·bears [fôr′bârz′] *n.* Ancestors; people from whom someone is descended.

fort·night [fôrt′nīt′] *n.* A two-week period: **A *fortnight* had passed before they heard from their brother.**

fres·co [fres′kō] *n.* A picture painted on moist plaster: **The artist frequently dampened the fresh plaster as he painted the *frescoes* on the palace walls.**

fru·gal [frōō′gəl] *adj.* Thrifty; not wasteful of money or materials: **Because she had very limited means, Mother learned to be a *frugal* housekeeper.**

fu·gi·tive [fyōō′jə·tiv] *n.* A person fleeing from justice.

fur·tive [fûr′tiv] *adj.* Secret; done by stealth. *syn.* surreptitious

fu·tile·ly [fyōō′təl·ē] *adv.* In an ineffective, fruitless way. *syn.* vainly

G

gaf·fer [gaf′ər] *n.* (*informal*) An old man: **The *gaffer* told us that he had been a childhood friend of my grandfather.**

gag·gle [gag′əl] *n.* Any group, flock, or cluster. *syn.* aggregate

gawk·y [gô′kē] *adj.* Out of proportion; awkward: **The *gawky* basketball player seemed to be all arms and legs as he walked to the free throw line.**

grat·i·fy [grat′ə·fī′] *v.* **grat·i·fied, grat·i·fy·ing** To be a source of or give pleasure or satisfaction to.

gren·a·dier [gren′ə·dir′] *n.* A member of a special corps of the British army: **The *grenadiers* were known to be fearless fighters.**

griev·ance [grē′vəns] *n.* Serious complaint: **The seniors took their *grievance* about the cancellation of the game to the student council.**

gri·mace [gri·mās′ *or* grim′əs] *n.* A twisted facial expression that shows pain or disapproval.

gris·ly [griz′lē] *adj.* Causing horror or fear. *syn.* gruesome

gro·tesque [grō·tesk′] *adj.* Distorted, ugly, or bizarre in style or appearance: **The villain in the film had horrid and *grotesque* facial features.**

guile [gīl] *n.* Cunning; slyness: **Foxes in Aesop's fables are usually crafty characters, using *guile* to get what they want.**

gun·nel [gun′əl] *n.* Gunwale; the upper edge of a boat's side: **We balanced the oar on the boat's *gunnel*.**

gyre [jīr] *n.* A circling or spiraling form or motion.

gy·ro·scope [jī′rə·skōp′] *n.* A free-turning wheel or disk mounted on an axis, used to indicate direction: **The captain used the *gyroscopes* to keep the ship on course.**

H

hal·lowed [hal′ōd] *adj.* Sacred; deserving of reverence: **When people are in *hallowed* places, they should behave respectfully.**

har·ry [har′ē] *v.* To make a raid upon; to torment: **The enemy fighter planes were able to *harry* our ground troops with a five-hour air attack.** *syn.* assault

haugh·ti·ly [hô′ti·lē] *adv.* With obvious pride in oneself and scorn for others; arrogantly: **The winner of the pageant looked *haughtily* at the losing contestants as she accepted the crown.**

hav·oc [hav′ək] *n.* Widespread destruction. *syns.* devastation, ruin

heft [heft] *v.* **heft·ed, heft·ing** To heave or lift up. *syn.* hoist

ho·gan [hō′gən] *n.* A Navajo house made from sticks and mud: **Some Navajo *hogans* have six sides, and their doors always face the east.**

huff·i·ly [huf′ə·lē] *adv.* In an offended or insulted way. *syn.* peevishly

hum·mock [hum′ək] *n.* A low mound or ridge: **While hiking across the meadow, they came across a *hummock* in their path.**

I

il·lu·sion [i·lo͞o′zhən] *n.* A false belief; a mistaken idea: **The stage props help create the *illusion* of a man walking on water.**

il·lus·tri·ous [i·lus′trē·əs] *adj.* Distinguished or famous: **The scholar's *illustrious* career was the subject of the magazine article.**

im·pel [im·pel′] *v.* **im·pelled, im·pel·ling** To force or urge to make a statement or take action. *syn.* insist

im·pend·ing [im·pen′ding] *adj.* About to occur; likely to happen soon.

im·pet·u·ous [im·pech′o͞o·əs] *adj.* Marked by impulsive action or violent force: **"Look before you leap" is good advice for *impetuous* people.** *syns.* rash, hasty

im·plore [im·plôr′] *v.* **im·plored, im·plor·ing** To beg; to ask with feeling and determination: **Rachel has been *imploring* me for three years to visit.** *syns.* entreat, beseech

im·promp·tu [im·promp′t(y)o͞o] *adj.* Not planned in advance. *syn.* improvised

im·pu·ni·ty [im·pyo͞o′nə·tē] *n.* Freedom from consequence or punishment; immunity: **Clarice thought she could lie with *impunity,* but her employer found out and fired her.**

in·ces·sant [in·ses′ənt] *adj.* Unending; continuous: **People who live near the airport get used to the *incessant* roar of airplanes coming and going.** *syns.* uninterrupted, constant

in·com·mu·ni·ca·do [in′kə·myo͞o′nə·kä′dō] *adv., adj.* Out of communication with anyone: **Todd was stranded *incommunicado* for thirty-six hours after the phone lines went down in the storm.**

in·er·tia [in·ûr′shə] *n.* A property of physics in which matter tends to stay in its present state of motion or rest unless acted upon by an outside force: **If it weren't for the force of Earth's gravity, *inertia* would keep a thrown ball moving forever.**

in·ev·i·ta·bly [in·ev′ə·tə·blē] *adv.* With certainty; unavoidably.

in·fal·li·bil·i·ty [in·fal′ə·bil′ə·tē] *n.* The condition of being unable to make an error.

in·fil·trate [in·fil′trāt′ *or* in′fil·trāt′] *v.* **in·fil·trat·ed, in·fil·trat·ing** To enter a substance, an organization, or an area gradually or secretly: **The old house would have been a good buy, but termites had *infiltrated* its walls.**

in·fringe·ment [in·frinj′mənt] *n.* Violation, usually of a law or privilege. *syn.* encroachment

havoc *Havoc* now means any ruin or devastation, but its origins are military. During the Middle Ages it meant "plunder." *Cry havoc* was a command to soldiers to grab and make off with the enemy's property. *Havoc* may derive from the Old French word *haver,* "to take." It is probably related to the English words *heave, heft, hawk,* and even *have.*

hogan

a	add	**o͝o**	took
ā	ace	**o͞o**	pool
â	care	**u**	up
ä	palm	**û**	burn
e	end	**yo͞o**	fuse
ē	equal	**oi**	oil
i	it	**ou**	pout
ī	ice	**ng**	ring
o	odd	**th**	thin
ō	open	**th̶**	this
ô	order	**zh**	vision

ə = a in *above*, e in *sicken*, i in *possible*, o in *melon*, u in *circus*

intricate

jauntily We don't tend to think that someone who acts *jauntily* might also be *gentle,* but these words do share a common history. Both can be traced to the Old French word *gentil,* meaning "noble" or "of good birth" (from which we derive *gentleman* and *gentlewoman*). *Gentil* was reintroduced into English in the 16th century as *genteel,* and attempts at mimicking a French accent changed *genteel* to *jaunty.*

in·so·lence [in′sə·ləns] *n.* The quality of being insulting or disrespectful: **Brittany had the *insolence* to go to the party without being invited.** *syns.* rudeness, arrogance

in·tact [in·takt′] *adj.* Whole; with no part taken away or injured. *syn.* entire

in·ter·cept [in′tər·sept′] *v.* **in·ter·cept·ed, in·ter·cept·ing** To seize or halt on the way to a destination: **The defensive tackle surprised us all by *intercepting* the quarterback's pass and scoring a touchdown.**

in·tern [in·tûrn′] *v.* **in·terned, in·tern·ing** To confine or imprison during a war.

in·ti·ma·tion [in′tə·mā′shən] *n.* Something made known indirectly; a hint: **Ms. Dillon's sad face was an *intimation* that the tour had been canceled.**

in·tim·i·date [in·tim′ə·dāt′] *v.* **in·tim·i·dat·ed, in·tim·i·dat·ing** To make fearful or timid. *syn.* scare

in·to·na·tion [in′tō·nā′shən] *n.* Tone of voice; the pitch and manner of speech: **You can usually tell from a person's *intonation* whether he or she is interested in talking.**

in·tri·cate [in′tri·kit] *adj.* Complicated; with much detail.

in·var·i·a·bly [in·vâr′ē·ə·blē] *adv.* Without change; constantly. *syn.* regularly

i·ron·i·cal·ly [ī·ron′ik·lē] *adv.* In a way that is or seems to be the opposite of what is normal or expected: ***Ironically* the Johnsons inherited a fortune just when their business was finally becoming successful.**

ir·re·sis·ti·ble [ir′i·zis′tə·bəl] *adj.* Incapable of being resisted, refused, or opposed: **She was an *irresistible* child, whose charm made it impossible for people to say no to her.**

ir·ri·ta·bly [ir′ə·tə·blē] *adv.* With anger or annoyance.

J

jaunt·i·ly [jôn′ti·lē] *adv.* In a lively, self-confident way: **Pleased with his new jacket, Rick turned the collar up and walked *jauntily* down the avenue.**

K

keen·ing [kēn′ing] *adj.* Piercing; sharp and mournful: **The *keening* cries of the dogs pierced the quiet night.**

L

lan·guish [lang′gwish] *v.* **lan·guished, lan·guish·ing** To droop or fade from restless longing; to pine or suffer: **The lost collie *languished* at the animal shelter waiting for her owners to claim her.**

la·tent [lā′tənt] *adj.* Underlying; hidden: **Beulah's *latent* talent for music surprised everyone—even her parents.**

laugh·ing·stock [laf′ing·stok′] *n.* The object of laughter or ridicule: **I was the *laughingstock* of the team when my first pitch went only three feet.**

lee [lē] *adj.* Sheltered from the wind.

lee·ward [lē′wərd *or* lo͞o′ərd] *n.* The direction that faces away from the wind; the sheltered side: **We lost most of the wind's power after we sailed to *leeward* of the island's rocky cliffs.**

lev·i·ta·tion [lev′ə·tā′shən] *n.* The illusion of causing an object to rise and float in the air: **The magician claimed he had used his powers of *levitation* to suspend his assistant in the air.**

liv·er·y [liv′ər·ē] *n.* A place that keeps horses and horse-drawn vehicles for hire: **To avoid the considerable expense of keeping a horse, many horseback riders hire their mounts from a *livery.***

lore [lôr] *n.* Traditional beliefs or knowledge of a particular subject: **After the dance, the Irish singers shared some old stories and other *lore* of their homeland.**

lu·cid [lo͞o′sid] *adj.* Clearly understood: **I finally understood the problem after the teacher's *lucid* explanation.** *syn.* intelligible

lus·trous [lus′trəs] *adj.* Shiny without sparkle or glitter; glossy. *syn.* bright

lyre [līr] *n.* A stringed instrument resembling a harp, used by the ancient Greeks to accompany poetry: **In ancient Greece, a poet would often sing poetry while playing a *lyre.***

M

man·ner·ism [man′ər·iz′əm] *n.* An unconscious characteristic of behavior. *syn.* peculiarity

mar·tyr [mär′tər] *n.* One who accepts death as the penalty for refusing to reject his or her religion or belief: **Joan of Arc was among the famous *martyrs* who were burned at the stake.**

max·im [mak′sim] *n.* A general truth or principle to live by: **"Live and let live" is one of Sonya's favorite *maxims.***

mea·ger [mē′gər] *adj.* Not enough; insufficient: **Aunt Marya complained that her *meager* portion of dessert was much too small.** *syns.* spare, scanty

me·men·to [mə·men′tō] *n.* A reminder. *syn.* souvenir

mer·ce·nar·y [mûr′sə·ner′ē] *adj.* Motivated only by the desire for money.

me·ter [mē′tər] *n.* A pattern of accented and unaccented syllables, used in poetry.

me·tic·u·lous·ly [mə·tik′yə·ləs·lē] *adv.* Thoroughly; with great care.

mi·rage [mi·räzh′] *n.* An optical illusion. *syns.* vision, hallucination

mol·ten [mōl′tən] *adj.* Melted; liquified through heat.

mo·men·tous [mō·men′təs] *adj.* Important; significant: **Sorie made the *momentous* decision to continue his college studies.**

mo·rose [mə·rōs′] *adj.* Gloomy; sullen.

mus·ket [mus′kit] *n.* An old form of firearm that was popular before the invention of the rifle: **On some of our country's old battlefield sites, you can still find lead shot from the *muskets* used by Revolutionary soldiers.**

N

neu·rol·o·gist [n(y)o͝o·rol′ə·jist] *n.* A physician who treats diseases of the nervous system (nerves, brain, and spinal cord): **The *neurologist* gave me some tests to find out whether my dizziness was caused by damage to my nervous system.**

noi·some [noi′səm] *adj.* Foul; offensive to the sense of smell: **The smell in the alley was particularly *noisome* during the garbage strike.** *syns.* disgusting, offensive

lyre

meager *Meager* comes into English, by way of French, from the Latin word *macer,* which meant "thin" or "lean." Oddly enough, *macer* shares its origin with the ancient Greek *makros,* "large." How did these opposites develop from the same source? Apparently, the ancient root *mac* meant "long and thin." The Greeks emphasized "long," and the Romans, "thin."

a	add	**o͝o**	took
ā	ace	**o͞o**	pool
â	care	**u**	up
ä	palm	**û**	burn
e	end	**yo͞o**	fuse
ē	equal	**oi**	oil
i	it	**ou**	pout
ī	ice	**ng**	ring
o	odd	**th**	thin
ō	open	**th̶**	this
ô	order	**zh**	vision

ə = a in *above*, e in *sicken*, i in *possible*, o in *melon*, u in *circus*

ominously As it was to the Romans, today an *omen* is any sign, good or bad, that seems to tell what will happen in the future. *Ominous* and *ominously*, however, have completely negative connotations. An *ominous* occurrence is one that threatens danger.

parapet

O

ob·scure [əb·skyo͝or′] *v.* **ob·scured, ob·scur·ing** To hide or make difficult to see: **The clouds drifted in and *obscured* our view of the moon.** *syn.* conceal

o·cher [ō′kər] *n.* An earthy material used as a pigment; it contains iron and varies in color from yellow to deep orange or red: **Maria mixed *ocher* into the white paint to create a muddy color.**

o·di·ous [ō′dē·əs] *adj.* Hateful or disgusting; detestable: **I find gardening work *odious* and would prefer doing almost anything else.**

om·i·nous·ly [om′ə·nəs·lē] *adv.* Threateningly: **Before the storm, the sky grew dark and rumbled *ominously.*** *syn.* forebodingly

out·land·ish [out·lan′dish] *adj.* Out of the ordinary; very strange: **The stranger's *outlandish* way of talking made us wonder where he was from.**

P

pains·tak·ing·ly [pānz′tā′king·lē] *adv.* With great care and effort: **The surgeon *painstakingly* sewed up the patient's wound.** *syns.* cautiously, diligently

par·a·noi·a [par′ə·noi′ə] *n.* A tendency toward unreasonable suspiciousness or distrustfulness of others: **Andy's *paranoia* made him so suspicious that he became increasingly difficult to work with.**

par·a·pet [par′ə·pit *or* par′ə·pet] *n.* A low wall around the edge of a balcony or roof: **The archers hid behind the *parapets* of the castle until the invaders got close.**

par·ti·tioned [pär·tish′ənd] *adj.* Separated; divided.

par·tu·ri·tion [pär′tyo͞o·rish′ən] *n.* The act of giving birth: **After *parturition,* both mother and baby need rest.**

pas·tor·al [pas′tər·əl] *adj.* Of or relating to simple and peaceful country life: **Walking in city traffic is very different from our *pastoral* walks in the country.** *syn.* restful

pat·i·na [pə·tē′nə *or* pat′ən·ə] *n.* A dull green film that forms on copper or bronze after long exposure to the elements: **The *patina* of the garden sculpture makes it blend with the trees.**

pen·dant [pen′dənt] *n.* An ornament that hangs down: **Sherri is known for the lovely *pendants* she wears around her neck.**

pe·riph·er·al [pə·rif′ər·əl] *adj.* On the outer edge or boundary.

per·pet·u·ate [pər·pech′o͞o·āt′] *v.* **per·pet·u·at·ed, per·pet·u·at·ing** To cause to be continued or remembered for a long time: **Unfortunately, James actually *perpetuated* the rumor by trying to find out who started it.** *syn.* immortalize

phe·nom·e·non [fi·nom′ə·non′] *n.* Any observable event, fact, or condition of scientific interest.

phys·i·ol·o·gy [fiz′ē·ol′ə·jē] *n.* The study of the activities of a living organism or the functions of its parts.

pil·fer [pil′fər] *v.* **pil·fered, pil·fer·ing** To steal in small amounts: **Months went by before we noticed the mouse's *pilfering;* by then he had gotten into almost everything in the cupboard.**

pir·ou·ette [pir′o͞o·et′] *n.* A rapid, whirling motion: **The ballet dancer's *pirouette* was so fast that she appeared as a blur.**

pit·tance [pit′əns] *n.* A small amount or portion of something, usually money: **Esteban complained that his allowance was a *pittance* compared with his sister's larger one.**

plain·tive [plān′tiv] *adj.* Sad, mournful: **The child gave a *plaintive* cry when he couldn't find his parents in the crowd.**

plum·age [plo͞o′mij] *n.* Feathers: **The *plumage* of parrots is usually brightly colored.**

plum·met [plum′it] *v.* **plum·met·ed, plum·met·ing** To drop or fall straight down: **When Peter shook the tree with all his might, apples *plummeted* to the ground.**

pon·der·ous [pon′dər·əs] *adj.* Of great weight; large and clumsy. *syn.* lumbering

por·rin·ger [pôr′in·jər] *n.* A shallow metal bowl with a flat handle, used for foods such as porridge or soup.

pos·ter·i·ty [pos·ter′ə·tē] *n.* Descendants; all future generations: **Famous words spoken by great leaders are kept for *posterity.***

prec·e·dent [pres′ə·dənt] *n.* Something done or said that is used as a guide or model for a later act of the same kind.

pre·pos·ter·ous [pri·pos′tər·əs] *adj.* Contrary to nature or reason: **Her story about the flying tuna fish was simply *preposterous.*** *syns.* absurd, ridiculous

pre·sum·a·bly [pri·zo͞o′mə·blē] *adv.* Supposedly; assumably: **Tanya didn't explain why she missed practice, but *presumably* she needed the time to study.**

pri·va·teer [prī′və·tir′] *n.* A privately owned, armed ship that has government permission to attack enemy ships in wartime: **Without the support of several *privateers,* the country's small fleet probably would have lost the sea battle.**

prob·a·bil·i·ty [prob′ə·bil′ə·tē] *n.* Likelihood; the chance that a condition or event will occur.

pro·ceeds [pro′sēdz′] *n. pl.* The money or profit gained from the sale of goods or work: **All the *proceeds* from our school's bake sale will be used to buy new band uniforms.**

pro·dig·ious [prə·dij′əs] *adj.* Very large in amount or size: **We picked a *prodigious* number of apples this year.** *syn.* enormous

pro·found [prə·found′] *adj.* Extreme; deeply felt.

pro·pel·lant [prə·pel′ənt] *n.* A substance or thing used to move an object: **We usually use gasoline as a *propellant* in our cars.**

prose [prōz] *n.* Ordinary speech or writing, without meter or rhyme: ***Prose* is the type of writing that is found in newspaper articles, book reports, essays, and most fiction.**

pru·dence [pro͞o′dəns] *n.* The ability to use good judgment; wisdom. *syn.* foresight

pun·gent [pun′jənt] *adj.* Strong smelling; with a sharp or bitter aroma.

Q

quad·ru·ped [kwod′ro͞o·ped′] *n.* An animal with four feet: **A *quadruped* has four feet, like a horse, and a biped has two feet, like a human.**

qualm [kwäm *or* kwälm] *n.* A feeling of uneasiness or fear.

que·ry [kwir′ē] *n.* A question: **In response to the reporter's *query,* the mayor said he knew nothing about the problem.** *syn.* inquiry

plummet If you *plummet* from the high diving board into the pool, you fall straight into the water like a ball of lead. A string with a lead weight at one end is a *plumb line* used to make straight vertical lines at right angles to the earth. The Latin word for "lead," *plumbum,* gave us *plummet* and *plunge.* It is also the source of *plumber* and *plumbing,* because water pipes and drains were once made out of lead.

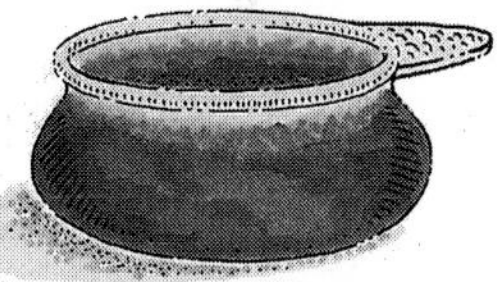

porringer

a	add	**o͝o**	took
ā	ace	**o͞o**	pool
â	care	**u**	up
ä	palm	**û**	burn
e	end	**yo͞o**	fuse
ē	equal	**oi**	oil
i	it	**ou**	pout
ī	ice	**ng**	ring
o	odd	**th**	thin
ō	open	**th̶**	this
ô	order	**zh**	vision

ə = a in *above*, e in *sicken*, i in *possible*, o in *melon*, u in *circus*

sabotage The word *sabotage* is derived from the French word *sabot,* meaning "wooden shoe." According to one theory, during a French labor dispute in the 1800s, unhappy factory workers threw their *sabots* into the machinery they were operating in order to cause damaging delays. Later, *sabotage* was used during World War I to describe acts of destruction that were committed by secret agents to hinder or delay an enemy.

R

rasp [rasp] *v.* **rasped, rasp·ing** To rub harshly; to scrape.

re·count [ri·kount′] *v.* **re·count·ed, re·count·ing** To remember or tell in detail. *syns.* tell, explain, recall

rec·ti·fy [rek′tə·fī] *v.* To make right; to correct: **The teacher asked us to *rectify* our own spelling errors before we turned in our papers.**

rec·ti·tude [rek′tə·t(y)o͞od′] *n.* The state of being morally right; honesty: **Lonnie's *rectitude* prompted him to return the wallet he found.**

re·ha·bil·i·tate [rē′hə·bil′ə·tāt′] *v.* To restore, as to good health or to a condition of useful and constructive activity: **The physical therapist helped to *rehabilitate* the injured athlete with exercises that strengthened her strained muscles.**

re·lent [ri·lent′] *v.* **re·lent·ed, re·lent·ing** To become less harsh; to become more compassionate: **At first the security guard refused to let us go backstage, but he finally *relented* after we promised to stay no longer than ten minutes.**

re·lent·less [ri·lent′lis] *adj.* Continuous and unforgiving. *syn.* persistent

rem·nant [rem′nənt] *n.* A remaining trace or leftover. *syn.* vestige

re·sheathe [ri·shē*th*′] *v.* **re·sheathed, re·sheath·ing** To cover or put in a case again: **After cleaning the fish he'd caught, Clint *resheathed* his hunting knife.**

res·i·due [rez′ə·d(y)o͞o′] *n.* A part remaining after another part has been removed. *syn.* remainder

re·sound·ing [ri·zound′ing] *adj.* Producing or filling with loud sound: **Our neighborhood rang with the *resounding* wail of the sirens.**

re·spec·tive [ri·spek′tiv] *adj.* Having to do with each person or item mentioned. *syns.* particular, separate

ret·ri·bu·tion [ret′rə·byo͞o′shən] *n.* Punishment given in return for a person's wrongdoing: **Litterers in our city are required to pay a sizable fine as *retribution.***

rev·el·ry [rev′əl·rē] *n.* Noisy and boisterous merrymaking or partying: **In their *revelry* after the championship game, the soccer team blocked traffic.**

re·vi·tal·ize [rē·vīt′(ə)l·īz′] *v.* To give new life to: **On a hot day, a swim in the pool *revitalizes* us.** *syn.* restore

rite [rīt] *n.* A ceremony: **Some cultures have special *rites* for welcoming their young people into adulthood.**

S

sab·o·tage [sab′ə·täzh′] *n.* The destruction of property by dissatisfied workers or by enemy agents in wartime: **Officials began to suspect that an act of *sabotage* was the cause of the factory explosion.**

sa·mite [sā′mīt′ *or* sam′īt′] *n.* A rich, medieval, silk fabric interwoven with gold or silver threads: **The queen's curtains were made of the very finest *samite.***

sa·vor [sā′vər] *v.* **sa·vored, sa·vor·ing** To take delight in the experience of; to enjoy: **Lucas spent most of the night *savoring* the memory of his touchdown pass in the afternoon's game.**

scrab·ble [skrab′əl] *v.* **scrab·bled, scrab·bling** To grope frantically or clumsily: **Sharon *scrabbled* around on the ground, trying to find the earring she had dropped.**

scrounge [skrounj] *v.* To forage; to gather by long, hard searching. *syns.* scavenge, rummage

scru·pu·lous [skrōōʹpyə·ləs] *adj.* With much care; thorough: **Mr. Donovan keeps such *scrupulous* records that we know nothing could ever be missing.** *syns.* precise, conscientious

scur·ri·lous [skûrʹə·ləs] *adj.* Coarse, vulgar, or evil: **The two candidates for mayor exchanged nasty and *scurrilous* remarks.** *syn.* abusive

seis·mol·o·gy [sīz·molʹə·jē] *n.* The study of earthquakes and other vibrations of the earth: **People knowledgeable about *seismology* are looking for ways to predict earthquakes.**

se·rene [si·rēnʹ] *adj.* Calm; suggesting tranquillity: **The soft sound of the crickets, the gentle breeze, and the cool temperature worked together to create a *serene* setting for the picnic.** *syn.* peaceful

sex·tant [seksʹtənt] *n.* An instrument for measuring the angular distance of celestial bodies such as stars in order to navigate a ship or rocket: **The ship's captain used a *sextant* to navigate by the position of the sun.**

shard [shärd] *n.* A fragment of a brittle object.

sheep·ish·ly [shēʹpish·lē] *adv.* In an embarrassed way: **Sarah *sheepishly* returned the brownie to the platter when her mother walked in.** *syn.* timidly

shift·less [shiftʹlis] *adj.* Lacking in energy or ambition; lazy: **The new employee turned out to be a *shiftless* liar who faked injuries to avoid any heavy lifting.**

shrap·nel [shrapʹnəl] *n.* Fragments scattered when a bomb explodes.

sim·u·la·tion [simʹyə·lāʹshən] *n.* A model or enactment of the real thing. *syn.* imitation

sin·ew·y [sinʹyōō·ē] *adj.* Firm, forceful, and strong: **During a summer of moving furniture, Aaron's body grew stronger and more *sinewy*.** *syn.* muscular

sin·gle-hand·ed·ly [singʹgəl·hanʹdid·lē] *adv.* By oneself; without assistance: **We expected Kim to ask for help and were surprised when he assembled the bicycle *single-handedly*.**

sin·gu·lar [singʹgyə·lər] *adj.* Unusual; the only one of its type: **On our trip to Greece last year we had some *singular* experiences that made it different from our previous vacations.** *syns.* uncommon, unique

skep·ti·cal [skepʹti·kəl] *adj.* Not believing readily; inclined to question or doubt: **She was *skeptical* about the beginner's ability to fly the airplane.** *syns.* doubtful, dubious

skulk [skulk] *v.* To move in a stealthy manner; to sneak about: **Cats often *skulk* around our yard when we put food out for the birds.**

slav·er [slavʹər] *v.* **slav·ered, slav·er·ing** To drool. *syn.* slobber

slith·er [sli*th*ʹər] *v.* **slith·ered, slith·er·ing** To slide on a loose or uneven surface.

smid·geon [smijʹən] *n. informal* (also spelled smidgen) Small amount: **I was looking forward to eating the leftover pizza for dinner last night, but my sister had left only a *smidgeon*.** *syn.* bit

sol·ace [solʹis] *n.* Comfort in difficult or unhappy circumstances: **Andrea was disappointed that she had lost the election, but she found *solace* in the knowledge that she had given it her best effort.**

som·ber [somʹbər] *adj.* Melancholy; of a sorrowful character: **Mr. Marjewski's face remained *somber* even after I tried to cheer him up.**

sextant

shard

a	add	**ŏŏ**	took
ā	ace	**ōō**	pool
â	care	**u**	up
ä	palm	**û**	burn
e	end	**yōō**	fuse
ē	equal	**oi**	oil
i	it	**ou**	pout
ī	ice	**ng**	ring
o	odd	**th**	thin
ō	open	***th***	this
ô	order	**zh**	vision

ə = a in *above*, e in *sicken*, i in *possible*, o in *melon*, u in *circus*

spar [spär] *v.* To box or pretend to box with an opponent; to argue back and forth: **The boys trade punches that never land when they *spar* in the living room.**

spasm [spaz′əm] *n.* Something that happens briefly and suddenly in bursts. *syn.* jerk

spe·cious [spē′shəs] *adj.* Seeming true, fair, or good, but actually not so: **We laughed about the car salesman's *specious* claims when we realized that the car wouldn't even start.**

spec·tral [spek′trəl] *adj.* Ghostly; eerie: **The fog and the emptiness made the slide on the playground a *spectral* sight.**

spend·thrift [spend′thrift′] *n.* A person who spends money wastefully.

squan·der [skwon′dər] *v.* **squan·dered, squan·der·ing** To spend foolishly or wastefully.

stal·wart [stôl′wərt] *adj.* Brave; determined; fearless: **Although the fire was out of control, several *stalwart* firefighters entered the building to search for victims.**

stan·chion [stan′shən] *n.* An upright bar, post, or support: **The canopy was supported by *stanchions*.**

stanchion

stip·u·la·tion [stip′yə·lā′shən] *n.* Condition or requirement: **My dad's *stipulation* for buying a new TV is that we watch it only on weekends.**

stu·pe·fac·tion [st(y)o͞o′pə·fak′shən] *n.* Great surprise; amazement.

stupefaction *Stup* in this word is the same Latin root that appears in *stupor* and *stupid*. All are related to a more ancient root *tup*, with a variation *stup*, which meant "to strike" or "to beat." If you are beaten about the head, you may fall into a *stupor* or act *stupidly*.

suav·i·ty [swäv′i·tē] *n.* Smooth and polished manner or behavior: **Marcelino's *suavity* did not seem to fit with what Lara had learned about his rough upbringing.** *syn.* sophistication

sub·side [səb·sīd′] *v.* **sub·sid·ed, sub·sid·ing** To become less active; to sink to a lower level. *syns.* settle, descend

sub·ter·fuge [sub′tər·fyo͞oj′] *n.* A strategy or trick to evade or conceal; deceit: **Using a clever *subterfuge*, she managed to escape her pursuers and cross the border to safety in a friendly country.** *syns.* fraud, trickery

sub·tle [sut′(ə)l] *adj.* Crafty and clever; indirect or difficult to see or understand: **I realized later that Luis had been giving me *subtle* hints all evening, but I hadn't understood them.** *syn.* cunning

suf·fused [sə·fyo͞ozd′] *adj.* Completely covered; spread over as with light or liquid.

sup·ple [sup′əl] *adj.* Easily bent or twisted; soft and pliant. *syn.* flexible

sur·mise [sər·mīz′] *v.* **sur·mised, sur·mis·ing** To guess; to base an idea on scanty evidence: **From Bridget's smug expression, we *surmised* that she had done well on the test.**

sus·te·nance [sus′tə·nəns] *n.* Something that gives strength and maintains life: **Caroline made sure the lost kitten had some *sustenance* before she looked for its mother.** *syn.* nourishment

syn·thet·ic [sin·thet′ik] *adj.* Produced artificially; not true or real. *syn.* unnatural

T

tack [tak] *v.* **tacked, tack·ing** To change a ship's direction by changing the position of its sails: **The sailing ship's captain was able to avoid the rocks by *tacking* several times.**

tac·tics [tak′tiks] *n.* The technique or science of accomplishing objectives through strategy.

taw·dry [tô′drē] *adj.* Cheap and gaudy: **The woman's *tawdry* costume contrasted strangely with her friend's tasteful and expensive clothing.**

ten·ta·tive [ten′tə·tiv] *adj.* Not certain; subject to change: **The two warring nations agreed to a *tentative* cease-fire while they tried to settle their differences at the negotiating table.**

ter·mi·nate [tûr′mə·nāt′] *v.* To stop or end. *syns.* conclude, finish

ter·ra-cot·ta [ter′ə·kot′ə] *adj.* Of or having to do with a hard, reddish-brown clay used for sculpture, pottery, and buildings: **Their patio was decorated with *terra-cotta* lamps and planters.**

ther·mal [thûr′məl] *adj.* Of, relating to, or caused by heat: **The cooling fan is designed to reduce *thermal* wear on the engine.**

thwart [thwôrt] *v.* **thwart·ed, thwart·ing** To keep from being hopeful or successful; to defeat. *syn.* foil

ti·rade [tī′rād *or* tə·rād′] *n.* An angry outburst: **The woman's *tirade* about careless riders seemed too long and harsh, considering the minor damage to her bike.** *syn.* tantrum

tog·gle [tog′(ə)l] *n.* A pin or rod that fits into a chain, loop, or hole for holding or securing something: ***Toggles* fasten the tent to the stakes in the ground.**

tor·ren·tial [tô·ren′shəl] *adj.* Of, like, or resulting from a violent stream of water.

tra·jec·to·ry [trə·jek′tər·ē] *n.* The curved path of a projectile or a comet in flight: **Scientists calculated the *trajectory* of the shuttle into space.**

tran·quil·li·ty [trang·kwil′ə·tē *or* tran·kwil′ə·tē] *n.* Peace; freedom from disturbance: **Mrs. Lazzara enjoys the *tranquillity* of early morning walks alone on the beach.** *syn.* calm

tran·sient [tran′shənt] *adj.* Passing quickly by; momentary. *syn.* temporary

tur·bu·lent [tûr′byə·lənt] *adj.* Agitated; restless: **The *turbulent* water made Kato seasick.**

tur·moil [tûr′moil] *n.* Disturbance; a feeling of agitation or confusion.

U

un·a·bashed [un′ə·basht′] *adj.* Not ashamed: **Lee took such *unabashed* delight in winning the contest that he couldn't stop smiling.** *syn.* undisguised

un·al·ien·able [un·āl′yən·ə·bəl] *adj.* Not able to be surrendered or taken away; inalienable: **The Declaration of Independence states that our *unalienable* rights were given to us by God.**

u·na·nim·i·ty [yo͞o′nə·nim′ə·tē] *n.* Unity; complete agreement: **The senior council's *unanimity* on the question of whether to have a picnic came as no surprise to anyone who was at the meeting.**

un·ob·tru·sive·ly [un′əb·tro͞o′siv·lē] *adv.* Without attracting attention; inconspicuously: **No one noticed that Susan had stepped *unobtrusively* into the room and stood listening intently.**

un·time·ly [un·tīm′lē] *adj.* Too early; happening at the wrong time: **Emiko's surprise party was spoiled by her *untimely* arrival.**

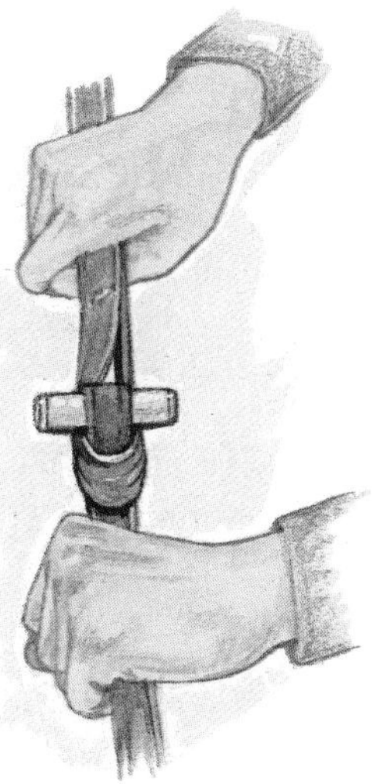

toggle

unalienable *Unalienable* is possibly a fine example of a printer's error. Apparently Thomas Jefferson, a masterful writer, wrote the word *inalienable* in his draft of the Declaration of Independence. It's likely that as the Declaration was revised, copied by hand, and printed, the initial *i* was changed to *u* and a variant spelling was created!

a	add	**o͝o**	took
ā	ace	**o͞o**	pool
â	care	**u**	up
ä	palm	**û**	burn
e	end	**yo͞o**	fuse
ē	equal	**oi**	oil
i	it	**ou**	pout
ī	ice	**ng**	ring
o	odd	**th**	thin
ō	open	**th̶**	this
ô	order	**zh**	vision

ə = a in *above*, e in *sicken*, i in *possible*, o in *melon*, u in *circus*

vermilion The source of this word—as well as the bright red dye that it signifies—is a "little worm." The cochineal insects from whose bodies this dye was produced were called *vermiculi,* the Latin for "little worms." Our word comes from the French version of *vermiculi.* If you like the pasta called *vermicelli,* you might not like thinking of it as the "little worms" the word means in Italian!

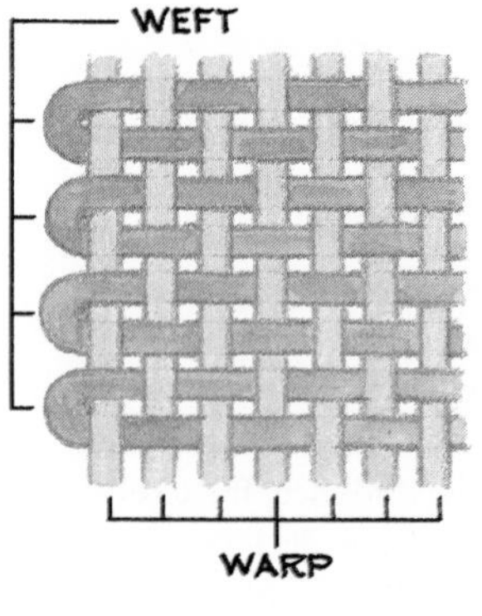

warp, weft

wolverine

un·wield·y [un·wēl′dē] *adj.* Difficult to manage or handle because of weight or size; awkward: **Corey almost dropped the *unwieldy* bundle of football gear as he carried it out to the car.**

u·sur·pa·tion [yo͞o′sər·pā′shən *or* yo͞o′zər·pā′shen] *n.* Takeover; the act of seizing by force: **The city council's actions were illegal *usurpations* of the city manager's responsibilities.**

V

val·et [val′ā *or* val′it] *n.* A servant; one who takes care of personal services: **Tell the hotel *valet* to have my suit cleaned by this evening.**

van·quish [vang′kwish] *v.* To overcome, subdue, or defeat: **The poem told about a knight who was able to *vanquish* his foes and win the hand of the princess.** *syn.* conquer

ver·mil·ion [vər·mil′yən] *adj.* Bright red in color.

ves·tig·i·al [ves·tij′ē·əl] *adj.* Of or relating to a part or organ that is small or useless and no longer functions: **A person can live without an appendix because it is a *vestigial* organ.**

vi·cin·i·ty [vi·sin′ə·tē] *n.* Surrounding area. *syns.* neighborhood, proximity

vo·lu·mi·nous [və·lo͞o′mə·nəs] *adj.* Having great volume or quantity; big: **Hideo's *voluminous* aquarium can hold thirty-five fish.** *syns.* bulky, ample

W

warp [wôrp] *n.* The threads that run along the length of a fabric: **The *warp* was pulled tight to keep the fabric even during weaving.**

weft [weft] *n.* The threads that crisscross the long warp threads in fabric: **The *weft* threads were woven from side to side on the loom.** *syn.* woof

wol·ver·ine [wo͝ol′və·rēn′] *n.* A wild animal related to the weasel, with a blackish coat striped with light brown: **The *wolverine* is said to be very intelligent.**

wraith [rāth] *n.* A barely visible gas or vapor; a ghostlike figure.

INDEX OF
TITLES AND AUTHORS

Page numbers in light type refer to biographical information.

Acknowledgments continued

Paul Fleischman: Comment on "The Passenger Pigeon." Text copyright © 1990 by Paul Fleischman.

David R. Godine, Publisher, Inc.: "The Delight Song of Tsoai-talee" from *Angle of Geese* by N. Scott Momaday. Text copyright © 1974 by N. Scott Momaday.

Linda Goss: "The Frog Who Wanted to Be a Singer" by Linda Goss. Text copyright © 1983 by Linda Goss.

Greenwillow Books, a division of William Morrow & Company, Inc.: Cover illustration from *The Trouble with Gramary* by Betty Levin. Copyright © 1988 by Betty Levin. From *The Hero and the Crown* by Robin McKinley. Text copyright © 1984 by Robin McKinley.

Harcourt Brace & Company: From *1787* by Joan Anderson. Text copyright © 1987 by Joan Anderson. "Macavity: The Mystery Cat" from *Old Possum's Book of Practical Cats* by T. S. Eliot, illustrated by Edward Gorey. Text copyright 1939 by T. S. Eliot, renewed 1967 by Esme Valerie Eliot; illustrations copyright © 1982 by Edward Gorey. Cover illustration by Bill Farnsworth from *The Fifth of March: A Story of the Boston Massacre* by Ann Rinaldi. Cover illustration copyright © 1993 by Bill Farnsworth. "Ever a Seeker" from *Honey and Salt* by Carl Sandburg. Text copyright © 1958 by Carl Sandburg, renewed 1986 by Margaret Sandburg, Janet Sandburg, and Helga Sandburg Crile. "Mother and Daughter" from *Baseball in April and Other Stories* by Gary Soto. Text copyright © 1990 by Gary Soto. Pronunciation Key from *HBJ School Dictionary*, Third Edition. Text copyright © 1990 by Harcourt Brace & Company.

HarperCollins Publishers: "The Dog on the Roof" from *Up the Chimney Down* by Joan Aiken. Text copyright © 1985 by Joan Aiken. Cover illustration by Richard Egielski from *A Telling of the Tales: Five Stories* by William J. Brooke. Illustration copyright © 1990 by Richard Egielski. Cover illustration by Hiroshige and Hokusai from *The Big Wave* by Pearl S. Buck. Copyright © 1973 by HarperCollins Publishers. "Water Striders" from *Joyful Noise* by Paul Fleischman. Text copyright © 1988 by Paul Fleischman. From pp. 128–149 in *The Talking Earth* by Jean Craighead George, cover illustration by Kam Mak. Text copyright © 1983 by Jean Craighead George; cover illustration © 1987 by HarperCollins Publishers. "I Have a Friend" from *Near the Window Tree* by Karla Kuskin. Text copyright © 1975 by Karla Kuskin. "Write About a Radish" from *Dogs & Dragons, Trees & Dreams* by Karla Kuskin. Text copyright © 1980 by Karla Kuskin. From *Listen for the Singing* by Jean Little. Text copyright © 1977 by Jean Little. From "We Hold These Truths" in *The American Revolutionaries: A History in Their Own Words, 1750–1800* by Milton Meltzer. Text copyright © 1987 by Milton Meltzer. "James Forten" from *Now Is Your Time: The African-American Struggle for Freedom* by Walter Dean Myers. Text and cover photograph copyright © 1991 by Walter Dean Myers. "Remember the Ladies" from *American Women: Their Lives in Their Words* by Doreen Rappaport. Text copyright © 1990 by Doreen Rappaport. "In Search of Cinderella" from *A Light in the Attic* by Shel Silverstein. Copyright © 1981 by Evil Eye Music, Inc. "One Time" from *A Glass Face in the Rain* by William Stafford. Text copyright © 1979, 1982 by William Stafford. "The Girl Who Cried Flowers" from *The Girl Who Cried Flowers and Other Tales* by Jane Yolen, illustrated by David Palladini. Text copyright © 1974 by Jane Yolen; illustrations copyright © 1974 by David Palladini.

Cristina Kenney Herdman, on behalf of the Estate of Nina Otero: From "The Bells of Santa Cruz" in *Old Spain in Our Southwest* by Nina Otero. Biographical information courtesy of Charlotte T. Whaley.

Houghton Mifflin Company: Cover illustration from *The Hobbit* by J. R. R. Tolkien. Illustration copyright © 1966 by J. R. R. Tolkien.

Trina Schart Hyman: Cover illustration by Trina Schart Hyman from *Dealing With Dragons* by Patricia C. Wrede.

Hyperion Books for Children, an imprint of Disney Book Publishing Group, Inc.: Cover photograph by Sigurgeir Jónasson from *Surtsey: The Newest Place on Earth* by Kathryn Lasky, photographs by Christopher G. Knight. Cover photograph © 1992 by Sigurgeir Jónasson.

Phyllis Janowitz: "There Was a Man" by Phyllis Janowitz. Text copyright © by Phyllis Janowitz. Published in *Event Magazine*, Douglas College, Vancouver, Spring 1973. Comment on "There Was a Man." Text copyright © 1990 by Phyllis Janowitz.

Kirchoff/Wohlberg, Inc.: Cover illustration by Floyd Cooper from *The Place My Words Are Looking For*, selected by Paul B. Janeczko. Illustration copyright © 1990 by Floyd Cooper.

Alfred A. Knopf, Inc.: "What the Twister Did" from *Hearing from Wayne and Other Stories* by Bill Franzen. Text copyright © 1988 by Bill Franzen. "Dreams" and "The Dream Keeper" from *The Dream Keeper and Other Poems* by Langston Hughes. Text copyright 1932 by Alfred A. Knopf, Inc.; text copyright renewed 1960 by Langston Hughes. "Icebox" from "A Cheerful Alphabet of Pleasant Objects" in *The Carpentered Hen and Other Tame Creatures* by John Updike. Text copyright © 1958 by John Updike. Comment on "Icebox" by John Updike. Text copyright © 1990 by John Updike.

Karla Kuskin: Comment on "Write About a Radish" by Karla Kuskin. Text copyright © 1990 by Karla Kuskin.

Patricia G. Lauber: From *Everglades Country: A Question of Life or Death* by Patricia Lauber. Text copyright © 1973 by Patricia Lauber.

Jeff Lavaty, on behalf of David McCall Johnston: Cover illustration by David McCall Johnston from *The Hero and The Crown* by Robin McKinley.

Lerner Publications: Cover illustration from *Julia Morgan: Architect of Dreams* by Ginger Wadsworth. Copyright © 1990 by Lerner Publications Company.

Little, Brown and Company: From "Superislands" in *The Book of Where, or How to Be Naturally Geographic* by Neill Bell, illustrations by Richard Wilson. Copyright © 1982 by the Yolla Bolly Press.

Little, Brown and Company, in conjunction with Sierra Club Books: Cover photograph from *The Sierra Club Book of Our National Parks* by Donald Young with Cynthia Overbeck Bix.

Lothrop, Lee & Shepard Books, a division of William Morrow & Company, Inc.: Cover illustration from *In the Forest: A Portfolio of Paintings* by Jim Arnosky. Copyright © 1989 by Jim Arnosky.

Macmillan Publishing Company: From *M. C. Higgins, The Great* by Virginia Hamilton, cover illustration by James McMullan. Text and cover illustration copyright © 1974 by Virginia Hamilton.

Alan Mazzetti: Cover illustration by Alan Mazzetti from *Taking Sides* by Gary Soto.

Margaret K. McElderry Books, an imprint of Macmillan Publishing Company: From "The Search for Early Americans" in *Searches in the American Desert* by Sheila Cowing, cover photograph by Walter C. Cowing. Text copyright © 1989 by Sheila Cowing; cover photograph copyright © 1989 by Walter C. Cowing.

Julian Messner, a division of Silver Burdett Press, Inc., Simon & Schuster, Inc.: From *The Invisible Thread* by Yoshiko Uchida. © 1991 by Yoshiko Uchida.

Howard Mohr: "How to Tell a Tornado" by Howard Mohr. Text copyright © 1973 by Howard Mohr. Originally published in *Minnesota English Journal*, Fall 1973.

Morrow Junior Books, a division of William Morrow & Company, Inc.: Cover illustration by Derek James from *Tales of a Dead King* by Walter Dean Myers. Copyright © 1983 by Walter Dean Myers. Cover illustration by David Wiesner from *The Star Fisher* by Laurence Yep. Cover illustration © 1991 by David Wiesner.

John Murray Publishers Ltd.: "The Speckled Band" by Sir Arthur Conan Doyle, dramatized by Michael and Mollie Hardwick.

Museum of New Mexico Press: "The Force of Luck" from *Cuentos: Tales from the Hispanic Southwest* by José Griego y Maestas and Rudolfo Anaya. Text copyright © 1980 by the Museum of New Mexico Press.

Penguin Books Canada Limited: Text and cover illustration from *Little by Little: A Writer's Education* by Jean Little. Text and cover illustration copyright © 1987 by Jean Little.

G. P. Putnam's Sons: Cover illustration from *The Great Little Madison* by Jean Fritz. Copyright © 1989 by Jean Fritz. "The Great Peanut Puzzle" from *Test-Tube Mysteries* by Gail Kay Haines. Text copyright © 1982 by Gail Kay Haines.

Random House, Inc.: Cover illustration from *The Diary of Anne Frank* by Frances Goodrich and Albert Hackett. Copyright © 1956 by Albert Hackett, Frances Goodrich Hackett and Otto Frank.

Charles Scribner's Sons, an imprint of Macmillan Publishing Company: "A Mother in Mannville" from *When the Whippoorwill* by Marjorie Kinnan Rawlings. Text copyright 1940 by Marjorie Kinnan Rawlings; text copyright renewed © 1968 by Norton Baskin.

Ian Serraillier: From *A Fall from the Sky* by Ian Serraillier. Text copyright © 1965 by Ian Serraillier.

Owen Seumptewa: Cover photograph by Owen Seumptewa from *Rising Voices: Writings of Young Native Americans*, selected by Arlene B. Hirschfelder and Beverly R. Singer. Photograph copyright © 1992 by Owen Seumptewa.

Leslie Marmon Silko: "The Time We Climbed Snake Mountain" by Leslie Marmon Silko.

William Stafford: Comment on "One Time" from *A Glass Face in the Rain* by William Stafford. Text copyright © 1990 by William Stafford.

Collection of State of South Carolina: Cover illustration by William Ranney from *Black Heroes of the American Revolution* by Burke Davis.

Sterling Publishing Company, Inc., 387 Park Ave. S., New York, NY 10016: "The Coin Expert" from *Super Sleuth: Mini-Mysteries for You to Solve* by Falcon Travis. Text © 1982 by Falcon Travis; American edition © 1985 by Sterling Publishing Company, Inc.

Larry Sternig Literary Agency: From *Touchmark* by Mildred Lawrence. Text copyright © 1975 by Mildred Lawrence.

Sunstone Press: "Song of the Sky Loom" from *Songs of the Tewa*, translated by Herbert J. Spinden.

Literary Estate of May Swenson: "The Cloud-Mobile" by May Swenson. Text © by May Swenson, renewed 1986 by May Swenson.

Rosemary A. Thurber: "The Princess and the Tin Box" from *The Beast in Me and Other Animals* by James Thurber. Copyright © 1948 by James Thurber; copyright © 1975 by Helen Thurber and Rosemary A. Thurber. Published by Harcourt Brace & Company.

The Estate of Yoshiko Uchida: "The Bracelet" by Yoshiko Uchida from *The Scribner Anthology for Young People*. Text © 1976 by Yoshiko Uchida. Published by The Japanese American Curriculum Project, Inc.

University of Southern California: "My Mother Pieced Quilts" by Teresa Palomo Acosta from *Festival de Flor y Canto: An Anthology of Chicano Literature*, edited by Alurista et al. Copyright 1976 by El Centro Chicano, University of Southern California.

Watkins/Loomis Agency on behalf of Geraldine Elliot: Cover illustration by Sheila Hawkins from *Where the Leopard Passes: A Book of African Folk Tales* by Geraldine Elliot. Copyright © 1949 by Geraldine Elliot.

Neil Waldman: Cover illustration by Neil Waldman from *Dogsong* by Gary Paulsen. Illustration copyright © 1985 by Bradbury Press.

Walker and Company: Cover illustration by Anthony Accardo from *Who Put the Cannon in the Courthouse Square?* by Kay Cooper. Copyright © 1985 by Kay Cooper.

Ramona Maher Weeks: "September–Bini'ant'aatsoh" from *Alice Yazzie's Year* by Ramona Maher. Text copyright © 1977 by Ramona Maher.

Wieser and Wieser, Inc., on behalf of Siv Cedering: "Nightmares" from *The Blue Horse and Other Night Poems* by Siv Cedering. Text copyright © 1979 by Siv Cedering Fox.

Alfred M. Worden: "Perspective" from *Hello Earth: Greetings from Endeavor* by Alfred M. Worden. Copyright © 1974 by Alfred M. Worden.

Illustration Credits

KEY: (t) top, (b) bottom, (l) left, (r) right, (c) center.

Theme Opening Art

Dave Bates, 342–343; Tim Bodendistel, 278–279; Britt Taylor Collins, 94–95, 372–373, 432–433; Joe Dinicola, 48–49, 404–405; Dave Gaadt, 126–127; Garth Glazier, 244–245; Ed Klautley, 222–223; Hank Kolodziej, 562–563; Brenda Losey, 540–541; Dean St. Clair, 160–161; Clarke W. Tate, 458–459; Amy Whitehead, 490–491

Theme Closing Art

Chris Armstrong, 431; Artist to Come, 243; Charles Cashwell, 539; Ken Hobson, 457; Brenda Losey, 187; Jackie Pittman, 483; Clarke W. Tate, 397

Connections Art

Lindy Burnett, 120–121, 398–399; Karen Strelecki, 216–217, 484–485; R.M. Schneider, 304–305, 600–601

Unit Opener, Bookshelf, & Connections Border Art (4/c)

Chris Armstrong, 16–17; Charles Cashwell, 400–401; Britt Taylor Collins, 486–487; Marilyn King, 122–123, 218–219; Drew Rose, 306–307

Selection Art

Bill Amend, 135, 158; Randy Chewning, 22–41; Floyd Cooper, 532–538; Don Dewitt, 344–353; Markn Elliot, 246–259; Richard Erickson, 110–118; Stephanie Garcia, 128–133; Byron Gin, 136–145; Edward Gorey, 44–46; David Groff, 82–91; HBJ, 408; Greg King, 168–175; Ronnie Knabel, 266–275; Berney Knox, 231, 344; Doug Knutson, 178–182; Kim LeFeve, 354–363; Sergio Martinez, 50–70; John Mattos, 190–210; Alan Mazzetti, 452–456; Wayne McLoughlin, 412–427; David Palladini, 336–340; Navin Patel, 465; S.M. Saelig, 492–507; Jill Karla Schwarz, 364–370; Slug Signorino, 434; Shel Silverstein, 375; Douglas Smith, 586–598; Martin Springett, 312–331; James Thurber, 376–379; Jack Unruh, 564–581; David Wilgus, 380–394; Richard Wilson, 436–443; Leslie Wu, 234–241